Digitization, Copyright and the Law

This book discusses copyleft and its impact on the traditional way to conceive of property. It is specifically focused on the European and international juridical framework.

Analysing the impact of digitalization on copyright and the potential effect of copyleft in the European market and within a European and international juridical framework, this book explores the complex evolutionary framework which charts the reduction of physical property and the progressive expansion of intangible assets. Although digitalization enables more accessibility than ever before, this impacts traditional intellectual property frameworks. Evaluating common traits of ownership structure, the book considers the challenges that intangible property, open source and creative commons present to the current legal system. Examining the impact of copyleft on copyright and the law of ownership, the book considers the rights of authors and creators, legal limits and complications arising from these new forms of ownership of intangible assets. The book is grounded in the European potential regulatory framework of copyleft through movements like open-source software.

The book will be of interest to students, academics and practitioners with an interest in contract law, property law and intellectual property law.

Ettore M. Lombardi, a Professor of Private Law and International Business Law at the University of Florence, is also a practicing lawyer. He co-directs the Executive Courses on Alternative Investment at Queen Mary University of London and on Art and Law at the University of Florence, Université de Genève, and Gallerie degli Uffizi. His academic qualifications include degrees from various prestigious institutions, an LL.M. at Harvard Law School, and advanced certificates in AI (Saïd Business School at Oxford University), Business Sustainability Management (Cambridge University) and Sustainable Finance (Cambridge University). Currently, he holds positions as Research Fellow and Visiting/Senior Fellow at various prestigious and globally recognized institutions.

Routledge Research in Intellectual Property

The Transformation of EU Geographical Indications Law
The Present, Past and Future of the Origin Link
Andrea Zappalaglio

Copyright Law and Translation
Access to Knowledge in Developing Economies
Chamila S. Talagala

Patent Law, Green Technology and Innovation
Ankit Singh and Yogendra Kumar Srivastava

Intellectual Property and Development
Geographical Indications in Practice
Barbara Pick

Collective Management of Music Copyright
A Comparative Analysis of China, the United States and Australia
Qinqing Xu

Intellectual Property Rights and Competition Law in India
Edited by Rajni Malhotra Dhingra and Nisha Dhanraj Dewani

Digitization, Copyright and the Law
Copyleft and the Future of Intellectual Property
Ettore M. Lombardi

For more information about this series, please visit www.routledge.com/Routledge-Research-in-Intellectual-Property/book-series/INTELLPROP

Digitization, Copyright and the Law

Copyleft and the Future of Intellectual Property

Ettore M. Lombardi

Routledge
Taylor & Francis Group
LONDON AND NEW YORK

First published 2025
by Routledge
4 Park Square, Milton Park, Abingdon, Oxon OX14 4RN

and by Routledge
605 Third Avenue, New York, NY 10158

Routledge is an imprint of the Taylor & Francis Group, an informa business

British Library Cataloguing-in-Publication Data
A catalogue record for this book is available from the British Library

ISBN: 978-1-032-54333-8 (hbk)
ISBN: 978-1-032-54345-1 (pbk)
ISBN: 978-1-003-42441-3 (ebk)

DOI: 10.4324/9781003424413

Typeset in Times New Roman
by Apex CoVantage, LLC

"To Eugenia, my gorgeous daughter, and to Beatrice, Filippo, Lorenzo and Edoardo, my four fabulous nephews, because the future is theirs and they are the future."

Contents

Foreword

The age of the digital revolution is upon us. The rapid development of artificial intelligence (AI) and other technologies in the 21st century is presenting many challenges to the application of the traditional doctrines of copyright law. The ability of AI to autonomously generate text, music and images, or in response to specific prompts by human users, is accelerating at a breathtaking pace, resulting in new scenarios that can be confounding to copyright lawyers as well as judges and policymakers.

Copyright as a form of an intangible property right is an odd creature. Unlike trademarks which one can presumably own in perpetuity so long as it is used commercially to designate the source of goods or services, copyright temporarily resides with an owner for his or her life plus 70 years, after which it dissipates into the hands of the public. Copyright supposedly exists to incentivize the progress of humankind through the creation of new art, books, music and entertainment, but at the same time, it can constrict learning, freedom of expression and entrepreneurship.

The doctrine of fair use in copyright law is capable of taking into account changes in technology in order to strike an appropriate balance between the enforcement of intangible property rights and other competing societal interests. However, computer programs differ to some extent from many other copyrightable works such as painting, dance and music because computer programs always serve a functional purpose. Because of these differences, fair use has an important role to play for computer programs by providing a context-based check that keeps the copyright monopoly afforded to computer programs within its lawful boundaries.[1] Copying was established in the US decision of *Authors Guild v. Google*, where books were digitized in order to make them searchable, but this was consequently held to be fair use,[2] in particular because "Google's making of a digital copy of Plaintiffs' books for the purpose of enabling a search for identification of books containing a term of interest to the searcher involves a highly transformative purpose."[3] In *Google LLC v. Oracle America, Inc.*, the US Supreme Court emphasized that the copier's use must add "something new, with a further purpose or different character, altering

1 *Google LLC v. Oracle America, Inc*, 141 S. Ct. 1183, 1198 (2021).
2 *Authors Guild v. Google Inc*, 804 F.3d 202, 207 (2nd Cir. 2015).
3 Ibid., 217.

the copyrighted work with new expression, meaning or message."[4] In finding fair use, the Court declared: "Google's use of the Sun Java API seeks to create new products. It seeks to expand the use and usefulness of Android-based smartphones. Its new product offers programmers a highly creative and innovative tool for a smartphone environment. To the extent that Google used parts of the Sun Java API to create a new platform that could be readily used by programmers, its use was consistent with that creative 'progress' that is the basic constitutional objective of copyright itself."[5] Arguably the Court had to resort to a more amorphous "public benefits" consideration outside the standard statutory fair use factors in order to reach a finding that the use by Google was fair where Google, through Android, provided a new collection of tasks operating in a distinct and different computing environment.[6] Those tasks were carried out through the use of new implementing code (that Google wrote) designed to operate within that new environment. Indeed, the new technology cases in copyright law are far more difficult to resolve compared to those involving parody and satire.

This book by Ettore M. Lombardi is a timely and important analysis of the fundamental rationales of copyright, and its nuanced reconceptualization of copyright provides us with a valuable framework to interrogate the application of traditional doctrines of copyright law to computer programs and software.

As the author contends, copyleft "represents a type of profoundly permissive license, so much so as to allow third parties to develop derivative works whose rules of use, dissemination and modification can assume, in the event of non-copyleft, traits completely different from those that the license of the original work foresaw." The advantages of a copyleft approach are identified with the freedom to use, exploit and modify, which manifests itself in the possibility of sub-licensing, creating and distributing derivative works without any limit. In summary, Lombardi's elegant argument from a legal point of view can be distilled to this: copyleft allows users to make use of the intellectual work, to modify it and to disseminate it in a less constrained manner than what one would derive from copyright.

One should note from the onset that copyleft does not consist of the complete denial of copyright, but in its weakening. Lombardi posits that copyleft presents a model of copyright management that is based on a licensing system designed to allow the creators, in their capacity as original owners of the rights on the work, to indicate to the users of the latter the ways in which it should be used, disseminated and often even modified, while respecting some essential conditions.

Do take time to uncover the gems within the pages of this book, and you may just be persuaded to rethink the monolithic and mythic proprietary nature of copyright.

Professor David Tan
Co-Director, Centre for Technology, Robotics,
Artificial Intelligence & the Law – Faculty of Law,
National University of Singapore

4 *Google LLC v. Oracle America, Inc*, 141 S. Ct. 1183, 1202 (2021).
5 Ibid., 1203.
6 Ibid., 1206–1208.

Foreword

In *Digitization, Copyright and the Law: Copyleft and the Future of Intellectual Property*, Professor Ettore Lombardi embarks on a compelling exploration of the interplay between technology, society and the evolving concept of property. Professor Lombardi delves into the heart of the digital revolution, unraveling its implications for social-economic dynamics, legal frameworks and the fabric of ownership itself.

The book begins with a comprehensive analysis of the transformative impact of digital technology on society, the economy and the law. Professor Lombardi examines how connectivity and technological innovation have reshaped traditional notions of ownership, giving rise to new ownership models and challenging established paradigms.

At least since the insights of the American Legal Realists, we have understood that all property involves a "bundle of entitlements" rather than a relationship of dominion over an object. Even in the paradigmatic cases of real estate and chattels, ownership involves legal relationships: my right to improve real property is necessarily contingent on my neighbors' rights to quiet enjoyment, lateral support or a fair proportion of subterranean resources; my right to exclude is limited by the rights of others to constructive easement to access adjacent land, etc. So, one might be tempted to conclude that intellectual property in the digital age poses no truly new challenges but only more obvious versions of familiar issues: old wine in new bottles.

Yet Professor Lombardi makes a compelling case that intellectual property, combined with novel technologies, confronts us with new conceptual and practical challenges. He examines the complexities of ownership in digital spaces, exploring the intricate balance between private law, regulatory frameworks and the rights of individuals in an online environment. As technology reshapes the logic of property rights, questions of access and inclusivity come to the forefront. These questions are more pronounced in the context of intellectual property, which in essence involves a state-granted monopoly on information, knowledge and communication. Why and when should government prevent competitors from copying a useful invention or making a creative work inspired by an existing text? These questions raise issues of social justice and equity and challenge familiar analogies between domains of intellectual property: should the very concept of ownership vary if a patent involves a life-saving drug as opposed to a luxury technology or if a derivative work makes a controversial political statement that invites critique? Here, Professor Lombardi explores the relationship between the new challenges of the digital age and older property rights logic, questioning whether access is merely a question of regulation or impinges on a fundamental manifestation of ownership.

Finally, Professor Lombardi delves into the realm of copyleft – a manifestation of digital liberty and the sharing culture. He explores the landscape of copyleft, from advancements in information technology to the emergence of community free/open source licenses, and he explores the implications of non-copyleft software, navigating "anomalous" licensing and substantive ownership in the digital sphere.

From the demise of the monolithic notion of property as dominion to the rise of new forms of virtual and digital property, we are invited to contemplate a world where the boundaries of ownership are constantly redrawn. Professor Lombardi is an ideal guide through the frontier of digital property.

Richard Thompson Ford
Professor of Law
Stanford University
Author of: *Dress Codes: How the Laws of Fashion Made History* (2021); *Dress code. Come la moda dà forma alla storia* (Il Saggiatore, 2023)

A Note

Dear readers,

The eternal question of what property right is has been addressed by scholars for centuries. Philosophers and jurists proposed various perceptions from various perspectives, including political, social and economic points of view. Yet, the current digital technology revolution, often described as disruptive, has raised unprecedented challenges to the legal notion of "property." This challenge lies at the heart of this book, *Digitization, Copyright and the Law: Copyleft and the Future of Intellectual Property*, written by Ettore M. Lombardi, which offers a novel and thought-provoking perspective on the proprietary nature of intellectual property rights (IPRs), particularly copyright, through the lens of digital technologies.

The notions of property in general and of property rights in intangible assets in particular have been divided over the years into different perceptions in the common law and continental legal worlds. Occasionally, the inter-legal discourse between these two separate legal worlds is reminiscent of a Tower of Babylon–style conversation. This book uses the emerging new reality created by digital technologies, characterized by their entirely global effects, to bridge the gap of the perceptions of property and build a unified notion adapted to digital assets, such as computer programs, and the digital environment, that is, the Internet. The profound understanding of both legal legacies, with special emphasis on Italian scholarship and jurisprudence, makes the book original and unique. In a comprehensive and outstanding analysis, step by step, it explores the evolution of proprietary perceptions of intangible assets, protected by IPRs such as copyright, and their new formations in the global digital sphere. The analysis delves into existing and ought-to-be legal transformations, making an important contribution to the study of the function of IPRs and copyright in promoting public goals in the digital era. The book adds a significant layer to the large body of scholarship on the meaning of property rights in intangible assets. It can enrich the knowledge of both scholars and legal practitioners who know that "there is nothing as practical as a good theory" (Kurt Levin).

Prof. Orit Fischman-Afori, March 2024

Professor of Law, The College of Management, Faculty of Law

President Elect, ATRIP – International Association for the Advancement of Teaching and Research in Intellectual Property

Introduction

Digital technologies have deeply affected every aspect of human life and also significantly affected the circulation of goods and the way in which ownership of them is expressed and translated.[1]

Technological progress has represented, in fact, the undisputed protagonist of the most profound changes that affected socio-legal architectures – as happened in the 19th century for the Industrial Revolution[2] – but never before have these transformations affected so much deep, rapid and broad existing structures.[3]

Obviously, the right of property has not remained immune to these transformations, which is increasingly linked to the idea of a dematerialization, operating

1 It shall be, as of now, noted that with the term "ownership" we mean the possibility to refer a certain object to a certain subjective situation. *See*, in this regard, P. Perlingieri, *Introduzione alla problematica della «proprietà»*, Napoli, 1971, where the author, at pp. 106 and 107, highlights that «[L]a nozione di titolarità [. . .] si può esprimere, manifestare in due modi: o attraverso la nozione di appartenenza o attraverso quella di spettanza. La spettanza è una forma di titolarità che non s'identifica con l'appartenenza. [. . .] Mentre l'appartenenza è una forma di titolarità che fa riferimento all'attualità della situazione soggettiva finale, personale o reale, la spettanza fa riferimento alla potenzialità della situazione soggettiva, cioè all'esistenza di un titolo idoneo all'acquisto di quella titolarità definitiva che è appunto l'appartenenza» ("[T]he notion of ownership [. . .] can be expressed, manifested in two ways: either through the notion of belonging or through that of ownership. Entitlement is a form of ownership that does not identify with membership. [. . .] While belonging is a form of ownership that refers to the actuality of the final subjective situation, personal or real, the due refers to the potential of the subjective situation, that is to say the existence of a title suitable for the purchase of that definitive ownership which is precisely membership.").

2 In this regard, it is possible to make reference to the recourse to new sources of energy that was carried out in successive periods and phases, as the Industrial Revolution led to radical social, political and economic changes. The same can be said for other economic phenomena that have profoundly impacted socio-economic structures, as demonstrated, for example, by the advent of pressing technics. *See*, for further information, M. Castells, *La sociedad red: una visión global*, Madrid, 2006, p. 1 ff.

3 Although modern information technologies do not represent (obviously) the only form of technological innovation that has profoundly changed human society, they are characterized by a new characteristic, the aptitude to converge or to operate jointly, simultaneously and with an effect of mutual reinforcement, which, combined with the technological development achieved so far, means that the conditions necessary to have an impact in a way never experienced before, because multifocal, multilevel and heterogeneous, on the current socio-juridical-economic architectures are expanded. See, for all, M. Castells, *La sociedad red: una visión global*, cit., p. 57 ff.

DOI: 10.4324/9781003424413-1

on the double level of ownership and enjoyment, as demonstrated by the fact that immateriality becomes the essential trait of a process of transformation that affects the way of perceiving the ownership of assets, and thus comes to affect the same way of conceiving the ownership scheme.[4]

In fact, legal circulation is no longer focused only on the exchange of physical goods, but is increasingly characterized by an easier access to the immaterial, and therefore by a tendency to favour the incorporeal over the corporeal: the broad and progressive dematerialization[5] is accompanied by the transition from an economy in which wealth is measured in terms of ownership of *res corporales* to an economy in which wealth is increasingly measured as the control of *res incorporales*,[6] which assume the guise of intangible assets.[7]

The reduction of physical property is accompanied by the progressive expansion of intangible property,[8] with consequences that are reflected on the environment in which the transfer takes place, no longer represented by a geographical space in which sellers and buyers exchange physical goods and services, but from a cybernetic arena, in which the exchange can take place between intangible assets.

The complex evolutionary framework now briefly outlined has strengthened the feeling of legal science, which, at least at the national level, has long since demonstrated the gradual tendency to abandon a purely monistic and formalistic logic in the light of which to frame the proprietary phenomenon, to enhance the

4 It is indubitable that technology simultaneously represents a powerful factor both for improving human life (and not only) and for changing traditional approaches and conceptual categories: if the law aspires to stability, new technologies seem to continually question the maintenance of established order. *See*, in this regard, for the icastic and evocative image of Minerva's owl that begins its flight at dusk without changing anything in the *status quo*, P. Grossi, *Società, diritto, Stato. Un recupero per il diritto*, Milano, 2006, p. 283 ff.

5 *See*, in broad terms on the notion of intangible asset, M. Are, voce *Beni. IV. – Beni immateriali. a) Diritto privato*, in *Enc. dir.*, V, Milano, 1959, p. 244 ff.; G. Pugliese, *Dalle* "res incorporales" *del diritto romano ai beni immateriali di alcuni sistemi giuridici odierni*, in *Riv. trim. dir. proc. civ.*, 1982, *passim*.

6 Just to give an example, think of the growing importance of personal data, their storage and their use for the most varied purposes (commercial, military, geo-political influence), with all the ensuing consequences, as in terms of privacy protection. *See*, on the subject, for all, S. Rodotà, *Intervista su privacy e libertà*, Roma-Bari, 2005, *passim*.

7 Both digital goods and those resulting from the creative and/or inventive human activity shall be linked to this concept.

8 *See*, in this regard, D. Bell, *The Coming of Post-Industrial Society. A Venture in Social Forecasting*, New York, NY, 1999, p. 127, where the author affirms that «[I]f an industrial society is defined by the quantity of goods as marking a standard of living, the post-industrial society is defined by the quantity of life as measured by the services and amenities – health, education, recreation, and the arts – which are deemed desirable». Beyond this peculiar manifestation, immateriality represents the functional condition to concretize a further coessential – if not exclusive – characteristic to this new juridical-economic scenario: ubiquity, or the possibility of existing and being present everywhere at the same time. Digital technologies have launched a phase in which goods can be replicated, transmitted, stored and manipulated with enormous simplicity, as the so-called ubiquitous computing. But, as happens with all *res humanae*, also for this type of ubiquity there are also negative traits, alongside evident positive traits, since both the potential damage and the potential violations that can be caused to the underlying subjective situations take on an equally ubiquitous character.

consideration of factual data and better identify the substance of the legal institution "property"[9] in order to reach a common goal: legal pluralism.[10]

The problem that a doctrinal reflection attentive to reality must raise becomes, then, the evaluation of which traits of the ownership structure are capable of qualifying its effective extent, considering the challenges that the contemporary world offers and the new types of goods that populate it.[11]

In fact, the possession of wealth, in all its forms, presupposes and requires a legal system that is capable of safeguarding and protecting it, especially where it is in the presence of intangible assets,[12] which, by their nature, are more easily

9 In broad terms, it can be considered that the origins of a process aimed at framing the proprietary right in a logic of greater proximity to the factual and phenomenal data are to be traced back to the well-known Pugliatti's approach that, overcoming a unitary definition of property, has recognized in an approach that favours the plurality of "proprietary statutes" is the keystone of the analysis of a more real property right, because it is closer to the factual data and less subject to formalistic influences. *See*, S. Pugliatti, *La proprietà nel nuovo diritto*, Milano, 1954, *passim*; and, for a reflection on juridical pluralism as the result of the elaboration of the most careful historiographical research on the subject of situations of belonging (Grossi) and comparative analysis (Pugliese and Gambaro), U. Mattei, voce *Proprietà*, in *Digesto delle Discipline Privatistiche – Sezione Civile*, XV, Torino, 1997, p. 433 e 434, according to whom «[T]ale pluralismo [. . .] non ha nulla a che spartire con la menzionata nozione della pluralità di statuti proprietari, un'idea quanto mai radicata nel positivismo legislativo e che anzi lo legittima, perché le differenti proprietà non ricevono i differenti statuti dalla natura del loro oggetto, ma dal diverso regime normativo. Né il pluralismo delegittima i tentativi di ricostruzione unitaria dell'istituto giuridico: proprietà privata» («[T]his pluralism [. . .] has nothing to do with the aforementioned notion of the plurality of proprietary statutes, an idea deeply rooted in legislative positivism and which indeed legitimizes it, because the different properties they do not receive the different statutes from the nature of their object, but from the different regulatory regime. Nor does pluralism de-legitimize attempts at a unitary reconstruction of the legal institution: private property»).

10 For further information, A. Gambaro, *Il diritto di proprietà*, in *Trattato di Diritto civile e commerciale*, già diretto da A. Cicu e F. Messineo e continuato da L. Mengoni, VIII, t. 2, Milano, 1995, *passim*.

11 To this effect, U. Mattei, voce *Proprietà*, in *Digesto delle Discipline Privatistiche – Sezione Civile*, cit., p. 434, where the author recalls, by way of example, «[. . .] l'informazione, il patrimonio genetico, il corpo, la ricchezza dematerializzata, la privatizzazione ecc. ecc.» («[. . .] information, genetic heritage, the body, dematerialized wealth, privatization, etc. etc.»).

12 *See* A. Gambaro, *Dai beni immobili ai beni virtuali*, in *Treccani*, 2009, available at www.treccani.it/enciclopedia/dai-beni-immobili-ai-beni-virtuali_%28XXI-Secolo%29/, where the author specifies that «La dizione *beni immateriali* è una delle tante in uso. Si parla anche di *beni intangibili* e di *beni virtuali*, locuzione quest'ultima che acquista una sfumatura di significato ulteriore indicando quei beni che esistono sulle reti telematiche, e, in questo caso, alla problematicità dell'inquadramento giuridico, si aggiungono le difficoltà di governare la rete con regole giuridiche efficaci. La parola più problematica rimane tuttavia: *bene/i*. La variabilità di significati è in questo caso enorme. Tale variabilità non deriva soltanto dagli usi, amplissimi, della parola *bene* nel linguaggio comune, ma anche dalle profonde diversità di concetti che tale termine evoca nel lessico delle diverse scienze sociali. Nei discorsi degli economisti, che sono pensati sostanzialmente in inglese, in qualunque idioma vengano poi veicolati, la parola *bene* traduce spesso *asset*, che indica qualsiasi elemento attivo del patrimonio oppure veicola l'idea di utilità economicamente sfruttabile. I depositi bancari sono quindi "beni," come lo sono i brevetti e i *trade secrets*. Ma, sempre nel linguaggio economico, anche la conoscenza è un bene, così come lo è la difesa nazionale, che viene considerato il bene pubblico per eccellenza. Il linguaggio giuridico richiede tassonomie più rigorose, posto che le categorie giuridiche hanno una funzione demarcativa: esse, cioè servono a indicare l'ambito di applicazione di una disciplina specifica, e, viceversa, a escludere l'applicazione di altre discipline specifiche».

exposed to acts of appropriation of others and, with the exception of trade secrets,[13] are not susceptible to forms of self-protection.[14]

The reference to immateriality therefore makes implicit the reference either to some form of private property or to some form of public property to be understood as being comparable to an organized community, especially because the legal categories are not very permeable to accept new and different forms of manifestation of wealth.

In this regard, it is noted that legal language poses a problem that is closely interrelated with the articulation of Western legal systems in the two well-known traditions of common law, extensively referable to English-speaking countries, and civil law, referable to continental Europe, to Latin America and Asia, where there are two different concepts of good in the legal sense that extend their differentiated effects also to the notion of ownership.

In the global world, also due to the systematic contribution made by numerous internal[15] and international[16] regulatory acts, we thus speak indiscriminately of ownership and intellectual property, to indicate new intangible assets, given the now peaceful extension of the concept of ownership beyond borders of corporal things. In this way, however, there is a tendency to evoke legal concepts and taxonomies[17] that certainly coincide only partially with each other[18] due to historical

(«The term intangible assets is one of the many in use. We also speak of intangible assets and virtual goods, the latter term acquiring a nuance of further meaning by indicating those goods that exist on telematic networks, and, in this case, the difficulties of governing the network with effective legal rules. However, the most problematic word remains: good(s). The variability of meanings in this case is enormous. This variability derives not only from the very broad uses of the word bene in common language, but also from the profound diversity of concepts that this term evokes in the lexicon of the various social sciences. In the speeches of economists, who are basically thought in English, in whatever language they are then conveyed, the word well often translates as asset, which indicates any active element of assets or conveys the idea of economically exploitable utility. Bank deposits are therefore "assets," as are patents and trade secrets. But, again in economic language, knowledge is also a good, as is national defense, which is considered the public good par excellence. Legal language requires more rigorous taxonomies, given that legal categories have a demarcating function: they, that is, they serve to indicate the scope of application of a specific discipline, and, conversely, to exclude the application of other specific disciplines»).

13 Before the 1995 reform that resulted from the conclusion of the international TRIPs agreements of 1994, trade secrets did not have a specific and autonomous regulatory qualification in the Italian legal system, but based their effectiveness on the principles of private contract law and competition law. Following the reform, however, a specific article was introduced (article 6-*bis*) in the Italian law on inventions (Royal Decree no. 1127 of 1939), which was then transfused and expanded into arts. 98 and 99 of the new industrial property code as also amended by Legislative Decree no. 63 of 2018.

14 A. Gambaro, *Dai beni immobili ai beni virtuali*, in *Treccani*, cit.

15 With regard to Italy, for example, consider Legislative Decree no. 30 of 2005 or the industrial property code.

16 Consider, in this sense, the Charter of Nice or the TRIPs agreements. See, for further information on the different regulatory uses to which the phrase "intellectual property" is subject, L.C. Ubertazzi, *Introduzione al diritto europeo della proprietà intellettuale*, in *Contr. e impr./Eur.*, 2003, p. 1081 ff.

17 See, on the importance that taxonomies play in order to better grasp the meaning of a legal culture and related legal institutions, A. Gambaro, *La proprietà nel* common law *anglo-americano*, in *Property, Propriété, Eigentum*, a cura di A. Candian, A. Gambaro, B. Pozzo, Padova, 1992, p. 33; and, with specific reference to intellectual property, L. Lessig, *The Future of Ideas. The Fate of the Commons in a Connected World*, New York, NY, 2002, p. 237 ff.

18 A. Candian, A. Gambaro, B. Pozzo, *Property, Propriété, Eigentum*, cit., *passim*.

factors traceable in the various legal systems and which have found clear expression in the civil codes of continental Europe.[19]

Various factors, in fact, led the codification to consider differently the discipline of ownership and possession in terms of corporal goods, both movable and immovable, as can be seen from the German BGB and its explicit referring to things in the sense of the law as things materials (§ 90), or by the Italian and French civil codes which do not adopt an explicit approach in this sense but articulate a discipline of ownership and possession capable of finding full application only if their materiality is assumed as a prerequisite.[20]

It is therefore no coincidence that the attention of Italian legal science has focused on the study of the object of ownership, enhancing the distinction that article 810 of the Italian Civil Code trace between things and goods.[21]

19 See, for an examination of the historical evolution that has characterized the way of conceiving the relationship between the individual, the right to property and the object thereof, A. Gambaro, A. Gambaro, *Dai beni immobili ai beni virtuali*, in *Treccani*, 2009, available at www.treccani.it/encyclopedia/dai-beni-immobili-ai-beni-virtuali_%28XXI-Secolo%29/, where the author observes, on the one hand, that «[. . .] in agricultural Europe the attitude of man towards things could sometimes be thought of as a function of the utilities linked to the rights of use of the land, rights that are ontologically intangible assets, and at other times in function of the fund itself which in the proprietary dimension and the quintessence of res corporales», and, on the other, that in Roman law «[. . .] since the first class of goods that formed the patrimony were the property rights and therefore the res (corporales), all the other patrimonial rights that made it up were called by counterpoint res incorporales, whose ontological characteristic was that of not being able to be an object of sensorial perception and therefore, by synecdoche, of touch»; A. Quarta, *Non-proprietà. Teoria e prassi dell'accesso ai beni*, Napoli, 2016, *passim*.

20 In this regard, it can be observed how, for example, real estate advertising and its effects have been structured according to the coincidence between property and corporal thing, with the exception of the transcription of limited real rights as an object of legislative typing.

21 On the subject of ownership, the terminological ambiguity that article 810 of the Italian Civil Code has engendered in the Italian legal system, and confirmed by the tendency to resort, both from the normative sources and from the legal literature, to use, in a promiscuous and undifferentiated way, the term "thing" or "good," often also using synonymously, where the same letter of article 810 of the Italian Civil Code it seems to distinguish, at least conceptually, the two terms. In this latter regard, it should be noted, however, that the same civil code contains numerous provisions that refer to the "thing," where one could expect the use of "good" for the consideration of the entity as an object of rights or part of an estate. By way of example only, it is sufficient to consider the reference to «a thing of the inheritance» pursuant to article 535 of the Italian Civil Code, to the «thing that is the subject of the provision» pursuant to article 625 of the Italian Civil Code, to the «movable thing» referred to in article 932 of the Italian Civil Code, or the «ownership of a thing» referred to in article 1470 of the Italian Civil Code. *See*, in the sense of believing that the property represents the only discrete criterion of the good with respect to the thing, K.P. Polanyi, *La grande trasformazione. Le origini economiche e politiche della nostra epoca*, Torino, 1974, p. 210 ff.; M. Barcellona, *Attribuzione normativa e mercato nella teoria dei beni giuridici*, in *Quadrimestre*, 1987, p. 607 ff.; P. Barcellona, *Diritto privato e società moderna*, Napoli, 1996, p. 245, where the author affirms that, following the criterion of equity, «[. . .] una situazione è o non è patrimoniale non in base a giudizi formulabili a priori, ma in base alla decisione che in ordine ad essa il mercato viene a maturare, ancorché entro limiti inderogabili eventualmente posti dal sistema medesimo» («[. . .] a situation is or is not patrimonial not on the basis of judgments that can be formulated a priori, but on the basis of the decision that the market comes to mature in relation to it, even if within mandatory limits posed by the system itself»). In a perspective of identification of the good with the thing, among others, B. Biondi, *I beni*, cit., p. 5, ove l'A. afferma che «[. . .] le nozioni di cosa e di bene coincidono» (*author's note*, "[. . .] the notions of thing and good coincide"); R. Franceschelli, *L'oggetto del rapporto giuridico (con riguardo ai*

In fact, the restrictive notion of property obtainable from the aforementioned provision has stimulated a long debate,[22] which, on the one hand, finding support in a purely literal interpretation, has led to identifying the object of the property right with only the *res corporales*,[23] with all the consequences that followed in terms of physicality and apprehension of the entity on which the subjective situation insists,[24]

---

rapporti di diritto industriale), in *Rivista trimestrale di diritto processuale civile*, 1957, p. 2 ff.; and, *contra*, V. Zeno-Zencovich, voce *Cosa*, cit., p. 439, where the author affirms that «Non vi è tuttavia una identificazione fra "bene" e "cosa" come da taluni sostenuto, giacché e chiaro che non tutte le cose sono beni, ma solo quelle suscettibili di formare oggetto di diritti (*author's note*, "There is, however, no identification between 'good' and 'thing' as claimed by some, since it is clear that not all things are goods, but only those capable of forming the object of rights"). The uncertain nature that characterizes the provision, however, has avoided the affirmation of those materialistic limitations which, for example, in the German legal system, § 90 BGB has instead determined, traditionally limiting ownership to the materiality of the goods. *See*, in favour of an ambiguity that avoided rigid classification divisions of normative origin, D. Messinetti, voce *Oggetto dei diritti*, in *Enc. dir.*, XXIX, Milano, 1979, p. 812; A. Jannarelli, *Beni, interessi e valori*, in *Diritto privato europeo. I*, a cura di N. Lipari, Milano, 1997, p. 337; U. Mattei, voce *Proprietà*, cit., p. 434; O.T. Scozzafava, *Dei beni. Artt. 810–821*, in *Il Codice civile. Commentario*, diretto da P. Schlesinger, Milano, 1999, p. 5 ff.; M. Costantino, *I beni in generale*, in *Tratt. di diritto privato. Proprietà. I*, diretto da P. Rescigno, Torino, 2005, p. 36; A. Gambaro, *La proprietà. Beni, proprietà, possesso*, cit., p. 165 ff. *See*, on the concept of immaterial good substantially identified with the creations of the human mind, F. Ferrarra, *Prefazione a Dunoyer. Teoria dei prodotti immateriali*, Torino, 1859, where the author considers essentially useless this category; R. Franceschelli, *Beni immateriali (Saggio di una critica del concetto)*, in *Riv. dir. ind.*, I, 1956, p. 381 ff., where the author declares the indispensability of such a juridical classification; P. Greco, voce *Beni immateriali*, in *Novissimo digesto italiano*, Torino, 1958, p. 356 ff.; M. Are, voce *Beni immateriali*, in *Enc. giur.*, V, Milano, 1959, p. 251 ff.; T. Ascarelli, *Teoria della concorrenza e dei beni immateriali*, Milano, 1960, p. 233 ff., where the author considers the intangible assets as entities that, unlike material things and energies, derive their origin and protection from the legal system not on the basis of their own essence, but on the basis of a legislative choice which, taking note of a pre-legal reality, governs its same constitutive case; D. Messinetti, voce *Beni immateriali (diritto privato)*, in *Enciclopedia del diritto*, V, Roma, 1988, p. 10 ff.; P. Perlingieri, *Il diritto civile nella legalità costituzionale*, Napoli, 1991, p. 459 ff.; S. Pugliatti, *Dottrine generali del diritto civile*, Napoli, 1997, p. 58 where the author affirms that «[I] beni immateriali si pongono accanto ai beni materiali, perché, come questi, costituiscono oggetti immediati di diritti assoluti, che sotto questo riguardo si comportano come i diritti reali, ma ne differiscono profondamente [. . .] in dipendenza della natura profondamente diversa dell'oggetto» («The intangible assets are placed next to material goods, because, like these, they constitute immediate objects of absolute rights, which in this respect behave like real rights, but differ profoundly from them [. . .] depending on their profound nature different from the object»).

22 On the specific subject of property, V. Zeno Zencovich, voce *Cosa*, in *Dig. disc. priv.*, *Sez. civ.*, IV, Torino, 1989, p. 438 ff.

23 The materialistic approach could be considered the result of the German experience, where § 90 BGB circumscribes the notion of ownership to the materiality of the assets. Nevertheless, even in Germany, analogical reasoning has been able to widen such tight meshes to allow the fullest exploitation of the institute's potential. See U. Mattei, voce *Proprietà*, cit., p. 434, where the author affirms that "(«[. . .] there is a relationship of inverse proportionality between the expansion potential of the civil notion of property and the circumscription of its object by a text of the law. [. . .] Therefore, the terminological ambiguity of article 810 of the Civil Code, because in order to adapt a well-known observation by Cardozo to the civil law context, the perplexity of the legislator makes the fortune of the educated interpreter»).

24 *See*, *ex multis*, A. Pino, *Contributo alla teoria giuridica dei beni*, in *Riv. trim. dir. proc. civ.*, I, 1948, p. 835 ff.; S. Satta, *Cose e beni nell'esecuzione forzata*, in *Riv. dir. comm.*, I, 1964, p. 350, where the author affirms that «[. . .] i beni sono sempre cose» (*author's note*, "[. . .] goods are always things").

and, on the other hand, overcoming the literal datum, he deemed such an interpretation inaccurate because of the legal link between goods and things, on which article 810 of the Italian Civil Code would not actually have a prescriptive character.[25]

In this regard, the dominant doctrine is in the sense of believing that the notions of "good" and "what" have an autonomous and distinct value, since the first lemma embodies a very broad legal concept that is substantially identified with the entities that are objects of significant interest and which, for this reason, are worthy of protection by the legal system; and the second lemma represents a classification criterion of an extra-legal matrix which, based on the physicality of the entity in question, can only be configured in the presence of the character of corporeality.

Such reasoning leads us to believe that things represent only a part of the entities qualifying as goods as worthy of protection, since the latter, following the Romanistic taxonomy,[26] include both the *res corporales*[27] and the *res incorporales*.[28]

In light of the proposed reconstruction, even intangible entities, where they are the subject of a relevant legal interest that makes them protectable by the legal

25 For an evaluation of the "thing" considered as a possible type of pre-legal entity, which represents a separate part of the surrounding matter considered by law to verify its qualification in terms of "good," or the object of a legally relevant interest, and consequently recognize a subjective juridical situation coinciding with the right of property, F. Santoro-Passarelli, *Dottrine generali del diritto civile*, cit., p. 56; V. Zeno-Zencovich, voce *Cosa*, in *Dig. disc. priv. – Sez. civ.*, III, Torino, 1998, p. 438 ff. e spec. p. 447ff.

26 For further information on the distinction between *res corporales* and *res incorporales*, C. Fadda, P.E. Bensa, *Note alla Pandette di Windscheid. IV*, Torino, 1925, p. 153, where the author highlights that «[. . .] seguendo l'esempio romano della traslazione ai *diritti* di concetti originariamente propri delle *cose*» («[. . .] following the Roman example of the translation to the rights of concepts originally proper to things») it is possible to assume that «[. . .] in questi vi è ciò che costituisce l'essenza della proprietà: l'unica differenza è nell'oggetto: nella proprietà vera è una cosa corporale, qua è una cosa incorporale. Ma ciò che per un diritto è decisivo non è già l'*oggetto*, sibbene la relazione giuridica fra il titolare e questo oggetto, relazione che poggia sui due momenti del *contenuto* e della *tutela giuridica*» («[. . .] in these rights there is what constitutes the essence of property: the only difference is in the object: in true property it is a corporal thing, here it is an incorporal thing. But what is decisive for a right is not the object, but the legal relationship between the owner and this object, a relationship that rests on the two moments of content and legal protection»). *See*, on the relationship between tangible and intangible assets, *ex multis*, S. Rodotà, *Note critiche in tema di proprietà*, cit., p. 1267 ff., where the author analyses the logical-functional relationship existing between property and other situations of belonging, such as those involving intangible assets; B. Biondi, *Istituzioni di diritto romano*, Milano, 1965, p. 152 ff.; F. Santoro-Passarelli, *Dottrine generali del diritto civile*, cit., p. 57, where the author, speaking of intangible assets and differentiating them from both cohesive and material assets, states that «[L] and intellectual, scientific, literary, artistic, interpretative, and industrial inventions (article 2575 cc) they are truly new goods, produced by the human spirit, more important than all the others, because the progress of humanity mainly depends on them [. . .]. These works are distinguished from things, precisely because, participating in the same spiritual nature of the creative or inventing intelligence of which they are projections, they are intangible goods, which should not be confused with the *corpus mechanicum* [book, painting, disc, etc.], that those works possibly contain»; L. Moccia, *Riflessioni sull'idea di proprietà*, in *Riv. trim. dir. proc. civ.*, 1, 2008, p. 21 ff., where the author underlines how the rights to intangible assets are offered to the interpreter as positivized legal figures in order to facilitate their allocation in a market that is as similar as much as possible to that of material assets.

27 These are material things that are the subject of property rights.

28 The reference is to the rights that are related to things but that are not identified with the right of ownership.

system – as happens with reference to intellectual property – can be traced back to the category of assets.

The incorporeal entity thus identified becomes an intangible asset, as it is worthy of protection, and the subject of a subjective right of enjoyment; for example, pursuant to article 832 of the Italian Civil Code or of § 90 BGB,[29] when it is expressed in a material element that allows it to be recognized by the legal system as an object of specific protection.[30]

Intangible assets, then, are included in the property right scheme, because an active subjective situation of an exclusive nature can insist on them, which, following a classic approach, gives its owner the full enjoyment of the related object and the possibility to oppose the *erga omnes* ownership yet to configure an authentic right of exclusion.[31]

Various legal systems, in fact, have long attributed importance to intangible assets, such as copyright, patent, trademark and distinctive signs, and in the same way as their discipline have operated the extension of the traditional theoretical-normative regulation of property rights to "new" intangible assets,[32] the discipline of which, due to the influence exercised by the common law, has created

29 Although, in fact, in Germany the legal system has long been refractory to the extension of the proprietary concept beyond corporeality, progressively the German civil dogmatic has perceived such a change of approach as peaceful, especially thanks to the theoretical and above all normative reference to the *geistiges Eigentum*. See, for all, M. Pierson, T. Ahrens, K.R. Fischer, *Recht des geistigen Eigentums*, Baden-Baden, 2018, *passim*.

30 In this regard, M. Are, voce *Beni immateriali*, in *Enc. del diritto*, V, 1959, p. 224, where the author, describing the evolutionary framework that has led to conferring legal importance on what follows from the exploitation of the intellectual abilities of the individual, states that «[T]ra queste nuove fonti di utilità assumono importanza prevalente le invenzioni industriali e le opere d'arte, che, al pari di altre produzioni di natura intellettuale, trovano in tutti i moderni ordinamenti, una tutela obiettiva, non alternativa, ma concorrente con la protezione del mezzo materiale di estrinsecazione o di realizzazione del contenuto intellettuale delle produzioni stesse» («[A]mong these new sources of utility assume prevalent importance industrial inventions and works of art, which, like other productions of an intellectual nature, find in all modern systems an objective protection, not an alternative, but concurrent with the protection of the material means of expression or realization of the intellectual content of the productions same»).

31 On the concept of exclusivity, for all, P. Perlingieri, *Introduzione alla problematica della «proprietà»*, cit., p. 60 ff. *See*, for a synoptic reading of the common law approach on property law, *ex multis*, B.C. Field, *The Evolution of Property Rights*, in *Kyklos*, 42, 1989, p. 319 ff.; and, in this context, for a perspective in favour of the identification of property with the concept of exclusivity, T.W. Merrill, *Property and the Right to Exclude*, in *Neb. Law Rev.*, 77, 1998, p. 730 ff., where the author speaks of this feature as a *sine qua non* of ownership; *contra*, for a more diluted vision, S. Balganesh, *Demystifying the Right to Exclude: Of Property, Inviolability, and Automatic Injunctions*, in *Harv. J. Law Pub. Pol.*, 31, 2008, p. 593 ff.; H.E. Smith, *Property as the Law of Things*, in *Harv. Law Rev.*, 125, 2012, p. 1691 ff.

32 *Ex multis*, D. Bell, *The Coming of Post-Industrial Society. A Venture in Social Forecasting*, New York, NY, 1999, p. 127, where the author affirms that «[I]f an industrial society is defined by the quantity of goods as marking a standard of living, the post-industrial society is defined by the quantity of life as measured by the services and amenities – health, education, recreation, and the arts – which are deemed desirable»; P. Spada, *Il paradigma proprietario e la protezione giuridica dell'innovazione e della nomenclatura commerciale*, in *Dir. ind.*, 2007, p. 269; Id., *La proprietà intellettuale tra "reale" e "virtuale": un guado difficile*, in *Diritto dell'Internet*, 2007, p. 437 ff.

considerable inconvenience to continental operators of law due to the offset that this nomenclature presents compared to the classic civil law setting,[33] where the category of intangible assets has usually represented a limited list;[34] at the same time, its classification among the assets object of effective ownership has always been doubtful.

However, the overseas legal experience proves to be of particular value when a consolidated approach is drawn in which property is considered as a variable bundle of rights, powers, privileges and immunities (so-called bundle of rights), which tends to enrich the theory of property as commonly perceived in the continental context with an articulated and dense juridical-cultural background.[35]

Reasoning on the terms of the problematic extension of proprietary protection to new intangible assets, we come to consider the plan of the instruments used to protect them and, in this way, to parameterize it to their evident ontological characteristics that materialize in the total dematerialization and potential universalization of access.

The first of these characteristics can be easily understood by using copyright as a reference parameter and the need for the disclosure of the literary, artistic or scientific work to be linked to a material support, resulting from this that the relative protection materializes only in the appropriation and destruction of copies that have been counterfeited, as similarly occurs for products bearing a counterfeit trademark.

On the contrary, from the moment in which goods not necessarily linked to material traits have gradually emerged, it has been possible to grasp how the legal remedies that can be used to protect them have revealed that they were conceived essentially for the circulation of material goods, as the fact clearly demonstrates that the computer program, for example, once entered and disseminated on the

33 The principle of the limited number of exclusives on intangible assets is found not only in Italy, but also in other civil law countries such as, for example, France. In this regard, F. Zenati-Castaing, T. Revet, *Les biens*, Paris, 2008, p. 114 ff.

34 *See* P. Auteri, *Diritti esclusivi sulle manifestazioni sportive e libertà di informazione*, in *AIDA*, 2003, p. 190, where the author affirms that «opinione da sempre accolta in dottrina e in giurisprudenza [. . .] che i beni immateriali, o altrimenti detti, o diritti di proprietà intellettuale sono in numero chiuso, nel senso che l'istituzione di diritti che riservino a determinati soggetti l'attività economica di sfruttamento di beni immateriali, imponendo correlativamente ai terzi di astenersi dall'interferire con tal attività, come pure la determinazione del contenuto e della durata di tali diritti, deve essere stabilita dalla legge come riguardo a ciascun tipo di bene e che viceversa non esiste nell'ordinamento un principio generale che riconosca a chiunque abbia creato un bene il diritto di sfruttarlo in esclusiva nei rapporti con i terzi in modo da trarne tutti i benefici economici di cui sia suscettibile» («an opinion that has always been accepted in doctrine and in jurisprudence [. . .] that intangible assets, or otherwise called, or intellectual property rights are limited in number, in the sense that the establishment of rights that reserve the economic activity of exploitation of intangible assets, by requiring third parties to refrain from interfering with such activity, as well as the determination of the content and duration of these rights, must be established by law as regards each type of asset and at the same time there is not general principle in the legal system which recognizes the right of anyone who has created an asset to exploit it exclusively in relations with third parties in order to derive all the economic benefits to which it is susceptible»).

35 *See infra* Chapter 2, § 4.

Internet, cannot materially return to the property of the copyright holder, since its existence is not necessarily linked to a *corpus mechanicum* but to the set of goods purely intangible,[36] whose protection is either compensatory (cash compensation for the loss or damage suffered) or is inhibitory (judicial authority orders aimed at preventing the perpetration of the harmful conduct).

On closer inspection, however, the described remedial apparatus requires the presence of a complex legal system capable of ensuring compliance with the judicial or arbitration decisions adopted, whose *ictu oculi* features cannot be traced in a prefigurable global system to which, in the case of the circulation of intangible assets, on the other hand, an appeal must often be made as it involves the use of computer networks.

The rights linked to intangible assets, such as copyright on software, are, in fact, generally separated from links with a specific national legal system and reverberate their effects on the ultra-state dimension typically referable to the Internet, unable to materialize actual forms of protection if not linked to an international framework based on the solidity of the judicial system and on the effectiveness of the measures adopted.

The evident difficulties just revealed have resulted, in the most advanced States, in the recognition, at internal level, of a particularly strong recognized protection in favour of intellectual property,[37] which in Europe has taken on particularly vivid features in the Community framework, such as, most recently, directive no. 790 of 2019 on copyright and related rights in the digital single market,[38] given the inability of agreements between states to ensure adequate protection. In this sense, in fact, we must read the experience linked to the TRIPs agreement[39] and the fact that not all States have joined the agreement establishing the World Trade Organization of which the first is an annex, and that, even when they have done so, they did not always actually respect the obligations they had assumed, exposing intellectual property to very weak international protection.

On the other hand, when compared to a framework that is characterized by the weaknesses of international protection just mentioned that derive from a systemic

36 *See* A. Gambaro, *Dai beni immobili ai beni virtuali*, in Treccani, cit.

37 See G. Resta, *Nuovi beni immateriali e numerus clausus dei diritti esclusivi*, in *Diritti esclusivi e nuovi beni immateriali*, a cura di G. Resta, Torino, 2011, p. 15, where the author highlights, in this regard, how it was an extension of the content of the reserves on a "vertical" dimension which was expressed in the identification of new exclusive faculties, in the expansion of the temporal space of duration of the right and in the compression of the area traditionally reserved for free use, with the consequent strengthening of the sanctioning system operated thanks to the use of civil and criminal instruments and the adoption of technological protection tools, as well as the increase of public and private subjects pushed to compete in the technological innovation market.

38 The reference is to the high level of protection in favour of intellectual property owners, which was well expressed, for example, by Recital nos. 4 and 9 of the Directive no. 29 of 2001 on the harmonization of copyright in the information society, by Recital no. 2 from Recital no. 10 of the Directive no. 48 of 2004 on the respect of intellectual property rights, and, lastly, by Recital no. 2 of the Directive no. 790 of 2019 on copyright and related rights in the digital single market.

39 The TRIPs agreement (Trade-Related Aspects of Intellectual Property Rights) was signed in Marrakech on 15 April 1994 and then merged into the World Trade Organization.

inability to ensure forms of protection plus accidents, a different attitude arises that belongs to the same holder of the right and which translates into the desire not to subject the asset that is the object of it to any form of protection or to subject it to forms of moderate protection in order to ensure maximum usability to third parties, thus opening the way to the configuration of the permit copyright or copyleft, as a model of copyright management.[40]

In this perspective, therefore, we do not move either in the sense of expanding the intellectual creations that can be protected or in the sense of extending the areas of exclusivity that the ownership of assets guarantees to the owner, but, by adopting an opposite behaviour, we try to ensure the greater possibility of use of the asset both in its moral component and in its economic component.

The boundaries between the two or more creative ideas, the original one and the derived one, thus become blurred and accentuate the faculty of elaboration of derivative works that the traditional discipline of copyright already allows, without, however, re-proposing, in the case of copyleft, the problem of the limits of the exclusive right by virtue of a consent to the full usability of the (main) work that its author has given since its creation.

The examination of the impact that copyleft can have on copyright and even more generally on the logic of ownership cannot, therefore, neglect some fundamental, albeit synthetic, clarifications on substantial concepts, such as copyright and licensing use, where the first term can be basically described as the indication of who is the owner of the copyright on a work, such as software, whose creative work is protected through rules that attribute various subjective situations that can be asserted towards the thirds (heteronomy), and the second term can be seen as the set of all the rules that the same author establishes for the distribution and use of his work (autonomy).

Therefore, the license of use has practically no value if the copyright is not present, or if the subject or subjects who are the owners of the rights on the work that is the object of it are not present, as only the latter can act to ensure compliance with the terms set out in the license itself.

A work of others, in fact, cannot be legitimately exploited to one's liking without the consent of the person who is the author, unless there is no copyright and the

40 In general, it has been noted, in fact, how copyleft represents a model of copyright management that is based on a licensing system designed to allow the creator, in his capacity as original owner of the rights on the work, to indicate to the users of the latter the ways in which it should be used, disseminated and often even modified, while respecting some essential conditions. In the stronger version of copyleft, the users of the work are obliged, in case they want to distribute it after having made changes, to do so under the same legal regime and generally under the same license provided *ab initio* by the author of the original work, so that he is guaranteed the possibility of providing a similar set of freedoms throughout the distribution chain and the possible elaboration of further licenses. Beyond the strictly technical-legal profiles, the term copyleft is also used to indicate a cultural orientation that aims to challenge the rigidity of copyright in its traditional setting. *See*, in the latter regard, P. Pisano, *Managing innovation. Creare, gestire e diffondere. Innovazione nei sistemi relazionali*, Limena, 2011, p. 224 ff.

work is not explicitly distributed to the public domain,[41] or there is no license of use or the methods of use are not indicated,[42] or both the copyright and the license of use are found, but unlawfully the user-distributor does not respect the latter.

On closer inspection, however, the reasons for openness that underlie the copyright permission scheme lie not only in the choice, one could almost say of thought, that the owner of the asset makes in allowing third parties to use and modify the works, but also in the facilitation that in this sense comes from the peculiarities that the digital age presents, where technology allows any figurative, linguistic or musical message to be transformed into files and, through binary codes and, therefore, without the necessary support material, to be transmitted throughout the planet in real time, allowing its receptor the possibility of finding its own and reworking it.[43]

If, then, the right to modify the work is based on a license, which as a legal technical term indicates the possibility of accessing an asset without committing an illegal act, it could hardly be paid in the presence of a real right, because no real-subjective position on the asset would derive from this contractual instrument, since the rights of the person who acquires the right could be restricted *ex contractu* by operating in an antagonistic manner to the active situations that are traditionally granted to the purchaser of an asset protected by copyright.

The situation, however, could change if a license derives, as happens in the milder forms of copyleft, a full right of the user not only to use the work that represents the object, but also to its modification with consequent economic exploitation of the transformations that have been perpetrated (transition from permissive license to proprietary license).

The possibility of the integral use of the good therefore imposes to evaluate its character in terms of reality or non-reality, having to understand whether the right, the power or the faculty that have been constituted have as their object the good (*in rem*) or derive from a personal relationship of the user with its owner (*in personam*), so as to entail the remediation of the concept of copyright through the expansion of the notion of property right, even in the awareness that there is an ontological difference between computer programs or digital messages and agricultural funds, for example, which cannot be inevitably transcended by basing some analogy of legal regime on an alleged incentive to creativity.

The aforementioned problem is not of secondary importance and has not only theoretical implications, but also and above all practical aspects that pass, among

41 In this regard, it is good to specify, on the one hand, that even if the work is completely anonymous, the author is well entitled to claim rights over it, and, on the other, that copyright represents a subjective situations term whose effectiveness varies according to the specific cases considered, so that when copyright prescribes the work can be used by everyone falling into the public domain.

42 In this case, in fact, it is necessary to make full reference to the legislation on copyright which will also operate in a supplementary key.

43 Consider, in addition to the more lax forms of copyleft applied to the software that allow the user to modify the computer program and its consequent economic exploitation, to the re-arrangement of musical pieces (CD sampling), or to the incorporation of previously recorded pieces in new musical compositions. *See*, on the impact of digital technologies on legal rules, G. Pascuzzi, *Come le tecnologie digitali cambiano le regole giuridiche*, in *Il diritto nell'era digitale*, a cura di G. Pascuzzi, Bologna, 2016, p. 205 ff.

other things, to the remedies that can be used in case of violation of the legal situation emerging from the use of the asset (actions of a petition or exact fulfillment) and for the complications deriving from the non-rival character of the intangible assets that populate the cyber space designed to allow a use that is not necessarily reserved for one or a few specific individuals.

The fact is, however, that the equivalence between ownership of corporal goods and belonging of incorporal goods to which, even within the community, the legislator refers for a systematic framework of incorporeality, which draws evident inspiration both from the precept contained in article 17, paragraph 2, of the Charter of Fundamental Rights of the European Union (Charter of Nice), according to which "intellectual property is protected" which by the precept contained in article 118 of the Treaty on the Functioning of the European Union (TFEU), according to which "Intellectual property designates the set of exclusive rights recognized on creations."[44] And, following the same perspective, both the European Court of Justice posed when it ruled, for example, in *Scarlet v. SABAM*, stating that "fundamental right to property, which includes the rights linked to intellectual property, must be balanced against the protection of other fundamental rights";[45] and the European Court of Human Rights, when it stated, for example, in *Anheuser Busch v. Portugal*,[46] that the property right, which is recognized as including intellectual property, is protected by article 1 of the First Protocol of the European Court of Human Rights.

Described in these terms the phenomenon of access to new intangible assets and, above all, to the good that tends to ensure maximally the management and control of cyber space, software, could be read in a logic in favour of its appropriability. It is assumed that computer programs represent the fruit of research and development investments which should ensure their author the benefits they could bring.[47]

44 *See*, for further information also based on different thinking perspectives, *ex multis*, S. Rodotà, *Il progetto della Carta europea e l'art. 42 Cost.*, in *La proprietà nella Carta europea dei diritti fondamentali. Atti del convegno di studi organizzato presso l'Università degli Studi di Siena, Siena 18–19 Ottobre 2002*, a cura di G.D. Comporti, Milano, 2005, p. 170 ff.; R. Mastroianni, *Proprietà intellettuale e costituzioni europee*, in *AIDA*, 2005, p. 9 ff.; Braegelmann, *The Constitutional Scope and Limits to Copyright Law in the United States, in Comparison with the Scope and Limits Imposed by Constitutional and European Law on Copyright Law in Germany*, in *Cardozo Arts Ent. L.J.*, 27, 2009, p. 137 ff.

45 Case C-70/10 *Scarlet/SABAM* [2011], § 44.

46 *Anheuser Busch v. Portugal*, App No. 73049/01 (ECtHR 11 January 2007), § 72, where it is stated that «[. . .] the Grand Chamber agrees with the Chamber's conclusion that Article 1 of Protocol No. 1 is applicable to intellectual property as such».

47 R. Caso, G. Pascuzzi, *Il diritto d'autore dell'era digitale*, in *Il diritto dell'era* digitale, cit., p. 161, note 31, where the author highlight how «[I]l riconoscimento al software della tutela propria del diritto d'autore [. . .] ha consentito la nascita di una fiorente industria di settore [. . .]. Tale logica rigidamente proprietaria [. . .] ha nel frattempo suscitato perplessità in quanti ritengono che la pratica di libera condivisione del software debba essere costitutiva dell'operare della comunità scientifica». («[T]he recognition of the software's copyright protection [. . .] has allowed the birth of a thriving industry in the sector [. . .]. This strictly proprietary logic [. . .] has in the meantime raised perplexity in those who believe that the practice of free sharing of software must be constitutive of the work of the scientific community»).

This approach, which in the TRIPs agreements has translated into the provision of a necessary protection of the software recognized in the individual Member States being a mandatory prerequisite for participation in the WTO, has implied in the United States, for example, the recognition of the program creator from elaborator of a proprietary protection that has implied, also at the international level, a protection of particular intensity.

It should be noted, however, how the described tendency to subject the computer program to a proprietary logic, even from a remedial perspective, is accompanied by a different, but equally pressing, orientation, which has found substance in the free/open source movement for then lead to the copyleft, according to which the software must be the object of a free enjoyment by users who are also free to be able to modify and exploit it, although it constitutes a derivative work from origin, due to its character of complex result that follows the development of programs already existing and elaborated after a free research.

More properly, in the case of software, the technical reason that is identified to recognize its free usability is that access to the source codes allows you to continuously improve the program through contributions from the users themselves, making it increasingly complex and, at the same time, they avoid its progressive aging.[48]

The philosophy underlying the mental attitude described is therefore concretized in the idea that the fruit of the work of a community must remain, as far as possible, at the disposal of the community of origin, allowing it to enjoy what are the results of an effort to collective character.

In these terms, the diffusion of innovative models of knowledge production is achieved, which appears to be facilitated by the use of so-called licenses non-proprietary and from the establishment of principles of circulation of knowledge that see their typical expression in free software.[49]

But if this is true, it is equally true that, with particular reference to copyleft in its weakest forms, the subsequent user is free to be able to transform the software he or she has used into an owner, obtaining ownership of both moral and economic exclusive exploitation.

A choice focused on exclusivity arises, however, in theoretical contrast with the well-known non-rival nature that tends to present the virtual good and which derives from its ability to provide utilities that are not always anchored to the exclusive use made of them, so that the justification principal to such closure can ideally be traced to the opportunity to incentivize their production which is obviously closely linked to the completion of investments.

48 Indeed, it is no coincidence that programs created through forms of spontaneous cooperation are usually able to compete, in qualitative terms, with products developed at an entrepreneurial level.

49 The GNU project (acronym which stands for "GNU's Not Unix") embodies the idea carried out by Richard Stallman to react to the emergence of a software that, thanks to the exclusive right, has moved to compress the user's freedom of use. In this sense it is worth reading the diffusion of the operating system for personal computers called Linux whose source code has been made available on the net, so as to allow any programmer who wishes to modify it and improve it. *See*, on the forms of collaborative and distributive creation in the IT sector, T. O'Reilly, *What Is Web 2.0: Design Patterns and Business Models for the Next Generation of Software*, in *Comm. Strat.*, 65, 2007, p. 17 ff.

It is argued, in fact, in the sense that, even if software is a non-rival good, programmers need hardware, and therefore rival goods, as well as other work tools that have the necessary character of exclusive goods.

But on closer inspection, this thesis lacks in excess because the incentive connected to the economic aspect of copyright can have even a minimal impact on scientific production per se, the results of which can be left freely usable, except for any possible charges of tax that can be linked to it.

Although, then, the extension to intangible assets of the concept of ownership is undeniable in a way almost analogous to what happens for material assets,[50] it is necessary to note, once again, the difficulty that they experience in being subject to a unique and exclusive use; in reality, it is problematic to exclude other subjects from their enjoyment, due to their intrinsic characteristics, among which the reproducibility[51] in an indefinite number of specimens is quite peculiar.[52]

It can be considered that the proprietary logic, with its typical implications in terms of exclusivity, is extended to intangible assets because, due to the easy possibility of use by third parties that characterizes them, it alone ensures and protects their development, when in reality is it within the owner's own right to choose the exclusivity regime or not to which the property is to be subjected?

Exclusivity as a trait referable to the proprietary scheme would not represent a necessary condition, but rather an element made available to the owner of the asset who, according to his own needs, could decide whether or not to use it in the fullest and most integral terms, as if to express a confirmatory or abdicative will.

In this perspective, the existence of exclusive rights would find a different light, read, among the other solutions proposed, or in the terms of the utilitarian theories that identify the basis in the promotion of knowledge[53] as demonstrated by Article I, sec. 8, cl. 8 of the US Constitution,[54] or in those of the personalistic theories that capture an expression of the author's personality in the work,[55] or in those of the natural law theories that read in the appropriability of intangible assets the just reward for the creative work carried out,[56] or in the more contemporary theories

50 U. Mattei, voce *Proprietà*, cit., p. 436, where the author affirms, in this regard, that «[. . .] l'istituzione giuridica della proprietà resta anche in questo campo uno strumento indispensabile di incentivo allo sviluppo economico e di efficiente allocazione delle risorse» («[. . .] the legal institution of ownership remains an indispensable tool in this field as well as an incentive for economic development and efficient allocation of resources»).

51 It is about the possibility of separating intellectual creation from the material support in which it is incorporated.

52 The economic doctrine of law speaks about the non-scarcity of intangible goods, to mark the difference with respect to material goods, which, per se, are instead characterized by a natural scarcity. *See*, for all, U. Mattei, voce *Proprietà*, cit., p. 435 ff.

53 T. Ascarelli, *Teoria della conoscenza e dei beni immateriali. Lezioni di diritto industriale*, Milano, 1957, *passim*.

54 *See*, in this regard, R. Caso, G. Pascuzzi, *Il diritto d'autore dell'era digitale*, in *Il diritto dell'era* digitale, cit., p. 149, where the author highlights how this constitutional provision ensures exclusive rights for limited periods of time in order to promote the progress of science and useful arts.

55 *See, ex multis*, R. Merges, *Justifying Intellectual Property*, Cambridge, MA, 2011, *passim*.

56 As it is well understood in article 27 of the 1948 Declaration of Human Rights which, on the one hand, expresses the right of every individual to take part in the cultural life of humanity, to enjoy the

that identify copyright as a means for the development of a pluralistic and democratic society,[57] or that apply the Aristotelian ethics of virtue to the balancing of the antagonistically involved interests divided between private exclusivity and public access to intellectual property.[58]

One could, then, grasp the philosophy underlying copyleft in this peculiarly proprietary perspective – because it is "inclusive"[59] – where, in the most extreme forms, the programmer completely frees the product he has created and makes it not only fully usable and enjoyable by anyone who wants it, but, unlike what the original programmer did, it can also be economically exploited by him, if the user has made changes to the software, as if he himself were the integral creator.

The study conducted in these pages therefore aims to analyse how emerging technologies, and especially the Internet, can affect the way goods circulate, transforming the fundamental rights and freedoms involved,[60] challenging the traditional categories and qualifications of properties,[61] and, in more general terms,

---

arts and to participate in scientific progress and its benefits, and, for the other, it affirms the right of every individual to the protection of the moral and material interests that derive from his scientific, literary and artistic production. *See* R. Caso, G. Pascuzzi, *Il diritto d'autore dell'era digitale*, in *Il diritto dell'era digitale*, cit., p. 149.

57 W.W. Fisher, *Theories of Intellectual Property*, in *New Essays in the Legal and Political Theory of Property*, Cambridge, 2001, p. 168 ff.

58 D. Lametti, *«Etica della virtù»: una rilettura della riforma del copyright canadese*, in *Dir. informazione e informtica*, 2013, p. 657.

59 The claimed inversion would derive from the fact that the owner of the intangible asset subject to copyleft would aim not to maintain the exclusive enjoyment of the asset but to its full usability, including economic ones, by third parties.

60 For a classic evaluation of the link between property and liberty, C.A. Reich, *The New Property*, in *Yale Law J.*, 73, 1964, p. 733 ff.; and, critically, U. Mattei, *"Senza proprietà non c'è libertà." Falso!*, Roma-Bari, 2014. See, for an approach that contrasts the same idea of centrality of the proprietary model, J. Boyle, *Foreword: The Opposite of Property*, in *Law Contemp. Probs.*, 1–2, 2003, p. 1 ff.

61 *See, ex multis*, in the vast literature on the subject, S. Rodotà, *Note critiche in tema di proprietà*, in *Rivista Trimestrale Di Diritto E Procedura Civile*, II, 1960, p. 1252 ff.; Id., voce *Proprietà (diritto vigente)*, in *Noviss. dig. it.*, XIV, Torino, 1964, p. 125 ff.; R. Sacco, *Il sistema delle fonti e il diritto di proprietà*, in *Riv. trim. dir. proc. civ.*, 1970, p. 462 ff.; P. Perlingieri, *Introduzione alla problematica della «proprietà»*, Napoli, 1971; P. Rescigno, *Per uno studio sulla proprietà*, in *Riv. dir. civ.*, I, 1972, p. 1 ff.; U. Natoli, *La proprietà*, Milano, 1976; S. Rodotà, *La logica proprietaria tra schemi ricostruttivi e interessi reali. 5–6 (1976–1977). Itinerari moderni della proprietà*, in *Quaderni fiorentini per la storia del pensiero giuridico moderno*, II, Milano, 1978, p. 881 ff.; F. Santoro-Passarelli, voce *Proprietà*, in *Enc. del Novecento*, V, Roma, 1981, p. 660 ff.; S. Rodotà, *Art. 42 Cost.*, in *Commentario della Costituzione*, a cura di G. Branca, Bologna-Roma, 1982, p. 69 ff.; P. Rescigno, voce *Proprietà (Diritto privato)*, in *Enc. dir.*, XXXVII, Milano, 1988, pp. 254 ff.; C. Salvi, *Il contenuto del diritto di proprietà. Artt. 832–833*, in *Il Codice civile. Commentario*, Milano, 1994; Id., *Il diritto di proprietà*, in *Tratt. di diritto civile e commerciale*, già diretto da A. Cicu e F. Messineo e continuato da L. Mengoni, Milano, 1995; U. Mattei, voce *Proprietà*, in *Digesto Disc. Priv. – Sez. Civ.*, XV, Torino, 1997, p. 432 ff.; G. Alpa, A. Fusaro, M. Bessone, *Poteri dei privati e statuto della proprietà*, Roma, 2001; G. Alpa, A. Fusaro, *Le metamorfosi del diritto di proprietà*, Matera, 2011; S. Rodotà, *Il terribile diritto*, Bologna, 2013; U. Mattei, *I Diritti Reali. 2. La proprietà*, in *Trattato di Diritto Civile*, Torino, 2015; C.M. Bianca, *Diritto civile. 6. La proprietà*, Milano, 2017; A. Gambaro, *La proprietà. Beni, proprietà, possesso*, in *Tratt. di diritto privato*, a cura di G. Iudica e P. Zatti, Milano, 2017.

stimulating, if necessary, a re-thinking of the relationship between man and good in the light of parameters and references other than those that have been traditionally used.[62]

The challenge that digitality launches to traditional models of copyright protection is played out on different levels, as demonstrated by the extreme ease of production and reproduction of the works made with the use of cheap machinery that express a widespread production capacity and practically unlimited, the impossibility of qualitatively distinguishing the copy from the original, the dematerialization of the digital copy which is neither scarce nor rival,[63] the ease of distribution of the works, the possibility of opening (i.e. open source code) and closing (i.e. cryptography) of information.[64]

More specifically, the idea of evaluating the evolution to which proprietary logic is exposed in a digital age leads to,[65] in the following pages, an analysis of the framework referable to intellectual property,[66] with special reference to licenses,

62 The impact capacity of technology, which is also called "exceptionalism," entails *ex se* the emergence of new problems which, by definition, imply, in turn, the need to develop new rules and principles. *See*, for further information, *ex multis*, G. Capogrossi, *L'ambiguità del diritto contemporaneo*, in *La crisi del diritto*, a cura di G. Balladore Pallieri, P. Calamandrei, A. Capograssi, F. Carnelutti, G. Delitala, A.C. Jemolo, A. Ravà, G. Ripert, Padova, 1953, p. 19 ff.; J. Mokyr, *The Lever of Riches. Technological Creativity and Economic Progress*, Oxford, 1990, *passim*; V.K. Vieweg, *Reaktionen des Rechts auf Entwicklungen der Technik*, in *Technische Innovation und Recht. Antrieb oder Hemmnis?*, Herausgeber von M. Schulte, Heidelberg, 1996, p. 35 ff.; N. Irti, *L'ordine giuridico del mercato*, Roma-Bari, 1998, *passim*; L. Mengoni, *Diritto e tecnica*, in *Riv. trim. dir. e proc. civ.*, 2001, p. 1 ff.; G. Bernstein, *Toward a General Theory on Law and Technology: Introduction*, in *Minn. J.L. Sci. Tech.*, 8, 2007, p. 441 ff.; F. Cafaggi, *New Foundations of Transnational Private Regulation*, in *J. Law Soc.*, 38, 2011, p. 20 ff.

63 This aspect is so true that some types of use of a certain digital asset do not require the physical possession of a copy of the file that contains it, since there is access to the file via the Internet and a temporary (ephemeral) copy on one's computer (i.e. vision of a streaming movie).

64 R. Caso, G. Pascuzzi, *Il diritto d'autore dell'era digitale*, in *Il diritto dell'era* digitale, cit., p. 154 ff.

65 *See*, F. Vassalli, *Il diritto di proprietà*, in *Studi giuridici*, II, 2, Milano, 1960, p. 417–418, where the author, referring prophetically to the property transformation process, describes it as «[. . .] da un lato, erosione del diritto di proprietà, per quanto riguarda il contenuto, cioè riduzione dei poteri riconosciuti al proprietario; dall'altro, erosione della sfera riservata alla proprietà individuale, e cioè riduzione degli oggetti sui quali ammettersi il diritto di proprietà nei privati» («[. . .] on the one hand, erosion of the property right, as regards the content, that is, reduction of the powers granted to the owner; on the other hand, erosion of the sphere reserved for individual property, that is, the reduction of the objects on which the right of ownership is admitted in private individuals»).

66 With specific reference to copyright, it should be noted that the right to authorship and integrity of the work, the right to publish the work or to keep it unpublished, the right to withdraw the work from the market, in their being as many profiles of copyright, are understood as inalienable, imprescriptible and non-transferable rights and, as such, not subject to negotiation. Cfr., *ex aliis*, T. Ascarelli, *Teoria della concorrenza e interesse del consumatore*, in *Saggi di diritto commerciale*, Milano, 1955, p. 52; Id., *Teoria della concorrenza e dei beni immateriali*, Milano, 1960, p. 854 ff.; L.C. Ubertazzi, *I diritti d'autore e connessi*, Milano, 2000, p. 12; P. Spada, *Il paradigma proprietario e la protezione giuridica dell'innovazione e della nomenclatura commerciale*, in *Dir. industriale*, 3, 2007, p. 269 ff., where the author highlights how the same proprietary paradigm, expressed by intellectual property and intangible assets, is in crisis, since the classic figures of legal knowledge brought back to the proprietary form need an adaptation to an economy that is more movable

free or open source software[67] (i.e. free/open source software [F/OSS] license)[68] with non-copyleft effect,[69] and therefore to free or open permissive licenses concerning computer programs that allow the user to use them fully, full modifiability and full exploitation, including economic, and which therefore translate from derivative licenses into substantially proprietary licenses.

In fact, from the study of copyleft and its consequent effects, we will try to understand more clearly whether the current conceptual apparatus in which the proprietary logic finds expression has problematic traits or whether the issues that

---

than real estate, more of production than of enjoyment, so much so as to lead to an authentic crisis of ownership of intangible assets.

67 With the term *open source*, in computer science we want to indicate a software whose authors make the source code public, that is the text of an algorithm of a program created in a programming language that is understood within a source file, favouring its diffusion and free study and allowing independent programmers, by means of user licenses, to modify and extend it. In this regard, the Open Source Definition (OSD) assumes particular importance which, elaborated by Perens, represents a sort of decalogue that aims to help the interpreter to correctly understand the value to be attributed to this concept. *See* B. Perens, *The Open Source Definition*, available at https://opensource.org/docs/osd; M. Bertani, *Guida alle licenze di software libero e open source*, cit., *passim*; V. Zeno-Zencovich, P. Sammarco, *Sistema e archetipi delle licenze open source*, cit., *passim*; A. Florio, *Il problema della qualificazione giuridica delle licenze software free ed open source*, in *dirittodellinformatica.it*, 2009, available at www.dirittodellinformatica.it/diritto-autore/copyright-focus/qualificazione-giuridica-licenze-software-free-open-source.html.

68 F. Martini, *Open Source, pubblica amministrazione e libero mercato concorrenziale*, in *Il diritto dell'economia*, 3–4, 2009, p. 676 ff., where the author, at p. 686, emphasizes the importance of free software in stimulating technological progress to the extent that it progressively replaces «[. . .] standardizzazione fino ad oggi generata dai modelli di diffusione del software proprietario che hanno fortemente ristretto la concorrenza sui mercati sfruttando il diritto di proprietà intellettuale in chiave protezionistica. La libera disponibilità del programma modificabile e utilizzabile da chiunque incentiva i produttori di programmi ad interagire e a migliorare il prodotto, può essere uno strumento di differenziazione delle imprese e, in ultima analisi, può svolgere un'importante funzione pro-concorrenziale» (*author's note*, "[. . .] the standardization up to now generated by the models of diffusion of proprietary software which have strongly restricted competition on the markets by exploiting the intellectual property right in a protectionist key. The free availability of the program that can be modified and used by anyone encourages program producers to interact and improve the product, can be a tool for differentiating companies and, ultimately, can play an important pro-competitive function").

69 Copyleft represents a type of profoundly permissive license, so much so as to allow third parties to develop derivative works whose rules of use, dissemination and modification can assume, in the event of non-copyleft, traits completely different from those that the license of the original work foresaw. More in detail, it can be noted that the advantages of copyleft *lato sensu* are identified with the freedom to use, exploit and modify, which manifests itself in the possibility of sub-licensing, creating and distributing derivative works without any limit of any kind, especially in the case of non-copyleft, with all the consequent advantages for programmers, also in terms of greater difficulty in emerging potential conflicts with other copyleft or proprietary licenses. However, embracing a perspective of complete promotion of the philosophy of sharing, non-copyleft can be perceived negatively precisely because of the possibility that it gives, in addition to the other freedoms mentioned above, to allow third-party users to subject the derivative works to proprietary licenses, so as to restrictively affect the full expression of the freedoms of future users.

the Internet poses can be managed in the legislative-conceptual framework already existing[70] in terms of both content and any applicable protection.[71]

If, in fact, the legislation on copyright hinges on the recognition of exclusive rights to the creators of intellectual works, these subjective situations and their coercibility are increasingly exposed to requests for modification that could perhaps reflect on the traditional conceptual and remedial structure,[72] as a movement in progress seems to manifest, at least for some intangible assets (i.e. software), which on the one hand would be marking a gradual turnaround compared to recent times, where the exclusive allocation of intangible resources it represented the rule,[73] and for the other it would translate into a return to the approaches adopted in the past, where freedom in their use has covered the traits of ordinariness.[74] And precisely the non-copyleft applied to computer programs would seem to embody this double and dichotomous tendency, allowing the author, on the one hand, to give full freedom to the use of the program that constitutes its object (perspective of inclusion), and on the other hand, to legitimize the user to operate in a perspective of exclusivity on the changes he has made to the derivative work (exclusion perspective).

70 *See*, for a general reflection on the institutional tools that can be used to incentivize or discourage the change in the regulatory framework that exists at a given historical moment, C.P. Gillette, *Lock-In Effects in Law and Norms*, in *Boston Univ. Law Rev*., 78, 1998, p. 813 ff.

71 In this regard, the reference is to the fungible nature of the assets considered here from which it derives that, should protection needs arise, the inhibitory protection would lose that specificity which, in the presence of non-fungible assets, it instead has compared to the compensatory one. For reasons of taxonomic completeness and therefore to grasp the different regime that follows the type of asset considered, it is then necessary to observe how the classic nomenclature on assets also considers the different movable/real estate plan. It follows that, as a rule, whoever has physical control of a movable property is the owner, as clearly evidenced in the Italian legal system, article 1153 of the Italian Civil Code, which operates with a view to facilitating the conferral of property rights through a reduction in transfer costs and an enhancement, albeit not absolute, of the factual situation found in most cases. With reference, on the other hand, to real estate property, only rarely does anyone who is physically on a land really own it, thus encountering greater difficulty in reducing transaction costs thanks to the use of the protection of possession, which is sacrificed to all advantage of special advertising rules. It is noted, however, that some movable property is also subject to a treatment similar to that reserved for landed property, as is the case for registered movable property, whose particular discipline, which focuses entirely on the privilege granted to specific forms of advertising, is justified not so much for their value or for their scarcity, according to an economic analysis of the law, as for their tracing to rules of responsibility that result from their ownership and, therefore, to their potential use. *See* U. Mattei, voce *Proprietà*, cit., p. 435 ff.

72 *See* G. Resta, *Nuovi beni immateriali e* numerus clausus *dei diritti esclusivi*, in *Diritti esclusivi e nuovi beni immateriali*, cit., p. 15, where the author, in this regard, speaks of an expansion, on a "horizontal" dimension, of the entities that may be subject to private protection due to the overcoming of the conceptual paradigms that operated as a margin for the expansion of intellectual monopolies.

73 *See, ex multis*, C. Caron, *L'irrésistible décadence du domaine public en droit de la propriété intellectuelle*, in *Etudes offerts à Jacques Dupichot*, Bruxelles, 2004, p. 61 ff.

74 *See*, to the contrary, G. Resta, *L'appropriazione dell'immateriale. Quali limiti?*, in *Dir. informaz. e informatica*, 2004, p. 21 ff.

As we have already considered in these introductory pages, the problematic nature of bringing *sic et simpliciter* back to intangible assets the same legal rules developed considering the characteristics of material assets has been entrusted to that set of legal principles and rules that are found in intellectual property and industrial property.[75]

In this perspective, an illustrative scope could be reconnected to the central theme of these pages, copyleft,[76] applied to computer programs (so-called software),

75 The term *intellectual property* refers to that set of intangible assets resulting from the creative and/or inventive activity of man, such as artistic and literary works, industrial inventions, design and trademarks, which belong to the three major areas of copyright, patent law and trademark law. In recent decades, in the wake of growing technological and digital innovation, there has been a trend towards a review of the principles that are the foundation of the intellectual property system. In fact, of until a few years ago, an intellectual work, such as a novel, disconnected from its physical support – the paper book – was not conceivable, and with the advent of digital technology the work has increasingly strained to dematerialize and be totally independent from the physical support. This led to a real revolution in the economic and legal balances that had been stabilizing for centuries. It follows that the most recent legal doctrine has deemed the term intellectual property no longer adequate since it would lead to improperly superimposing contemporary concepts (such as intellectual property, invention, trademark, brand, design) with concepts relating to property in the more classical (i.e. that relating to material goods, inherited from Roman law). Therefore we tend to speak more appropriately of "industrial property" with regard to innovation from a technological point of view. Industrial property is one of two broad categories – the other is literary and artistic property (copyright) – which constitute intellectual property. More specifically, the works of human ingenuity, by nature and discipline, can be classified into three macro categories, represented by the works of creative ingenuity, which refer to the world of art and culture (literary works, theatrical performances, cinema and television, photographs, paintings, architectural projects, organizational schemes, etc.), with distinctive signs, such as the brand, the company, the sign, the geographical indication, the designation of origin, and technical and design innovations, which concern inventions, utility models, industrial designs and models, topographies of semiconductor products and new plant varieties. We can therefore speak of industrial property rights only with reference to these last two categories. Indeed, art. 1 of Codice della Proprietà Industriale (Code of Intellectual Property) states that «Ai fini del presente Codice, l'espressione proprietà industriale comprende marchi e altri segni distintivi, indicazioni geografiche, denominazioni di origine, disegni e modelli, invenzioni, modelli di utilità, topografie dei prodotti a semiconduttori, informazioni aziendali riservate e nuove varietà vegetali» («For the purposes of this Code, the term industrial property includes trademarks and other distinctive signs, geographical indications, designations of origin, designs and models, inventions, utility models, topographies of semiconductor products, confidential company information and new plant varieties»). Article 2 of the Code then specifies that the methods of purchasing industrial property rights are represented by patenting (inventions, utility models, new plant varieties) and registration (trademarks, designs and models, topographies of semiconductor products).

76 According to the major orientation followed by the jurists who have dealt with the copyleft argument, these licenses must be qualified as contracts, in which the licensor expresses the will to distribute his work according to the terms provided in the license when he attaches it to the work, and the licensee expresses his willingness to accept the terms of the license through an attitude that unequivocally expresses his adhesive will. If the contractual nature of copyleft licenses derives their general collocation within the Italian legal system, at least, since they are expressive forms of autonomy sanctioned by article 1322 of the Italian Civil Code, the question they raise concerns rather their compatibility with the limits and schemes within which private individuals

as a possible expression of a different way of behaving of the property (traditionally understood) that follows the impact exercised by the intangible on the legal circulation of goods.

Resuming further the necessary insights, it is now necessary to point out that, from a semantic point of view, the phrase copyleft represents the exact opposite of

can regulate their relationships: are the clauses contained in copyleft licenses valid and effective in the light, for example, of the discipline of unfair clauses? Certainly, in the absence of a general discipline that defines in detail the operating procedures of these licenses, it is the contract that must be referred to. *See*, in general on the subject of the legal qualification of copyleft licenses, M. Bertani, *Guida alle licenze di Software Libero e Open Source*, Milano, 2004, *passim*; V. Zeno-Zencovich, P. Sammarco, *Sistema e archetipi delle Licenze Open Source*, Milano, 2004, *passim*. A very different problem, which can only be mentioned here due to its complexity, is the application of copyleft in Italy, where the Italian Society of Authors and Publishers (SIAE), in its capacity as an associative body in charge of managing collective rights of use of intellectual works, in fact exercises an authentic monopolistic function that finds its legitimacy in article 180, § 1, of law no. 633 of 1941 (copyright law), according to which «L'attività di intermediario, comunque attuata, sotto ogni forma diretta o indiretta di intervento, mediazione, mandato, rappresentanza ed anche di cessione per l'esercizio dei diritti di rappresentazione, di esecuzione, di recitazione, di radiodiffusione ivi compresa la comunicazione al pubblico via satellite e di riproduzione meccanica e cinematografica di opere tutelate, è riservata in via esclusiva alla Società italiana degli autori ed editori (SIAE)» («The activity of intermediary, however carried out, in any direct or indirect form of intervention, mediation, mandate, representation and also of assignment for the exercise of the rights of representation, performance, acting, broadcasting including communication to the public via satellite and mechanical and cinematographic reproduction of protected works, is reserved exclusively to the Italian Society of Authors and Publishers (SIAE)»). On closer inspection, however, since in these pages the topic dealt with essentially focuses on the impact that the circulation of F/OSS software with a non-copyleft effect has on the proprietary logic, the question of the harmonization of copyleft with the activity of the SIAE, although of certain importance, it fades into the general economy of discourse. See, with regard to the copyleft-SIAE relationship, S. Aliprandi, *Teoria e pratica del Copyleft*, cit., p. 44 ff., where the author, at p. 44, after underlining the exclusive nature of the SIAE activity, underlines how it is «[. . .] facile intuire come una simile impostazione difficilmente possa convivere con la scelta di rilasciare opere in regime di *copyleft*. È vero che gli autori sono liberi di scegliere di non usufruire dei servizi di tutela offerti dalla Siae e a maggior ragione di non associarsi all'ente. Ma è anche vero che attualmente in Italia e solo la Siae ad avere i mezzi per garantire certi servizi determinanti relativi alla distribuzione e allo sfruttamento economico di opere dell'ingegno [. . .]. Da ciò deriva che: primo, vista la situazione di monopolio l'autore che voglia avvantaggiarsi di tali servizi non può far altro che affidare la gestione dei diritti sulla sua opera alla Siae; secondo, vista l'impostazione esclusiva, l'autore che effettuasse questa scelta perderebbe la possibilità di promuovere e diffondere la propria opera attraverso altri canali, compresa la possibilità di applicazione di una licenza copyleft» («[. . .] easy to understand how such an approach can hardly coexist with the choice to release works under copyleft. It is true that the authors are free to choose not to use the protection services offered by SIAE and, even more so, not to join the body. But it is also true that currently in Italy it is only SIAE that has the means to guarantee certain crucial services relating to the distribution and economic exploitation of intellectual property [. . .]. From this it follows that: first, given the monopoly situation, the author who wants to take advantage of these services can only entrust the management of the rights on his work to SIAE; second, given the exclusive setting, the author who made this choice would lose the opportunity to promote and disseminate his work through other channels, including the possibility of applying a copyleft license»).

copyright,[77] given that right, in English, means right, but also right (right side), and left, on the contrary, it means left.[78]

From a legal point of view, copyleft allows users to make use of the intellectual work, to modify it and to disseminate it in a less constrained manner than what would derive from copyright.

In addition, although copyleft can relate to any intellectual work (just like copyright), it generally relates to computer programs (software).[79]

77 It should be noted right now that between copyright and copyright there is not a synonymic relationship, but a side difference, which consists in a greater conceptual extension of the first than the second. Copyright, typical of common law systems, aims to protect primarily the interest of the entrepreneur (publisher, producer, distributor) who invests in the marketing of the work, also achieving the protection, thanks to copyright, of every work that may be object of commercialization, regardless of its originality and creativity traits. It follows that every author can boast of patrimonial rights on his work that he can assign, usually for a cash consideration, to an entrepreneur who will take care of its management and marketing. The copyright, on the other hand, at least in Italy, imposes on the author a certain control over the work, even after the possible transfer of the patrimonial rights that gravitate there, because alongside subjective patrimonial profiles, transferable to third parties (*ex* article 107 Law no. 633 of 1941 and article 2581 of Italian Civil Code), there are others of a moral nature, as they are connected to honor and reputation, theoretically indispensable, non-transferable and perpetual, pending their existence even after the author's death and the entire duration of the patrimonial rights (*ex* article 25 Law no. 633 of 1941; 70 years from the death of the author). *See* P. Spada, *Introduzione*, in *Diritto industriale. Proprietà intellettuale e concorrenza*, a cura di P. Auteri, G. Floridia, V. Mangini, G. Olivieri, M. Ricolfi, P. Spada, Torino, 2016, *passim*.

78 Therefore, copyleft would present itself as the opposite of copyright.

79 A software consists of a series of mathematical calculation procedures, codes, diagrams and/or algorithms, consisting of a set of instructions given to the computer to allow it to perform certain functional operations to achieve data results. These instructions materialize in the so-called object code (processed by the machine) which essentially represents the translation into the so-called machine language of an antecedent expression of the idea at the basis of intellectual creation in a language that is characterized by a remarkable technicality, which in any case does not make it incomprehensible to man, the CD source code or program (developed by man). In Italy, significant questions have been raised about the type of protection to be granted to software and the adequacy of the copyright discipline to ensure protection for computer programs, especially with reference to the object code. More specifically, initially, there was a discussion on the applicability to software or the protection provided by the law on copyright or the protection provided for industrial patents, also in light of the peaceful understanding according to which industrial invention rights arise when in which the patent is obtained, while the copyrights on intellectual works arise at the very moment of the creation of the work. Observing that the software materializes in impulses that take on an expressive form that is difficult to refer to the traditional idea of a protected literary work, some authors have encountered a problem of communicative capacity that makes the program incompatible with the regulatory logic of protection of intellectual works provided for by arts. 1 and 2 of the Law no. 633 of 1941. In fact, precisely by enhancing the technical nature of the programs and their direct purpose for the operation of the machine and not for communicating ideas and feelings to others, it was considered that the software could not be traced back to intellectual works. Currently the majority doctrinal orientation is in the sense of believing that software is an asset belonging to the category of intangible assets, and this has caused the shift of its analysis towards the field of copyright. *See*, among the authors who claimed the qualification of the software as a work of ingenuity, G. Santini, *La tutela giuridica della programmazione elettronica*, in *Giur. it.*, 1968, IV, p. 225 ff.; G. Galtieri, *Note sulla proteggibilità dei programmi*, in *Diritto di autore*, 1971, p. 425 ff.; G. Sena, *Software: problemi di definizione e di protezione giuridica*, in *Riv. dir. ind.*, II, 1983, p. 479

Because copyleft, as a particular expression of copyright, is based on a system of licenses through which the creator of the intellectual work, as the original owner of the rights on the work, indicates to the users of the latter that it can be used, disseminated and often even modified freely, its inclusive capacity could be affirmed towards third parties who make use of the goods that are subject to it.[80]

---

ff.; C. Ciampi, *La proteggibilità dei programmi elettronici e dei relativi manuali applicativi quali opere dell'ingegno di carattere creativo*, in *Dir. dell'informazione e dell'informatica*, 1985, p. 258 ff.; and, *contra*, E. Luzzato, *Una norma di legge francese da non imitare (a proposito della brevettabilità o meno dei programmi o serie di istruzioni per lo svolgimento delle operazioni dei calcolatori elettronici)*, in *Riv. dir. ind.*, I, 1968, p. 297 ff.; E. Luzzato, *La crisi del software*, in *Problemi attuali del diritto industriale*, Milano, 1977, p. 719 ff.; G. Ghidini, *I programmi per computers fra brevetto e diritto d'autore*, in *Giur. comm.*, I, 1984, p. 251 ff.; R. Borruso, *L'Algoritmo per computer e la sua brevettabilità*, in *Dir. dell'informazione e dell'informatica*, 1987, p. 75 ff.; G. Floridia, *La protezione del software nel sistema delle esclusive sulle creazioni intellettuali*, in *Dir. dell'informazione e dell'informatica*, 1989, p. 71 ff.; G. Guglielmetti, *L'invenzione di software*, Milano, 1997, p. 214 ff.; M. Bertani, *Open source ed elaborazione del software proprietario*, in *Open Source*, cit., p. 116 ff., where the author speaks, on the one hand, of the source code as an expressive form belonging to the areas of human knowledge in which intellectual creativity cannot substantially express itself, and, on the other, of the object code as being protected, exceptionally, thanks to the copyright. The impossibility of recognizing patent protection for software is, however, reinforced by the express prohibition contained in article 12 from the R.D. no. 1127 of 1939 (*Testo delle disposizioni legislative in materia di brevetti per invenzioni industriali*), as amended by the D.P.R. no. 338 of 1979. *See*, on the impracticability of software patent protection, S. Pastore, *Il cammino della tutela giuridica del software, opera dell'ingegno di carattere creativo*, in *Dir. d'Autore*, 1987, p. 177, where the author points out that «[. . .] la disciplina del diritto d'autore non subordina la protezione all'adempimento di alcuna formalità di deposito o di registrazione; con la tutela del diritto d'autore il software consegue una protezione erga omnes; la proteggibilità del software attraverso il diritto d'autore è più ampia di quella brevettuale, anche dal punto di vista quantitativo, oltre che qualitativo, in quanto può riguardare qualsiasi tipo di programma e concernere sia il programma che le istruzioni; la tutela del diritto d'autore è meno rigorosa di quella brevettuale, richiedendo, anche sul piano tecnico, un accenno modesto di originalità personale; la tutela attraverso il diritto d'autore, infine, comporta il riconoscimento dei vari diritti esclusivi previsti dal legislatore in capo al titolare dell'opera dell'ingegno» (*author's note*, "the discipline of copyright does not make the protection subject to the fulfilment of any filing or registration formalities; with copyright protection, the software achieves *erga omnes* protection; the protectability of the software through copyright is wider than the patent one, also from a quantitative point of view, as well as qualitative, as it can concern any type of program and concern both the program and the instructions; copyright protection is less stringent than patent protection, requiring, even on a technical level, a modest hint of personal originality; protection through copyright, finally, involves the recognition of the various exclusive rights provided by the legislator for the owner of the intellectual work»). *See*, for further details, G. Alpa, *La tutela giuridica del Software*, Milano, 1984, *passim*; S. Gatti, voce *Software*, in *Enc. Dir.*, XLII, Milano, 1990, p. 1208 ff.; L. Bosotti, G. Jacobacci, *I brevetti. La valorizzazione dell'innovazione d'impresa*, Torino, 1993, *passim*.

80 Inverted because it is not aimed at exercising a domain over the asset, but at ensuring its free enjoyment and exploitation to third parties. In fact, if, on the one hand, whoever distributes the program with proprietary licenses takes advantage of the copyright protection on the program to reserve for himself the copying, modification and distribution activities as exclusive rights of economic use, licensing the mere use of the program, on the other hand, those who distribute a program through a free license with copyright permission, in its most classic form, want to ensure, on the one hand, that the freedoms granted remain such for all subsequent users, and on the other hand, that changes and improvements made to the program by users remain available to the whole community.

If, in fact, like a traditional feeling, ownership has typically been read in the light of exclusivity,[81] since this trait was perceived as a useful tool for managing the allocation of resources and stimulating the production of new goods, today, with particular reference to new intangible assets and under certain legal conditions,

81 In civil law systems, where the trait of exclusivity is generally presented as one of the supporting elements of property together with individuality, the notion of ownership hinges on the absolute character of the right, resulting in the fact that the owner, in addition to enjoying all the benefits of the well that is the object, has the right to exclude, in fact, any other individual from the benefits that can be drawn from the *res*. A similar approach is also found in common law systems, where the majority orientation is in the sense of considering the right of exclusion as an essential element of the property right, albeit tempered by numerous exceptions. *See*, with reference to civil law, *ex multis*, R.J. Pothier, *Traité du droit de domaine de propriété*, in *Œuvres de Pothier. IX*, Paris, 1846, p. 197, where the author states that «[. . .] il est de l'essence de ce droit, que deux personnes ne puissent avoir chacune pour le total le domaine de propriété d'une même chose»; P. Perlingieri, *Introduzione alla problematica della «proprietà»*, cit., p. 60, where the author highlights that the «[. . .] caratteristica che solitamente si attribuisce al diritto di proprietà, nella scía della tradizione romanistica, cioè la "esclusività" almeno tendenziale del godimento del proprietario, non deve ritenersi essenziale ed assoluta [. . .]. Se poi si vuole intendere per esclusività qualcosa di diverso dall'esclusività del godimento, e cioè il fatto che ogni situazione giuridica soggettiva spetta o appartiene a un titolare e quindi a costui in sostanza spetta esclusivamente quella situazione giuridica soggettiva, se in altre parole nell'esclusività si vuol sottolineare quel legame tra la situazione giuridica soggettiva e il suo titolare, in sostanza questa non sarà più una caratteristica peculiare del diritto di proprietà, ma costituirà una delle caratteristiche tipiche delle situazioni giuridiche soggettive, giacche le situazioni giuridiche soggettive non possono che spettare a determinati soggetti. Quando la titolarità appartiene o spetta ad uno solo, è evidente che la situazione giuridica soggettiva è di esclusiva spettanza o appartenenza di un determinato soggetto» *(author's note*, "a characteristic that is usually attributed to the right of property, in the wake of the Roman tradition, that is the 'exclusivity' at least tendential of the enjoyment of the owner, must not be considered essential and absolute [. . .]. If, then, exclusivity is to be understood as something different from the exclusivity of enjoyment, that is, the fact that every subjective legal situation belongs to or belongs to a holder and therefore he is essentially entitled to that subjective legal situation only, if in other words in the exclusivity we want to emphasize that link between the subjective legal situation and its owner, in essence this will no longer be a peculiar characteristic of the property right, but will constitute one of the typical characteristics of subjective legal situations, since subjective legal situations can only belong to certain subjects. When the ownership belongs or belongs to only one, it is clear that the subjective legal situation is the exclusive property of or belonging to a specific subject"); F. De Martino, *Beni in generale*, in *Commentario del codice civile*, a cura di A. Scialoja e G. Branca, Bologna-Roma, 1976, p. 146, where the author, identifying exclusivity with the absoluteness of law, states that «[. . .] il proprietario ha diritto che tutti i terzi si astengano da qualsiasi invasione nella sfera del suo diritto [. . .]. Il suo diritto cioè opera *erga omnes*» (*author's note*, "The owner has the right that all third parties refrain from any invasion of the sphere of his right [. . .]. His right that is, operates *erga omnes*"); F.A. Hayek, *Law, Legislation, and Liberty. I*, Chicago, IL and London, 1973, p. 107, where the author believes that property rights were essentially perceived as a legal and social set of «expectations [. . .] designating [. . .] ranges of objects over which only particular individuals are allowed to dispose and from the control of which others are excluded»; M. Xifaras, *La propriété. Etudes de philosophie du droit*, Paris, 2004, p. 145 ff. *See*, with reference to the common law, T.W. Merrill, *Property and the Right to Exclude*, in *Neb. Law Rev*., 77, 1998, p. 730 ff., according to which the exclusivity and the *condicio sine qua non* of ownership; J.E. Penner, *The Idea of Property in Law*, Oxford, 1997, p. 68, where the author affirms that «[T]he right to property is a right to exclude others from things which is grounded by the interest we have in the use of things»; *contra*, S. Balganesh, *Demystifying the Right to Exclude: Of Property, Inviolability, and Automatic Injunctions*, in *Harv. J. Law Pol*., 31, 2008, p. 593 ff.

should rather be enriched by the opposite attribute of inclusiveness, understood as a characteristic of a property predisposed to participation and extension through access.

Copyleft (or author's permission) poses the problem of assessing what type of relationship with the (intangible) asset can be configured: would it be an authentic property, or a different subjective situation?

On closer inspection, copyleft does not consist in the complete denial of copyright, but in its weakening, which can be seen at least in its less radical forms (strong copyleft and weak copyleft), where the creator remains the holder of the moral right that it is connected, although it can assign the relative property right.

In the perspective adopted here, a profoundly innovative trait, however, is captured in non-copyleft, where its original owner completely frees the intellectual work, allowing the subjects who sign the relative license not only to be able to use it freely, but also to modify it *ad libitum*, enjoying, if they so wish, the relative economic advantages, transforming it from derivative into proprietary.

While maintaining the classic dualistic theory, which is based on a *tutela bifronte*[82] (or "two-faced protection") characterized, on the patrimonial level, by the possibility of direct or indirect exploitation guaranteed to the author, and, on the moral level, by the protection that he receives and that he materializes in the right of paternity on the work created which manifests itself in the right to be recognized as the author, therefore, there would be the purchase by any user of an ownership, with respect to the good used, which previously did not have and which allows to pose about creative elaboration in a manner analogous to what was allowed to its creator.

Basically, considering the inalienability of the author's moral right, at least for the national framework (article 7 of the Inv. Law), the non-copyleft allows the transfer, in addition to the right to economic exploitation of the intangible asset, of the right to its use and modification, without addressing a specific subject, but *ad incertam personam*.

In other words, the innovative trait that characterizes the situation described coincides with a *quid pluris* with respect to the regime that is usually typical of the derivative work, since, for the same modalities in which non-copyleft operates, which see it strongly linked to digital products and an intangible world, it is anchored to a situation of uncertainty on the level of the user and subsequent holder by way of derivative of the asset referable in its first existence to a different subject.

It is therefore necessary to evaluate whether the changes taking place are determining the shift from a traditional one to a different ownership logic in the wake of a new way of operating exchanges that focuses on the transition from an economic-spatial dimension, because it is related to geographical features, to a different one. -spatial, because it is digital, and on a profound change in the circulation of goods that from purely material becomes more and more immaterial.

82 N. Abriani, G. Cottino, *Diritto industriale*, in *Trattato di diritto commerciale*, diretto da *G. Cottino*, II, Padova, 2001, p. 210.

When we talk about the "inclusion" of the property right with reference to the copyleft hypothesis, we simply want to highlight how the ownership scheme that derives from it is linked precisely to the particular attitude that the owner of the intangible asset – for example, the program – he has towards the latter, left by his choice completely free in the enjoyment, modification and economic exploitation by anyone who has an interest in it.

The application of a proprietary logic to intangible assets and copyleft, as its particular declination, thus implies that, for example, the programmer has such a possibility of impact on the asset and its circulation, that he chooses to deprive himself entirely of any right to influence on the same,[83] both in terms of usability by third parties and economic enjoyment, while remaining the original owner. And this as if it were moved by an animus that, although it concretely strips itself of the ownership of the asset, actually wants to maintain a demeanor that, in fact, stands as an expression of this ownership, allowing its enjoyment and economic exploitation by parties of anyone who wants it.

This animus, therefore, does not impact on the good by transforming it into a *res derelicta stricto sensu intesa*, since its theoretical[84] traceability to the original programmer, the lack of an authentic objective state of abandonment (so-called *corpus derelictionis*) and the recognition of this state still remains (the so-called *animus derelinquendi* in fact), but the mode of legal circulation is altered, making it completely free without, among other things, referring to a specific user.

If, following a legal approach, the recognition of intellectual property is justified because it is necessary to ensure a certain legal protection to the creator of the asset, in order to stimulate its development and diffusion, as if to say that without adequate legal protection the creative spirit would not find sufficient stimulus, in order to ensure the need to protect the intellectual work through specific mechanisms, of which copyright would be a clear expression, it could be hypothesized that, again as an expression of ownership of the intangible asset, the creator is also granted the possibility of choosing whether or not to enjoy this protection, giving, in the latter case, the opening to full freedom of movement of the asset.

Therefore, since the choice of whether or not to opt for its free circulation and its free economic exploitation is left to the will of the owner of the intangible asset, the assumption that the legal institution of property would operate in this sector would lose its effectiveness as an indispensable incentive aimed at channeling energy and investments to the development, for example, of computer programs, which, in the absence of adequate legal protection, would otherwise be left without an incentive that could stimulate their creation.

The whole picture thus reconstructed would lead back to the free will of the owner of the intangible asset and the choice of the circulation regime to which to

83 Except, as it often happens, the provision of the obligation placed on users/any modifiers of the computer program by the original programmer to respect the philosophy of free use underlying the copyleft itself, as an open or free resource.

84 In reality, in fact, it can be concretely difficult to grasp who the original programmer is, especially when the same software subject to the copyleft "regime" has been modified several times by different subjects.

submit it, also in a perspective of free exploitation by others, would be nothing more than his choice, among other things, expressive of the availability juridical that the latter has on the good.

Technological development, in fact, has the intrinsic ability to alter the very concept of ownership that is invested in it, being able to move it from a traditional vision to a technologically oriented vision, capable of modifying the perception of the subjective situation touched and the interests that underlie it.[85]

The fruitful interchange that is taking place today between technology and law, as concepts that were previously deeply distinct and now increasingly close, certainly involves the substance of subjective law, its sources, its attitude towards the one who is its owner, its aptitude to adapt to intrinsically dynamic legal areas, the mechanism to be used for its exercise, and, in general, its legal essence.

Therefore, all the antinomic tensions related to the complexity of a technology-law relationship that is characterized by a deep and growing interconnection are polarized on the subjective situation involved.

The problem of the definition and regulation of subjective rights influenced by innovative technological realities, in fact, arises not only from the affirmation of very recent technologies in the light of which the law must update and adapt,[86] but also from technologies that although well established and widespread at the moment present – as often happens – an innate propensity for change, transformation and impact on one's object.[87]

The technology is thus characterized *ex natura* by an intrinsic changeability, from which it follows that analogous legal approaches, which are initially valid,

85 *See*, on this point, S. Rodotà, *Il terribile diritto*, cit., p. 58, where the author, precisely with reference to the adoption of an analytical and realistic perspective, the one of properties, compared to an exclusively dogmatic approach centred on an abstract and artificial unity of the proprietary concept, notes that «[. . .] tutte le indagini tendenti a sostituire ad un riferimento concettuale unico una molteplicità di assunzioni concrete (come accade ormai anche in materie diverse dalla proprietà, quali l'impresa o il negozio giuridico) devono decifrare una dialettica complessa: se non possono trascurare il fatto che, per un periodo sufficientemente lungo e rappresentativo, proprio il concetto "astratto" ha costituito il "reale" punto d'avvio di operazioni legislative, giurisprudenziali e scientifiche (per non parlare delle sue utilizzazioni fuori dello stretto ambito giuridico), neppure possono rinunciare, già nella prospettiva storica e non solo ricostruendo i lineamenti dell'ordinamento vigente, a misurare la rilevanza effettiva dei singoli statuti» («[. . .] all investigations tending to replace a single conceptual reference with a multiplicity of concrete assumptions (as is now also the case in matters other than property, such as the company or the legal transaction) must decipher a complex dialectic: if they cannot overlook the fact that, for a sufficiently long and representative period, precisely the "abstract" concept constituted the "real" starting point of legislative, jurisprudential and scientific operations (not to mention its uses outside the strict juridical context), nor can they renounce, already in the historical perspective and not only by reconstructing the features of the current legal system, to measure the actual relevance of the individual stands all»).

86 *See*, on the concept of legal updating to technology that is expressed in the three legal moments of "connecting," "staying connected" and "fighting disconnection," R. Brownsword, M. Goodwin, *Law and Technology of the Twenty-First Century, Texts and Materials*, cit., p. 63 ff. and p. 371 ff.

87 *See*, on the difficulties of giving an adequate and prompt legal response to technological innovations, M. Kirby, *New Frontiers: Regulating Technology by Law and "Code,"* in *Regulating Technologies: Legal Futures, Regulatory Frames and Technological Fixes*, cit., p. 367 ff.

could subsequently become, in fact, no longer effective due to the gradual technical advancement.

In essence, the relationship between law and technology can find a twofold and antithetical development, reflecting either the prevalence of the former, which seeks to resist technological evolution in contrast with the very dynamic essence of the human being, or the prevalence of the latter, to which power the law cannot offer a valid and efficient resistance, also losing its regulatory purpose.[88] Technology, therefore, seems just in appearance a concept with a neutral character, having to be addressed and conditioned in such a way as to take the form that is best suited to the objectives that may eventually be achieved by means of it.[89]

Therefore, if what has been traced up to now is a path aimed at highlighting, on the one hand, the mutability of technology, and, on the other, the influence exercised by the latter on its relationship with the law, it must also be noted that binomial right (even subjective)-technology will always find a configuration that ensures respect for dignity and fundamental rights.

This, therefore, must represent the irreplaceable and solid mooring on which to anchor any legal conceptualization, especially when it concerns the examination of the subjective right par excellence, the right of property, of which they should represent the privileged angle of observation:[90] technology, being at the service of the human being, should conform to fundamental rights and human dignity.

On a theoretical level, however, it is observed how the transition from the physical world to the digital world is marked by the potential affirmation of a structure that looks at the human being in increasingly impersonal terms, thanks to the diffusion of algorithms used to regulate ownership and the exercise of the legal situation possibly referable to the subject.

Thus, we can speak of a "digital" ownership of the property right that derives from the extremist reduction of the person to the object of an algorithm, capable of profoundly conditioning the exercise of the subjective situation that belongs to them both in the relationship with the object of the right in itself and in the relationship with the other subjects with whom it enters into a relationship. Can we propose a reasoning on the ownership of intangible assets in a new sense because it is capable of effectively considering what the right to property and its strict boundaries are today?[91]

An answer in this sense is profoundly influenced by the nature of the reference technology, so much so that looking at the Internet, for example, one should

88 *See*, on the relationship between law and technology, for all, N. Irti, *Il diritto nell'età della tecnica*, Napoli, 2007, *passim*.

89 *See*, on this point, C. Schmitt, *Das Zeitalter der Neutralisierungen und Entpolitisierungen*, in *Der Begriff des Politischen, mit einem Vorwort und drei Korollarien*, München and Leipzig, 1932, p. 76 ff.

90 *See* P. Perlingieri, *Introduzione alla problematica della «proprietà»*, cit., p. 21 ff.; Id., *La personalità umana nell'ordinamento giuridico*, Napoli, 1972, p. 150 ff.

91 For an in-depth analysis of the debate around the concept of ownership and the classical theory of assets, M. Bertani, *Proprietà intellettuale, antitrust e rifiuto di licenze*, in *Quaderni di AIDA*, 2004, p. 10 ff.

distinguish between web management and problems related to the subjective rights on which it imposes:[92] a constitutionalization of the Internet capable of extending its reflections to the subjective positions that arise and find fulfillment in it.[93]

However, this profile does not exclude that the unexpected perspectives opened by new technologies refer to frontiers centred on the single human subject, which, although perceived in its enormous complexity, is captured in its multifaceted and multifaceted nature, so as to constitute a field of action internal and no longer external to the investigation to be conducted.

It is here that a series of interesting legal problems emerge that concern, just to name a few, responsibility, the protection of property (including intellectual)[94] and respect for fundamental rights, and which require, among other things, to rethink the adequacy of the conceptual language used up to now.

Indeed, if sometimes innovative results spontaneously follow the way in which fundamental issues inherent to individuals and their intrinsic conceptual background are addressed without such changes being accompanied by a full awareness and willingness to the actual change that follows, other times such changes derive from the conscious will to overcome specific conceptual schemes thanks to the effect of innovation, so as to realize, in a perspective diametrically opposite to the other experience, the conscious attempt to overcome the juridical-political-philosophical knots and the problems that similar changes could pose.

This work, without claiming to fully resolve these issues, seeks to give voice to the need to clarify the conceptual issues deriving from the close relationship established, in the digital market, between property rights (and its exercise) and technologies to which one makes use, if necessary, by attempting a reformulation and restructuring of the conceptual vocabulary that accompanies the applicable discipline.

It is no coincidence, in fact, that the change in the linguistic approach that took place in Western philosophy of the 20th century translated into a significant transformation of the sense of reality, which from the realm of thought passed to the realm of language, since the word is not it is a simple label firmly linked to concepts, but rather a part of the language that makes up reality: the meaning of the object it refers to requires language to be well expressed.[95]

92 Recent years have been characterized by the growing violation of rights on the Internet by both public (*see*, for example, the China and the exercise of freedom of expression) and private (*see*, for example, the companies operating in the cybernetic field of Big Data).

93 *See*, *ex multis*, G. Teubner, *Constitutionalizing Polycontexturality*, in *Soc. Leg. Stud.*, 20, 2011, p. 210 ff.

94 *See*, for a careful critical and systematic examination of the dogmatic and structural dualism that exists between the notions of property and intellectual property, J. Janich, *Geistiges Eigentum: eine Komplementärerscheinung zum Sacheigentum?*, Tübingen, 2002, specially p. 193 ff. *See*, for a complete analysis of the doctrinal framework not only German developed on the subject, G. Resta, *Persona, proprietà, mercato: alcune indicazioni sul dibattito tedesco*, in *Riv. critic. dir. priv.*, 2, 2003, p. 373 ff.

95 More specifically, the concept "tree" is not a representation of the real living being "tree," but rather a representation of the meaning of that living being called "tree."

Such a change resulted both in the description of the "factual" reality of nature (naturalistic level) and in the description of the "factual" reality of the institutions (institutional level), causing the abandonment of the objective model centred on a "neutral observer" in favour of a "participating observer" who does not necessarily have a neutral and external gaze, but who, based on the attitude assumed, can be more or less involved in the description of the facts that involve him and of the relations he has with them.[96]

Technological innovations have, then, generated profound and unprecedented consequences in the legal framework which, invested by an authentic revolution, places the self-determination of subjects at the centre of the system, the construction of new identities, both individual and collective, and the development of new ways of conceiving social and real ties.[97]

Emerging technologies not only reconstruct the relationship that the individual has with himself, but, by doing so, they profoundly change what was previously defined the "normal" relationship of the person with his/her good (ownership), and, at the same time, they challenge traditional philosophical and juridical approaches, especially with regard to the conceptual vocabulary and the definition of rights found in new and old territories, always articulated and elusive.[98]

Thus, various points of reflection open up, which could feed the possible need to reformulate the semantic meaning of part of the traditional conceptual and legal lexicon, while respecting two cardinal principles: autonomy and correctness.

The first, autonomy, which represents an almost sacred concept that takes its first philosophical-juridical steps with Descartes, strengthens its path, through

96 *See*, cfr. K. Olivecrona, *Il diritto come fatto*, Milano, 1967, *passim*, where the author highlights how the decisions taken by law are the result of the interaction of various factors, such as social forces, legal awareness, the ideologies of social groups, the centres of economic power, which, to varying degrees, cooperate and influence each other in the attempt to achieve the most appropriate balance to achieve the interests to be protected; J. McDowell, *Mind and World*, Cambridge, MA, 1994, esp. p. 66 ff. and p. 87 ff.; and, lastly, F. Capra, U. Mattei, *Ecologia del diritto. Scienza, politica, beni comuni*, Sansepolcro, 2017, *passim*.

97 *See*, on the subject, Y. Benkler, *The Wealth of Networks: How Social Production Transforms Markets and Freedom*, New Haven, CT, 2007, *passim*; R.J. Deibert, J.G. Palfrey, R. Rohozinski, J. Zittrain (eds.), *Access Denied: The Practice and Policy of Global Internet Filtering*, Cambridge, MA, 2008, *passim*; S. Rodotà, *Il diritto ad avere diritti*, Roma-Bari, 2012, p. 12 ff., where the author, operating on the more specific level of rights, speaks of a «rivoluzione dell'uguaglianza» ("revolution of equality") and of «rivoluzione della dignità» ("revolution of dignity").

98 *See*, on the topic, R.R. Nelson, *Linkages Between the Market Economy and the Scientific Commons*, in *International Public Goods and Transfer of Technology Under a Globalized Intellectual Property Regime*, edited by K.E. Maskus and J.H. Reichmann Cambridge, 2005, p. 121 ff.; D. Bollier, S. Helfrich (eds.), *The Wealth of the Commons. A World beyond Market & State*, Amherst, MA, 2012, *passim*. It is no coincidence, then, that precisely with reference to the subject of ownership in these pages, S. Pugliatti, *La proprietà nel nuovo diritto*, cit., p. 126, affirms that «[. . .] una definizione della proprietà non può che essere, per il suo contenuto, generica, sì da delineare lo schema massimamente ampio nel quale ogni specificazione dell'istituto dovrà essere contenuta» («[. . .] a definition of the property can only be, for its content, generic, so as to outline the maximally broad scheme in which each specification of the institution must be contained»).

Locke, with Mill and the liberal tradition, and is definitively structured with Kant, poses significant challenges when placed in relation with the "technique."

In the current technological era, in fact, one of the key problems that a reflection on autonomy can pose is: to what extent can a person who owns an intangible asset actually be the sole owner and freely dispose of it? Does it make sense to speak of the autonomous exercise of ownership of the right over the asset – whether it be a manifestation of a strictly sense of ownership or an intellectual property – to trace an argumentative path on which to structure the individual's legitimacy for its use and transfer?[99]

The second, correctness, whose positive and constant affirmation represents one of the most interesting socio-economic challenges posed by the contemporary age, has accentuated, in recent years, its problematic profiles following the incessant development of more and more sophisticated technologies that, on the one hand, gradually make the legal relationships that technology invests less personal, and, on the other hand, and consequently, automate and mechanize the relationships by blurring that necessary aura of loyalty that must be at the base.

99 As of now, however, it is necessary to keep in mind the words of P. Perlingieri, *Introduzione alla problematica della «proprietà»*, cit., p. 87, where the author, analysing the relevance that the good plays in the concept of ownership, states that «[I]l bene e la proprietà sono [. . .] due diversi istituti, non due definizioni legislative che vogliono rappresentare punti di vista convergenti di uno stesso fenomeno socialmente rilevante, qual è il bene; due diversi istituti, due complessi di norme che regolano fatti e rapporti socialmente rilevanti e autonomi. [. . .] più che una disciplina dei beni in sé considerati, lo studio della proprietà dev'essere rivolto all'individuazione della disciplina dei singoli diritti che convergono sul bene ed in ispecie all'individuazione di quella particolare disciplina che si riferisce a quel rapporto col bene che è il rapporto di proprietà, cioè all'individuazione di quel complesso di norme che sono tipiche del diritto di proprietà e che caratterizzano dunque l'istituto "proprietà"» (*author's note*, "Good and property are [. . .] two different institutions, not two legislative definitions that want to represent converging points of view of the same socially relevant phenomenon, which is the good; two different institutes, two sets of rules that regulate socially relevant and autonomous facts and relationships. [. . .] more than a discipline of the assets considered in themselves, the study of the property must be aimed at identifying the discipline of the individual rights that converge on the asset and in particular at the identification of that particular discipline that refers to that relationship with the good which is the property relationship, that is, to the identification of that set of norms which are typical of the right of property and which therefore characterize the institution *property*"); but, on the contrary, for an approach that has favoured an authentic identification of the law with the thing over which the owner exercises his powers, S. Pugliatti, *La proprietà nel nuovo diritto*, cit., p. 135 ff., where the author, on p. 135, in highlighting the nature of the property right «diritto reale "fondamentale," rispetto al quale tutti gli altri diritti reali (di godimento o di garanzia), siccome *iura in re aliena*, sono dipendenti ed al quale si appoggiano» («as a "fundamental" real right, with respect to which all the other real rights (enjoyment or guarantee), as *iura in re aliena*, are dependent and on which they rely»), states, at p. 138, that this right must be understood in a double sense, given that «*a)* esso si costituisce come diritto "autonomo" non solo perché non dipendente, ma perché per sua essenza non può "dipendere" da altro diritto reale; *b)* "ogni altro diritto reale" presuppone "di necessità," come immancabile piedistallo, il diritto di proprietà» («a) it constitutes itself as an" autonomous "right not only because it is not dependent, but because by its very essence it cannot "depend" on another real right; b) "every other real right" presupposes "of necessity," as an inevitable pedestal, the right of ownership»); Salv. Romano, *Sulla nozione di proprietà*, in *Riv. trim. dir. e proc. civ.*, 1960, p. 342 ff. *See*, for further information in a non-objective sense, *infra* Chapter 1, § 4.

Trying, therefore, to overcome the empty reference to a generic right of equality, the fundamental objective of the analysis is to evaluate how it is possible to avoid that individuals or groups are excluded from being full owners and users of goods that the digital market makes available to them.

In fact, emerging technologies allow access to a vast list of new *res* that contemplate innovative possibilities for sharing positive effects – especially in terms of access and use – as well as the ability to react to subtle forms of technological division, and not necessarily of an economic nature, which can nestle in the medium used.

The issues considered so far represent only some of the possible complex intersections that challenge the law as a whole and that pose as a crucial junction in grasping the new attitude of the legal relationships between the subject and the asset and their effects in the era of the digital market.

The attempt to respond to this titanic confrontation can only spring from an approach that is built on the interpenetration of disciplinary horizons and which, consequently, derives from a certainly juridical, but also profoundly philosophical vision, from which new energies and motivations can be drawn that, sinking into the past and tradition, give adequate importance to the future and innovation.[100]

In essence, digital technology has profoundly changed the classic balances on which both society and economic relations were based, offering new models of exchange, business and circulation of goods, and thereby raising challenges that affect numerous aspects of law.[101]

Doctrine, jurisprudence, policy-makers and regulators are therefore all involved in a lively debate aimed at elaborating the most appropriate answers to give to the complex evidence that the digital revolution reserves.

Responding to the logic of private law which in order to contribute to the correct functioning of intersubjective relationships must ensure a general legal framework based on efficient tools, the creation of an authentically interconnected digital

100 M.J. Copps, *Disruptive Technology . . . Disruptive Regulation*, cit., p. 309, where the author highlights the need to ensure that regulatory changes, aimed at addressing the challenges posed by new technologies, are capable of creating «[. . .] landscape which really fosters innovation».
See, ex multis, R. Schulze, D. Staudenmayer, *Digital Revolution – Challenges for Contract Law*, in *Digital Revolution: Challenges for Contract Law in Practice*, edited by R. Schulze, D. Staudenmayer, Baden-Baden, 2016, p. 19 ff.

101 *See*, C. Koopman, M. Mitchell, A. Thierer, *The Sharing Economy and Consumer Protection Regulation – The Case for Policy Change*, in *J. Bus. Entrep. Law*, 8, 2015, p. 529 ff.; K. Schwab, *The Fourth Industrial Revolution*, Cologny-Geneva, 2016, p. 11, where the author qualifies in terms of «fourth industrial revolution» the era characterized by robotics, artificial intelligence, the Internet of things, self-driving vehicles, 3D printing, as it follows «[T]he first industrial revolution spanned from about 1760 to around 1840. Triggered by the construction of railroads and the invention of the steam engine, it ushered in mechanical production. The second industrial revolution, which started in the late 19th century and into the early 20th century, made mass production possible, fostered by the advent of electricity and the assembly line. The third industrial revolution began in the 1960's. It is usually called the computer or digital revolution because it was catalysed by the development of semiconductors, mainframe computing (1960s), personal computing (1970s and 80s) and the internet (1990s)».

world seeks to respond effectively to the challenges of the digital revolution in order to make the most possible economic implications.

Thus, the European Commission, within the framework of its *Digital Single Market Strategy*, has envisaged a series of measures aimed at facilitating access to digital goods and services for EU consumers and entrepreneurs, underlining that the absence of shared and common policies in the European Union can create barriers to entry, hinder competition and limit investors' foresight.[102]

The harmonization of European private law represents, in fact, an increasingly important test bed that has inspired significant developments, as demonstrated, most recently, by the publication on 29 September 2017 of the Guidelines for *Online Platforms to Tackle Illegal Content*, as part of the *Digital Single Market Strategy* of the European Commission.[103]

102 European Commission, *Communication from the Commission to the European Parliament, the Council, the European Economic and Social Committee and the Committee of the Regions. Strategy for the Digital Single Market in Europe* – COM (2015) 192 final, Brussels, 6.5.2015, p. 3 ff., available at http://eur-lex.europa.eu/legal-content/EN/TXT/PDF/?uri=CELEX:52015DC0192&from=EN.

103 *See* European Commission, *Tackling Illegal Content Online Towards an Enhanced Responsibility of Online Platforms – COM(2017) 555 Final*, Brussels, 28 September 2017, p. 2 ff., available at the page https://eur-lex.europa.eu/legal-content/IT/TXT/PDF/?uri=CELEX:52015DC0192&from=IT. In reality, the actual presence of a single digital market must be questioned since, even from a competition law point of view, it is not possible to find a single entity but rather a macroeconomic aggregate in which there are different sectors corresponding to a different market or set of markets. *See*, in this regard, G. Olivieri, *Del mercato delle cose al mercato delle idee*, in *Riv. soc.*, 4, 2017, p. 818, where the author affirms that «[. . .] i mercati di Internet (o mercato digitali) possono essere utilmente pensati come un sistema a strati sovrapposti così composto: Dispositivi e sistemi (hardware); Software e soluzioni ICT (accesso alla rete, programmi); Servizi di navigazione in rete (piattaforme, motori di ricerca *ecc.*); Advertising (Google); E-commerce (Amazon). All'interno di ciascuno di questi strati sono poi a loro volta individuabili distinti mercati dal punto di vista merceologico e concorrenziale. [. . .] può essere utile ricordare come l'immagine più frequentemente evocata dagli economisti per rappresentare questo fenomeno sia quella dell'ecosistema digitale (*internet web ecosystem*), ovvero un sistema nel quale ciascuno degli strati di cui esso si compone interagisce con gli altri in base a dinamiche influenzate in pari misura dalla evoluzione tecnologica e dal comportamento dei consumatori. Le principali caratteristiche di questo ecosistema digitale e dei mercati in esso operanti (in particolare di quelli *advertising* e *e-commerce*) sono: a) la esistenza di effetti di rete molto rilevanti (*network effects*); b) la struttura economica a più versanti; c) la notevole riduzione dei costi di produzione e dei c.d. *sunk costs*» («[. . .] Internet markets (or digital markets) can usefully be thought of as a system of superimposed layers composed as follows: Devices and systems (hardware); ICT software and solutions (network access, programs); Network navigation services (platforms, search engines, etc.); Advertising (Google); E-commerce (Amazon). Within each of these layers, distinct markets can be identified from a product and competitive point of view. [. . .] It may be useful to remember how the image most frequently evoked by economists to represent this phenomenon is that of the digital ecosystem (internet web ecosystem), i.e. a system in which each of the layers of which it is composed interacts with the others in based on dynamics influenced in equal measure by technological evolution and consumer behavior. The main characteristics of this digital ecosystem and of the markets operating in it (in particular those of advertising and e-commerce) are: a) the existence of very relevant network effects; b) the multi-sided economic structure; c) the significant reduction in production costs and the so-called sunk costs»).

It therefore appears of crucial importance to evaluate how the digital revolution influences the development of law and to respond adequately to the new challenges that result from it, giving primary importance to the impact that digital technology has on the relationship with the digital work, on its qualification and on the (new) means of protecting the subjective positions that are involved.

Can I address and solve the problems that the digital world brings with it by adapting the application and interpretation of existing national and EU rules? Is it necessary to reformulate the laws already in force to a greater or lesser extent or to simplify some of the problems that digitization poses? Is it necessary to adopt new rules governing situations not yet provided for by current legislation?

In some cases, a disruptive point is reached such that it is no longer possible to adapt the existing rules to the new situation and, consequently, it is inappropriate, as well as useless, to adapt them to the new.

The risk that is run, in these situations, is, on the one hand, that the desire to ensure a rapid response to new developments leads the regulator to develop standards that are not adequately weighted in their composition and formulation, so as to create problems instead of resolve, and, on the other, that new rules that are too stringent and that limiting could generate a distorting effect on technological progress and consequent economic developments.[104]

In this context, numerous problematic profiles are raised that hinge on digital content, on the belonging of the digital asset and on its use,[105] achieving the usefulness of categorizing digital content and tracing a general framework that allows to face and resolve situations that characterize the digital market.[106] More specifically, it must be assessed whether the existing regulatory instruments, with the conceptual apparatus that accompanies them, are able to respond to the needs that emerge with the digital economy, as well as with the so-called Internet of things[107] and the

104 R. Podszun, S. Kreifels, *Digital Platforms and Competition Law*, in *J. Eur. Consumer Market Law*, 5, 2016, p. 33 ff.

105 In general, it can be said that we are dealing with a digital work when it is expressed in a format that uses a bit encoding to circulate on the electronic communication networks defined and regulated, as far as Italy is concerned, by Legislative Decree no. 259 of 2003. The digital work, therefore, is not associated with a support that represents the essential element for its circulation, since if an association occurs it must not be such as to imply the qualification of the work as an "edition on support," but must in any case preserve the original format of the work and take on the temporary character of a service copy. It follows, therefore, that when, for example, an MP3 file is recorded on a CD, it will keep its nature as a copy of an MP3 on a support without becoming a music CD.

106 Evocative, in this regard, is the pronunciation *Sony Corp. of Am. v. Universal City Studios Inc.*, 464 US 417, 442 (1984), where, with reference to copyright law, it is stated that it shall reach «[. . .] a balance between the legitimate request for effective protection [. . .] by the owner of copyright [. . .] And the right of others to freely engage in substantially unrelated areas of commerce». *See*, for further information, S. Van Erp, *Ownership of Digital Assets?*, in *J. Eur. Consumer Market Law*, 5, 2016, p. 73 ff.

107 N. Helberger, *Profiling and Targeting Consumers in the Internet of Things – A New Challenge for Consumer Protection*, in *Digital Revolution: Challenges for Contract Law in Practice*, edited by R. Schulze and D. Staudenmayer, Baden-Baden and Oxford, 2016, p. 135 ff.

links between the objects it creates.[108] In essence, the advent of the Internet has given rise to new and unexpected challenges that make it more difficult to achieve stable (legal) balances between the actual ownership of digital assets and the protection of their controllability and use.[109] At the same time, digital technologies allow, in addition to a very extensive dissemination of their contents, also almost complete and perfect access and use, inexpensive and unlimited, so much so that it can be observed, without fear of denial, how times are changing substantially and the needs of the "information society" are very different from those characterizing the previous "industrial society."[110] Given the new possibilities in terms of appropriation and distribution that the Internet offers, it can therefore be considered that the owner of the copyright on a digital asset responds to the same logic of the past technology and is homologous to the figures that emerge from the application of the new media characterizing the digital world. Must the rules governing ownership logic be amended in light of the new potential offered by the circulation of digital goods,[111] or can they absorb the "impact" of innovation? And again, can digital works be considered, in essence, on the same level as physical goods or "traditional" intangible goods, or do they have features of more marked originality? What are the economic models, legal protections and technological measures to be used to manage the use, distribution and control of digital assets?[112]

108 The Internet of things is, for example, linked to the use of robotics in "smart" companies, intuitive home applications or cars that drive alone. *See*, for further information, also in terms of responsibility, *European Commission, A Digital Market Strategy for Europe* – COM (2015) 192 Final, cit., passim; E. Palmerini, A. Bertolini, *Liability and Risk Management in Robotics*, in *Digital Revolution: Challenges for Contract Law in Practice*, cit., p. 189 ff.; R.H. Weber, *Contractual Duties and Allocation of Liability in Automated Digital Contracts*, ibidem, p. 163 ff.; P. Bräutigam, T. Klindt, *Industrie 4.0, das Internet der Dinge und das Recht*, in *Neue Jurist. Wochenschr.*, 68, 2015, p. 1137 ff.

109 T. Ascarelli, *Teoria della concorrenza e dei beni immateriali*, Milano, 1960, p. 353 ff.

110 M. Castells, *The Rise of the Network Society*, Oxford and Malden, MA, 2000, p. 33 ff.

111 Within the concept of digital good a large complex of *res* and services must be included, among which, in addition to digital intellectual works, databases, digital archives, as well as any other set of information whose processing and whose supply are subject to economic evaluation. *See*, with regard to the regulation of digital circulation, E. Prosperetti, *L'opera digitale tra regole e mercato*, Torino, 2013, p. 2, where the author affirms that its discipline «[. . .] e frammentata tra vari settori, competenze e materie che non trovano coordinamento unitario: si studiano i temi relativi alla responsabilità dei prestatori di servizi, ai diritti sui contenuti, ai dati personali che vengono scambiati, agli illeciti derivanti dalla circolazione, al regime dei nomi a dominio ed altri ancora [. . .]. Ulteriore frammentazione viene dai distinti criteri, giurisprudenziali e territoriali di applicazione delle varie "regole" della circolazione e dalla pluralità di autorità e giurisdizioni competenti a regolarne ogni singolo aspetto, nonché a dirimerne le controversie» («[. . .] is fragmented between various sectors, skills and subjects that do not find unitary coordination: the issues relating to the liability of service providers, rights to content, personal data that are exchanged, illicit acts are studied deriving from circulation, the regime of domain names and others [. . .]. Further fragmentation comes from the distinct jurisprudential and territorial criteria of application of the various "rules" of circulation and from the plurality of authorities and jurisdictions competent to regulate every single aspect, as well as to settle disputes»).

112 *See*, for a clear perception of the innovation needs of conceptual schemes that are linked to the change in economic models, T. Ascarelli, *Teoria della concorrenza e interesse del consumatore*, in *Riv. trim. dir. proc. civ.*, 1954, p. 42, where the author affirms that «[. . .] il trionfo della produzione industriale di massa e la conseguente trasformazione di tutta la nostra vita» (*author's note*, "the

Although some of these questions have already found a reasonable answer, a greater awareness of their significance and the broad debate – both national and international – that continues to affect them can represent a sure aid in solving the problems that are connected to them and which are related to them and will try to address in the next few pages.

From this point of view, comparative considerations between systems will certainly be relevant in the perspective of which to grasp and evaluate current legal and technological approaches.[113]

Ultimately, this work aims to evaluate the compatibility of the object of (intellectual) property, as classically understood, with new technologies, in order to understand whether the architecture traditionally built around this fundamental right[114] can conform and adapt to the new digital age, while fully aware of the need to find a harmonious balance between the holder of the right and users that favours the necessary protection requests involved and facilitates the use of the digital assets to which it refers.

Must the principles and legal concepts on which the right to property rests as traditionally understood be redefined or can they continue to apply to the new challenges posed by the digital age? Can the digital revolution underway be regulated by resorting to the existing proprietary discipline or is a new and more adequate approach required?

These are just some of the problems and questions that we will try to answer in the following pages.

---

triumph of industrial mass production and the consequent transformation of our whole life") reverberates on the private categories «quasi tutte ispirate alla premessa di una economia anteriore alla produzione industriale di massa» (*author's note*, "almost all inspired by the premise of an economy prior to mass industrial production").

113 The analysis of different legal systems appears to be of particular importance also in terms of a marked ethnocentrism that we tend to recognize when dealing with the digital world: often reference is made to a single country. A comparative study, in fact, aims to achieve a dual purpose, trying to improve, on the one hand, the understanding of the institutions considered, and, on the other, the clarification of their causal inference.

114 *See*, in this regard, A. Gambaro, *La proprietà*, cit., p. 86, where the author considering the typical connotation that is classically attributed to property, affirms that this right is fundamental in a double meaning, since it serves both «[. . .] per costruire un certo ordine politico e sociale» (*author's note*, "To build a certain political and social order") and «[. . .] per costruire concettualmente tutto il sistema giuridico relativo alla situazione di appartenenza» (*author's note*, "to conceptually build the whole legal system relating to the situation of belonging").

1 The Digital Revolution and Evolving Social-Economic Dynamics

1 The Impact of New Technologies on Society: From the Emergence of the So-Called Network Society to the Transition to the Digital Economy

Digital technologies have profoundly touched every aspect of human life, significantly affecting also the circulation of goods and the way in which ownership is expressed and translated[1] on them.

In nature, in fact, the process of transformation is uninterrupted and continuous, and from this permanent movement the course of man is not immune, revealing itself, among other things, in the connatural inclination of individuals both to adapt to their surroundings and to adapt the latter to their own needs.

However, the extent and intensity of the changes that the social framework has undergone in recent years has assumed such proportions as to appear unprecedented, and, certainly, the development of this new phenomenology is to be attributed primarily to technical development, by reason of its aptitude to pervade *ab externo* and condition, in essence, every sector of human activity.

Technological development has, in fact, been the undisputed protagonist of the most profound changes that have affected social architectures, as witnessed in the past by the Industrial Revolution,[2] but never before have these transformations

1 It should be made clear from the outset that ownership here means the generic possibility to refer a certain subjective situation to a certain subject.

2 In this regard, we need only think of the recourse to new sources of energy that took place in successive periods and phases as the Industrial Revolution led to radical social, political and economic changes. The same can be said of other economic phenomena that profoundly impacted socio-economic structures, as demonstrated, for example, by the advent of the printing press that took place, first in China and then in Europe. *See*, for further information, J. Rifkin, *The Age of Access*, New York, NY, 2000, p. 101, where the author underlines «[I]n the old industrial economy, each person's own labor power was considered a form of property that could be sold in the marketplace. In the new network economy, selling access to one's day-to-day living patterns and life experiences, as reflected in purchasing decisions, becomes equally coveted and a much sought-after intangible asset»; A. Widuto, C. Evroux, S. Spinaci, *From Growth to "Behind Growth": Concepts and Challenges*, in *European Parliamentary Research Service – Briefing*, May 2023, p. 1 ff.

DOI: 10.4324/9781003424413-2

affected existing structures in such a profound, rapid and wide-ranging way as has happened with information and communication technologies.[3]

Information and communication technologies (ICTs), in fact, have undergone such a development that they have penetrated into the everyday life of the present generation, becoming its actual characterizing feature, as demonstrated by the recurring use made of concepts that emphasize the relevance either of information (so-called information society) or of knowledge (so-called knowledge society).

At a closer look, however, those just indicated are expressions that only partially succeed in marking the phenomenon that today's society is experiencing, not so much because, albeit with gradations and intensities quite different from today's, information and knowledge have always characterized the human community, but especially because the real element that makes the contemporary socio-economic structure absolutely original and different from previous ones is its interpenetration in a network that is not limited to amplifying the information-knowledge traits, but goes so far as to condition all the folds of human life.

More appropriately, then, one should speak of a network society[4] in order to better describe today's phenomenon and grasp how current developments have

3 Although ICTs are not, of course, the only form of technological innovation that has profoundly changed human society, especially in terms of the dissemination of information and knowledge, these modern technologies are characterized by a new feature, the aptitude to converge, i.e. to operate jointly, simultaneously and with a mutually reinforcing effect, which, combined with the technological development achieved so far, means that the conditions necessary to impact current socio-economic architectures in a way never experienced before, because they are multifocal, multi-level and heterogeneous, are broadened. *See*, for further details, S. Si, J. Hall, R. Suddaby, D. Ahlstrom, J. Wei, *Technology, Entrepreneurship, Innovation and Social Change in Digital Economics*, in *Technovation*, 119, 2023, p. 1 ff., where the authors affirm that «Technology and digitalization are increasingly core subjects for researchers across disciplines, from economics and management to engineering and the humanities. Digital innovations, such as the Internet of Things, big data, cloud computing, artificial intelligence and various digital technology-based platforms, are influencing business venturing and changing the ways that extend beyond entrepreneurship and innovation practices to influence culture, politics and society. Social media platforms and digital communications have even restructured social relations. [. . .] We elaborate the emerging new business models, their antecedents, and their economic and social consequences. The issue also highlights key emerging research areas of digital technology-based entrepreneurship/innovation and articulates an agenda for future scholarship».

4 The concept of the network society was coined and developed by Jan van Dijk and Manuel Castells in the wake of the "wired society" referred to by James Martin in 1978 to refer to a society that is connected by mass and telecommunication networks. More specifically, van Dijk defined the "network society" as a form of society that progressively organizes its relationships through media networks that gradually replace or complement social networks based on *de visu* communication. Indeed, personal and social network-based communication is supported by digital technology, which implies that media and social networks shape the most important organization modes and structures of modern society. Thus, van Dijk defines the network society as a society in which a set of media and social networks realize both their main modes of organization and the most important structures at every level (individual, organizational and social), in such a way as to configure a mass society that is formed by groups, organizations and communities (so-called masses) organized through physical co-presence. Ultimately, for van Dijk, information structures the substance of contemporary society, while networks structure the organizational forms and (infra)structures of that society. According to Castells, on the other hand, networks constitute the new social morphology of contemporary human

enabled the Internet not only to maintain but to strengthen its elasticity and adaptability, providing individuals with the necessary tools to overcome the coordination shortcomings that had been practically experienced in the past and that had prevented those possibilities of sharing and collaboration that are now, instead, more easily viable.

On a more properly economic front, the proliferation of global electronic networks, among which the Internet stands out, of course, entails a repositioning of economic circulation on the very plane of cyberspace.

Therefore, the centrality assumed by technologies in contemporary society, also qualified as socio-digitization[5] to refer to that process of transformation in which the dynamics of information and digital communication condition the logic of social organization, interaction and socio-economic space in general, is strongly linked to the idea of dematerialization:[6] intangibility becomes the essential trait of a transformation process that leads to a different perception of information and communication from that of the analogue age, thereby encroaching on the notion of ownership itself.

In a world where personalized production, continuous innovation, a massive flow of goods and services, accompanied by their rapid and short life cycle, albeit characterized by their uninterrupted improvement, concepts such as "having," "possessing," and "disposing" take on a different guise, conditioned, of necessity, by an economy where change in and of itself appears to be the only possible constant.

In this network economy, the winning trait of marketing is to capture the attention of potential users,[7] not only through physical resources, but also through digital

---

communities, as the network society surpasses the information society itself. According to Castells, it is not technology that, purely and simply, qualifies modern societies, but cultural, economic and political factors that operate to construct the network society also contribute to this defining process: religion, culture, politics and social states all contribute to shaping the network society, either by elevating it or by exhausting it. *See* M. Castells, *The Network Society Revisited*, in *Am. Behav. Sci.*, 67(7), 2023, p. 940 ff. *See*, on a specular side, M. Weiser, *The Computer for the 21st Century*, in *Sci. Am.*, September 1991, p. 94 ff., where the author, at p. 94, affirming that «[T]he constant background presence of these products of "literacy technology" does not require active attention, but the information to be conveyed is ready for use at a glance», expresses the idea that the computer is in the best condition to help the human being perform the activities he performs on a daily basis, so that individuals, favoured by this external support, are placed in the condition to optimize and make better use of their own performance.

5 A. Rahmatian, *Intellectual Property and the Concept of Dematerialised Property*, in *Modern Studies in Property Law. Volume 6*, edited by S. Bright, Oxford, 2011, p. 361 ff.

6 It is worth to notice that the terms *assets* or *patrimonium* or *wherewithal* make reference to the sum total of assets minus the liabilities allocated by law to a person in the form of tangible and intangible (including purely intangible) objects (rights and obligations), which constitutes the person's estate and which can typically be expressed in a monetary value, for example in the case of succession or insolvency. *See*, for further information, D. Messinetti, voce *Beni immateriali (diritto privato)*, in *Enc. giur. Treccani*, V, Roma, 1989, p. 10 ff.

7 Jisun An, Haewoon Kwak, Soon-gyo Jung, Joni Salminen, Bernard J. Jansen, *Customer Segmentation Using Online Platforms: Isolating Behavioral and Demographic Segments for Persona Creation via Aggregated User Data*, in *Soc. Netw. Anal. Min.*, 54(8), 2018, p. 1 ff., where the authors say that

assets characterized not only by their inherent incorporeality, but also by their ability to foster the establishment of long-term legal relationships between providers and users.[8]

In these terms, therefore, the economic framework is no longer based on the mere exchange of *res*, but on facilitated access to the immaterial, and thus on a tendency to favour the incorporeal over the corporeal: one is no longer in the presence of an order that makes things tradable that will be exchanged in a specific area designated to this, the market, but of a juridical-economic process aimed at allowing reciprocal access to one's goods, one's time, one's skills, putting them at the disposal of others and considering them as an activity or an event that one uses for a more or less limited period of time.

In essence, the exchange system would seem to conceal its purely material origins to gradually become governed by the immaterial.

Beyond this peculiar manifestation, intangibility represents the essential condition to realize a further characteristic that is coessential – if not unique – to this new juridical-economic scenario: ubiquity, i.e. the possibility of existing and being present everywhere at the same time.

Digital technologies have initiated a phase in which goods can be replicated, transmitted, stored and manipulated with enormous ease, as is well demonstrated by ubiquitous computing, according to which innovations are so far-reaching that individuals no longer perceive the interactions they establish with technology to achieve certain results.[9]

Technology, understood in this way, becomes a sort of "background noise" in which every human being is immersed and by which he is surrounded, insofar as the subject is in a position to benefit from a ubiquitous technological support because, placed in the background of his everyday life, it allows him, at all times and in an almost unconscious manner, to resort to it through devices that are ordinarily and regularly present in his everyday life.

«»; X. Jiang, J. Lin, C. Wang, L. Zhou, *Seize Market Opportunities: Market Segmentation, Profile and Monitoring Through User-Generated Content*, in *Kybernetes*, 12 July 2023, p. 1 ff.

8 A. Kamalaldin, L. Linde, D. Sjödin, V. Parida, *Transforming Provider-Customer Relationships in Digital Servitization: A Relational View on Digitalization*, in *Ind. Mark. Manag.*, 89, 2020, p. 306 ff.

9 R. Milner, *Ubiquitous Computing: Shall We Understand It?*, in *Comp. J.*, 49(4), July 2006, p. 383 ff., where the author, at p. 383, states that «Pervasive or ubiquitous computing has become an aspiration of the computing community over the past 15 years. Its vision, pioneered by Mark Weiser, is that populations of computing entities – hardware and software – will become an integral part of our environment, performing tasks that support our overall purposes without us being continually guided by them, thus allowing us to be largely unaware of them. The vision arises because technology begins to be within our reach. This simple aspiration raises questions that range across computing and beyond. Here are some of them. Social questions: what ubiquitous computing (UCS) systems do people want or need and how will they change people's behaviour? Technological questions: how will the hardware entities – the sensors and devices whose cooperation represents such a system – acquire power and by what means will they communicate? Engineering questions: for the populations and sub-populations – including software agents – that make up a system, what design principles should be adopted at each order of magnitude to ensure reliable performance? Fundamental questions: what concepts are needed to specify and describe pervasive systems, their subsystems and interactions?»

But, as is the case with all *res humanae*, this type of ubiquity also has not only the positive traits now briefly described, but also obvious negative profiles, given that both the potential damage and the potential violations to the underlying subjective situations are equally ubiquitous,[10] especially when intangible goods are involved.

The influences that digital technologies exert on social interactions are, then, amplified by the increased possibilities of cooperation that increasingly powerful and fast technological tools make possible: relationships, both personal and professional, are facilitated by the elimination of physical-temporal differences, so that heterogeneous, multiform and multilevel forms of collaboration become increasingly natural and evidently useful and attractive tools for promoting, cultivating and achieving common interests and results.[11]

The combination of microelectronics, computers and telecommunication enables the realization of a single integrated communication grid that unfolds in the creation of new models of collaboration and sharing.

Thus, accentuating their inherent dynamism, networked digital technologies enable the initiation and facilitation of participatory structures on a global scale, capable of reinforcing an already constantly changing environment.

All these changes are reflected in the notion of ownership, because while in a geographically based system of legal circulation, sellers and buyers exchange physical goods and services, in the space created by the Internet, servers and users are increasingly facilitated in transferring information and knowledge.

Therefore, if the objective of the traditional economic system is the transfer of ownership, the objective of the digital economic system is to allow access that

10 J.P.A. Galgano, *Tackling the Intangible: Why the Supreme Court Needs to Define Intellectual Property and What Facebook Stands to Lose (or Win)*, in *Notre Dame J. L. Ethics Pub. Poly.*, 2023, 37, p. 323 ff.

11 C. Zhang, Y. Xu, *Institutional Innovation Essence and Knowledge Innovation Goal of Intellectual Property Law in the Big Data Era*, in *J. Innov. Knowl.*, 8(4), 2023, p. 1 ff., where the authors, at p. 1, affirm their will «[. . .] to expand the understanding on the nature of institutional innovation and the goal of knowledge innovation of intellectual property (IP) law in the era of big data (BD) and to avoid the risks of information security in the IP service system. On the basis of the era of BD, the nature of institutional innovation and the goal of knowledge innovation in IP law are systematically discussed. Combined with smart contract (SC) technology, an IP service system based on blockchain technology is designed to ensure the security of IP services. The SC is optimized from the perspective of concurrency, and the contract transactions (CTs) are clustered. Moreover, considering the execution time (ET) and available resources of CTs, a speculative concurrency control algorithm that can realize intelligent contract scheduling is proposed. On the basis of the ciphertext-policy attribute-based encryption (CP-ABE) algorithm, a policy-updatable attribute encryption algorithm is designed. The improved CP-ABE algorithm includes six steps: system initialization, attribute private key generation, encryption, decryption, ciphertext policy generation, and ciphertext policy update. The identity parameter of the traceability manager is introduced into the improved CP-ABE scheme, which significantly increases the amount of computation of bilinear mapping, thus resulting in the time cost of encryption and decryption being approximately 350 ms and 300 ms higher than that of the CP-ABE scheme. Using the technical mode of "blockchain+SC," the design of the IP service system is realized, which has important reference value for the institutional innovation of IP law».

enables the individual not so much to purchase and accumulate goods with the idea of excluding other individuals from their enjoyment, but to enjoy goods that can also be contextually enjoyed by other users without their full enjoyment being compromised.

It is in this way that the so-called digital economy, based on information technologies that constitute its backbone, comes into being and develops.[12]

2 Connectivity and the Shift Towards New Forms of Ownership as the Defining Trait of the Digital Age Economy

If one were to identify the distinctive trait of the digital economy, this could only be identified with connectivity, so much so that one usually speaks of the so-called connected economy: computer networks, by their very nature, tend to break every boundary and barrier and to impose themselves thanks to connections that overcome every space-time limit.

Unlike the economic systems of the industrial era, characterized by a development in a geographical sense, facilitated by the affirmation of an idea of sovereignty and autonomy of operators, involved in individual, autonomous and independent exchanges, the contemporary economy unravels in a network of relationships, mutually interdependent, in which individuals share their activities and goals.[13]

Markets increasingly see suppliers and users in contact with each other to share both corporeal and incorporeal goods,[14] in the full conviction that by pooling their resources everyone will benefit from a better and fuller satisfaction of their needs.[15]

12 *See, ex multis*, E. Brynjolfsson, Brian Kahin (edited by), *Understanding the Digital Economy: Data, Tools, and Research*, Cambridge, MA, 2002, *passim*; B. Carlsson, *The Digital Economy: What Is New and What Is Not?*, in *Struct. Change Econ. Dyn.*, 15(3), 2004, p. 245 ff.; R. Bukht, R. Heeks, *Defining, Conceptualising and Measuring the Digital Economy*, in *Development Informatics – Working Paper Series*, 68, 2017, p. 1 ff., where the authors, at p. 1, affirm that «[T]he digital economy is growing fast, especially in developing countries. [. . .] there are three scopes of relevance. The core of the digital economy is the "*digital sector*": the IT/ICT sector producing foundational digital goods and services. The true "*digital economy*" – defined as "that part of economic output derived solely or primarily from digital technologies with a business model based on digital goods or services" – consists of the digital sector plus emerging digital and platform services. The widest scope – use of ICTs in all economic fields – is here referred to as the "*digitalised economy*"».

13 S. Ammirato, A.M. Felicetti, R. Linzalone, V. Corvello, S. Kumar, *Still Our Most Important Asset: A Systematic Review on Human Resource Management in the Midst of the Fourth Industrial Revolution*, in *J. Innov. Knowl.*, 8(3), 2023, p. 1 ff., where the authors, at p. 1, affirms that «[T]he digital transition is transforming society in general and industry in particular, so much so that the concept of Industry 4.0 is by now widespread and consolidated. However, there is the risk that too pronounced a focus on technology may lead to losing sight of the centrality of human resources. Among others, the European Commission has urged greater attention from research and industry on the human factor. There is a need for further theorizing concerning the role of humans in a digitalized industry. Understanding what is known in the literature on human resource management in an Industry 4.0 context is an important first step toward defining a roadmap for enhancing the human factor in a digitized industry».

14 In this respect, digital assets such as, for instance, information, specific skills, intangible assets, etc. shall be considered.

15 J. Hanlan, D. Fuller, S. Wilde, *Destination Decision Making: The Need for a Strategic Planning and Management Approach*, in *Tour. Hosp. Plan. Dev.*, 3, 2006, p. 209 ff.; T. Papawadee, *The Boundary*

Thus, as we have just seen,[16] the very Smithian idea of the invisible hand, which governed the entire industrial age and preached the subject's ability to achieve and accumulate ownership of goods, to the exclusion of others, as a demeanour capable of benefiting the individual directly, but society as a whole indirectly, appears to be in crisis.[17]

If, then, the accumulation and ownership of physical goods are inherent to the industrial age, the ownership of intangible goods is appropriate to the digital age, where physical goods, which have long represented the industrialized world's own form of wealth, are increasingly dematerializing and becoming identified with bundles of data or intellectual goods.[18]

Between Digital Goods and E-Services in Cross-Border E-Commerce and Implication for Non-Discrimination Under the WTO System, in *Intern. J. Law Inform. Techn.*, 31(3), 2023, p. 213 ff., where the author, although by a tax point of view, analyses various approaches to classify goods and services including technological neutrality and tradability.

16 *See supra* § 1.

17 R. Koselleck, *Critique and Crisis: Enlightenment and the Pathogenesis of Modern Society*, Cambridge, MA, 1988, p. 1 ff., where the author argues that it was the split that developed between state and society during the Enlightenment that fostered the emergence of this intellectual elite divorced from the realities of politics. This disjunction between political authority proper and its subjects, therefore, led to private spheres that later became centres of moral authority and, eventually, models for political society that took little or no notice of the constraints under which politicians must inevitably work. In this way progressive bourgeois philosophy, which seemed to offer the promise of a unified and peaceful world, in fact produced just the opposite.

18 Factors such as new and lighter building materials, miniaturization, the substitution of information for physical content and the increasing role played by services are all contributing to the contraction of an economy based on mere corporatism. On the other hand, not even money is immune from this process of dematerialization, as the phenomenon of bitcoins, cryptocurrencies and blockchains demonstrates. *See*, for further details, M. Cogoy, *Dematerialisation, Time Allocation, and the Service Economy*, in *Struct. Change Econ. Dyn.*, 15(2), 2004, p. 165 ff., where the author «[. . .] investigates the role of human capital and knowledge-based services in determining the materials intensity, and therefore the environmental impacts of consumption. The model presented generates a stylised structural dynamics of the economy: a phase of growing materials throughput is superseded by a phase of dematerialisation and service-intensive consumption. It is assumed, that consumption is a time-requiring activity, and that knowledge-based services play an important role in shaping the material requirements of consumption. The accumulation of human capital can therefore enable consumers to substitute service time for commodities as the economy develops. In this way, both the allocation of time and the material intensity of the life-process is endogenously determined in a dynamic model of economic development». Therefore, «[I]t is necessary to distinguish between *relative* and *absolute* dematerialisation, the first expression denoting a reduction in the flow of materials and energy per unit of output, or of consumption service, and the second denoting the final overall result, after the economy has dynamically adapted to the stimulus represented by the original increase in ecological efficiency. A reduction of materials and energy inputs per unit of output, or of consumption service (*relative* dematerialisation), will not necessarily lead to a global, or *absolute*, dematerialisation of the economy, if the gains in terms of ecological efficiency are neutralised by the overall effects of economic growth [. . .]. Since the overall impact of human activities on the environment depends on the absolute level of materials and energy flows mobilised by the economy, it is absolute, and not relative dematerialisation that contributes to sustainability [. . .]». *See*, on the cryptocurrencies, *ex multis*, R.H. Huang, H. Deng, A.F. Lok Chan, *The Legal Nature of Cryptocurrency as Property: Accounting and Taxation Implications*, in *Comp. Law Sec. Rev.*, 51, 2023, p. 1 ff. where the authors, by taking an interdisciplinary approach to examining the property nature of crypto and its accounting and taxation implications for companies holding crypto, underline, at p. 1, that «[C]ryptocurrencies have recently attracted much attention and intense discourse.

In a network economy, in fact, individual interest seems to play a different role as it is embedded in a network of relationships centred on potentially mutual, reciprocal benefits and directed towards optimizing the achievement of the participants' goals, so that the well-being of each individual can be potentially better guaranteed.[19]

A further and fundamental element typical of a global network economy is its stimulating and concomitant intense acceleration of technological innovation:[20] in

---

In Hong Kong, according to a statement issued by the Securities and Futures Commission ("SFC") in 2018, the term "cryptocurrency" has been used interchangeably with "crypto-asset," "digital token" and "virtual asset," which, by virtue of their names, may be seen as a recognized "currency" and "asset."[1] Meanwhile, different jurisdictions are also adopting a wide variety of terms, including "virtual currency" and "digital currency."[2] However, such terms may be misleading because in many jurisdictions there are strict legal definitions as to what constitutes "currency."[3] In fact, cryptocurrencies may not have the characteristics of currencies or commodities.[4] For the purpose of our discussion, cryptocurrencies will be referred to as "crypto" in order to be neutral as to their nature. [. . .] In the absence of clear rules to classify crypto as cash or cash equivalents, financial instruments, inventories or intangible assets, it has created uncertainties in the accounting treatment of crypto. If the accounting treatments do not fit well with the legal nature of crypto, accounting issues such as distorted financial figures and valuation difficulties may arise. For instance, earnings can be distorted, and asset values can be understated, on financial statements. This will also have important impacts on its treatment for taxation purposes, including profits tax, capital gains tax and transaction tax. Indeed, while the legal nature of crypto as property has now been well explored, its implications for the accounting and tax treatments of crypto remain understudied. There is a great need to think about the property, accounting and taxation aspects together».

19 In usual economic parlance, this mutual profit approach is qualified as a win-win strategy. With regard to the so-called network economy, Castells identifies five main types of networks that characterize the new global markets: the so-called supplier networks, in which companies operate through a series of sub-contracts covering a wide range of activities, from design to the production of different components; the so-called producer networks, consisting of companies that pool their production means, human and financial resources to produce different components; and the so-called win-win networks, consisting of companies that pool their production means, human and financial resources to produce different components. d. producer networks, made up of companies that pool their production means, human and financial resources to increase the range of goods and services they are able to offer users, to increase the geographical reference market and to reduce operating risks; the c. d. customer networks, which link manufacturers, suppliers, marketing circuits, resellers and users; the so-called standard coalitions, which unite, in a given field, as many companies as possible with the intention of binding them to technical standards set by a sector leader; and the so-called technology cooperation networks, which enable companies to share knowledge and expertise useful for research and development of product lines. *See* M. Castells, *The Information Age. Economy, Society and Culture. I. The Rise of the Network Society*, Chichester, 2010, p. 191 ff. *See*, for details on the technical informatic standards, *ex multis*, J.R. Reidenberg, *Lex Informatica: The Formulation of Information Policy Rules Through Technology*, in *Texas Law Rev.*, 76, 1998, p. 553 ff.

20 I. Irtyshcheva, M. Stehnei, N. Popadynets, K. Bogatyrev, Y. Boiko, I. Kramarenko, O. Senkevich, N. Hryshyna, I. Kozak, O. Ishchenko, *The Effect of Digital Technology Development on Economic Growth*, in *Intern. J. Data Netw. Sci.*, 5, 2021, p. 25 ff., where the authors, at pp. 25 and 26, affirm that «[T]he development of relationships in a social environment depends on the level of economic development. This applies to any level: global, European, national, regional, territorial, etc. The digitalization of the economy is a specific economic technology with its own characteristics, trends and patterns. Many countries of the world use this technology to improve the efficiency of economic development, increase competitiveness, and etc. The results of the digital economy are the same

a highly digitalized environment, production mechanisms, equipment, goods and services are subject to a rapid obsolescence process, a long-term ownership logic becomes less attractive than models centred on short-term exploitation.

Thus, the acceleration of technological innovations, combined with the continuous need for asset turnover, profoundly conditions the nature of the network economy[21] and related ownership positions.

The temporal contraction of the life cycle of products has repercussions, then, on the very idea of ownership, favouring models of more or less long-term access to goods and services that become increasingly attractive and alternative to traditional forms of ownership.[22]

---

products as in ordinary economic activity. Thus, the digital economy is not a separate industry, but simply acts as a virtual addition to the real traditional economy. The digitalization of society provides for the formation of relationships between government, business and society using the latest information technologies, covers socio-economic events on the Internet platform, mobile and sensor networks. The digital economy is based on the ability to access the Internet. The introduction of the digital economy makes it possible to increase labor productivity, business competitiveness and the well-being of citizens. To implement the digital economy, first of all, it is necessary to provide expanded access to the Internet, because today the Internet is the most important element of economic development. The current stage of socio-economic systems development is characterized by rapid structural and qualitative transformations under the influence of the rapid spread of innovative technologies, including digital technologies. The processes of digitalization of the economy and social relations contribute to the deepening of interaction between all subjects of the market environment that go beyond national borders, create the preconditions for GDP growth, increase labor productivity, introduce and spread innovations in all spheres of life. At the same time, rapid technological changes that have a multiplier effect require the formation of qualitatively new, adaptive approaches and models for managing economic processes at all levels. Without taking into account the influence of the main trends in the digitalization of society on the development of economic and social processes, the formation of strategies for the economic development of the state, regions and individual industries has no practical meaning. The digital economy is based on the introduction and widespread use of technologies for storing and processing large amounts of information (Big data, cloud computing), the Internet of Things, end-to-end information technologies, cyber security technologies, robotization and comprehensive automation of most processes and industries and other areas of development of innovative technologies that change the human role in the economic system».

21 R. Glazer, *Marketing in an Information-Intensive Environment: Strategic Implications of Knowledge as an Asset*, in *J. Market.*, 55, 1991, p. 7, where the author affirms that «[T]he result is a more rapid evolution in the basic product form and a shift in emphasis toward successive generations of the product, with the life cycle of any one generation or "version" [. . .] assuming less importance».

22 D. Clarke, J. Östlund, I. Sergey, T. Wrigstad, *Ownership Types: A Survey*, in *Aliasing in Object-Oriented Programming. Types, Analysis and Verification. Lecture Notes in Computer Science*, edited by D. Clarke, J. Noble, T. Wrigstad, 7850, Berlin and Heidelberg, 2013, p. 15 ff., where the authors, analysing the various flavours of ownership types that have been developed over the years, along with the many applications and other developments, underline at p. 15 that «[O]wnership types were devised nearly 15 years ago to provide a stronger notion of protection to object-oriented programming languages. Rather than simply protecting the fields of an object from external access, ownership types protect also the objects stored in the fields, thereby enabling an object to claim (exclusive) ownership of and access to other objects. Furthermore, this notion is statically enforced by now-standard type-checking techniques. Originating as the formalisation of the core of Flexible Alias Protection, ownership types have since been extended and adapted in many ways, and the notion of protection provided has been refined into topological and encapsulation dimensions».

But, beyond the affirmation of alternative forms of property, has digitality caused or could cause a change in the very way property law is understood?

Certainly, the general dematerialization to which the concept of property is exposed in the digital age is accompanied by the transition from an economy in which wealth is measured in terms of ownership of *res corporales* to an economy in which wealth is increasingly measured as control of *res incorporales*, which take on the guise of intellectual and intangible goods: the reduction of physical property is accompanied by progressive access to digital goods.[23]

The classical industrial age presented itself as a world dominated by physicality, whose dominant idea was the reconstruction of the corporeal world in the image of man, and where the materiality of nature was reconstituted by the individual in the form of corporeal ownership in which the owner, as an authentic *minor deus*, acted as *dominus* in his private regnum, populated by corporeal objects drawn from the surrounding world that continually reminded him of their origin, creation precisely.

The digital cosmos, on the contrary, is more immaterial and incorporeal, populated by Platonic forms, ideas, images, archetypes, concepts and *fictiones*: if the individual of the industrial world was beset by the idea of expropriating and remodelling materiality according to his own needs, that of the digital world is certainly more interested in affecting the incorporeal.

In an era characterized by the privilege accorded to access over having, where the immaterial has become a fundamental object of exchange, the ability to penetrate and expand the network, to be connected, to share and to exploit all the possible potential that digitality offers is the real motivation that activates and fuels the transfer of goods.

Just as the circulation of tangible goods characterizes the epoch that has just passed, so the circulation of intangible goods characterizes the contemporary period, due to the loss of importance and centrality to which property in its traditional forms is increasingly exposed.

23 W. Prayitno, T. Tumangkar, S. Mulyani, *The Metaverse Symbol of Civilization Transfer in the Middle of Digital Economic Hegemony: Synthesis of Progressive Law of the Post-Modern Era*, in *Seven Editora*, 2023, p. 1 ff., where the authors, at p. 1, stress that «[T]he problem that arises with the presence of avatars, NFT, crypto, virtual land, and others in the midst of the hegemony of the digital economy is whether progressive law in the post-modern era can: (1) ensure the direction of digital transformation can run according to the desired corridor in the midst of digital economic hegemony; (2) paying attention to social elements such as culture and social conditions of society, although it is absolutely related to the use of digital technology, digital transformation is not only about technology; (3) accelerating the process of digital transformation is not impossible to create an increasingly polarized digital divide; and (4) ensuring that digital transformation does not have a counter-productive impact, but there must be a guarantee that it will not only benefit certain groups, while at the same time marginalizing the existence of other groups. The world has now arrived at the progress of spiritual intelligence that breaks through the tradition of thinking that only relies on logic or linear thinking (Intellectual Quotient), even thinking with feelings (Emotional Quotient). Intuitive spiritual intelligence (Spiritual Quotient) will make a leap that does not exist in the workings of the intellectual quotient and emotional quotient. In contrast to machines that work according to rules, human life has many aspects that cannot be understood and captured by machines».

On the other hand, a gradual process of dematerialization and transformation of the very concept of ownership of property is accompanied by a progressive increase in the risks associated with an exploitation of concepts, ideas, persons and *res* that exceeds space-time limits because it is not linked to corporeality but driven by the use of a ubiquitous computer and digital network.

Ultimately, the advent of the Internet coincides with a substantial change that has affected the legal circulation of goods and its primary purposes: from being an instrument for the expansion of markets and the easy realization of the exchange of material property between seller and buyer, it is increasingly characterized by a process of deconstruction of its own institutional foundations and founding principles.

The contemporary economic system,[24] articulated in the network and exploiting its characteristics and potential, is undergoing a phase of radical reinvention thanks to a process of transformation populated by new forms of power and economic influence far more incisive than those experienced by the traditional market.[25]

These changes, therefore, while they obviously cannot fail to affect the right that most expresses the individual's economic personality and status, property, do not entail its extinction but its apparent articulation in a plurality of guises,[26] ranging

24 *See*, for further details, T.K. Hopkins, I. Wallerstein, *Structural Transformations of the World-Economy*, in *Review (Fernand Braudel Center)*, 39(1/4), 2016, p. 171 ff., where the authors, at p. 171, state that «[A] set of interrelated processes affects the capitalist development of the modern world-system. These processes work through a massive, world-scale complex of relational networks or social structures, which the processes produced, continually reproduce, and also continually modify. Together this ensemble of generative processes and channelling structures forms a coherent, historical, social system – the capitalist world-economy. As a historical social system, this world-economy is time-specified in two constitutive ways: it is temporally bounded, having beginnings, middles, and end points that can in principle be located on conventional time scales; and it is temporally patterned, having distinctive periodicities and durations», and continue at p. 173 stating that «[A] distinction is often drawn between two directions of structural transformation, the broadening of the capitalist world-economy and its deepening, to use the well-known pair of terms. One refers to the historical expansion of its geographical space by the successive elimination via incorporation of areas external to it. The capitalist world economy thus broadens geographically, from the limited arena in which its axial division of labor took shape during the sixteenth century (an arena thereby formed into a locus of a world-economy) to its present occupancy of the whole of the globe (and, indeed, even beyond, if the minuscule footholds on outer space provided by orbiting satellites may be counted). The other refers to the historical extension of its social space (to use that metaphor) via the successive elimination, or the fundamental reconstitution, of social relations external to it. The world-economy thus deepens socially, from the highly circumscribed and subordinate place its organizing processes occupied initially, in the geographical area where they operated, to their present place of dominance and reach throughout the length and breadth of contemporary human affairs».

25 A. Phillips, *The Global Transformation, Multiple Early Modernities, and International System Change*, in *Int. Theory*, 8(3), 2016, p. 481 ff., where the author, at p. 487, observes that «[A]s we move into a world of "de-centered globalism" (Buzan and Lawson 2015, 273), where the return of non-Western Great Powers is again yielding diverse regional orders, it is imperative that we acknowledge the deeper historical roots of this resurgent diversity».

26 *See*, for a classic view along these lines, L. Josserand, *Cours de droit civil positif français. I*, Paris 1938, p. 839 ff.; S. Rodotà, *Il terribile diritto*, Bologna, 2013, esp. at p. 53 ff. and p. 129 ff., where the author, at p. 56, affirms that «[A]ll'osservatore di oggi, quindi, la proprietà non si presenta

from the genuine act of alienation, centred on the negotiated exchange between seller and buyer, to short-term or long-term types of access, centred on a relationship between parties to access or share ownership of tangible or intangible goods.[27]

Therefore, the network economy, in its becoming a system in which the contemporary market expresses itself, is characterized, on the one hand, by forms of ownership based more on fruition than on actual purchase, and, on the other, by the growing marginality of tangible property in favour of the pressing affirmation of intangible property as a trait that qualifies and defines the era based on access.

From the perspective of dematerialization, the very legal relationship of sharing that exists between two or more parties seems to be transfigured into an authentic asset that is legally transferable and circulable, thus becoming a true commodity.[28]

A legal circulation characterized today by the presence of different forms of ownership, as well as by the intangibility of the goods that are the subject of it, is the cause of both the shift from the seller-buyer binomial towards the supplier-user binomial and the shift of long-term ownership towards short-term access-use of goods, services and capital.[29]

---

come un blocco monolitico, da misurare nella sua compattezza e, se mai, da levigare in qualche spigolo troppo acuto. Essa, anche quando viene presentata come un a oggetto da considerare nel suo insieme, è piuttosto un τόπος, intorno al quale una stratificazione secolare è venuta raccogliendo problemi, i cui nessi, però, non possono essere arbitrariamente recisi: questi nessi, anzi, vanno analizzati, sia per accertarne l'effettiva portata storica, sia per saggiarne la corrispondenza alla realtà attuale. Infatti, non si può certo dire che, per effetto della frammentazione della categoria giuridica della proprietà, sia venuto meno nella nostra cultura il riferimento allo schema proprietario per descrivere o connotare nel loro insieme tipi di rapporti esistenti nell'organizzazione sociale. Ed è agevole constatare come questi descrizioni o connotazioni, critiche o apologetiche che siano, trapassino poi dall'originario loro terreno filosofico, economico, sociologico nel campo giuridico, fondando la pretesa o la ripulsa di forme di tutela proprietaria, nell'ottica, già ricordata, di chi la considera ancora la più forte tra le tecniche giuridiche disponibili. L'innegabile rilevanza di questi fenomeni, da una parte, obbliga a fare ancora i conti con nozioni di proprietà assai comprensive: ma, d'altra parte, impone l'attenzione per criteri ricostruttivi diversi da quelli logico-formali, determinando così una ulteriore dissoluzione della categoria giuridica tradizionale».

27 If the negotiated exchange of ownership of an asset represent the circulation mechanism of ownership typical of the traditional market system, access to assets would constitute the heart of the network economy.

28 To sum up, digital assets, included in the form of patents, trademarks, copyrights, trade secrets, and legal relationships aimed at access, contribute to the new market structure.

29 *See*, B. Lee, E. LiPuma, *Cultures of Circulation: The Imaginations of Modernity*, in *Publ. Cult.*, 14(1), 2002, p. 191 ff., where the authors, at p. 192, underline that «[I]f circulation is to serve as a useful analytic construct for cultural analysis, it must be conceived as more than simply the movement of people, ideas, and commodities from one culture to another. Instead, recent work indicates that circulation is a cultural process with its own forms of abstraction, evaluation, and constraint, which are created by the interactions between specific types of circulating forms and the interpretive communities built around them. It is in these structured circulations that we identify cultures of circulation. [. . .] Cultures of circulation are created and animated by the cultural forms that circulate through them, including – critically – the abstract nature of the forms that underwrite and propel the process of circulation itself. The circulation of such forms – whether the novels and newspapers of the imagined community or the equity-based derivatives and currency swaps of the modern market – always presupposes the existence of their respective interpretive communities, with their own forms of interpretation and evaluation. These interpretive communities determine

Thus, a series of issues are generated – to be addressed in the following pages – that touch on the impact of this legal-economic phenomenon on the nature of the right to property and its concrete scope.

3 Property as a Fluid Constant in Human Historical Progression

Throughout history, the concept of property, in its individual or collective form,[30] has progressively assumed and gained such importance that it has become an authentic constant that has accompanied human existence since the beginnings of civilization and the first forms of organized society.[31]

The right to property, in fact, represents an instrument that, due to its ability to conventionally delimit reciprocal spheres of influence, allows, at a social level, the establishment between individuals of economic-legal relations aimed at distinguishing their own from others[32] – so much so that, as long as human relations are also expressed in material, spatial and geographical terms, some proprietary regime will have to exist.

Property, however, has always presented a strong conceptual elusiveness, which leads it to appear, on the one hand, easy to perceive and grasp in its various forms, and, on the other hand, and at the same time, difficult to decline in its various identifying characteristics.[33]

Certainly, a factor that might explain the considerable difficulty encountered historically in clearly perceiving and exhaustively describing ownership is linked to the very flexibility inherent in the image of ownership: property varies with the

---

lines of interpretation, found institutions, and set boundaries based principally on their own internal dynamics».

30 *See*, for a classic study on the subject, P. Lafargue, *The Evolution of Property: From Savagery to Civilization*, New York, NY, 1901, *passim*.

31 *See*, for a synopsis of the origin of property, H. Demsetz, *Toward a Theory of Property Rights*, in *Am. Econ. Rev.*, 57(2), 1967, p. 347 ff.; J.E. Krier, *Evolutionary Theory and the Origin of Property Rights*, in *Cornell Law Rev.*, 95, 2009, p. 139 ff.; and, for an original view of the relationship between property and freedom, U. Mattei, *"Senza proprietà non c'è libertà." Falso!*, Roma-Bari, 2014, esp. p. 25 ff. e p. 71 ff.

32 *See* P. Grossi, *Il dominio e le cose. Percezioni medievali e moderne dei diritti reali*, Milano, 1992, p. 603 ff., where the author observes that «[L]a nostra insegna, col pressante richiamo al "proprio," al "mio," non deve bendare i nostri occhi e farci ritenere esclusivo un paesaggio giuridico per la semplicistica ragione che ci è vicino e familiare. Vivere all'interno dell'universo della appartenenza, com'è nostra sorte, senza aprire ideali finestre sull'esterno, rischia non soltanto di farci considerare unica quella che è semplicemente una soluzione storica dominante, ma di farcela considerare la migliore possibile, con la conseguente condanna di ogni altra soluzione come anomala e deteriore».

33 Cfr. P. Lafargue, *The Evolution of Property: From Savagery to Civilization*, London, 1890, p. 6, where the author affirms that «[S]o great were the zeal, and ardour which economists brought to bear on their search for capitalistic property in prehistoric times, that they succeeded, in the course of their investigations, in discovering the existence of property outside the human species, to wit, among the invertebrates: for the ant, in her foresight, is a hoarder of provisions. It is a pity that they should not have gone a step farther, and affirmed that, if the ant lays up stores, she does so with a view to sell the same and realise a profit by the circulation of her capital». *See*, for more on this subject, *infra* Chapter 2.

flow of time and adapts to the evolution of economic systems and legal systems, proving to be – as, moreover, is the case for any other "invention" attributable to a structured social complex – a fluid notion exposed to the heterogeneity of the intentions, conceptions and perceptions of each era.[34]

Property, in fact, more than any other juridical concept, is subject to the influence of the forces that condition human society in its most qualifying juridical-economic traits, as is well demonstrated by the authentic transfiguration to which the organization of human relations has been subjected in the transition from an economy centred on the production and exchange of goods to access to services transformed into authentic *res* commodities.

Ownership continues, however, to be perceived as a trait congenital to human relations, although no longer exclusively referring to physicality, but also to immateriality, implying a profound change in the very way interrelationships are perceived.

The transition, in fact, towards a world in which the exchange of material *res* no longer represents the sole characterizing feature of legal relations, but only one of its possible developments, marks a change that extends to the most profound way of perceiving intersubjective relations and the world in which they are immersed and from which they draw life, no longer mediated by a traditional proprietary logic strongly linked to a physical good, but by a *modus cogitandi* that, less material and less limited by specific space-time boundaries, certainly becomes more intangible and incorporeal, but at the same time capable of affecting the very scope of ownership.

Evidence of this is the way in which services, as tradable goods, have undergone an evolution that has led them to be, from the distinct and autonomous object of transfer that they were, to the current object of a legal relationship between supplier and user, which, thanks to digitalization, is multifaceted and long-lasting.

Digital goods, in short, are characterized by being subject to continuous evolution and by resorting to information and interaction, gradually losing their material status and acquiring a condition that progressively transcends corporeity: their value relies less and less on material supports to become increasingly linked to digitality.

This progressive change in the nature of the good also affects its way of being considered, so much so that from the fixity of the product conceived as a *res* whose

34 *See* P. Grossi, *Il dominio e le cose. Percezioni medievali e moderne dei diritti reali*, cit., esp. pp. 609 and 619, where the author affirms that «[N]essun discorso giuridico è forse tanto intriso di bene e di male, tanto condìto da visioni manichee quanto quello che verte sul rapporto uomo-beni. Perché sono così grossi gli interessi in gioco, che inevitabilmente le scelte economico-giuridiche vengono difese dalle corazze non usurabili delle connotazioni etiche e religiose. La soluzione storica tende a diventare ideologia facendo un clamoroso salto di piani, e il modesto istituto giuridico che è conveniente tutelare di determinanti interessi di ceto e di classe, è sottratto alla relatività del divenire e connotato di assolutezza. L'istituto da coagulo sociale rischia di diventare modello, la rappresentazione della validità suprema, l'apice espressivo d'una ricerca del bene sociale. All'interno dell'universo chiuso dell'appartenenza c'è il pericolo immanente del condizionamento da parte di un archetipo pesantissimo».

value is mainly linked to a single and unique transfer, we pass to its consideration as a platform exposed to all sorts of services that update it and add meaning to it.[35]

There is, therefore, a gradual transformation of goods towards immaterial forms that allow, among other things, considerable economic savings, significant reductions in emissions related to production and its waste, and, in general, a lower environmental impact.

At the same time, the digital age is characterized by an emblematic shift from the simple manufacture and sale of products to the establishment and maintenance of long-lasting relationships, which marks a profound change in the very way business is conceived: whereas in the industrial age the imperative of order was only to increase production in order to increase sales, this approach has now been superseded by a vision of marketing that sees processing as only an activity not included in direct contact with the user (so-called back-office function).

The establishment of a relationship with the latter becomes, in fact, the absolute priority even when goods are brought back to platforms to improve their fruition, and the related services become the main engine of trade.[36]

Enabled by the digital, this new approach to the thing, based on its incorporeality, has thus favoured not only a different way of using the good, but also a different way of conceiving its ownership.

The shift from a geographical and material space to a digital space, from the substantial materiality of goods to their substantial immateriality, and from an ownership expressed through physical apprehension to an ownership expressed

35 The platform is merely a vehicle to which services are added that increase the value of the digital good, so that it becomes a bridgehead or a way of establishing a physical presence made available to the user. In this way, the seller is put in a position to initiate a stable and long-term relationship with the latter, thus explaining why access to so-called platforms is often allowed for a cost higher than the actual sale value of the good itself, as it discounts the expectation of its greater usability made possible, during the life of the product, by an enrichment of its meaning and content. *See*, for various examples of shifting of materiality towards the immateriality, J. van Dijck, T. Poell, M. de Waal, *The Platform Society: Public Values in a Connective World*, Oxford, 2018, p. 49 ff.; A. Hein, M. Schreieck, T. Riasanow, D. Soto Setzke, M. Wiesche, M. Böhm, H. Krcmar, *Digital Platform Ecosystems*, in *Electron. Mark.*, 30, 2020, p. 87 ff., where the authors, at p. 90, underline that «[. . .] we propose the following definition: *a digital platform ecosystem comprises a platform owner that implements governance mechanisms to facilitate value creating mechanisms on a digital platform between the platform owner and an ecosystem of autonomous complementors and consumers*. [. . .] Applying the definition on established and emerging digital platform ecosystems, we conclude three different building blocks to characterize digital platform ecosystems: status of platform ownership; value-creating mechanisms in the ecosystem; and autonomy of complementors». *See*, for further details, *infra* Chapter 2, § 3.

36 Here, let it be emphasized, without, however, wishing to delve into issues that are not properly legal, that in the industrial age, individual buying and selling operations gave the user almost complete control over every step of the decision-making process, whereas in the digital age, the user runs the risk of progressively losing the management of long-term relationships that he has established either directly or through appointed intermediaries. In essence, digitality means that the purchase of goods gives way to the contracting of a wide range of services that extend to virtually every aspect of the relationship between supplier and user. The latter, therefore, would see himself bound by a dense network of ongoing relationships and could become completely dependent on commercial forces that have little understanding of his needs and little subservience to his power of disposition.

through digital access could lead to a rethinking of the man-goods relationship based on the sharing of content, knowledge and skills.[37]

Does this signal, then, the crisis of the notion of property that matured in the modern age from the perspective of its individuality, its exclusivity and its interchangeability in the legal system, and understood as the fulcrum of the industrial age?[38]

Now, this approach, which constituted an authentic paradigm of civilization centred on a viewpoint that saw the cooperation between seller and buyer as the focal moment of the transfer of ownership, would seem to have been undermined by the advent of the age of digitalization and its immateriality and multiple, unlimited and simultaneous use.[39]

The notion of access, permitted and favoured by the Internet and the network, becomes increasingly important in reparameterizing and redefining not only the social dynamics, but with them and through them, the logics of ownership, determining the affirmation of a new idea of property, multifocal and multifaceted, the result of a new way of conceiving ownership coming from a digital market.

In general terms, therefore, access-fruition becomes a term that can be used to distinguish, within the broad category of individuals, those to be included and those to be excluded in the use, employment and enjoyment of certain goods, thus becoming a conceptual tool to reconsider the same proprietary Weltanschauung in its current and imminent juridical-economic becoming.

Throughout the modern era, property and the economic system have appeared synonymous voices, as exchanges, imbued with a physicality that has permeated

37 *See*, for an interesting example regarding the project management and the value chain of construction projects, S. Li, J.T. Martins, A.C. Vasconcelos, G. Peng, *Knowledge Sharing in Project Work: The Dynamic Interplay of Knowledge Domains and Skills*, in *J. Knowl. Manag.*, 27(2), 2023, p. 328 ff., where the authors realize a novel framework that theorizes the dynamic interplay between knowledge domains and the skills that facilitate knowledge sharing (KS) for successful project work throughout the construction project.

38 A right to property declined in the aforementioned terms has dictated the times of everyday life, has imbued the political world with itself, and has represented a factor in the light of which the status of the individual has been forged. *See*, in this regard, S. Rodotà, *Il terribile diritto*, cit., p. 263, where the author states that «[. . .] se percorriamo la storia della definizione, dalla glossa fino a quelle più recenti, avremo modo di notare che il termine proprietà e stato quasi sempre impiegato per indicare strutture giuridiche che non corrispondevano affatto, o corrispondevano soltanto parzialmente, alla definizione che di quel termine veniva data nel medesimo contesto: e ciò per ragioni varie, di carattere politico talvolta, derivanti dallo scarto tra sistematica e realtà in altri casi».

39 In this regard, one should note, for example, the growing tendency of companies to make their products available free of charge in order to attract potential customers and then to charge them costs, such as management and updating costs. This strategy is particularly evident in the computer industry, where operators are driven by the idea that the more parties that are linked together by similar computer programmes, the more are, on the one hand, the benefits that each user can achieve, and the more, on the other hand, the economic advantages, in terms of services, that the company can ultimately obtain. This phenomenon, which is known as the network effect, implies that the greater the amplitude of the network of users, the greater the interconnections and, consequently, the benefits that can be achieved by the individuals that make up the so-called network.

them to the core, have been realized in a physical and geographical space dedicated to them, where legal operators have carried out their trades.

It was only in the course of the 19th century that the two terms took on a connotation and valence that tended to diverge, the market becoming a place no longer coinciding with a physical reality in which physical resources were traded, but an ἀγορά that was conceptually used to describe the system deputed to the abstract process of selling and buying.

Therefore, we have gradually witnessed the birth of a new economic framework, the so-called digital economy, marked by high-tech, in which heterogeneous factors coexist, each exerting its own influence: a strong dematerialization of goods, an increasing decline of physical resources to the benefit of intangible resources, the gradual transformation of the enjoyment of *res* into the enjoyment of services, the change in the way of conceiving the exercise of economic activity, which from a productive perspective shifts to a marketing perspective.

After centuries in which the primary juridical-economic objective was identified with the transformation of physical resources into goods subject to ownership, today we are witnessing a tendency to dematerialize this process, which is thus hinged on the concept of enjoyment-access.

In a world of symbols, computer codes, networks and feedback circuits, populated by theoretically individual-monadic concepts, such as "connectivity," and social-collective ones, such as "interconnectivity," the boundaries and barriers, proper to each space-time dimension, become blurred, and everything that was previously solidified now tends to liquefy.

The present is a new technological era, in which daily life is continuously mediated by innovative digital devices that enhance and amplify the human being's visual, expressive, communicative, and cognitive capabilities, making him a part of a network that he can access anywhere and in any way.

A whole world that for centuries existed in a semi-independent realm, only occasionally touched by the logic of the market but never fully absorbed by it, such as, for example, culture and experience, are now part of a realm of exchanges that, by exploiting new technologies, allows them to penetrate the existence of each.[40]

The latest generation of electronic devices, combined with the possibilities of the Internet, represents an extraordinary set of tools to capture the quintessence of any cultural experience and transform it into digital data that can be communicated vividly and with a very high degree of fidelity thanks to images, shapes and sounds.[41]

40 If culture in general represents an experience to be shared, insofar as it is the result of a co-participation that develops around common values, cultural production is a section of it that becomes the object of individual re-appropriation thanks to cultural entertainment operated on a personal level. *See* J. Rifkin, *The Age of Access*, cit., p. 163, where the author states that «[T]he meteoric rise of the entertainment economy bears witness to a generation in transition from accumulating things to accumulating experiences and from property to access relationships».

41 It seems appropriate to note here that the most extreme forms of this technological process can lead to the transformation of the real into virtual reality, i.e. into a simulated experience that post-modern philosophers and media define as hyper-real. See E. Dzardanova, V. Kasapakis, *Virtual Reality:*

In essence, the digital revolution has the potential to transform most cultural expressions into fungible goods and make them tradable in a digital space in the same way that money makes physical goods fungible in geographical space, being a different representation of them.[42]

In an economic system, therefore, that, due to its digitalization, can be said to be truly global because it is immaterial, potentially every resource can become an object of commercialization thanks to the access that is allowed to it, so much so that accessibility itself appears to be the pivot of the system in a similar way to what had already happened with material availability until the industrial or pre-digital era.[43]

Goods, therefore, that until a few decades ago were "indivisible" in their use and enjoyment have now become "divisible" in their fruition, because they too, like man, have become part of a global digital network that, depriving them of their most elementary physicality, extends their reach in almost unlimited terms.

It is precisely in this perspective that the particular relationship that digitality has enabled between technology and communication is inserted,[44] especially in

---

A Journey From Vision to Commodity, in *IEEE Ann. Hist. Comput.*, 45(1), 2023, p. 18 ff., where the authors, at p. 18, affirm that «[V]irtual reality (VR) is a technology-induced experience that exploits mechanisms of human perception to falsify the sense of embodied presence in synthetic, computer-generated, three-dimensional (3-D) environments. That is a pragmatic way of defining VR but the answer to *what is virtual reality* is far more intricate».

42 *See* M. Castells, *The Information Age. Economy, Society and Culture. I. The Rise of the Network Society*, cit., p. 373, where the author states that «[A]ll messages of all kinds become enclosed in the medium, because the medium has become so comprehensive, so diversified, so malleable, that it absorbs in the same multi-media text the whole of human experience, past, present, and future».

43 T. Stroiko, L. Nazarova, N. Danik, *Transformation of Economic Processes on the Basis of Digitalisation*, in *Balt. J. Econ. Stud.*, 7(1), 2021, p. 102 ff., where the authors, at p. 105, affirm that «The global digital economy is seen as a driving force for economic growth, capable of leading to significant economic changes and affecting the goals of the business, the labour market, and people's way of life; it has significant potential for developing countries, for which such economic shifts can mean economic growth, increased productivity of capital and labour, reduce transaction costs and expand access to world markets [. . .]. [. . .] The global digital economy provides companies with new business opportunities: – unimpeded access to the best suppliers, customers, workforce, financial resources, in whatever country they are located; – doing business "without borders": real-time interaction with foreign clients and partners, supply chain management on a global scale, supporting the activities of foreign employees in conducting operations and customer service, instant cross-border operations in distant markets; – reduction of costs for transactions, marketing, interaction with customers in emerging market; – organisation of virtual teams through the effective use of digital platforms interacting online; – transition of small businesses and startups to the category of transnational since its inception. The rapid development of information and computer technologies and the active Internet penetration into all spheres of human life have led to the transformation of economic processes according to the level of digitalisation. Digitalisation of the economy requires the development of new business models. Network organisations based on collective methods of production and consumption transform traditional market relations and require the development of new solutions in the field of modern company management. The further development of digital technologies is important for the economy as a whole».

44 It seems appropriate to point out that forms of communication should be understood as meaning not only language, but also art, music, cinema, etc., i.e. all those instruments that are capable of embodying and expressing human culture.

the form it takes in culture, so as to forge a new tool for interpreting, reproducing, storing and transforming the meaning of human expression.[45]

Culture, in fact, because it is born and develops in a human community as a particular form of externality of creativity (communitarian form of expression), profoundly benefits from the logic of access and inclusion that the digital world allows, increasing its potential: it becomes a good subject to legal circulation when it is separated from the human group of origin and is made available to individuals, who, although external to the reference complex, are able to pay to use it,[46] sees its relevant features enhanced, also in legal-economic terms, when it is placed in a network that enhances its meaning and scope to a very large extent.[47]

The subject, therefore, if, from a sociological point of view, he is an integral part – provided he is not excluded – of a community and a culture to which he has access as a tessera of a broader mosaic of shared meanings and experiences, from a purely economic-legal point of view he can resort, if he has the means, to digitality to extend and to strengthen this participation by accessing a network that goes beyond the boundaries of his own reference group and allows him to tap into a reality that is still participatory, but global and timeless because it is no longer purely physical.

With the gradual fragmentation of aspects of shared culture into a series of commercial transactions conducted within a digital economic network, we are thus witnessing the passage of access rights from the realm of the social to the realm of the economic.[48]

This intensely technologized, or rather digitized, environment must be looked at, then, to grasp the contemporary proprietary statute and try to intuit the logics that actually underlie it and that seem no longer or not only governed by "apprehension" but driven towards access.[49]

45 *See*, for more details, *infra* esp. Chapter 2, § 4.

46 *See* H.I. Schiller, *Culture Inc. The Corporate Takeover of Public Expression*, Oxford, 1989, p. 30 ff., where the author, at p. 31, affirms that «[S]peech, dance, drama (ritual), music, and the visual and plastic arts have been vita, indeed necessary, features of human experience from earliest time. What distinguishes their situation in the industrial-capitalist rea, and especially in its most recent development, are the relentless and successful efforts to separate these elemental expressions of human creativity from their group and community origins for the purpose of selling them to those who can pay for them».

47 *See*, for an icastic description of this progressive transition, J. Rifkin, *The Age of Access*, cit., p. 144, where the author points out that «[T]he new communications technologies and artistic mediums gave the capitalist market a powerful advantage over traditional cultural mediums like paintings, dance, song, theater, pageantry, parades, festivals, sports and games, and civic involvement, all of which relied heavily on intimate face-to-face engagement to reproduce shared experiences. Culture now could be harnessed in bits and pieces to electronic, mediums and spread quickly over great distances, bringing the masses of people together in simulated kinds of shared cultural experiences that, while less intimate, were often more seductive and entertaining».

48 Once filtered into the legal-economic world, access becomes an operation no longer based on intrinsic criteria, such as, for example, tradition, family, ethnicity, religion, gender, but essentially on economic availability. *See* J. Rifkin, *The Age of Access*, cit., p. 140.

49 *See*, for an intriguing application of these concepts to art, Y. Chen, *Possession and Access: Consumer Desires and Value Perceptions Regarding Contemporary Art Collection and Exhibit Visits*,

In contemporary times, then, when almost everything becomes a dematerialized good, the traditional notion of ownership becomes more elusive and less meaningful, as digital production eclipses industrial production, and access becomes the basis of fruition.

Without prejudice to the need to explore this issue further in the following pages,[50] it can already be observed that, beyond the profiles of relationship with the *res*, whether material or immaterial, both property in the classical sense and access-use represent concepts – one of a more technical-juridical nature and the other of a more factual nature – governed by the idea of distinction, inasmuch as, if the former distinguishes those who possess the good from those who do not, the latter generally distinguishes individuals who are connected to the network to make use of the digital *res* from those who are not.[51]

Therefore, in both cases, we are in the presence of concepts that are based on the reference to inclusion or exclusion: just as property operates a quantitative differentiation, which is based on the value of the ownership of the good, and a qualitative one, which refers to the power and control that can be exercised over the good, so too fruition-access distinguishes the subjects who are in the network from those who are outside it, resorting both to the number of networks of which one is part (quantitative profile) and the level of integration and connection that the reciprocal relations are capable of expressing among themselves (qualitative profile).[52]

---

in *J. Cons. Res.*, 35(6), 2009, p. 925 ff., where the author develops «a multilevel and multifaceted perspective on art consumption behaviour by separating consumption modes from the consumption products (artworks), by comparing possession (collection) with access (exhibit visits), and by distinguishing desire from value. The findings challenge the presupposition that possession is the ultimate expression of consumer desire and illustrate that contemporary art collectors and visitors choose collection or visits based on different desires. While artwork is perceived similarly, collection and visits have different impact on consumers' perception of value».

50 *See infra* esp. Chapter 3.

51 *See* R.D. Watkins, J. Denegri-Knott, M. Molesworth, *The Relationship Between Ownership and Possession: Observations from the Context of Digital Virtual Goods*, in *J. Mark. Manag.*, 32(1–2), 2016, p. 44 ff., where the authors highlight limitations in the current trend towards dichotomizing full ownership and access-based consumption by recognizing a broader, more complex array of "fragmented" ownership configurations in the context of digital virtual goods (DVGs). The challenge of this dichotomy determines that the relationship between ownership and possession becomes particularly significant. Indeed, DVG ownership configurations may shape the way in which possession is assembled, potentially reducing consumers' scope of action relative to DVGs and leaving possession susceptible to disruption. Conversely, the ways in which consumers' continued attempts at possession may impinge upon the agency of ownership mechanisms within the market.

52 In this regard, it is worth emphasizing the essential function that, in a reality dominated by digitality, the so-called gatekeepers play, i.e. those subjects that essentially allow access and permanence in this world governed by the network. If, in fact, in a pre-digital era, material property represented the only title to participate in a full economic-legal life, in a digitized and dematerialized cosmos, the possibility of accessing the web constitutes an essential feature in the conduct of human existence. *See*, in this point, J. Rifkin, *The Age of Access*, cit., p. 177 ff., where the author, at p. 178, underlines that «[G]ateways is used increasingly to define the various passages and routes into networks, parallel worlds, and virtual realities of one sort or another. Gatekeepers refers to the institutions and individuals who determine the rules and conditions of admittance and control who gains access and who is shut out of a network-based society».

If in a society governed by private property, those who own capital and control the means of production are able to "prevail" over others, in a society governed by access, those who oversee the channels of communication and access to the network are able to manage the legal circulation.[53]

In this becoming, different forms of ownership seem, then, to assert themselves and gradually overlap the configuration that property has traditionally assumed.

The new digital age no longer seems to rest on that having, that possessing and that excluding which in a pre-digital world have represented the *raison d'être* of human existence, but appears inclined towards the immaterial. Indeed, there is no longer the mere tendency to make material places and things tradable in order to exchange them in a physical-geographical space, but there is a gradual move towards an incorporeality stimulated and favoured by technology. Therefore, the role played until now by material ownership seems to be changed profoundly, losing the presumed monolithic traits that classicism tried to impose on it and taking on a new and multifaceted immaterial guises that shows how "[L]ong is the way and hard, that out of Hell leads up to light."[54] In fact, as Milton well described in this sentence, that encapsulates the arduous journey towards redemption and enlightenment. Putting it in different terms, the actual evolution towards digitalization shows properly the struggles faced by humankind as it strives to attain a change of juridical and economic perspective. The path out of Hell is portrayed as lengthy and challenging, emphasizing the steepness of the climb to achieve a new way of thinking and approaching the perception of things. But, as Milton expressed through these words, it shall be always vivid the idea that the path is clearly indicated although the true enlightenment and new understanding often require perseverance and overcoming significant obstacles.

53 *See* N. Holmstrom, *Exploitation*, in *Canad. J. Phil.*, 7(2), 1977, p. 353 ff., where the author, at p. 353, affirms that «According to Marx one of the primary evils of capitalism (and any other class society) is that it is exploitative-and necessarily so. Socialist and communist societies will (necessarily) not be exploitative and this is one of the reasons why they will in some sense be better. To understand such claims we have to determine exactly what Marx means by "exploitation" and what it is about exploitation that Marx finds to be bad. Neither of these questions is as simple as it might seem. A common misunderstanding of Marx is this: exploitation consists simply in an unequal distribution of social wealth. Workers are exploited because they get so much less of the pie than do capitalists. Another interpretation of Marx's concept is that exploitation consists in the fact that workers to not get the whole pie. They produce all value and, therefore, deserve to get it all back. I will show that both of these interpretations are inadequate or simply mistaken. An error common to both is an overemphasis on distribution»; but, J. Rifkin, *The Age of Access*, cit., p. 179, underlines that «[I]n the era of property relations, ownership was the precondition for exercising one's will in the world. [. . .] In a wired world, however, having access to networks is the guarantor of full engagement in society».

54 J. Milton, *Paradise Lost*, bk. 2, l., 1667, p. 432.

2 Property in the Frame of the Digital Domain

1 Unraveling Ownership in the Social Fabric of the Digital Realm

The shift of legal circulation from a geographical to a digital space represents a phenomenon[1] that, made possible by the technological revolution, appears capable of opening up new avenues to the configuration and organization of relations that can be established both between humans and between humans and things.[2]

The Internet, as a global medium, makes it possible to reach a potentially unlimited number of people at the same time, at a minimum cost and without any limitation of either time or space:[3] a ubiquitous network and very low-cost access that offers an environment in which products that were previously distributed physically as tangible goods can now be enjoyed in a fully digital format,[4] thereby affecting

1 *See*, E. Katsh, *Law in a Digital World: Computer Networks and Cyberspace*, in *Vill. Law Rev.*, 38, 1993, p. 403 ff.; M. Nicolini, *The Legal, the Digital, and the Global Production of Space*, in *Pólemos*, 17(1), 2023, p. 45 ff., where the author, at p. 45, affirms that we need to consider «[. . .] the law at the intersections between the humanities, technology, and the production of digital space. Interactions like these are relevant in the present age, where humankind is outcompeting natural resources and changing the earth. The Anthropocene is an epoch of environmental crisis; despite this, we turn such a crisis into a process of sublimation servient to the control of the earth. Blurring the divide between the digital and the human is functional to such a process. The strategic use of the law makes climate-change policies compatible with global markets. [. . .] Blending real-word performances with internet- and media-related contents, they are functional to sublimation, convincing us that we can tackle climate change without rearranging our economic paradigms».

2 There is no doubt that the development and diffusion of technologies, such as computers, telecommunications, cable television, and the Internet, has made possible the establishment of new forms of human-human and human-*res* relationships that until recently were not even imaginable.

3 In a socio-political dimension, the new era seems to be undermining the very idea of the nation-state, which was conceived until now to oversee and administer a territory, is now being undermined in its deep geographical roots: if the socio-economic life of humanity is shifting towards an immaterial and a-geographical dimension, could political institutions, due to their territorial nature, progressively lose relevance? In a world where the most basic socio-economic activities are increasingly carried out in a digital space, governments are forced to play a severely depowered role. Thus, while personal and commercial property classically understood gradually loses centrality, there is the growing relevance of ownership in the form of access.

4 *See* I. Trotter Hardy, *Not So Different: Tangible, Intangible, Digital, and Analog Works and Their Comparison for Copyright Purposes*, in *U. Dayton Law Rev.*, 26(2), 2001, p. 212 ff.; T. Rayna, *Understanding the Challenges of the Digital Economy: The Nature of Digital Goods*, in *Comm.*

DOI: 10.4324/9781003424413-3

not only costs and distribution strategies,[5] but in the same way of understanding the ownerships that are touched and involved.[6]

And the scale of the revolutionary effects thus produced is such that they affect – as will be seen below[7] – not only on the perception and attitude of tangible (dominical) property but also on the perception and attitude of intangible (intellectual) property.[8]

In fact, digitization represents both a revolution and a challenge that could provide great opportunities for the development of new businesses and new distribution models,[9] as demonstrated by the web as an instrument for the circulation of goods characterized by its great breadth and remarkable low cost.

In this regard, Samuelson argued, as early as 1990, that the digital world presented six peculiar traits capable, in perspective, of profoundly changing the law:[10] (a) the ease with which digitally developed works can be reproduced,[11] (b) the ease

---

Strat., 71, 2008, p. 13 ff., where the author, investigating the economic nature and characteristics of digital goods, describes as such goods that are, due to their replicability, shown to be public goods (albeit in an evolutionary way) and durable goods. Furthermore, the content of such goods, combined with their durability, makes them experience goods. As a consequence of this view, while only one of these characteristics would be sufficient to create difficulties for producers and lead to market failure, the author demonstrates that each of the characteristics reinforces the other, as it is well shown by the new trend of massive consumer piracy and the overall problem of value of digital goods.

5 *See* E. Nelson, *Windows Into the Digital World: Distributor Strategies and Consumer Choice in an Era of Connected Viewing*, in *Connected Viewing*, edited by J. Holt and K. Sanson, Abingdon, 2013, p. 62 ff.; A. Bharadwaj, O.A. El Sawy, P.A. Pavlou, N. Venkatraman, *Digital Business Strategy: Toward a Next Generation of Insights*, in *MIS Quart.*, 37(2), 2013, p. 471 ff.; M.T. Nuseir, G.A. El Refae, A. Aljumah, M. Alshurideh, S. Urabi, B.A. Kurdi, *Digital Marketing Strategies and the Impact on Customer Experience: A Systematic Review*, in *The Effect of Information Technology on Business and Marketing Intelligence Systems. Studies in Computational Intelligence*, edited by M. Alshurideh, B.H. Al Kurdi, R. Masa'deh, H.M., Alzoubi, S. Salloum, 2023, p. 21 ff., where the authors explore, by one side, the contemporary digital marketing strategies and tools and the role played by these in various marketing activities or areas, and, by the other, the market segmentation in the digital era to improve customer experience tools. Moreover, a study is conducted to determine which strategy has been suggested to be most optimized for enhancing customer experience.

6 *See* J. Käll, *Posthuman Property and Law: Commodification and Control through Information*, Abingdon, 2023, *passim*.

7 *See infra* esp. Chapter 4.

8 *See* M. Kelly, *Owning Our Future: The Emerging Ownership Revolution*, San Francisco, CA, 2012, p. 19 ff.

9 The fruit of the digital revolution is already there for all to see, as demonstrated by the combination of MP3 technology – which allows the compression of stored data down to 1/22 of its original size – with peer-to-peer technology – which ensures autonomy with respect to the central server so as to ensure a direct transfer of files through users' computers – which has favoured a substantial transformation of the concepts of appropriation use and distribution of the goods enjoyed, certainly amplifying the opportunities for knowledge and culture dissemination, but at the same time, on the side of the intellectual property right holder, also facilitating the possibilities of illegal appropriation, distribution of "pirated" files, counterfeiting and unauthorized reproduction.

10 Cfr. P. Samuelson, *Digital Media and the Changing Face of Intellectual Property Law*, in *Rutgers Computer Tech. Law J.*, 16, 1990, p. 324 ff.

11 The ease of replication of digital goods implies that their content can theoretically be reproduced indefinitely without any deterioration in quality. This characteristic may raise copyright issues.

with which they can be transmitted,[12] (c) the ease with which they can be modified and manipulated,[13] (d) the absolute identity that digital goods have with each other,[14] (e) their compactness,[15] and (f) the aptitude of digital assets to foster the study of new methods of interconnection and research in the digital space.[16]

From a point of view more closely related to the physical nature of digital assets, one can then add that their further characteristic is the intangibility stemming from their inherent immateriality.[17].

In the light of the framework just outlined, it is clear how the owner of the digital asset may fear the loss of his or her full control, if he or she ever had it, since the emergence of new technologies leads to the development of new dissemination systems characterized by decentralization, loss of materiality and almost contextual and unlimited use of the assets involved.[18]

12 *See* P. Samuelson, *Digital Media and the Changing Face of Intellectual Property Law*, cit., p. 327, where the author points out that ease of transmission and multiple use means that the same digital asset can be «[. . .] loaded into a computer booked up to a network of computers or a network of users of a large computer systems, each of whom can have ready and virtually simultaneous use of the same copy».

13 The third characteristic is identified with the flexibility of the digital world, whose contents, such as music and images, can be easily modified, manipulated and transformed to the point of becoming unrecognizable with respect to their original source. *See* P. Samuelson, *Digital Media and the Changing Face of Intellectual Property Law*, cit., p. 328 ff.

14 The absolute identity that goods in digital format have with each other means, for example, that works, once digitized, no longer tend to be distinguishable from each other in terms of copyright. *See* P. Samuelson, *Digital Media and the Changing Face of Intellectual Property Law*, cit., p. 332 ff.

15 The possibility of compacting digital assets could be the cause of new legal problems, given, for example, the possibility of storing them with great ease in the tiny memory of various computer devices despite their extreme complexity. *See* A. Perzanowski, J. Schultz, *The End of Ownership: Personal Property in the Digital Economy*, Cambridge, MA, 2016, p. 15 ff.

16 The sixth characteristic of digital assets is identified with the so-called non-linearity, i.e. the possibility of creating new techniques of investigation and study such as, for instance, the development of connected navigation systems that allow users to easily find and download the desired information. *See* P. Samuelson, *Digital Media and the Changing Face of Intellectual Property Law*, cit., p. 336 ff.

17 Binary data, peculiar to the digital world, cannot be seen or perceived in the same way as analogue data. Clear evidence of this can be seen by observing the completely different human behaviour when faced with the illegitimate appropriation of digital content: although the consequences for artists and the music industry are essentially the same, music lovers may have less qualms about downloading an MP3 song from a peer-to-peer distribution system than they may have when they misappropriate a CD from a shop shelf. *See* A. Spahn, *Digital Objects, Digital Subjects and Digital Societies: Deontology in the Age of Digitalization*, in *Information*, 11(4), 2020, p. 228, where the author re-examines the three categories "subject," "object" and "intersubjectivity" in light of digital behaviour change technologies (BCTs) and suggests deontological guidelines for digital objects, digital subjects and a digitally mediated intersubjectivity, based on a re-examination of the requirements of epistemic, motivational and deliberational rationalism.

18 *See*, for further details, H. Singh, *Decentralized Web, Distributed Ledgers, and Build-up to Blockchain*, in *Distributed Computing to Blockchain: Architecture, Technology, and Applications*, edited by R. Pandey, S. Goundar, S. Fatima, London, San Diego, CA, Cambridge, MA and Oxford, 2023, p. 8 ff.

The flow of information, content and data, which the new distribution technologies allow, thus presents a broad flexibility that may also translate into greater ease in overcoming the associated legal protections, but which, at the same time, is characterized by interesting positive profiles, such as, for example, a considerable reduction in the costs of production and circulation of digital goods, given that these are no longer indispensably linked to a material "support" but become completely accessible in digital and therefore "immaterial" mode.[19]

Digital products, in fact, thanks to their full online accessibility, can often be easily broken down into their wide variety of content and distributed on demand, thus explaining the strong incentive that web services, such as pay-per-view or pay-per-download, increasingly show.[20]

In essence, the awareness of the possibilities that the Internet offers in overcoming the traditional distribution-usage model that directly addresses the individual and autonomous recipient, in addition to provoking a profound change in the relationship that the owner has with the digital asset and, therefore, in the ownership idea itself, generates the need to develop and maintain, both locally and globally, secure information infrastructures that improve the use of resources, reduce costs, and incentivize the application of technological measures that are directed towards a standardized protection of operators.[21]

The digital good, as *res intra commercium* and thus as a tradeable commodity, "impacts" on the classical scope of both contract and property law, raising new questions that may require specific answers.[22]

19 See, for further considerations, Y. Ibrahim, *Transacting Memory in the Digital Age: Modernity, Fluidity and Immateriality*, in *Fudan J. Humanit. Soc. Sci.*, 11, 2018, p. 453 ff., where the author operates a re-contextualization of history and memory through a technological gaze that implicates us within new forms of vulnerabilities. By reviewing the politics of looking and watching online in digital platforms, the author invites to ponder over the flattening of memory and history through algorithms and a "digital morality" and "mortality" encoded through "user agreements" and "community standards." «The repressing of this moral gaze weaves us into a social media economy where morality and ethics are refashioned through a viral economy where images are circulated, altered and reframed through digital technologies. The wider implications of this "virality" for humanity, memory making and historicity are explored» (p. 453).

20 As the functionality of Apple iTunes well demonstrates, providers can generate profit by focusing more on user needs than on doing business directly and controlling the related opportunities. *See*, in this regard, C. Peukert, M. Windisch, *The Economics of Copyright in the Digital Age*, in *CESifo Working Paper No. 10687*, 2023, p. 1 ff., where the authors, at p. 14, well represent that «[I]n the empirical context of Spotify's entry into the music streaming market, Aguiar and Waldfogel (2018b) estimate that the lower revenues from selling less digital music in the transaction model (e.g., iTunes) are, on average, countered by the additional royalty income from streaming. In addition, licensed music consumption options, where consumers can choose between fee-based or free and ad-supported models, can reduce the demand for piracy (Wlömert and Papies, 2016; Aguiar and Waldfogel, 2018b). Evidence from the video streaming context suggests similar effects».

21 *See, ex multis*, I. Brown, C.T. Marsden, *Regulating Code: Good Governance and Better Regulation in the Information Age*, Cambridge, MA, 2013, p. 117 ff. See, for further details, *infra* § 2.

22 *See* C. Wendehorst, *Proprietary Rights in Digital Assets and the Conflict of Laws*, in *Blockchain and Private International Law*, edited by A. Bonomi, M. Lehmann and S. Lalani, Leiden, 2023, p. 101 ff., where the author, at p. 101, affirms that «Digital assets – from raw data to software to Bitcoin – are among the most valuable assets in our modern economies. Their sheer variety and their novelty

Already Directive 2011/83/EU on consumer rights, for instance, provides for a special discipline intended to protect digital content, which Article 2(11) defines as "data which are produced and supplied in digital form," which is accompanied by the possibility of precluding the consumer from the ordinary right to withdraw from the contract when the digital content is supplied online in accordance with the law on distance selling or off-premises (Articles 9 and 16[m]).[23]

On the other hand, the Common European Sales Law (CESL) itself,[24] according to Article 2(j), defines digital content as "[. . .] data which are produced and supplied in digital form, whether or not according to the buyer's specifications, including video, audio, picture or written digital content, digital games, software and digital content which makes it possible to personalise existing hardware or software."

It also appears significant that Article 5(b) CESL considers digital data in the same way as any other object susceptible of being purchased, regardless of whether it was obtained online or offline or by downloading, providing that "The Common European Sales Law may be used for: (a) sales contracts; (b) contracts for the supply of digital content whether or not supplied on a tangible medium which can be stored, processed or accessed, and re-used by the user, irrespective of whether the digital content is supplied in exchange for the payment of a price [. . .]."

---

pose challenges not only for substantive law, but also for conflict of laws. This is partly due to the speed of technological progress, but also to grey areas between the law of obligations, intellectual property law, (tangible) property law and a range of overriding mandatory provisions of a more regulatory nature, which results in a challenge for both classification and the identification of the most appropriate connecting factor(s). While the contractual aspects of transactions may be covered by the Rome I Regulation and similar conflict-of-laws legislation outside the EU, including the 2015 Hague Principles on Choice of Law in International Commercial Contracts, the proprietary aspects are still very much unchartered territory. This includes, for example, the question of who has rights in crypto assets that take effect vis-à-vis third parties and how such rights can be assigned, with assignment meaning anything from full transfer of title to transfer of title by way of security to the provision of a security interest such as a pledge. Rights that take effect vis-à-vis third parties may be akin to ownership, but they may also be of a very different, data-specific nature. Recently, the debate has focused on crypto assets, but it seems worthwhile to set the broader scene of digital assets in general».

23 *See* R. Schulze, J. Morgan, *The Right of Withdrawal*, in *The Common European Sales Law in Context*, edited by G. Dannemann and S. Vogenauer, Oxford, 2013, p. 294 ff.; and, more in general terms on the Directive 2011/83/EU on consumer rights and its function, C. Franco, *Consumer Protection Measures – Legal Basis Objectives Achievements*, in *The European Agency for Safety and Health at Work*, Spain, 2023, p. 1 ff., where the author, at p. 1, specifies that «[T]his new directive amended Council Directive 93/13/EEC (on unfair terms in consumer contracts) and Directives 98/6/EC (on consumer protection in the indication of the prices of products offered to consumers), 2005/29/EC (concerning unfair business-to-consumer commercial practices in the internal market) and 2011/83/EU (on consumer rights) of the European Parliament and of the Council. [. . .] Directive (EU) 2020/1828 expanded the scope of the injunctions system in order to cover various horizontal and sector-specific EU instruments relevant to the protection of the collective interests of consumers and laid down procedures for compensatory redress».

24 *Proposal for a Regulation of the European Parliament and of the Council on a Common European Sales Law – COM/2011/0635 Final – 2011/0284 (COD)*, Brussels, 11 October 2011, available at http://eur-lex.europa.eu/legal-content/EN/TXT/?uri=CELEX%3A52011PC0635.

The approach followed by CESL thus implies that in cross-border commercial transactions digital goods are considered and protected like all other alienable goods.

A similar approach is found in *UsedSoft GmbH v. Oracle International Corp.*, where the European Court of Justice (ECJ), although applying an argument from Directive 2009/42/EU on the legal protection of computer programs[25] and ruling on a specific issue (prescription) concerning the sale of software, holds, in harmony with the principles of the European Single Market, that digital goods are fully "tradeable" goods to be treated, in cross-border trade, as goods in respect of which a full ownership right can be transferred.[26]

A similar solution also extends to the case of downloads from cloud systems, i.e. when, during cloud computing, digital goods are transferred in terms of both ownership and use: a digital good, in the described context, is considered a real good and must be treated in those terms in light of private law principles.

It follows, then, how the Consumer Rights Directive, the CESL and the European Court of Justice have all contributed, more or less clearly, to the identification of the treatment to be reserved to digital goods, providing, in general, for the extension of contractual and proprietary logics[27] and thus influencing the behaviour of the various operators in the *Digital Single Market* and the resulting business practices.

The problem that arises is thus to assess whether the scheme now outlined can exert any influence on the way of conceiving the very ownership of digital goods, bringing it closer to the traditional approach, or, instead,[28] may represent a mere

25 *Directive 2009/42/EC of the European Parliament and of the Council of 6 May 2009 on Statistical Returns in Respect of Carriage of Goods and Passengers by Sea*, in *OJ L* 141, 6 June 2009, p. 29 ff.

26 *See UsedSoft v. Oracle*, where the Grand Chamber of the European Court of Justice, at paragraph 46 of its judgment, states that «[I]n those circumstances, the operations mentioned in paragraph 44 above, examined as a whole, involve the transfer of the right of ownership of the copy of the computer program in question».

27 S.E. Phelan, N.G. Wenzel, *Big Data, Quantum Computing, and the Economic Calculation Debate: Will Roasted Cyberpigeons Fly into the Mouths of Comrades?*, in *J. Econ. Behav. Org.*, 206, 2023, p. 172 ff., where the authors, at p. 172, affirm that «[A]dvancements in cloud computing, machine learning and quantum processing are starting to erase long-standing conceptions on the scarcity of information. [. . .] removing all limits on the volume, velocity, and variety of data will allow the messiness of the market process to be replaced by a more rational system of resource allocation and distribution that would generate less waste and more equity. [. . .] unlimited access to information will not solve the problem of economic calculation, as some have conjectured. The market process provides valuable benefits beyond the simple aggregation of spatially and temporally dispersed information. As such, it is unlikely to be displaced by more centralized forms of economic organization».

28 In essence, it is a question of grasping whether the digital world pushes the development of law and its traditional categories, especially in terms of property law, towards new territories rather than towards attempts to adapt classical concepts to digitality. S. Zenin, A. Kornev, S. Lipen, D. Shepelev, O. Tanimov, *Transformation of Law and Legal Activity in the Context of the Development of Digital Technologies*, in *Lex Hum.*, 15(1), 2023, p. 277 ff., where the authors, at p. 277, focusing on the transformation of law and legal activity caused by the active introduction of information and communication technologies in the legal sphere, assume that «[. . .] the most important areas of the existence of law, such as law-making, legal realization, and legal protection are increasingly

appearance that does not invalidate the whole prima facie disruptive character of legal concepts linked to the existing relationship between subject and good, such as joint and contextual use and enjoyment: do the principles and concepts that are classically linked to the ownership of property rights have to be redefined or could they also be applied to the new situations created by the digital world? If the traditionally existing principles and concepts could have found suitable application in the legal world of a few decades ago, can the same be argued now that digitalization has led to the intense developments related to the Internet of things and, as a consequence, has generated new situations in which such principles and concepts might struggle to be applied?[29]

Certainly, as mentioned in the previous pages,[30] the digital revolution may require an adaptation of the regulatory system to enable it to cope with the new conditions.

It follows that, where regulations are sufficiently flexible in character,[31] these adjustments will be quasi-automatic, but where they are not actually practicable, a genuine reform of the regulatory framework of reference will be required, as is well demonstrated by the large number of new instruments and proposals that have been envisaged, at Community level, since the drafting of the *Digital Single Market Strategy*.[32]

---

digitalized», and, therefore, it appears of paramount importance «[. . .] to consider the transformation of law and legal activity in the context of the development of digital technologies». The authors stress not only the positive aspects of the introduction of new, primarily digital technologies but «also identifies individual problems that are caused by this process», and they conclude that the law will acquire more and more a technologized character today and in the future. As a consequence, if the purpose of law has always been to establish social discipline in society, in the conditions of the formation of a network society and the state, «behavioral models that are fixed in legal norms acquire the character of algorithms peculiar to technological civilization». In fact, two factors will most of all determine the transformation of law – economic and technological. But the digital transformation of law represents only a change in the forms of law, that is, the forms of its objectification.

29 *See*, for further thoughts, S. Galle, A. Rodríguez-Clare, M. Yi, *Slicing the Pie: Quantifying the Aggregate and Distributional Effects of Trade*, in *Rev. Econ. Stud.*, 90(1), 2023, p. 331, where the authors, also using an econometric approach, try to establish a bridge between two separate literatures. Indeed, on the one hand, they register a recent wave of empirical work that have shown that trade shocks have important distributional implications, but without deriving welfare effects. While, on the other hand, other researches show how to quantify the welfare effects of trade for a wide class of gravity models, but with so far little to say about distributional implications. The authors, therefore, extend the multi-sector gravity model of trade to allow for heterogeneous labour and with multiple groups of *ex ante* identical workers and use the resulting framework to derive a simple approach to computing group-level and aggregate welfare effects of trade shocks.

30 *See supra* Introduction.

31 Y. Quan, X. Liang, Q. Jian, W. Wei, M. Qian, Z. Qiang, S. Yujun, Y. Huihong, L. Xiaoweng, *Flexibility Demand Analysis and Regulation Capacity Sharing Decisions Between Interconnected Power Systems Considering Differences in Regulation Performance*, in *IEEE Access*, 11, 2023, p. 93968 ff., where the authors, adopting especially an economic approach, underline how to cope with the demand for large amount of flexibility regulation that is caused by high penetration of intermittent renewable energy: «it is necessary to classify and measure the demand capacity for different regulation performance, and to reasonably allocate flexibility resources for different regions and different regulation capacities».

32 In this regard, consider, for example, the *Proposal for a Directive on the online and other distance sales of goods*, the *Proposal for a Regulation on ensuring the cross-border portability of online*

2 Balancing Act: How Digital Technology Shapes Private Law

The growing affirmation of the platform economy[33] is having distorting effects on both the established economic models and the related regulatory system,[34] so much so that, recently, both case law and regulators in most EU countries have been dealing with electronic platform issues with increasing interest.[35]

---

content services in the internal market, or the *Directive (EU) 2019/770 of the European Parliament and of the Council of 20 May 2019 on certain aspects concerning contracts for the supply of digital content and digital services*.

33 In a simplified form, the online platform is identified with an intermediary that brings supplier and user of goods, services and digital content closer together, so as to facilitate the conclusion of agreements between them. Some platforms, then, provide additional services, such as the possibility of processing payments, but also of guaranteeing agreements and resolving any disputes that may arise. Others go even further and provide the supplier with detailed rules for offering products on the same platform used. In general terms, then, online platforms represent a key tool for suppliers who do not wish to have their own website in order to reach more consumers or increase the number of online channels in which to conduct their existing business (so-called marketplace platforms). *See*, for further details, J.P. Vazquez Sampere, *Why Platform Disruption Is So Much Bigger Than Product Disruption*, in *Harv. Bus. Rev.*, 8 April 2016, where the author, describing the "platform economy," affirms that «For the sake of clarity, let's call a product "a platform that is used for one or very few products" and a platform "a structure upon which many variations of products are built." These definitions recognize that product vs. platform isn't black-and-white, but let's use them for practical purposes. For example, using this definition, a Tesla car battery is a product, because it powers only a few cars. But as more electric cars enter the market (including more Tesla models) and there are more uses for rechargeable electric batteries, perhaps the battery will one day move up the scale to become more like a platform»; Z.J. Acs, A.K. Song, L. Szerb, D.B. Audretsch, É. Komlósi, *The Evolution of the Global Digital Platform Economy: 1971–2021*, in *Small Bus. Econ.*, 57, 2021, p. 1629 ff.; A. Bisultanova, *Platform Economy: The Path to Sustainable Development*, in *E3S Web of Conferences*, 431, 2023, p. 1 ff., where the author, with a special view to the experiences of platform market leaders, such as the United States and China, observes how platforms are becoming powerful tools for providing access to resources, supporting economic growth, improving resource management and creating sustainable consumer patterns.

34 *See*, for more details, C. Koopman, M. Mitchell, A. Thierer, *The Sharing Economy and Consumer Protection Regulation: The Case for Policy Change*, in *J. Bus. Entrep. Law*, 8(2), 2015, p. 529 ff.; A. Jabłonowska, *EU Consumer Law and Technology*, in *Research Handbook on Law and Technology*, edited by B. Brożek, O. Kanevskaia and P. Pałka, Cheltenham, 2023, p. 174; Z. Khan, J. Zeng, G. Knight, T. Rajwani, C. Pattnaik, *Non-Market Strategies and Disruptive Innovation in the Platform Economy*, in *J. Int. Manag.*, 29(5), 2023, p. 1 ff., where the authors, at p. 1, affirm that «[D]ue to their direct and indirect network effects, platform firms play a significant role in the global economy. These firms have disrupted the innovation value chain by creating and capturing value from the scaling up of their business activities. Despite the role they play in disruptive innovation, we know relatively little about the ways in which platform firms engage with their institutional and other stakeholders through non-market corporate political activities and social strategies».

35 *See*, for further information, European Commission, *Communication from the Commission to the European Parliament, the Council, the European Economic and Social Committee and the Committee of the Regions – Online Platforms and the Digital Single Market – Opportunities and Challenges for Europe – COM(2016) 288 Final*, Brussels, 25 May 2016, reperibile alla pagina http://eur-lex.europa.eu/legal-content/EN/TXT/HTML/?uri=CELEX:52016DC0288&from=EN; and, in doctrine, E. Wibisono, *The Digital Entrepreneurial Ecosystem in the European Union: Evidence from the Digital Platform Economy Index*, in *Eur. Plan. Stud.*, 31(6), 2023, p. 1270 ff.

In broad terms, it can be considered that the existing regulatory systems do not seem fully capable of providing adequate legal solutions to the numerous problems linked to the platform economy, its nature and function: do these exchange mechanisms consist of a mere intermediary that stands between those who offer and those who require the good or service, or of a *quid pluris*?

This is precisely the effect that disruptive technology has on law, in general, and on property law, in particular:[36] the digital revolution, with the increasing digitization of many activities, has created new opportunities for trade and the movement of goods, which, also taking advantage of the interaction of new technological tools,[37] are capable of profoundly affecting legal concepts that are taken for granted under a classical approach.

More specifically, two types of technological evolution can be grasped: on the one hand, one can speak of sustaining technology – a concept referring to a technology that either gradually evolves or simply improves on already existing technologies – and, on the other, of disruptive technology – a concept referring to a new type of technology that, as soon as it is introduced, might appear less reliable than already existing technologies, but which would tend to acquire rapid credibility.[38]

This last notion concerns, then, technological tools that, at an early stage, appear to be of uncertain application, and that, once they gain a certain recognition, can profoundly affect the reality in which they are applied, and, consequently, the operating modes of the economic models that are in place.

It is at this stage that the distorting effects of the new technology are produced and the new models of conducting business, which benefit from the innovative

36 *See*, for the first elaboration of the concept of "disruptive technology," C. Christensen, *The Innovator's Dilemma. When New Technology Causes Great Firms to Fail*, Boston, MA, 1997, p. 69 ff.; and, for further details, M.L.P. Magalhães, *Disruptive Technologies and the Rule of Law: Autopoiesis on an Interconnected Society*, in *Braz. J. Law Techn. Innov.*, 1(1), 2023, p. 23 ff., where the author, at p. 23, affirms that «[D]isruptive technologies are expanding and information flow increasing. Due to the new technologies, we are facing unavoidable new challenges and ongoing changes. However, the law as the meta-technology crucial for the fourth revolution still thrives on an algorithmic and data-driven world. The law adjusts itself to the new realities, framing the ought to be's of society, being reshaped by progressive developments. As such a mirror held up against life, it now reflects an interconnected, cosmopolitan, and global world. As a result, following the wishes and needs of markets and societies per si, corporations, private parties, universities, and even governments and natural persons are in a constant process of global legal rules creation. A process similar to the *Lex mercatoria*, able to effectively frame the fast-paced advances, as an autopoietic legal process – now driven by nontraditional players. A variety of technologies and processes are getting incorporated into the law – such as dispute resolution over algorithms, simplified international contracts, social "quasi-legal" sanctions widely spread by social media, protection of intellectual property, through and especially by the use of machine learning, AI and autonomous technologies – growing in importance and being materialized in previously inconceivable ways. Binding and self-enforceable, the reshaped rule of law follows society's expectations, framing autonomous technologies and artificial intelligence, yet being framed by those, ensuring our rights globally, in an effective but innovative way».

37 Consider, for example, the fruitful combination of the Internet and smart-technology.

38 Cfr. C. Christensen, *The Innovator's Dilemma. When New Technology Causes Great Firms to Fail*, cit., p. xiv ff.

application of technology, begin to threaten the existence of the traditional models that have hitherto been drawn upon.[39]

Certainly, the invention of the Internet and the affirmation of intelligent technologies have produced obvious distorting consequences, as is well demonstrated, for example, by e-commerce, which the market initially approached timidly as a purely alternative form to the material exchange mechanisms that see the physical shop as their point of reference (s.c. bricks-and-mortar stores).[40]

Since then, the use of the Internet and digital technology has expanded enormously, stimulating the emergence of ever new business models that make the digital world their own, and causing interesting issues to surface in numerous branches of law.

There is, therefore, an increasing need to develop a homogeneous and systematic approach that, at least on a theoretical level, is capable of overcoming both the possible structural shortcomings that the application and dissemination of disruptive technologies has produced and the problems associated with the adoption of fragmented and differentiated solutions.[41]

In broad terms, then, if technological developments were to take on a distorting character, it would seem necessary to proceed with a change even at the regulatory-categorical level, thereby highlighting the lack of resilience of the standards referred to and, therefore, the inappropriateness of their mere adaptation to problems created precisely by the distortion produced by the new technology.[42]

39 A. Warren, *Disruptive Technologies and New Threat Multipliers*, in *The Digital Global Condition*, edited by E. Kath, J.C.H. Lee and A. Warren, Singapore, 2023, p. 53 ff., where the author, at p. 53, affirms that «[I]n the current era of omnipresent and near-instant communication, rapid technological changes are disrupting many sectors of domestic economies, while also transforming the broader global security arena. Diplomacy, deterrence and direct military action, tools that have long been utilized to safeguard the national interest, are being tested by precipitously evolving technologies – including, uninhabited aerial vehicles (UAVs), lethal autonomous weapons (LAWs), cyber and artificial intelligence (AI) – and are presenting new problems with limited guardrails to "balance" their usage. As these technologies mature, they could hold significant implications for defence authorizations and appropriations, military concepts of operations and the future of war. Moreover, as they evolve, they will continue to pose ethical and reliability questions about the use (and misuse) of technological power».

40 It should be noted, in this respect, how the distorting effect of e-commerce has become more and more evident over the years, so much so that it has caused either the disappearance of numerous brands that were famous in the past or the transformation of their market presence from a physical reality to an online reality.

41 An appropriate cost-benefit analysis could make a valuable contribution in this respect, especially with a view to introducing a unified regulatory framework of reference and achieving an appropriate balance between the opposing and conflicting interests of, on the one hand, the parties that put digital goods online and, on the other hand, the users.

42 *See*, for a clear example, G.P. Ranjitha, K. Jeesha, *Collaborative Consumption: The Future of Sharing Economy*, in *Dealing with Socially Responsible Consumers*, edited by J. Bhattacharyya, Singapore, 2022, p. 69 ff., where the author, introducing the concept of collaborative consumption under the domain of sharing economy and covering the definition of collaborative consumption, the nature of collaborations and the process of it thereby, demystifies the traditional ownership aspect toward collective ownership and brings in the motivations of a consumer for CC, such as economic, social, environmental and hedonic utilities. The author discusses than the dimensions and a triadic framework of CC (the

Alternatively, and provided that the changes brought about by technological innovation are not such as to entail excessive alterations in the system, one could hypothesize maintaining the existing approaches, clarifying their application in the context of a new framework: the distorting effect would be minimal, proving the organic and flexible structure of the existing regulatory system and its potential extension to the new system that has been created.[43]

If, then, the technological change, while having a distorting effect on the conduct of business, does not reverberate in the legal world and makes minor changes sufficient, a further possibility arises: assessing whether proceeding with moderate reforms – such as, for example, clarifying or modifying the main definitions, amending the wording of existing legal rules, or extending the scope of rules already in place – is sufficient to address the new and specific issues that technological change has generated.[44]

---

consumer, the provider and the interface), and, finally, investigates a few practical cases from different industries to augment the conceptual exploration. More in particular, at p. 69, the author affirms that «[T]he marketing world is witnessing a transformation from an exclusive ownership-driven consumption to a sustainable shared consumption. The attitude of collective ownership toward the larger canvas in terms of environment, society and its well-being are realized by the empowered consumers today resulting in a drive toward collaborative consumption (CC). This shift is fueled further by technology and its influence on the digital consumers. In this chapter, the authors draw upon past research to explore the concept, discuss its dimensionalities, motives and consequences. With various service providers/brands venturing into the space of CC, this chapter will also bring in the practitioners' perspective through multiple case examples. [. . .] Sustainable and responsible consumption is the key marketing principle for tomorrow and CC is the key driver toward turning the vision into reality. The future of marketing lies in dismantling the consumers' mind from ownership to collaboration. This essence of collective ownership and consumption applies equally to consumers, companies, brands and service providers». E. Dekker, K. Pavel, *Markets and Knowledge Commons: Is There a Difference Between Private and Community Governance of Markets?*, in *Public Choice*, 2023, p. 1 ff., where the author underlines that, if market governance can be provided by both public (state) and private organizations, the concept of private governance has been used to refer to two distinct forms of non-state governance, such as private governance and community governance. The author distinguishes between these two forms, arguing that private governance should be understood as the provision of market governance by (external) private parties, while community governance refers to a process where a group, a community, or society has the autonomy to govern its own affairs without interference from external authorities. «[T]he former internalizes the externalities associated with governance, while the latter comes about mainly as an unintended externality of social interaction in markets» (p. 1). To further illuminate the differences, and the relative strengths of these types of non-state governance, the author distinguishes among three elements of market governance: the formation and interpretation of rules, the administration of rules of ownership and exchange, and the enforcement of rules. Finally, the author argues that community governance is of great relevance for the formation and interpretation of the rules of ownership and exchange, which are consequently very hard to outsource to external parties, private or public.

43 Consider in this sense, and just as an example, the guidance issued by the European Commission on the Unfair Commercial Practices Directive. *See* European Commission, *Guidance on the Interpretation and Application of Directive 2005/29/EC of the European Parliament and of the Council Concerning Unfair Business-to-Consumer Commercial Practices in the Internal Market (2021/C 526/01)*, Brussels, 29 December 2021, available at https://eur-lex.europa.eu/legal-content/EN/TXT/PDF/?uri=CELEX:52021XC1229(05).

44 A commonly invoked principle in this regard is that of "functional equivalence," according to which, for example, once the essential characteristics of new approaches developed in the light of existing legislation have been identified, consideration is given to how they can be extended to any other new situation requiring regulatory intervention.

Consequently, if such an approach were not possible or sufficient, and it appeared appropriate to proceed to the elaboration of a new set of rules, expressing new principles and normative-doctrinal orientations, technological innovation would be the harbinger of a real distortion of the regulatory framework.

In this perspective, the need to conceive property law on digital goods in such a way as to consider the effects of market changes, which originate in the gradual affirmation of online platforms, seems clear.

The digital revolution, in fact, forces the current regulatory system to deal with entirely new situations, which only a regulatory framework characterized by a sufficient degree of flexibility is able to address without pressing for the elaboration of a new set of instruments capable of solving the innovative problems that the digital world brings with it.

Perhaps it is in the latter sense that one should read the set of proposals that, at EU level, have been put forward in the *Digital Single Market Strategy*, given the EU's commitment to bringing the single market in step with the digital age.

Indeed, many of the issues created by the digital revolution involve aspects that cannot be left to the mere input of scholars, judges and national legislators, since they must be framed within a coherent EU logical-legal framework that favours the use of an interdisciplinary approach.

It may be considered, then, that the first objective referable to the Community legal community is to favour the analysis and development of private law, with all its facets, in such a way as to take into account all the force exerted by the digital revolution:[45] it is fundamental to achieve a fair balance that, on the one hand, does not leave the new markets unregulated, and, on the other, prevents an excess of regulation that ensures both the protection of users and the possibility of the development of new socio-economic models.[46]

Ultimately, once the law has been affected by the technological developments that have occurred up to a given point in time, it becomes essential to consider the degree of distortion that has taken place.

Here, then, it is sufficient to note that only by making a correct assessment of the relationship between the existing regulatory framework and the technological innovation in place could one foster, at the domestic level, the affirmation of a regulatory system in step with technological developments, and, at the EU level, the development of a genuine single market centred on real legal transparency and certainty, so as to increase the overall attractiveness of digital commerce.

The digital revolution, in essence, has an inherent distorting force that, by allowing people to resort to the digital world to perform activities that in the past required recourse to other means, appears to be closely linked to the combination

45 A. Janssen, M. Lehmann, R. Schulze (edited by), *The Future of European Private Law*, Baden-Baden, 2023, *passim*.

46 *See*, for further details, E. Bechard-Torres, *Social Rights and Transformative Private Law*, in *Osgoode Hall Law J.*, 60(2), 2023, p. 373, where the author considers the legal environments that foster each path, as well as their normative dynamics, internal limits, and shortcomings. In this effort, the author aims to recentre private law in discussions of how social rights participate in transformative constitutionalism.

of three factors: wide access to fast Internet, widespread use of smartphones, and an increasing evolution of both software and hardware.[47]

At first, digitalization, through online trading, paved the way for the use of the Internet as a complement to the possibility of shopping in physical shops,[48] to then turn in favour of an individual use of the network to enjoy goods and services thanks to the spread of online platforms.

The spread of online platforms has thus enabled the development of a new business model that allows individuals to share their goods with others.[49]

The digital revolution was, therefore, facilitated by the remarkable technical development of numerous devices that were previously mainly mechanical or elementary electronic in nature and were not capable of connecting to the Internet

47 *See*, for further details, M. Fuster Morell, *Multidisciplinary Commons Collaborative Economy Framework: A Commons Balance of the Collaborative Economy*, in *Multidisciplinary Framework on Commons Collaborative Economy*, edited by M. Fuster Morell, B. Carballa Smichowski, G. Smorto, R. Espelt Rodrigo, P. Imperatore, M. Rebordosa, M. Rocas, N. Rodríguez, E. Senabre, M. Ciurcina, in *DECODE (DEcentralised Citizens centralised Owned Data Ecosystem)*, Barcelona, 2017, esp. p. 10 ff.

48 *See supra* at the beginning of this section.

49 There are many opportunities to bring people (individuals and traders) who are underusing their goods closer together with other individuals who would like to use them instead, and mobile technology has greatly facilitated the establishment of such relationships. This phenomenon is often referred to as the sharing economy or peer-to-peer economy (P2P) to indicate those intersubjective relationships that take place between non-professional individuals, at the basis of which online platforms such as sharing platforms or collaborative economy platforms operate. *See*, for more details, European Commission, *A European Agenda for the Collaborative Economy – COM(2016) 356 Final*, Brussels, 2 June 2016, available at http://europa.eu/rapid/press-release_IP-16-2001_en.htm; and, in doctrine, S.R. Miller, *First Principles for Regulating the Sharing Economy*, in *Harv. J. Legis*., 53, 2016, p. 147 ff.; M. Gerlich, *The Rise of Collaborative Consumption in EU Member States: Exploring the Impact of Collaborative Economy Platforms on Consumer Behavior and Sustainable Consumption*, in *Sustainability*, 15, 2023, p. 1 ff., where the author, at p. 1, affirms that «[S]ignificant changes in the global economy over the past ten years will be the economy's defining difficulties. The most important megatrends today and in the future are climate change, the cost of living crisis, and geo-economic conflicts. Megatrends have caused changes in the global economy's hierarchy and its composition. Collaborative consumption understood as a system of sharing resources between individuals and service providers via online platforms as an alternative to residential/car rental is a potentially growing economic trend. According to statistics, the collaborative economy is currently being used by a sizeable portion of the global population. They take part as both a service provider and a service consumer. This demonstrates the popularity of this practice and its viability alongside traditional economic models. In 2023, the collaborative economy has grown to include over 10,000 businesses, providing a wide range of goods and services in 133 of the world's 196 nations». Therefore, although it has been discovered that collaborative consumption practices in European society are still expanding despite changes in global economic trends, it has been determined that the physical goods sector is the collaborative economy's priority. In fact, it is demonstrated that online platforms of the collaborative economy primarily contribute to the redistribution of consumption centred on behaviour patterns such as economic value quality, social responsibility, and rational consumption. In conclusion, the author deepens the comprehension of collaborative consumption while also furnishing decision-makers and business leaders with information that can be put into practice to encourage responsible and sustainable consumption behaviours within the collaborative economy.

via a Wi-Fi connection that would allow them to be interconnected and controlled through a single control station, such as a smartphone.[50]

It is precisely this ability of the most advanced electronic equipment to share data online, so that it can be processed and used, that constitutes the so-called Internet of things.[51]

Lastly, a significant development was the combination of a mechanical process with a digitally conceived technology aimed at creating a new form of technological production, such as the 3D printer, also known as additive manufacturing (AM).

In addition to the many interesting features present in this technology,[52] it is worth mentioning, for affinity with the subject of the investigation, the possibility of design files being marketed separately from the physical good they represent: some websites allow designers – whether professionals or private individuals – to develop a design and download it online so that other individuals can purchase a copy or order a printed version through the same website.

Thus, while the circulation of 3D-printable goods has a very broad potential to contribute to changing the way goods are made and adapted to the preferences of the individual user, it also raises significant legal issues.

In this respect, if, at an early stage, the doctrine focused on the implications that 3D printing creates in the area of intellectual property strictly understood,[53]

50 Electronic equipment can now collect information on its status and performance and share it with users, the manufacturer or third parties.

51 *See*, in this regard, L.B. Furstenau, Y.P. Reckziegel Rodrigues, M. Kremer Sott, P. Leivas, M.S. Dohan, J.R. López-Robles, M.J. Cobo, N.L. Bragazzi, K.-K.R. Choo, *Internet of Things: Conceptual Network Structure, Main Challenges and Future Directions*, in *Digit. Commun. Netw.*, 9(3), 2023, p. 677 ff., where the author, at p. 677, states that «[I]nternet of Things (IoT) is a key technology trend that supports our digitalized society in applications such as smart countries and smart cities»; and, for an analysis of the IoT's backlash, B. Kaur, S. Dadkhah, F. Shoeleh, E.C. Pinto Neto, P. Xiong, S. Iqbal, P. Lamontagne, S. Ray, A.A. Ghorbani, *Internet of Things (IoT) Security Dataset Evolution: Challenges and Future Directions*, in *Intern. Things*, 22, 2023, p. 1 ff., where the authors, trying to catalogue and compare attacks, datasets and machine learning algorithms and architectures for intrusion detection systems for IoT devices, underline, at p. 1, that «[T]he evolution of mobile technologies has introduced smarter and more connected objects into our day-to-day lives. This trend, known as the Internet of Things (IoT), has applications in smart homes, smart cities, industrial automation, health monitoring systems, and has become an essential component of the communication and networking industry. However, different communication and protocol standards, weak security defaults and the difficulty of distributing updates have exacerbated cybersecurity threats to critical applications that employ IoT. To mitigate the threats and counter these attacks, a promising approach is to develop a robust intrusion detection framework specifically aimed at securing IoT». The authors classify attacks aimed at IoT devices at different layers and protocols and also highlight potential features that can be used by machine learning-based intrusion detection systems to detect different types of attacks.

52 The use of 3D technology makes it possible to produce goods by continuously "printing" thin layers that, superimposed one on top of the other, eventually make it possible to compose the object that was designed. The common feature of the various ways in which additive manufacturing can be expressed is the use of a computer file, developed using appropriate design software (so-called computer-aided design [CAD]), which is sent to a physical device – the 3D printer – that produces a corporeal product based on a CAD file.

53 *See, ex multis*, J.F. Hornick, *3D Printing and the Future (or Demise) of Intellectual Property*, in *3D Print. Addit. Manuf.*, 1(1), 2014, p. 34 ff.; M. Rimock, *An Introduction to the Intellectual Property*

and then the discussion turned to considering the liability implications of damage created by goods printed in this format,[54] we now point out the need to broaden the debate to more extensive private law implications, such as, in particular, the ownership of an asset that was originally dematerialized and then highly usable and sharable, as software is.[55]

3 Navigating Digital Spaces: Regulatory Taking and Online Platforms

The digital revolution has manifested itself essentially in the way in which digital content has been deployed and used, as demonstrated, for instance, by the vast operational scope of the applications (so-called apps) of a smartphone, or the fact that, in numerous hypotheses, the digital enables the operation of numerous physical devices.

It is no coincidence that the possibility of legal circulation of the digital sign is particularly broad and can be the subject both of a specific and autonomous contract that is completed with the downloading of a given programme,[56] as much as of a broader negotiation – also consisting in the purchase of a tangible good – of which it constitutes a more or less important part.[57]

Consequently, and in principle, the centrality that digital goods have progressively assumed poses the inevitable problem of whether there are, firstly, legal rules and concepts currently in force that can be drawn upon in consideration of digital quality and form, and secondly, remedies to be resorted to when either the digital content does not sufficiently present those qualities that the user expected or it has caused damage to another digital good, a physical device, or to the data that the user of the digital content has stored in a device.

Law Implications of 3D Printing, in *Can. J. Law Techn.*, 13(1), 2015, p. 1 ff.; L.S. Osborn, *3D Printing and Intellectual Property*, Cambridge, 2019, p. 9 ff.

54 *See*, for all, D. Mendis, J. Nordemann, R. Ballardini, H. Brorsen, M.D.C. Calatrava Moreno, J. Robson, P. Dickens, *The Intellectual Property Implications of the Development of Industrial 3D Printing*, in *Project Report. Brussels: European Commission*, Luxembourg, 2020, p. 116 ff.

55 *See*, for more on 3D printing, G. Howells, C. Willett, *3D Printing: The Limits of Contract and Challenges for Tort*, in *Digital Revolution: Challenges for Contract Law*, edited by R. Schulze and D. Staudenmayer, Baden-Baden, 2016, p. 67 ff.; H.K. Chan, M. Guo, F. Zeng, Y. Chen, T. Xiao, J. Griffin, *Blockchain-Enabled Authentication Platform for the Protection of 3D Printing Intellectual Property: A Conceptual Framework Study*, in *Enterp. Inf. Syst.*, 17(11), 2023, p. 1471 ff., where the authors, at p. 1472, underline that «[T]he openness of the Internet and characteristics of 3DP designs, such as the value of co-creation, sharing and co-ownership, further impede the evidence collection and responsibility confirmation for the infringement of digital IP rights. As a result, there are growing demands from innovators and creators for the adequate protection of their digital products [. . .]. Due to the lack of an existing solution to offer protection for IP in the 3DP supply chain, the development of distributed 3DP production networks for established products has been inhibited [. . .]. Various IP-related risks can partially contribute to the situation that 3DP has not yet realised its full commercial potential [. . .]». *See*, for more on software and its circulation, *infra* esp. Chapter 4.

56 Think of the purchase of an office package.

57 Think of the case of software to control the functions of a car.

Thus, these profiles are accompanied by other problems related to digitality, such as the need to identify the most appropriate type of contract for the transfer of software or digital content (e.g. service contract, sales contract), but above all – and for what is of interest here – the status of digital content in terms of ownership.

Certainly, digital goods are, by their very nature, immaterial and, although especially in the past they often circulated thanks to a physical medium, they are currently and increasingly the subject of a simple download that is directly and integrally realized via the Internet, thus operating on an entirely immaterial level.

It could be considered, then, that the exchange of a digital good, not implying the transfer of the right of ownership over a physical *res*, implies, thanks to a license of use, the simple right to acquire a copy of the digital content, provided that the good is not enjoyed online and therefore in the absence of any passage on the user's device.[58]

Whatever the answer to the question given below, the issues inherent to the classification of the digital asset and its ownership are relevant in light of the fact that, on the one hand, some legal systems resort to a *numerus clausus* of real rights and, on the other, that certain remedies are used to ensure that the person acquiring a digital content is protected by the right it has become the owner of or the existence in the asset of a certain quality standard recognized *ex lege*.[59]

Let it be said in passing here that if the former situation occurs, the digital revolution could also translate into the need to reform the already existing regulatory framework, requiring, hypothetically, the development of new subjective situations linked to the *res* that reflect the particular relationship that binds the digital asset to its owner.

Such an eventuality could easily be pursued in some legal systems more than in others as it could be linked only to specific subjective situations that, operating in the digital world and thus being influenced by specific and distinct characteristics referable to the good, could concern digitality alone without having general application.

The second situation, on the other hand, would be linked to the provision of specific rules applicable to digital goods, if certain types of use were envisaged associated with instruments of protection to be resorted to when the digital good does not have the envisaged characteristics or the interaction of its content with the physical device or other digital good causes damage.

58 *See* T. Karger, *Bounded Ownership: Lessons Learned from Online Platforms in Creating Inclusive Goods*, in *Soc. Med. Soc.*, 9(2), 2023, p. 1 ff.

59 J.-H. Jhang-Li, and R. Chiang, *Licensing and Revenue Sharing for Digital Content Co-Production*, in *Rising Like a Phoenix: Emerging from the Pandemic and Reshaping Human Endeavors with Digital Technologies – Forty-Second International Conference on Information Systems 2023*, Hyderabad, 16, 2023, p. 1 ff. where the authors develop a content co-production mechanism for copyright owners to set a revenue-sharing split with content creators («Content creators, aiming for higher ad revenue, can dispute the copyright claim within a specific time frame» [p. 1]). They suggest how the proposed mechanism can help the two sides settle and avoid a trial in court with a sensible revenue-sharing ratio and dispute time frame. Furthermore, they show how the share of ad revenue can be made proportional to the contribution of the baseline materials.

One could, then, hypothesize starting a process of adaptation that, by resorting to the most relevant norms on the subject of ownership and related instruments of protection, would then move on to modify them according to the needs that the digital form makes appear more convenient.

On the other hand, new rules could also be developed based both on the relationship with the asset and on specific profiles related to the digital content.

Lastly, the rules concerning digital ownership could reflect the possibility for the subject to avail himself of the many avenues granting him access to the digital good, given that the latter can be enjoyed through a physical medium, or download via the Internet, or through online retrieval without being installed on any device of the user.

In general terms, one can grasp some key issues that need to be addressed and resolved when a subject has access to a digital good, starting from the possible specification of the title that the individual has in his relationship with a digital content, up to the remedies that he can resort to, by virtue of his position with respect to the good.

It is quite clear that there is no single, simple answer to the questions that may arise on the subject, both because of the different subjects potentially involved in the mechanism of use of the digital good (creator of the digital good, its supplier and its user), and because of the numerous ways in which it may be used or made available to the user.[60]

It should be noted, on the side, how the digital revolution has fostered, among other things, the emergence of online platforms,[61] which, as mentioned in the previous section, is in essence a new type of online intermediary, whose function is to act as an intercessor between the provider of a good, service or digital content and its user.

While the function of such platforms is to connect supplier and user, often the benefit for the former is to access a larger number of potential users without having to invest in the creation of a web portal.

However, sometimes, online platforms do not operate as mere passive intermediaries, but, in addition to defining a set of rules to which supplier and user must adhere in order to use their service, they also identify mechanisms for placing

60 For reasons of thematic coherence, I cannot consider here a further problematic profile pertaining to the actual position that the party assumes in the contractual relationship having as its object the goods, given the possibility that the private party has of becoming a supplier of goods, services and digital content through various online platforms (for example, if Airbnb and Uber allow parties to share their resources with others, other platforms, such as Shapeways, allow them to dispose of their CAD files necessary to proceed to any 3D prints or, like Etsy, to sell goods produced at home). More specifically, the described qualifying profiles take on a particular, for obvious reasons of applicable law (consumer law or not), relevance in these circumstances because just as the party receiving the good or service often does not know whether the other party to the contract is another private individual or a professional, so too the private individual who regularly offers a good, service or digital content may not know to what extent the activities performed take on professional traits.

61 This could be a private individual who occasionally acts as an intermediary as well as a trader who independently, and thus on a voluntary basis, decides to do so on a regular basis.

orders and making payments, in exchange for a small percentage of the transfer fee (so-called processing fee).[62]

The framework outlined is important because, especially with reference to the latter hypotheses, it could make even more complex the framing of the legal relations underlying the relationship that actually exists between the subject/user and the digital good, raising new legal questions in terms of legal ownership and involving the problem of the actual transfer of a property right on the digital good.

In this sense, in fact, the very regulation of one or more technologies relates back to the search for the way in which legislation can legitimize an organization of social and economic relations that already finds its structure in practice, and which, due to its operation also on a supranational level, may exceed the scope of national rules consolidated over time.

Here again, an answer could come from a careful analysis of the way platforms operate, the problems they create, and the limit within which existing rules and conceptual categories can be applied to resolve the issues that have arisen in this way: has the growing relevance that digital goods have progressively assumed had a profound effect on the way traditional rules on property could be applied? In other words, has the traditional discipline of ownership expressed or not the ability to promote effective innovation in the digital field in terms of digital circulation of creative content?

If, *prima facie*, one might find it difficult to grasp an alteration of the classical categorical fabric when dealing with the transfer of a physical good via the web – whether or not through online platforms – the situation seems to change when it comes to digital goods simultaneously usable by several subjects, where the need for a renewed approach to the matter seems to be felt, capable of going beyond the traditional approaches in the light of which to evaluate the relationship with the *res*.[63]

Indeed, in such cases, what could happen if the user were prevented from making total or partial use of the digital good? Could he resort to petitory actions to protect his proprietary position, or could he in fact not speak of real ownership? Does the user therefore have true ownership of the good, or a mere right of use thereof?[64]

62 Other platforms take on an even more active role, such as those operating in the 3D printing sector, which can allow designers to publish their designs (e.g. CAD files) on the platform and thus create virtual "shops," which allow interested parties to analyse the designs and order the desired good.

63 Cfr. C. Wendehorst, *Consumer Contracts and the Internet of Things*, in *Digital Revolution – Challenges for Contract Law*, edited by R. Schulze and D. Staudenmayer, Baden-Baden, 2016, p. 189 ff., che dopo aver evidenziato che la rivoluzione digitale, sotto forma dell'*internet of things*, rappresenta una seria sfida alle regole tradizionali, specie con riferimento al diritto di proprietà, afferma, a p. 222, che gli *smart devices* (who after highlighting that the digital revolution, in the form of the internet of things, represents a serious challenge to traditional rules, especially with reference to property rights, he states, at p. 222, that smart devices) «[. . .] combine the features of goods and digital content, and their supply combines the features of sales and of services».

64 F. Tietze, T. Pieper, C. Herstatt, *To Own or Not to Own: How Ownership Impacts User Innovation – An Empirical Study*, in *Technovation*, 38, 2015, p. 50 ff., where the authors, at p. 50, underline that «[. . .] users also use products that they do not own, in which case ownership and control are separated. Property rights theory predicts that the separation of ownership and control is a user innovation barrier. When innovating, users need to accommodate an additional actor: the owner. Separation of ownership and control thus induces uncertainty and complexity in the user innovation

In addressing these issues, it does not seem possible to disregard one fact, namely that – as happens, for instance, in the context of the Internet of things – the legal system cannot focus on the mere physicality of the device, but must consider that the primary function of these devices is not linked to their materiality but to their digital content and the related data that are processed, stored and transferred.

Certainly, and once again, it appears evident how the digital revolution, with all its potentially distorting effect, can lead to a fundamental alternative: a reasoning in the sign either of a simple categorical adjustment, or of a more profound reconsideration of the approach to the subject-thing relationship as classically understood.

Ultimately, there is no doubt that digitality has had and continues to have a distorting effect, but it must be borne in mind that the latter with respect to the regulatory framework, and especially to proprietary situations, may not be as profound and deflagrating as it may *prima facie* appear.

It is indeed necessary to carefully consider the legal and systemic implications that may be attached to the disruptive effects attributable to the digital revolution and to identify whether they actually affect the reference legal system in such a way as to require the development of new rules or new systemic approaches: both the search for solutions to address these specific problems and the broader implications for the affected legal areas as a whole must be considered before innovative rules or approaches are concretely adopted.

So-called distorting technology poses legal problems that may lead to legislation resulting from the same distortion, with the result that legal practitioners must be driven by the objective of identifying, evaluating and possibly adopting solutions more appropriate to the changes that have actually occurred.[65]

If, therefore, the development of rules, principles and legal models was caused by problems that emerged in the past, which consequently forged the resulting value system, the law, which has undergone a distorting effect, requires new rules and principles to deal with the innovative issues that disruptive technology has produced: since doctrine, policy-makers and standardizers will have to identify new legal models and concepts to refer to, new knowledge and skills will have to be developed and cultivated.

---

process, increasing users' costs to innovate»; M. Zhou, M.A.A.M. Leenders, L.M. Cong, *Ownership in the Virtual World and the Implications for Long-Term User Innovation Success*, in *Technovation*, 78, 2018, p. 56 ff., where the authors, at p. 56, affirm that «[. . .] the findings reveal that the separation of content and platform ownership and their inherent interdependencies are a source of ownership tensions posing significant challenges to entrepreneurs. Moreover, the virtual world business model favors the platform's ownership rights while undermining other kinds of competing ownership interests. The current structures around ownership rights and control seem detrimental for successful business creation, profitable technology development and long-term user innovation success. The implications for theory and the practical implications for virtual entrepreneurs are discussed».

65 *See*, for further details, S. Jung, P.J. Wisniewski, C.E. Hughes, *In Limbo: The Effect of Gradual Visual Transition Between Real and Virtual on Virtual Body Ownership Illusion and Presence*, in *IEEE Conference on Virtual Reality and 3D User Interfaces (VR)* – Tuebingen/Reutlingen, 2018, p. 267 ff.

4 Real Rights and Shared Goods in the Digital Age

A particular profile that the digital revolution brings to light as a trait that, while affecting the subject of personal data, hints at the overall incidence of the phenomenon on the subject-thing relationship, concerns the possibility of identifying a counter-performance that stands as an alternative to money: a given digital good is not provided against payment of a sum of money, since the recipient, in lieu of payment, gives his willingness to communicate certain personal data to the provider.[66]

The scenario envisaged, in addition to raising numerous other legal issues, is an undoubted illustration of the influence of the digital revolution on the subject-personal relationship that is of interest here: if, in principle, once the exchange of digital goods–personal data has taken place, Community law states that consent to the use of the data may be withdrawn at any time,[67] this general provision may, however, create uncertainties precisely because personal data represent the counter-performance to the receipt of the digital good or content as to the effects that such a withdrawal may have on the relationship that has been established.

More specifically, if the revocation of consent to the use of one's personal data implies that the person concerned must regain full access to them and, therefore, has the right to their definitive deletion by whoever received them (the so-called right to be forgotten), it seems to follow that the data owner may lose, in turn, the possibility of making use of the digital content he had received in exchange.

In this regard, among the various possible solutions, one plausible perspective would be to consider the relationship established between the subject and the asset as governed by a mere licence to use the data in exchange for a mere licence to use the digital asset, so that, on the one hand, the revocation of the consent to use the personal data would entail the termination of the relevant licence to use, and, on the other hand, the licence to use the digital asset would terminate *ex se*.

According to a different approach, resulting, for instance, from the possible combination of the personal data that the subject has received from the various users of the digital content for the purpose of processing new data,[68] even though the individual referrer of the personal data withdraws consent to their use for further processing, all the results of the research he has already carried out and the results of which may also go beyond the specific limit marked by the consent of use originally given will remain with the subject who has used them.

66 It should be noted, in fact, that users are often not fully aware that a digital good is often offered for free only in appearance, since, in reality, the consideration is access to personal data.

67 *See* European Parliament and the Council, *Regulation (EU) 2016/679 of the European Parliament and of the Council of 27 April 2016 on the Protection of Individuals With Regard to the Processing of Perso*nal Data and on the Free Movement of Such Data, and Repealing Directive 95/46/EC (General Data Protection Regulation, in OJEU L119, 4). 5.2016, p. 1 ff. which, as a new Data Protection Regulation, provides, on the one hand, in Article 6(1)(a) and 9(2), for the necessary consent of the subject to the use of his or her personal data for one or more specific purposes, and, on the other hand, in Article 17 the right to be forgotten (so-called right to erasure or right to be forgotten).

68 For instance, when added value has been generated by the combination and analysis of a subject's personal data with those of other subjects.

In such a case, precisely because of the benefits that remain for the person who has used the information in exchange for the use that the other party has had of the digital asset, the person to whom the data, then reprocessed, are referable should be allowed to continue using the same digital assets even in the presence of a revocation of the consent of use initially given.

In essence, one can see how the inevitable effects of a distorting change are not produced, in their full extent, in the immediate future, but generally emerge clearly only with the passage of time: some consequences of the change occurred in the circulation of goods will become evident before others, stimulating doctrine and policy-makers to act to assess whether the distortions operated are such as to require their reparative-corrective intervention.

It is in this perspective that the *Digital Agenda*[69] should be read, which is an expression of the primary commitment undertaken by the European Union to address the issues that have emerged, also at the legal level, as a result of the digital revolution, as is well demonstrated by the numerous initiatives undertaken to foster the *Digital Single Market* and the new proposals and communications launched since May 2016,[70] which have highlighted the cautious attitude taken by the European Commission on the subject and aimed at planning each regulatory reform gradually and carefully.[71]

69 *See* European Commission, *A Digital Single Market Strategy for Europe – COM(2015) 192 Final*, Brussels, 6 May 2015, where, at p. 3, this central document of the *Digital Agenda* states that «[T]he global economy is rapidly becoming digital. Information and communication technologies (ICT) are no longer a specific sector but the foundation of all modern innovative economic systems. The Internet and digital technologies are transforming our lives and the way we work – as individuals, in businesses and in our communities – and are increasingly being integrated into all sectors of our economy and society. These changes are happening at a scale and speed that offer immense opportunities for innovation, growth and jobs. But they also raise challenging policy issues for public authorities that require coordinated EU action. All Member States are struggling with similar issues, but on too narrow a national basis to allow them to grasp all the opportunities and address all the challenges of this transformational change. For many issues, the European level offers the right framework. This is why the European Commission has made the creation of a digital single market one of its top priorities. A digital single market is a market in which the free movement of goods, persons, services and capital is ensured and in which individuals and businesses can access and operate online seamlessly under conditions of fair competition and with a high level of consumer and personal data protection, regardless of their nationality or place of residence. The realization of a *Digital Single Market* will ensure that Europe maintains its position as a world leader in the digital economy, helping European businesses to grow globally».

70 In 2016, for instance, it launched a review of regulatory measures in the area of consumer protection of parcel delivery cooperation, the legislative proposals to reform the current telecom rules, the review of the *Audiovisual Media Services Directive*, the initiatives on data ownership, free movement of data and the European cloud, the review of the e-privacy directive, while on 2017, among other measures, it launched the *VAT Package on the Digital Single Market*.

71 *See*, for example, on the subject of online platforms, European Commission, *Communication on Online Platforms and the Digital Single Market – Opportunities and Challenges for Europe – COM(2016) 288 Final*, Brussels, 25 May 2016, p. 5, where it is stated that «[. . .] the need to foster the innovation-promoting role of platforms requires that any future regulatory measures proposed at EU level only address clearly identified problems related to a specific type or activity of online platforms in line with better regulation principles. This problem-oriented approach should start with an assessment of when the existing framework is still appropriate».

At the Community level, one can thus grasp the methodological tendency to act on a dual line that goes from the clear identification of problems, in such a way as to move more in the direction of reaction rather than prevention, to the attempt to apply, in the first instance, the already existing rules to the newly identified problems, to then move on, in the event of impossibility in this sense, to the introduction of new legislation, in the full awareness that "[. . .] where rules designed with traditional [. . .] provision in mind may impede"[72] the development of new models for the circulation of goods.

In essence, it appears evident how this method allows with flexibility to respond to all the problems identified without necessarily adopting new and specific regulations, being, if necessary, sufficient to assess whether the rules already in force can respond to the discipline of the specific case: the key idea is that, in the presence of the more or less apparent alterations that the digital revolution has caused and is causing to the classic ownership structure, one must always act cautiously in filling the gaps that seem to have affected the regulatory system.

In essence, the problems and distorting legal implications that the aforementioned developments may cause to the regulatory system and to classical methodological approaches must be clearly identified, and only then, if necessary, should one proceed to a genuinely innovative reflection that breaks with the traditional past.

Now, if we change the terms of the discourse, and move from the major regulatory or macro-system frameworks (legislative policy) to the consideration of the more punctual micro-system frameworks (scientific-doctrinal policy), we need to assess whether such a methodology can also be applied to the reference models drawn on in this study: does the digital revolution, with all the changes it has fostered, allow us to maintain the traditional approaches through which to read and interpret the thing-subject relationship, or does it profoundly alter its structure?

The circulation of digital goods raises important questions in terms of both contract law and property law, so much so that the very concept of a digital good as a circulating thing raises not insignificant questions of exclusivity in fact and in law.

One thinks, for instance, of personal data, which, initially conceived as pertaining exclusively to the protection of personality, can instead also be used, within certain limits, as a *res* of exchange: if one considers the intellectual property law currently in force, the right of the person who develops a database can be licensed and transferred, without, however, the protection of the individual data.

The question then arises as to whether the development of a new concept of property rights is desirable or possible.

In reality, however, in what do realty and the property that constitutes its object concretize themselves? What concepts, in general terms, do they express? Is their meaning unambiguous?

72 *See* European Commission, *Communication from the Commission to the European Parliament, the Council, the European Economic and Social Committee and the Committee of the Regions – Online Platforms and the Digital Single Market – Opportunities and Challenges for Europe, COM(2016) 288 Final*, 25 May 2016. Brussels, p. 5.

An answer that strives for comprehensiveness cannot disregard certain semiotic considerations: the absolute importance that signs in the broadest sense have is linked to their ability to communicate information.[73]

The distinction that is usually made between the semantic level of information (meaning), the syntactic level of information (signs and their interrelation) and the communicative channel of information (at the physical level) leads to the possibility of making further differentiations between the content level, the code level and the physical level.[74]

Indeed, it appears useful to distinguish the three described planes in order to define the good and elevate it to an object of potential transfer, since, through them, its content can be distinguished and defined, precisely, at the semantic level (content having a certain meaning), at the syntactic level (content represented through a certain number of signs) and also through its material support (content present in a certain physical support or, in a broader sense, represented through the structure of a physical object).[75]

While the different planes are certainly interconnected, when considered in their legal and economic individuality, they also make it possible to grasp and define distinct and specific content, and consequently digital content can be defined on the basis of each of the three levels.

In fact, transfer of a digital good can mean either transfer of a certain meaning or content, or transfer of a set of signs – especially if stored digitally as is the case for a file or MP3, or, as was often the case before powerful and efficient technological

73 *See* U. Eco, *Trattato di semiotica generale*, Milano, 2016, *passim*.

74 It is no coincidence that, in the world of modern information technology, when talking about digital content transfer, a differentiation is made between the three levels described. *See* L. Lessig, *The Future of Ideas, the Fate of the Commons in a Connected World*, New York, NY, 2002, p. 23, where the author, referring to the thesis expressed by Y. Benkler, *From Consumers to Users: Shifting the Deeper Structures of Regulation Toward Sustainable Commons and User Access*, in *Fed. Comm. Law J.*, 52, 2000, p. 562 ff., states that «[T]he layers that I mean here are the different layers within a communications system that together make communications possible. Following the technique of network architects, Benkler suggests that we understand a communications system by dividing it into three distinct "layers bottom is a "physical" layer, across which communication travels. This is the computer, or wires, that link computers on the Internet. In the middle is a "logical" or "code" layer – the code that makes the hardware run. Here we might include the protocols that define the Internet and the software upon which those protocols run. At the top is a "content" layer – the actual stuff that gets said or transmitted across these wires. Here we include digital images, texts, on-line movies, and the like. These three layers function together to define any particular communications system. Each of these layers in principle could be controlled or could be free. Each, that is, could be owned or each could be organized in a common. We could imagine a world where the physical layer was free but the logical and content layers were not. Or we could imagine a world where the physical and code layers were controlled but the content layer was not. And so on».

75 Each of the three types of information can be traced in everyday life. In fact, when talking about a story and the content of a book we refer to the semantic level, when working on a file we refer to the syntactic level, and when dealing with a CD or a book we refer to the structural level. Obviously, the three levels are interconnected, given that a meaning can be contained in a text and a text can be printed: the physical level brings with it the syntactic level, and the syntactic level brings with it the semantic level.

networks were developed, transfer of a physical support to digitized content such as a CD or key drive.[76]

It should be noted, in this regard, that Directive 2011/83/EU uses the term "digital content" and defines it, in Article 2(10), as "data which are produced and supplied in digital form," while the Proposal for a Directive on certain aspects concerning contracts for the supply of digital content, on the one hand, provides an authentic definition of digital goods in Article 2(1),[77] and, on the other hand, considers the need to differentiate digital content from the relevant physical medium by extending, in Article 3(3), its application "to any durable medium incorporating digital content where the durable medium has been used exclusively as carrier of digital content."[78]

Article 3(5)(a) of the Proposal then distinguishes digital content from the digital service, excluding its extension to "services performed with a predominant element of human intervention by the supplier where the digital format is used mainly as a carrier."[79]

Considering, then, that the same European Court of Justice, in the *UsedSoft*[80] ruling with which it decided a case of software resale, clarified that digital goods must be treated as a tertium genus with respect to physical goods and physical services, it seems useful to clarify the value of the concept of "digital content."

When digital contents are the object of legal circulation, they are considered and treated as goods in the strict sense, so that the concept of good, if, from an

76 Consider, in this respect, the *General Data Protection Regulation – Regulation (EU) 2016/679 of the European Parliament and of the Council of 27 April 2016 on the Protection of Individuals with Regard to the Processing of Personal Data and on the Free Movement of Such Data, and Repealing Directive 95/46/EC*, which makes a distinction, at the level of meaning (semantic content), with regard to personal data, defined, pursuant to Article 4(1), as information concerning the person. More specifically, the provision in question provides that «"personal" data means any information relating to an identified or identifiable natural person ('data subject'); an identifiable natural person is one who can be identified, directly or indirectly, in particular by reference to an identifier such as a name, an identification number, location data, an online identifier or to one or more factors specific to the physical, physiological, genetic, mental, economic, cultural or social identity of that natural person».

77 *See* European Commission, Directive (EU) 2019/770 of the European Parliament and of the Council of 20 May 2019 on certain aspects concerning contracts for the supply of digital content and digital services, 22.5.2019, L136/1, Brussels, according to which Article 2, «(1) "digital content" means data which are produced and supplied in digital form, (2) "digital service" means: (a) a service that allows the consumer to create, process, store or access data in digital form; or (b) a service that allows the sharing of or any other interaction with data in digital form uploaded or created by the consumer or other users of that service; (3) "goods with digital elements" means any tangible movable items that incorporate, or are inter-connected with, digital content or a digital service in such a way that the absence of that digital content or digital service would prevent the goods from performing their functions».

78 The provision thus covers digital content embedded in a physical medium but not the physical medium used exclusively to provide digital data.

79 Article 2(2) and (3) considers, however, as digital goods subject to the discipline of the Directive, respectively, both so-called storage services, such as, for instance, cloud services, and so-called data sharing services.

80 *See supra* § 1.

economic point of view, it is linked to the use that is made of it,[81] from a legal point of view, it poses the problem of assessing whether or not it is subject to the right(s) of ownership, even before analysing the contract to which it is subject.

It is no coincidence that, in the national legal system, Article 810 of the Civil Code[82] defines as property the object of the right, whether absolute or relative, and that the German legal system, for example, often identifies the object of the right with the property in the same vein.

If, therefore, it can be said, in general terms, that a good is the *res* subject to rights, according to an economic approach the *discrimen* is identified with the use to which the thing is subject, given that the good is the result of the summation of its possible uses, thus arriving at a concept of property understood as a set of rights or possible uses from which its owner can benefit.

Starting from concepts traditionally linked to the right of ownership,[83] three different types of rights can be grasped that, beyond circulation,[84] are linked to the ownership of the *res*, understood also in its digital form: the possession of the good, its use and its destruction.

Possession of the tangible good, which when translated into digital terms becomes access to the intangible-digital good,[85] represents the first concept that tends to be exclusively linked to the owner of the right: owning an object allows the owner to potentially carry out any kind of activity concerning it, and especially to make use of it as he wishes.

The use of the good, whether physical or digital, constitutes the second key step of a perception, in exclusive terms, of the right of ownership, although access can be differentiated, as is well shown, *ex parte alienantis*, on the one hand, by the patent, which is aimed at limiting the use of digital content without conditioning access,[86] and, on the other, by copyright, which is aimed at limiting the use of the content by limiting access itself.[87]

81 In this sense, goods are objects that are defined according to their use.

82 According to Article 810 of the Italian Civil Code, «goods are those things that can be the subject of rights». *See*, for an in-depth examination of the distinction between "good" and "thing," *ex aliis*, B. Biondi, *I beni*, in *Tratt. di diritto civile italiano*, IV, 1, a cura di F. Vassalli, Torino, 1956, p. 15, where the author maintains that a legal asset is «[. . .] qualsiasi entità materiale o ideale giuridicamente rilevante»; S. Pugliatti, *Beni e cose in senso giuridico*, Milano, 1962, esp. p. 56 ff., where the author, at p. 58, states that «[L]e cose, per poter formare oggetto di rapporti giuridici, debbono essere beni: ciò vuol dire che debbono essere utili, atte a soddisfare un bisogno umano, senza di che mancherebbe persino l'interesse giuridicamente tutelabile»; A. Gambaro, *I beni*, in *Tratt. di diritto civile e commerciale*, già diretto da A. Cicu, F. Messineo e L. Mengoni e continuato da P. Schlesinger, Milano, 2012, p. 16 ff.

83 The reference is to concepts such as use (*usus*), enjoyment of the property and its fruits (*usus fructus*), improper or unauthorized use of the property (*abusus*) and transfer of ownership.

84 The transfer of the right of ownership is not understood as typically and specifically pertaining to ownership – as, on the other hand, is the case for possession, use and destruction of the thing – because it concerns a different level that does not necessarily and exclusively pertain to the holder of the right, but can also be assigned to a higher or meta-level.

85 *See*, for more details, J. Rifkin, *The Age of Access*, cit., esp. p. 3 ff. and p. 114 ff.

86 The patent, on the other hand, aims at facilitating the distribution of technical information to the public.

87 Copyright, in particular, prevents the copying and distribution of works that fall under its protection.

Lastly, the destruction of both corporeal and digital goods can result from the alteration of the relevant syntactic information or the falsification of the relevant semantic information. More specifically, if, on the one hand, syntactic content can be completely destroyed through its deletion, which occurs through the elimination of every possible support[88] in which the specific syntactic content is stored, on the other hand, knowledge, which in the human mind represents semantic information, cannot be destroyed at all, or cannot be destroyed without violating the integrity of those to whom it is accessed.

Ultimately, the outlined picture shows how the concept of exclusive enjoyment or use of the good as a coessential characteristic of the right to property in its traditional construction, undergoes a profound attenuation in the presence of goods characterized by a strong digitality, since, unlike the possession of a corporeal or physical *res*, the enjoyment of this type of *res* is in contrast neither with the use of the object that others make of it at the same time and in the same manner nor with an exclusivity of use, deriving from this that the right of ownership, when related to the digital world and based on the concept of access, seems to require a reconstruction that is set on different terms than those classically resorted to.

As is well known,[89] the development of technologies has largely reduced the cost, size and weight of sensors, computer memory, telematic networks, computers and control devices, so that digital content can be more effectively, more quickly and more economically stored, transmitted and analysed.

Three aspects can therefore be distinguished, as one can see, firstly, that conventional physical goods are now able to operate in a profoundly digitized world, generating, storing and transmitting content and information;[90] secondly, that traditional tools are increasingly being replaced by digital content;[91] and thirdly, that the latter has become a real tradable commodity.[92]

The typology and extent of transferable rights to digital goods therefore becomes a very central issue, and in this regard, the distinction between production, retrieval

88 This is what is known as structural information.

89 *See supra* Introduction and Chapter 1.

90 Consider, for example, the latest generation of cars that have become authentic computers on wheels. This is a phenomenon that is often linked to the idea of being smart and concerns a wide range of commercial and everyday objects, such as mobile phones, household appliances, clothes, agricultural machinery and machines in general.

91 The digital content economy is not only an economy governed or controlled by data, but also sees data as freely tradable goods because they have an intrinsic economic value.

92 Evidence of this can be found, for example, in Directive 96/9/EC of the European Parliament and of the Council of 11 March 1996 on the legal protection of databases, which solves the problem of legally considering data as economic goods: unlike the rights that traditionally make up intellectual property, this discipline does not limit itself to protecting the creation of human ingenuity, but rather the result of an investment that is identified not with the data individually understood, but with the database or with the expenditure incurred to create a database. See, on this subject, A. Steinbeck, *Immaterialgüterrechte und Informationsinteresse*, in *Kölner Schrift zum Wirtschaftsrecht*, 2010, p. 223 ff., where the author, at p. 224, affirms that «Nicht nur der Schöpfer einer geistigen Leistung, sondern auch derjenige, der mit organisatorischen Einsatz und finanziellen Investitionen dazu beiträgt, dass Informationen generiert und/oder verbreitet werden, hat regelmäßig ein Interesse daran, diese Informationen zunächst ausschließlich selbst zu nutzen und auszuwerten».

and analysis of digital content becomes relevant: rights of use or exclusive rights act on different levels depending on their origin and the way they are exercised.

It is, therefore, of primary importance to assess whether and how a reserved legal protection, which can be linked to the exclusive nature of the ownership of the right,[93] can also be recognized in the presence of digital goods that are accessed and enjoyed.

As in any economic system, even in those that recognize the circulation of content of a digital nature, two potential groups of actors – on the one hand, the companies and, on the other, the consumers-users – are grasped, but the particularity of systems with digital circulation is the ease with which these two subjective categories can be mixed.

Indeed, the proliferation of increasingly complex, yet simple-to-use devices has made it easy for individual users to take on the role of producers of digital content disseminators, and, at the same time, has allowed companies to participate in the process of developing and circulating digital content, even though such activities would, in theory, be far removed from their chosen economic activity.[94]

However, two particular positions can be distinguished that, in general, can be assumed with respect to digital goods: on the one hand, access to data, which, in essence, expresses a factual relationship (having the data in one's material

93 L. Katz, *Exclusion and Exclusivity in Property Law*, in *Univ. Tor. Law J.*, 58(3), 2008, p. 275 ff., where the author, at p. 275, states that «[L]ike many of the contemporary critics of the "bundle of rights" approach to ownership, I insist that ownership is a legal concept with a well-defined structure. I differ from most of them, however, in the model of ownership that I believe to be at work in property law. Most of these critics propose a model of ownership that emphasizes the owner's right to exclude non-owners from the owned thing as the central defining feature of ownership. I call this the "boundary approach" to highlight its fixation on the owner's power to decide who may cross the boundaries of the owned thing. But this, I argue, makes it impossible for the boundary approach to explain adequately the many subsidiary rights in things that coexist with the rights of owners. Indeed, I argue that when we look more closely at the structure of ownership in property law, its central concern is not the exclusion of all non-owners from the owned thing but, rather, the preservation of the owner's position as the exclusive agenda setter for the owned thing. So long as others – whether they be holders of subsidiary property rights or strangers to the property – act in a way that is consistent with the owner's agenda, they pose no threat to the owner's exclusive position as agenda setter»; P. Dhliwayo, A.J. Van Derwalt, *The Notion of Absolute and Exclusive Ownership: A Doctrinal Analysis*, in *S. Afr. Law J.*, 134(1), p. 34 ff. where the authors, exploring doctrinal perspectives on limitations on ownership and specifically on the right to exclude, consider the idea that the absoluteness of ownership implies that the right to exclude is either absolute or central to ownership and, consequently, affirm that «[T]he idea of absoluteness can be understood as an indication that ownership is the most complete real right, to distinguish it from limited real rights, or that ownership allows the owner freedom in using the property, but only in so far as the law allows. However, even with these qualifications it remains problematic to describe ownership as an absolute right». Therefore, it is affirmed that neither ownership nor the right to exclude is absolute in any meaningful sense because ownership is limited by limited real rights and by constitutional and statutory law. Stated differently, ownership and the right to exclude are limited by and within the legal system in which they function.

94 This is the so-called fourth industrial revolution or *Industrie 4.0*, which can be briefly described as the result of the application of the Internet of things to production processes.

possession), and, on the other, data ownership, which, in essence, configures a legal relationship (having the data in one's legal possession).

As far as the factual profile is concerned, since access, and not possession, which typically refers to physical *res*, represents the characteristic trait of the individual's relationship with digital goods, the rights that have this as their object aim to ensure precisely access to certain contents, so that, once their use is guaranteed, the user can make the use to which he is legitimized and which pleases him most (i.e. copy, distribute or analyse them).[95]

A special case is, however, exclusive access, which is permitted to the extent that the digital content is kept secret or used confidentially.

As far as the legal profile is concerned, since digitality concerns goods whose boundaries cannot always be as clear and defined as those of physical *res*, access to digital content may or may not be accompanied by the transfer of a right of ownership, with the result that ownership in these cases should be conceived not so much as a predefined monolith, but rather as a bundle of different and variable faculties.

It should also be considered that digital goods, by their intrinsic nature, tend to be subject to non-exclusive and concurrent use, which does not theoretically alter their value structure.

It is precisely from this perspective that the legal system, in some cases, can prevent the use of certain digital content that goes beyond the prior assignment of full ownership, as occurs, for instance, in the area of data protection. As is the case with personality rights, in fact, data protection does not respond to a need for allocation of resources, and, unlike property rights, cannot be assigned, although it can still be the subject of contractual relations, thus raising the problem of assessing data protection as a form of quasi–intellectual property.[96]

In this regard, in fact, a classic distinction must be drawn between movable and immovable property, where only with respect to the former, ownership follows whoever has physical control over it, where, with respect to the latter, only possibly, whoever is physically on a piece of land and enjoys it is its owner.

In the Italian legal system, an approach aimed at protecting de facto control over the movable thing is confirmed by the rule under Article 1153 of the Italian Civil

95 H. Zech, *Data as a Tradeable Commodity*, in *European Contract Law and the Digital Single Market. The Implications of the Digital Revolution*, edited by A. De Franceschi, Cambridge, 2016, p. 51 ff.; N. Filatova-Bilous, *Data as a Tradeable Commodity: Propertization vs. the Concept of Exclusive Rights*, in *Teisė*, 124, 2022, p. 55 ff., *Law/Teisė*, 85, where the author, at pp. 63 and 64, states that «[I]n the modern world data (including personal data, nonpersonal data, masses of data etc.) have a significant economic value and often become objects or a payment in various contracts. That is why it is important to determine the legal nature of data and rights to them both at the theoretical and legislative levels. The theory of propertization which nowadays is one of the most prominent in the world allows lawyers to consider data as a separate alienable object, whereas rights to data have an absolute nature.

However, this theory is hardly compatible with the classical doctrine of ownership under continental law. That is why the exclusive rights theory which considers rights to data as the rights similar to IP rights seems to be preferable».

96 *See* C. Langhanke, M. Schmidt-Kessel, *Consumer Data as Consideration*, in *J. Eur. Consumer Market Law*, 2015, p. 221 ff.

Code, which meets the need both to introduce presumptions (albeit not *iuris et de iure*)[97] based on the *id quod plerumque accidit* and to clarify, in economic terms, the proprietary situations involved: Italian law places a burden of verification on the owner which, at the same time, spares the purchaser.

The result is an increase in the value of ownership of furniture because the economic system incorporates, in its favour, a (juridical) correspondence between physical control and ownership that enhances the security of traffic,[98] but this model, strongly centred on the protection of the purchaser *a non domino* (who bought from person who was not the real owner) against the eventual owner, is not fully reflected in all systems.

In common law, in fact, the proprietary scheme used contemplates much less protection of the *non-domino* purchaser than of the owner, so that the owner is incentivized to check the provenance of the goods more carefully, on the one hand, and, at the same time, discouraged from taking adequate precautions, on the other.

With regard to real estate, the scarcity of land ownership means that individuals with a title other than dominical title often insist on the same parcel of land,[99] hence the need to ensure certainty to the subjective situations by means of verification other than mere material availability.[100]

It becomes necessary, then, to specify the spheres of ownership, so as to break down the uncertainty that follows the mere recognition of possession and to encourage the use of instruments to formalize the right: the precise identification of legal ownership takes on a value of public importance that is better guaranteed and protected with the use of collective instruments.[101]

It is in this perspective, in fact, that the analyses conducted using economic methodologies and dealing with the system of property rights, focus on a definition of property as a complex of socio-economic relations that qualify the position of the individual with respect to the use of scarce resources.[102]

97 The need to provide for balancing is expressed, in the Italian legal system, by the requirement in Article 1153 of the Italian Civil Code that "good faith" and "suitable title" are required in order for an effective non-domino purchase to actually take place. In other systems, however, the rules of non-domino purchase exclude, for example, stolen goods.

98 *See*, for further details, A. Gambaro, *Il diritto di proprietà*, Milano, 1995, p. 672 ff. and p. 708 ff.

99 *See, ex multis*, C.B. MacPherson, *Democratic Theory. Essays in Retrieval*, Oxford, 1973, p. 131 ff., according to whom property would represent a means of constructing human relations in a reality characterized by an inevitable physical scarcity: proprietary relations configure legal instruments aimed at ensuring that the subject owner has a right to a material income.

100 A similar approach is found, however, with respect to special categories of movable property, i.e. registered movable property, which, differing from other movable property, are subject to a regime similar to that reserved to landed property, by reason of their connatural tendency to be a potential source of liability and damage that need to be subjectively allocated.

101 It is no coincidence, then, that movable and immovable property cannot be subject to similar rules of disclosure.

102 *See, ex multis*, H. Demesetz, *Toward a Theory of Property Rights*, in *Am. Econ. Rev.*, 2, 1957, p. 347 ff.; E.G. Furutbom, S. Pejovich, *Property Rights and Economic Theory: A Survey of Recent Literature*, in *J. Econ. Lit.*, 4, 1972, p. 1137 ff.; B.A. Ackermann, *Economic Foundations of Property Law*, Boston, MA and Toronto, 1975; S. Rodotà, *Il terribile diritto*, cit, p. 61, where the author, referring to these economic approaches to property, speaks of a «[D]efinizione nella sostanza tutt'altro che originale, ma che spinge a riflettere sui limiti entro cui è possibile utilizzare

Nonetheless, de facto control also assumes significant importance in the real estate sphere for relevant legal consequences, such as usucaption, to occur.

In essence, the profound connection between property and *res (mobile) corporalis*, which appears so evident in civil law systems (Italy, France and Germany), is rooted, even historically, in the expulsion from the logic of ownership of those powers which, although relative to the property, do not present a physical connection with it.[103]

Thus, a divergence is realized with respect to the attitude matured in common law, where this classic contraposition is not realized, and, at an epistemological level, the distinction is made between absolute and relative property in all the nuances and meanings that this concept can assume,[104] although, in the end, the complex reality underlying the proprietary institution is the multifocal vision typical of Anglo-Saxon jurists that disentangles property, according to Hohfeld's approach and his so-called bundle of rights,[105] into rights, privileges, powers, immunities, duties and subjugations.[106]

---

il riferimento alla proprietà» («[D]efinition that is in essence far from original, but which prompts reflection on the limits within which it is possible to use the reference to property»); R.A. Posner, *Economic Analysis of Law*, New York, NY, 2014, *passim*.

103 Relevant on this subject are classics such as R. Sacco, *La proprietà*, Milano, 1968; A. De Vita, *La proprietà nell'esperienza giuridica contemporanea. Analisi comparativa del diritto francese*, Milano, 1969; P.G. Monateri, *La sineddoche*, Milano, 1984; and, from a historical point of view, cfr. P. Grossi, *Il dominio e le cose. Percezioni medievali e moderne dei diritti reali*, in *Per la storia del pensiero giuridico moderno*, 41, Milano, 1992, p. 57 ff.; id., *L'ordine giuridico medievale*, Bari, 1995.

104 The common law even subtracts the major problems related to land enjoyment or land use from the proprietary sphere, bringing them back to tort law in the species of the law of nuisances, thus demonstrating how land use is perceived in the dimension of subjection (to the neighbour) and not in that of powers. See, for more details, A. Candian, A. Gambaro, B. Pozzo, *Property, Propriété, Eigentum*, Padova, 1992; U. Mattei, *Common law. Il diritto anglo-americano*, Torino, 1992, p. 79 ff.

105 *See* W.N. Hohfeld, *Fundamental Legal Conceptions as Applied in Judicial Reasoning by Wesley Newcomb Hohfeld*, edited by D. Campbell and P. Thomas, Abingdon and New York, NY, 2016, p. 7 ff., wherein the author describes property as a so-called bundle of rights, i.e. as a set of legal relations between persons centred on the dominion of the thing, on the relationship between owner and good and on every bodily consideration of its object. *See*, for more on the Hohfeldian approach, T.C. Grey, *The Disintegration of Property*, in *Property: Nomos XXII*, edited by J.R. Pennock and J.W. Chapman, New York, NY, 1980, p. 69, where the author underlines that «[B]y contrast, the theory of property rights held by the modern specialist tends both to dissolve the notion of ownership and to eliminate any necessary connection between property rights and thing»; K.J. Vandevelde, *The New Property of Nineteenth Century. The Development of the Modern Concept of Property*, in *Buffalo Law Rev.*, 29, 1980, p. 325 ff.; J. Waldron, *What Is Private Property?*, in *Oxford J. Legal Stud.*, 3, 1985, p. 313 ff.: J.E. Cribbet, *Concepts in Transition: the Search for a New Definition of Property*, in *Univ. Ill. Law Rev.*, 1, 1986, p. 1 ff.; J.E. Penner, *The Bundle of Rights Picture of Property*, in *UCLA Law Rev.*, 43, 1996, p. 711 ff.; S.R. Munzer, *Property as Social Relations*, in *New Essays in the Legal and Political Theory of Property*, edited by S.R. Munzer, Cambridge, 2001, p. 36 ff.; J.W. Singer, *Property*, New York, NY, 2017, spec. p. 2 ff.; and, against the idea of a so-called bundle of rights approach, for all, A. Mossoff, *What Is Property? Putting the Pieces Back Together*, in *Ariz. Law Rev.*, 45, 2003, p. 371 ff., where the author states, at p. 374, that «[. . .] as with any bundle of items – say a shopping bag of fruit, filled with oranges, apples, bananas and peaches – people are free to pack it and rearrange it in whatever way they see fit». *See*, for more details, *infra* Chapter 3, § 4.

106 *See*, for an interesting application of the bundle of rights theory to the digital dimension also as a consequence of the launch of the Data Act, M. Eckart, W. Kerber, *Property Rights Theory,*

More specifically, Hohfeld's analysis, later taken up by Honoré,[107] identifies a series of fundamental aspects that should characterize the notion of property rights and be useful to grasp, once broken down, the founding features of dominical law.[108]

Thus, beyond their abstract character that allows one to go beyond the specificities of the individual positive system, the qualifying importance of the characteristics identified would be such as to bind to their presence the concrete existence of the proprietary institution, but with the clear peculiarity that their integral and contextual presence would not be necessary to configure a property right.

In fact, the bundle of powers thus identified, in addition to being characterized by a reciprocal independence that allows their possible disjointed circulation, would make it possible to distinguish property from other legal situations, without any necessary exclusion from the abstract scheme of ownership being derived from the possible absence of certain traits.

From a legal-economic perspective, on the other hand, it can be seen that the more evident are the features of mobility of an asset, the more utility will derive from the circulation of the *res*, where, on the contrary, the more marked are the features of immobility, the more utility will be connected to the enjoyment of the *res*.

With regard to this last profile, it follows, then, that the easier it is to resolve the problems connected to the immobile nature of the *res*, the more accentuated is its proximity to the property itself and, therefore, its public and local nature.[109]

Bundles of Rights on IoT Data, and the Data Act, in *Eur. J. Law Econ.*, 2024, forthcoming, available at https://ssrn.com/abstract=4376833, where the authors, analysing how the DA will change the bundle of rights on non-personal IoT data regarding who can control, access, use, share, and monetize this data, affirm that «[W]ith the advance of smart IoT devices (Internet of Things) the amount of valuable data will increase dramatically. With its recently enacted Data Act (DA) the EU introduces new data access and sharing rights for the users of IoT devices. [. . .] Since the DA is not very clear and partly contradictory, three different concepts for the design of this bundle of rights are analyzed and compared: A data holder-centric IP-like concept, a user-centric concept, and the concept of co-generated data. [. . .] For achieving the objectives of the DA, especially regarding unlocking of data for innovation, bundles of rights should be chosen which reject notions of exclusivity and enable broad access and sharing of IoT data. The enacted Data Act, which still clings too much to the exclusivity of data and includes too many hurdles for data sharing, cannot be expected to contribute much to achieving these objectives».

107 A.M. Honoré, *Ownership*, in *Oxford Essays on Jurisprudence*, edited by A.G. Guest, Oxford, 1961, p. 107 ff., who, in defining the proprietary prerogatives that make up the bundle regardless of the material type of scarce resource owned, identifies its objective traits in the right to possess (right to exclusive possession), in the right to use (right to personal enjoyment), in the right to manage (right to control and monitor the use that others may make of it), in the right to the income (right to the income that follows the use of it by others), in the right to the capital (right to the value of the capital), the right to security (right to the security of the subjective proprietary situation), in the incident of transmissibility (right to transfer), in the incident of absence of term (right to the absence of conditionings in the exercise of the various proprietary rights), in the prohibition of harmful use (duty to use the scarce resource without harming others), in the liability to execution (subjection to forced execution for the payment of debts) and in the residuary character (residual rights linked to the elasticity of the domain).

108 *See infra* Chapter 3, § 4.

109 In this regard, it is possible to make reference, for example, to the problem of immissions that Article 844 of the Italian Civil Code resolves by providing an explicit limit anchored to a "normal

In general terms, and always from the point of view of the economic analysis of law, the competitive mechanism directed to the acquisition of the ownership of a specific asset, to which the corresponding interest of the individual is linked, will be activated if the difference between the benefits that he can obtain by exercising the faculties and powers linked to the *res*, and the costs that he can derive from the relative obligations and subjection, is positive.[110]

The positivity or negativity of land enjoyment is, thus, influenced by the complex character of the landed property that results from the potential conditioning arising from neighbouring properties.[111]

An expression of the positive signs deriving from land ownership is found in Articles 840 and 841 of the Italian Civil Code,[112] which, albeit with due exceptions, identify, on the one hand, the possible extension of the proprietary right, and, on the other, the power to exclude outsiders from the material boundaries of the property, linking up, in general, with the Anglo-Saxon land law tradition on the subject of fencing's power, and revealing, at the same time, the influence that has been exercised on this subject on the Italian Civil Code by both Article 544 of the French Civil Code and by the doctrine of the right of exclusion (*Verbietungsrecht*) taken from § 903 of the German BGB.

The examination of real property highlights the complex nature of this right, which, however, does not seem to be repeated for the ownership of movable property, whose content, from the point of view of enjoyment, appears much more simplified.

Precisely because the right is differentiated in the face of two subjective situations that can be read as expressions of an analogous juridical-economic phenomenon, it follows that the right of ownership seems to represent a (juridical) form of wealth allocation and organization whose efficiency is conditioned by the nature of the asset that is its object.

The truthfulness of this assumption is such that the most relevant legal problems related to property emerge precisely at the moment when one proceeds to the legal organization of the effects of its substitution or, more technically, its disposition:

---

tolerability" that refers, however, to the "condition of the premises." *See*, in general on the subject, A. Gambaro, *La proprietà. Beni, proprietà, possesso*, cit., p. 304 ff.

110 *See* A. Gambaro, *La proprietà. Beni, proprietà, possesso*, cit., p. 218 ff.

111 It should be noted that, unlike modern property logic, which does not focus on a vision of ownership as a unitary, autonomous and isolated entity, the Romanist tradition considered the various landed estates as non-communicating and impermeable monads. *See*, for further discussion, P. Barcellona, *L'individualismo proprietario*, Torino, 1987, *passim*; P. Grossi, *Il dominio e le cose. Percezioni medievali e moderne dei diritti reali*, cit., p. 153 ff.

112 Articles 840 and 841 of the Italian Civil Code, like the provisions of similar scope found in other legal systems, express the owner's freedom to do what he pleases with the whole of his property, where there are no foreclosures preventing him from doing so. This approach, in fact, turns out to be the fruit of the provision of Article 832 of the Civil Code, according to which «[I]l proprietario ha diritto di godere delle cose in modo pieno ed esclusivo entro i limiti e con l'osservanza degli obblighi stabiliti dall'ordinamento giuridico» («[T]he owner has the right to enjoy things fully and exclusively within the limits and with the observance of the obligations established by the legal system»).

due, on the one hand, to the easy substitutability of the *res* mobile, and, on the other, to the difficulty of controlling the consequences connected to its substitution, the scope of which increases due to the possibility of easily moving the property from its place.[113]

But could such a vision become even more dynamic and liquid when referring to intellectual property and, *a fortiori*, to digital goods?

One may, therefore, consider that, just as enjoyment seems to be the benchmark to be used for the analysis of immovable property, so the provision seems to stand as the paradigm to be appealed to for the study of movable property, all reflecting the structural diversity existing between movable property and real estate.[114]

On closer inspection, in fact, property, as an institution of civil law, presents a complex and not fully univocal structure, although civil law tradition has identified the *ius excludendi omnes alios* as an indisputable trait.

The right to exclude, better than any other fundamental character of property, succeeds in giving legal substance to the economic character of the institution, as recognition of the idiosyncratic evaluations of the owner,[115] linking it to the market, i.e. to the place that, through the price mechanism, informs the complex of evaluations of attraction or repulsion that are the responsibility of the individual.[116]

This assumption appears valid, although the utility of the goods constituting the object of the property not only does not appear, since it is common ground that the non-use of the *res* does not entail any legal consequences,[117] but it cannot appear

113 It is worth noting, in fact, that the most significant legal questions arise precisely at the moment when the movable property is transferred.

114 *See* U. Mattei, voce *Proprietà (nuove forme di)*, in *Enciclopedia del diritto*, V, Milano, 2012, p. 434.

115 In the world of common law the particular and exclusive relationship between subject and property is framed in the concept of entitlement. *See*, in this regard, U. Mattei, *Tutela inibitoria e tutela risarcitoria*, Milan, 1987, p. 89, where the author states that «[U]n *entitlement* viene definito come la legittimazione di una parte a prevalere su di un'altra nel caso di conflitto fra le due dovuto ad interessi incompatibili. Quale delle due o più parti debba prevalere va deciso dall'ordinamento giuridico se si vuole evitare che la legittimazione sia decisa dalle legge del più forte. Una volta allocato, l'*entitlement* va protetto in maniera da garantirne l'effettività» («[A]n entitlement is defined as the legitimacy of one party to prevail over another in the case of conflict between the two due to incompatible interests. Which of the two or more parties should prevail is to be decided by the legal system if legitimacy is not to be decided by the law of the stronger party. Once allocated, the entitlement must be protected in a manner that ensures its effectiveness»).

116 *See* A. Gambaro, *La proprietà*, in *Trattato dei diritti reali. I. Proprietà e possesso*, a cura di A. Gambaro e U. Morello, Milano, 2008, p. 307; U. Mattei, voce *Proprietà (nuove forme di)*, cit., p. 439.

117 Although the traditional and widely shared thesis whereby utility characterizes the good, representing its essential characteristic, gives force to the assumption that it is up to the legal system to identify, on the basis of its own scale of values, the goods worthy of protection, the direct connection between utility for man and susceptibility to individual appropriation does not follow. Such an approach, in fact, is easily called into doubt by observing how the legal system does not cease to protect the owner of a good merely because the good that is the subject of the right does not realize any advantage for its owner. *See* O.T. Scozzafava, *I beni e le forme giuridiche di appartenenza*, Milano, 1982, p. 8 ff.

if not as an evaluation of subjective and idiosyncratic utility, precisely, which can certainly enhance individual advantages not shared by other subjects.[118]

A further structural datum of property is the power relationship that the owner (subjective valence) establishes with a given object (objective valence), from which derives, as a potential negative consequence,[119] the responsibility that, according to a legal-economic approach, makes property the natural centre of reference and absorption of externalities.[120]

In essence, in order to grasp the actual legal scope of the ownership structure, also in order to recognize its role as an ordering concept suitable for organizing and understanding the articulated private relationships of the current digital world, it is necessary to go beyond the idea of formal ownership alone in order to also focus on factual situations, and therefore on the possession and actual material availability of the asset.[121]

118 *See* A. Gambaro, *I beni*, cit., p. 15.

119 From the perspective of an economic analysis of law concerning the relationship between property rights and property rules, it is observed that an entitlement can only be effectively strengthened by the provision of an adequate remedy *in rem*. Only in these terms can full protection and, consequently, an authentic property right be achieved. The entitlement-property rule pair, however, would place the holder in such an advantageous position as to enable him to take advantage of conflict situations: only a discretionary intervention of the judicial authority directed to the possible granting of the remedy could redress this imbalance. *See* U. Mattei, *Tutela inibitoria e tutela risarcitoria*, cit., p. 122 ff. and p. 129 ff.

120 An externality is present when the outcome of a market transaction conditions the welfare of subjects who are not involved in it, because they are third parties to the buyer and seller. The impact on the overall welfare of third parties implies, therefore, that externalities do not guarantee an efficient allocation of resources if they are not taken into account in the analysis of the effects of the negotiation due to the so-called collective interest in the market outcome. *See*, for more details, U. Mattei, *Tutela inibitoria e tutela risarcitoria*, cit., p. 113 ff.; R. Cooter, U. Mattei, P.G. Monateri, R. pardolesi, T. Ulen, *Il mercato delle regole. Analisi economica del diritto civile. I*, Bologna, 2006, p. 61 ff.

121 If we go beyond what is affirmed by monistic-positivistic logic, in fact, we realize how property is a right that is anything but simple to grasp in its actual scope, because, in reality, it requires, in addition to the state production rules concerning it, further sources of a constitutional, codictic, legal and regulatory nature, without neglecting the jurisprudential and factual sources. In essence, a complex of factors contribute to the regulation of property, some of which have a political value, and others a technical-legal-cultural value. Cfr., for in-depth studies in this sense, A. Gambaro, *Il diritto di proprietà*, cit., p. 675 ff.; P. Grossi, *L'ordine giuridico medievale*, Roma-Bari, 1997, esp. p. 52 ff. This perspective thus goes beyond the identification of law in the set of written norms in force in a given national system to embrace the idea that Sacco had expressed many years ago, according to which the law of a country is produced by a plurality of sources of which positive law is an expression: the law is also formed by doctrine (think, for example, of the vast problem of the so-called new properties, of which the law is a part, and which is an expression of the law of the Middle Ages). so called new properties, of which digital property is an expression) and by jurisprudence (think, for example, of the evolutionary interpretation to which article 700 c.p.c. on the subject of radio-television property has been subjected), from which the rules of fact applied originate. *See*, most recently, R. Sacco, *Introduzione al diritto comparato*, Torino, 2015, *passim*; A. Gambaro, *La proprietà*, cit., p. 160 ff., where the author, at pp. 162 and 163, observes that «[. . .] il sistema delle fonti dell'istituzione proprietaria è complesso, e comprende, non sorprendentemente data la rilevanza centrale dell'istituzione nel sistema giuridico complessivo, tutte le possibili fonti del diritto: costituzioni, codici, altre leggi generali e speciali, regolamenti ed altre fonti sub legali,

Are similar assumptions also valid for intellectual property and intangible goods?[122]

ed anche, sebbene il punto sia disputato, gli atti di autonomia privata. La pluralità di fonti implica una gerarchia, ma anche una specializzazione, posto che tale pluralità non dipende da un capriccio della storia, ma dalla ricerca razionale del tipo di fonte più adatto a regolare lo specifico aspetto che in ciascuna di esse viene considerato» («[. . .] the system of sources of the proprietary institution is complex, and includes, not surprisingly given the central importance of the institution in the overall legal system, all the possible sources of law: constitutions, codes, other general and special laws, regulations and other sub-legal sources, and also, although the point is disputed, acts of private autonomy. The plurality of sources implies a hierarchy, but also a specialisation, given that this plurality does not depend on a whim of history, but on the rational search for the type of source best suited to regulating the specific aspect considered in each of them»).

122 On the subject of property, the terminological ambiguity that Article 810 of the Italian Civil Code has engendered in the Italian legal system is confirmed by the tendency of both regulatory sources and legal literature to use, in a promiscuous and undifferentiated manner, the term "thing" or "good," often even using it synonymously, where the very letter of Article 810 of the Italian Civil Code seems to distinguish, at least conceptually, the two terms. In this latter respect, it should be noted, however, how the Civil Code itself contains numerous provisions referring to the "thing," where one might expect the use of "good" for the consideration of the entity as the object of rights or part of a patrimony. By way of example only, it is sufficient to consider the reference to "a thing of the estate" in Article 535 of the Italian Civil Code, to the "thing that forms the subject matter of the disposition" in Article 625 of the Italian Civil Code, to the "movable thing" in Article 932 of the Italian Civil Code, or to the "ownership of a thing" in Article 1470 of the Italian Civil Code. *See*, in the sense of considering that patrimoniality represents the only discretional criterion of the good with respect to the thing, K.P. Polanyi, *La grande trasformazione. Le origini economiche e politiche della nostra epoca*, Torino, 1974, p. 210 ff.; M. Barcellona, *Attribuzione normativa e mercato nella teoria dei beni giuridici*, in Quadr., 1987, p. 607 ff.; P. Barcellona, *Diritto privato e società moderna*, Napoli, 1996, p. 245, where the author states that, following the criterion of patrimoniality, «[. . .] una situazione è o non è patrimoniale non in base a giudizi formulabili a priori, ma in base alla decisione che in ordine ad essa il mercato viene a maturare, ancorché entro limiti inderogabili eventualmente posti dal sistema medesimo» («[. . .] a situation is or is not patrimonial not on the basis of a priori formulated judgments, but on the basis of the decision that the market makes regarding it, even if within the mandatory limits that may be set by the system itself»). *See*, in a perspective of identification of the good with the thing, among others, B. Biondi, *I beni*, cit., p. 5, where the author states that «[. . .] le nozioni di cosa e di bene coincidono» («[. . .] the notions of thing and good coincide»); R. Franceschelli, *L'oggetto del rapporto giuridico (con riguardo ai rapporti di diritto industriale)*, in *Riv. trim. dir. proc. civ.*, 1957, p. 2 ff.; e, *contra*, V. Zeno-Zencovich, voce *Cosa*, in *Digesto discipline privatistiche – Sez. civ.*, IX, Torino, 1989, p. 439, where the author states that «Non vi è tuttavia una identificazione fra "bene" e "cosa" come da taluni sostenuto, giacché e chiaro che non tutte le cose sono beni, ma solo quelle suscettibili di formare oggetto di diritti» («There is however no identification between "good" and "thing" as claimed by some, since it is clear that not all things are goods, but only those susceptible of forming the subject matter of rights»). The uncertain nature that characterizes the provision, however, has avoided the affirmation of those materialistic limitations that, for example, in the German legal system, § 90 BGB has, on the contrary, determined, traditionally circumscribing property to the materiality of goods. *See*, in favour of an ambiguity that avoided rigid classificatory divisions of normative origin, D. Messinetti, voce *Oggetto dei diritti*, in *Enciclopedia del diritto*, XXIX, Milano, 1979, p. 812; A. Jannarelli, *Beni, interessi e valori*, in *Diritto privato europeo. I*, a cura di N. Lipari, Milano, 1997, p. 337; U. Mattei, voce *Proprietà (nuove forme di)*, cit., p. 434; O.T. Scozzafava, *Dei beni. Artt. 810–821*, in *Il Codice civile. Commentario*, diretto da P. Schlesinger, Milano, 1999, p. 5 ff.; M. Costantino, *I beni in generale*, in *Tratt. di diritto privato. Proprietà. I*, diretto da P. Rescigno, Torino, 2005, p. 36; A. Gambaro, *La proprietà. Beni, proprietà, possesso*,

Without prejudice to the partition that is classically made, at a material level, between movable and immovable property – which, in part, has been overcome by the unitary vision affirmed by Article 832 of the Italian Civil Code[123] – it can be considered that property on intangible goods is not differentiated from property on tangible goods.

Immateriality is a characteristic that brings with it the extreme difficulty of excluding other subjects from the enjoyment of the same asset, hence, theoretically, the non-full practicability of the legal rules that, drawn up considering only tangible assets and their particular needs, focus on the enhancement of exclusivity.

Therefore, even in the absolute awareness that the ownership rules in force in the national system do not, of necessity, require the presence of a tangible asset to refer to,[124] property remains, even in its immateriality, an indispensable legal institution both to stimulate economic development and to allocate resources effectively.

---

cit., p. 165 ff. *See*, on the concept of immaterial good substantially identified with the creations of the human mind, Franceschelli, *Beni immateriali (Saggio di una critica del concetto)*, in *Riv. dir. ind.*, I, 1956, p. 381 ff., where the author pronounces himself in the sense of the indispensability of such a juridical qualification; P. Greco, voce *Beni immateriali*, in *Novissimo digesto italiano*, Torino, 1958, p. 356 ff.; M. Are, voce *Beni immateriali*, in *Enciclopedia del diritto*, V, Milano, 1959, p. 251 ff.; T. Ascarelli, *Teoria della concorrenza e dei beni immateriali*, Milano, 1960, p. 233 ff., where the author speaks of intangible assets as entities that, unlike tangible things and energies, originate and are protected by the legal system not on the basis of their essence, but by reason of a normative choice that, taking note of a pre-legal reality, regulates the constitutive case in point; F. Ferrarra, *Prefazione a Dunoyer. Teoria dei prodotti immateriali*, Torino, 1961, p. 357 ff., where the author pronounces himself substantially in the sense of the uselessness of the category; D. Messinetti, voce *Beni immateriali (diritto privato)*, in *Enciclopedia del diritto*, V, Rome, 1988, p. 10 ff.; P. Perlingieri, *Il diritto civile nella legalità costituzionale*, Napoli, 1991, p. 459 ff.; S. Pugliatti, *Dottrine generali del diritto civile*, Napoli, 1997, p. 58, where the author states that «[I] beni immateriali (diritto privato), in Enc. affirms that «[I]ntangible goods stand alongside tangible goods, because, like the latter, they constitute immediate objects of absolute rights, which in this respect behave like real rights, but differ profoundly from them [. . .] depending on the profoundly different nature of the object». *See*, for further discussion, *supra* note 82.

123 *See*, on the actual defining scope of article 832 of the Civil Code, P. Perlingieri, Introduction to the problem of "property," cit., p. 81 ff., where the author, at p. 85, criticizing the objectivist theory of property, states that «[L']art. 810 c.c. [. . .] definisce "beni" le cose che possono formare oggetto di diritti; orbene, si può osservare in generale che il bene oggetto di diritti non è il diritto, quindi il diritto di proprietà definito dall'art. 832 c.c. non e il bene in sé e per sé, ma semmai è la situazione giuridica soggettiva relativa al bene. [. . .] pertanto dire che la proprietà, o la teoria della proprietà, s'identifica con la teoria del bene, o dei beni, significa dire cosa solo parzialmente esatta, in quanto non esiste un'identificazione tra la teoria dei beni e la teoria della proprietà: la teoria dei beni, se c'è, è una teoria più ampia della teoria della proprietà» («[A]rt. 810 of the (Italian) Civil Code defines "goods" as the things that can be the subject of rights; well, it can be observed in general that the object of rights is not the right, therefore, the right of ownership as defined in Article 832 of the Civil Code is not the property in and of itself, but rather the subjective legal situation relating to the property. [. . .] therefore to say that property, or the theory of property, is identified with the theory of the good, or of goods, is to say something only partially accurate, since there is no identification between the theory of goods and the theory of property: the theory of goods, if there is one, is a broader theory than the theory of property»).

124 *See* U. Mattei, voce *Proprietà*, cit., p. 436; A. Gambaro, *La proprietà. Beni, proprietà, possesso*, cit., p. 218 ff.

To affirm, therefore, that, in the Italian legal system, legal situations having as their object intangible assets do not have a proprietary nature, is tantamount to denying, for the most part, the reality of things, even though, in the presence of such *res*, account must be taken of their particularities in order to respect and enhance their nature.

Allow it to be mentioned here that intangible goods could be allocated in accordance with the rule either protecting the first individual capable of controlling them (in essence, apprehension) or framing them in the light of the criteria belonging to land ownership (in essence, enjoyment).

According to the first canon, if, on the one hand, control would be associated with the disadvantageous effect of not being able to identify an owner until someone occupies the property, thus creating the so-called tragedy of the commons,[125] on the other hand, the rule based on first possession would be efficient insofar as it would facilitate the demonstration of ownership and, at the same time and consequently, discourage litigation.

According to the second canon, precisely because one is operating in the field of immateriality, the resulting proprietary rights would still be less delimited than with classical land ownership, but, conversely, the link established between ownership of the right and the property already allocated in ownership would avoid the possible so-called tragedy of the commons.

Ultimately, the particular immateriality associated with the digital world does nothing but re-propose in new declinations the traditional issues that jurists have long sought to address, but which, nevertheless, receive new impetus in a highly digitalized world.

125 G. Hardin, *The Tragedy of the Commons*, in *Science*, 162, 1968, p. 1243, where the author, at p. 1244, describing the idea of "tragedy in the commons," affirms that «[T]he tragedy of the commons develops in this way. Picture a pasture open to all. It is to be expected that each herdsman will try to keep as many cattle as possible on the commons. Such an arrangement may work reasonably satisfactorily for centuries because tribal wars, poaching, and disease keep the numbers of both man and beast well below the carrying capacity of the land. Finally, however, comes the day of reckoning, that is, the day when the long-desired goal of social stability becomes a reality. At this point, the inherent logic of the commons remorselessly generates tragedy. As a rational being, each herdsman seeks to maximize his gain. Explicitly or implicitly, more or less consciously, he asks, "What is the utility *to me* of adding one more animal to my herd?" This utility has one negative and one positive component. 1) The positive component is a function of the increment of one animal. Since the herdsman receives all the proceeds from the sale of the additional animal, the positive utility is nearly + 1) The negative component is a function of the additional overgrazing created by one more animal. Since, however, the effects of overgrazing are shared by all the herdsmen, the negative utility for any particular decision-making herdsman is only a fraction of – 1. Adding together the component partial utilities, the rational herdsman concludes that the only sensible course for him to pursue is to add another animal to his herd. And another; and another . . . . But this is the conclusion reached by each and every rational herdsman sharing a commons. Therein is the tragedy. Each man is locked into a system that compels him to increase his herd without limit – in a world that is limited. Ruin is the destination toward which all men rush, each pursuing his own best interest in a society that believes in the freedom of the commons. Freedom in a commons brings ruin to all».

5 Ownership and Access in the Digital Realm

Contracts whose subject matter is digital content may be based either on contractual obligations or on exclusive rights owned by one of the parties, so that if the party transfers its assets on a merely mandatory basis, the resulting legal certainty will be limited insofar as the contract will create binding relationships only for the contracting parties (so-called *inter partes* bindingness), unlike the case in which the contract provides for the transfer of a genuine right of ownership that per se is protectable vis-à-vis the entire community (so-called *erga omnes* bindingness).

More in detail, in the case of *inter partes* bindingness, the *de facto* exclusivity, which is secrecy, is only hardly marketable profile: even if know-how contracts are permissible and binding,[126] they require careful drafting which, despite best efforts, may not nullify possible causes of uncertainty.

Therefore, although the adoption of technical protection measures allows, at a practical level, a certain degree of exclusivity of use, without necessarily resorting to absolute secrecy, these instruments still appear difficult to use and articulate for the user, unlike what happens, on the other hand, in the presence of genuine exclusive rights concerning the use of digital content.[127]

126 *See Directive 2016/943 of the European Parliament and of the Council of 8 June 2016 on the Protection of Undisclosed Know-How and Business Information (Trade Secrets) Against Their Unlawful Acquisition, Use and Disclosure*, in *OJ L*, 157, 16 June 2016, p. 1 ff.

127 Technical protection measures are aimed at making the use of content confidential, without resorting to secrecy, so that the party can provide goods while retaining de facto control over their use. Clearly, these means of protection can be used not only with contents present on physical supports, but, without doubt, also with completely digital goods, so much so that these means have become an important instrument of control of this type of goods both in the case in which they are the subject of material supports, and in the case in which they are the object of downloading, and in the case where they are the object of streaming. The protection provided for by law operates in the same perspective, as evidenced, for example, by Directive 2001/29/EC of the European Parliament and of the Council of 22 May 2001 on the harmonisation of certain aspects of copyright and related rights in the information society (the so-called Infosac Directive), whose Articles 6 et seq. structure a de facto intellectual property whose operativeness is strictly correlated to the protection deriving from trade secret: exclusivity in fact is reinforced by the legal prohibition as expected by article 6(1) when it states that «Member States shall provide adequate legal protection against the circumvention of any effective technological measures [. . .]». *See Directive 2001/29/EC of the European Parliament and of the Council of 22 May 2001 on the Harmonisation of Certain Aspects of Copyright and Related Rights in the Information Society*, in *OJ L*, 167, 22 June 2001, p. 10 ff. As far as contracts concerning digital goods are concerned, there is a structural simplification of them, if they have technical protection measures, because the goods that are the subject matter, whether digital or corporeal, are in fact subject to reservation of use. In this regard, however, there is a risk that such protective measures could be used to unilaterally create exclusivity effects similar to those arising from intellectual property, without, however, following its system of "checks and balances." Contract law, however, especially thanks to the implicit mandatory guarantees and the verification of terms and conditions, can provide for effective control mechanisms, as demonstrated, for example, by the Proposal for a Directive of the European Parliament and of the Council on certain aspects concerning contracts for the supply of digital content, whose Article 6(1) (a), by providing that «[I]n order to conform with the contract, the digital content shall, where relevant [. . .] be of the quantity, quality, duration and version and shall possess functionality,

The presence of the latter subjective situations, in effect, would make the legal circulation of digital goods economically less burdensome,[128] since, on the one hand, standardized obligations are established and implemented, and, on the other hand, it is determined that the supplying party either transfers the entire right of ownership or simply ensures the use of the goods regardless of the presence of exclusive rights, as, for example, in the case of granting a licence.

In the case of situations governed by an *erga omnes* binding nature, on the other hand, the establishment of rights of use of digital assets or of rights analogous to ownership exercised over them must be considered as the way forward for the allocation of content that is realized through or in conjunction with exclusive rights: on the one hand, the classic property right that stands as a comprehensive right exercised over tangible *res*, and, on the other, the traditional intellectual property that manifests itself in the forms of patent law and copyright, operate in this matter as a model, albeit surrounded by neighbouring rights that appear less defined in their actual scope.

Before proceeding to a clearer definition of the profiles outlined above, it appears interesting to note that a primary criterion for assessing whether an attribution of power over an asset is realized in a manner similar to that found in the transfer of ownership, is represented by the shift in economic values.[129]

There is, in fact, a hierarchical relationship between the transferability of rights and the allocation of assets, since the former usually requires the transferability of economic entities, whereas the latter does not necessarily presuppose the assignability of active subjective positions.[130]

---

interoperability and other performance features such as accessibility, continuity and security, as required by the contract including in any pre-contractual information which forms integral part of the contract», could be objectively interpreted as being based on the reasonable expectation of the user and, in this way, used to counteract the unjustified recourse to technical protection measures. *See*, for more details, K. Sein, *What Rules Should Apply to Smart Consumer Goods: Goods With Embedded Digital Content in the Borderland Between the Digital Content Directive and Normal Contract Law*, in *J. Intellect. Prop. Inf. Technol. Elec. Com. Law*, 8(2), 2017, p. 96 ff.; S. Lohsse, R. Schulze, D. Staudenmayer, *Smart Products – A Focal Point for Legal Developments in the Digital Economy*, in *Smart Products*, Baden-Baden, 2022. p. 11 ff.

128 E.T. Vargas, E. Torres, *Legal Challenges of Digital Copyright Laws in the Circulation of Digital Content*, in *Law Econ.*, 3(1), 2024, p. 1 ff.

129 Consider, for example, Article 2(1)(b) which defines «trade secret» as «[. . .] information which [. . .] (b) [. . .] has commercial value because it is secret [. . .]».

130 B.T. Runolfsson, *Measuring Quality of Property Rights: Development of User Rights Quality in the Icelandic Fisheries*, in *Marine Pol.*, 160, 2024, p. 1 ff., where the author, at p. 1, asking herself if property law can have a consumer protection purpose, affirms that «one of the most important consumer law concerns today is the limited control consumers have over the digital assets and software-embedded products they purchase». Indeed, current proposals for reform focus on classifying the transaction as either "license" or "sale" and rely mostly on contract law and consumer protection regulation with a few calls for restoring ownership rights. As a consequence, the author affirms that property law can protect consumers by setting a minimal bundle of rights for consumers, the s.c. "the consumer bundle." Therefore, working with property theory and an analysis of property values, the author tries to explain the importance of users' ability to use and alienate digital and technological assets as part of a new property category for consumers. «These assets represent a new emerging resource that is currently managed and controlled by manufacturers and

Rather, it is sufficient that the subjective position being allocated, provided it is actually transferable,[131] confers a right of (commercial) use in a manner that does not imply its complete and definitive transfer to the user.

In more general terms, the notion of property classically established in the Italian legal system is characterized by the presence of certain essential elements, which are identified, as to the object of the right, with the corporeal thing,[132] as to the type of right, with typicality (so-called *numerus clausus*),[133] and as to the manner of exercising the right, with absoluteness, exclusiveness, fullness, perpetuity.[134]

Indeed, although we are aware that it is not possible here to fully reconstruct the map of the problems related to the definition of property, the restrictive notion of property derived from Article 810 of the Italian Civil Code[135] has stimulated a long debate that, in light of a literal interpretation of the provision, has led to identify the object of the right of ownership with only *res corporalis*.

Thus, the exercise of the right to property has traditionally been confined within the narrow limits of the physicality and apprehensibility of the entity on which the subjective situation lies.[136]

On the other hand, a different reading of Article 810 of the Italian Civil Code has held this interpretation to be incorrect because the legal nexus between goods and things on which the provision in question seems to be based is not, in reality, prescriptive in nature.[137]

---

platforms. The suggested consumer's bundle limits platforms' control, and protects use, alienability, and repair».

131 The faculties assigned must be able to be effectively exercised by a natural or legal person.

132 An exception to this assumption could, however, be found in intellectual property centred on an intellectual or creative work which, taken in and of itself, has very little material content. *See*, with reference to this effect, *infra*.

133 On closer inspection, this characteristic is more broadly referable to rights *in rem* in general. See, for an analysis of the rights *in rem*, M. Giorgianni, voce *Diritti reali*, in *Novississimo digesto italiano*, V, Torino, 1960, p. 748 ff.; G. Pugliese, voce *Diritti reali*, in *Enciclopedia del diritto*, XII, Milano, 1964, p. 758 ff.; L. Bigliazzi Geri, U. Breccia, F.D. Busnelli, U. Natoli, *Diritto civile. 2. I diritti reali*, Torino, 1996; M. Comporti, *Diritti reali in genere*, in *Trattato di diritto civile e commerciale*, già diretto da A. Cicu, F. Messineo e L. Mengoni continuato da P. Schlesinger, Milano, 2011, *passim*; A. Gambaro, U. Morello (diretto da), *Trattato dei diritti reali. Volume II. Diritti reali parziari*, 2011.

134 *See* C.M. Bianca, *Diritto civile. 6. La proprietà*, Milano, 2016, p. 151 ff.

135 According to Article 810 c.c. «Sono beni le cose che possono formare oggetto di diritti» (*author's note*, "goods are things that can be the subject of rights").

136 *See, ex multis*, A. Pino, *Contributo alla teoria giuridica dei beni*, in *Riv. trim. dir. proc. civ.*, I, 1948, p. 835 ff.; S. Satta, *Cose e beni nell'esecuzione forzata*, in *Riv. dir. comm.*, I, 1964, p. 350, where the author states that «[. . .] i beni sono sempre cose» (*author's note*, goods are always things).

137 *See*, for a view of the "thing" seen as a possible type of pre-legal entity, representing a separate part of the surrounding matter considered by law to verify its qualification in terms of the "good," i.e. the object of a legally relevant interest, and consequently recognizing a subjective legal situation coinciding with the right to property, F. Santoro-Passarelli, *Dottrine generali del diritto civile*, Napoli, 1964, p. 56; V. Zeno-Zencovich, voce *Cosa*, in *Dig. disc. priv. – Sez. civ.*, III, Torino, 1998, p. 438 ff. and esp. p. 447 ff.

In this regard, the dominant doctrine is in the sense of considering that the notions of "good" and "thing" present an autonomous and distinct value, since, on the one hand, the first lemma embodies a very broad legal concept substantially identifiable with the entities that are the subject of a relevant interest and that, for this reason, are worthy of protection by the legal system, and, on the other hand, the second lemma represents a classificatory criterion of extra-legal matrix that, based on the physicality of the entity considered, can be configured only in the presence of the character of corporality. It follows that things constitute only a part of the entities qualifiable as goods as worthy of protection, since they include in them both *res corporales*[138] and *res incorporales*[139] of Roman matrix.[140]

According to the proposed reconstruction, therefore, even intangible entities, where they are the subject of a relevant legal interest that makes them protectable by the legal system, can be brought back to the category of goods: by the will of the same legislator, the intangible entity thus identified becomes an intangible asset, or

138 It is about the material things that are the subject of property rights.

139 It is about the rights that insist on things, but which are not identified with property rights.

140 *See*, for further details on the distinction between *res corporales* and *res incorporales*, C. Fadda, P.E. Bensa, *Note alla Pandette di Windscheid. IV*, Torino, 1925, p. 153, where the authors underline that «[. . .] seguendo l'esempio romano della traslazione ai *diritti* di concetti originariamente propri delle *cose*» (*author's note*, following the Roman example of the transfer to rights of concepts originally belonging to things) it is possible to believe that «[. . .] in questi vi è ciò che costituisce l'essenza della proprietà: l'unica differenza e nell'oggetto: nella proprietà vera è una cosa corporale, qua è una cosa incorporale. Ma ciò che per un diritto è decisivo non è già l'*oggetto*, sibbene la relazione giuridica fra il titolare e questo oggetto, relazione che poggia sui due momenti del *contenuto* e della *tutela giuridica*» (*author's note*, "in these there is what constitutes the essence of property: the only difference is in the object: in real property it is a corporeal thing, here it is an incorporeal thing. But what is decisive for a right is not the object, but the legal relationship between the owner and this object, a relationship that rests on the two moments of content and legal protection"). *See*, on the relationship between tangible and intangible assets, *ex multis*, S. Rodotà, *Note critiche in tema di proprietà*, Milano, 1960, p. 1267 ff., where the author analyses the logical-functional relationship between property and other situations of ownership, such as those involving intangible assets; B. Biondi, *Istituzioni di diritto romano*, Milano, 1965, p. 152 ff.; F. Santoro-Passarelli, *Dottrine generali del diritto civile*, cit., p. 57, where the author, speaking of intangible goods and differentiating them from both coextensive and tangible goods, states that «[L]e opere dell'ingegno, scientifiche, letterarie, artistiche, interpretative, e le invenzioni industriali (art. 2575 c.c.) sono beni veramente nuovi, prodotti dallo spirito umano, importanti più di tutti gli altri, perché da essi principalmente dipende il progresso dell'umanità [. . .]. Queste opere si distinguono dalle cose, appunto perché, partecipando della stessa natura spirituale dell'intelligenza creatrice o inventrice di cui sono proiezioni, sono beni immateriali, i quali non vanno confusi col *corpus mechanicum* (libro, quadro, disco, ecc.), che quelle opere eventualmente racchiude» (*author's note*, "The intellectual, scientific, literary, artistic, interpretative works and industrial inventions – Article 2575 of the Italian Civil Code – are truly new goods, produced by the human spirit, more important than all the others, because the progress of mankind depends on them [. . .]. These works are distinguished from things, precisely because, participating in the same spiritual nature of the creative or inventing intelligence of which they are projections, they are immaterial goods, which are not to be confused with the corpus mechanicum [book, painting, disc, etc.], which those works may contain"); L. Moccia, *Riflessioni sull'idea di proprietà*, in *Riv. trim. dir. proc. civ.*, 1, 2008, p. 21 ff., where the author emphasizes how rights to intangible goods are offered to the interpreter as positive legal figures in order to facilitate their allocation in a market as similar as possible to that of tangible goods.

an asset worthy of protection, which when its object is a thing, pursuant to Article 832 of the Civil Code, becomes the subject of a subjective right of enjoyment.[141]

Intangible goods, then, are subject to the right of ownership and other real rights, because they are subject to an active subjective situation of an exclusive nature, which confers on its owner the full enjoyment of the relative object and the possibility of being opposed erga omnes, so as to configure a genuine right of exclusion.[142]

In a classical view, then, such a power of exclusion conditions the scope of the modern property right to such an extent that it is identified with it and constitutes its primary characteristic.

This *forma mentis*, however, which manifested its full maturity in the 18th and 19th centuries,[143] if not reinterpreted in the reality of the facts, runs the risk of being orbiting and losing a profound sense that is equally inherent in property and coincides with a character that is other than exclusion: property was expressed in the past and is also expressed in the present as the right not to be excluded from the use or benefit of something.

In this sense, then, one is induced to speak also of a different configuration that property can assume, the public one, which makes it a right legitimizing each member of the community of reference to benefit from the enjoyment and use of the goods of which this public dimension can be composed.[144]

The full spectrum of property can thus only be grasped by embracing both its public and private character, so as to encompass the set of individual rights that each human being can enjoy as a member of a given social body: if the first profile assures each individual the right to exclude others from the use or benefit of something (right of exclusion), the second assures him the right not to be excluded from the use or benefit of something else (right of inclusion).[145]

141 *See*, for further details, G. Pugliese, voce *Diritti reali*, in Enciclopedia del diritto, XII, Milano, 1964, p. 774 ff.; P. Rescigno, voce *Proprietà (diritto privato)*, in *Trattato di diritto privato*, Torino, 2002, p. 281 ff.; A. Gambaro, *La proprietà*, Milano, 2017, p. 38 ff.; L. Bigliazzi Geri, U. Breccia, F.D. Busnelli, U. Natoli, *Diritto civile. 2. I diritti reali*, Toriuno, 2007, p. 3 ff.; C. Salvi, *Il contenuto del diritto di proprietà. Artt. 832–833*, Milano, 1994, p. 83 ff.; M. Comporti, *Diritti reali in generale*, Milano, 1980, p. 124 ff.

142 *See*, on the concept of exclusivity, for all, P. Perlingieri, *Introduzione alla problematica della «proprietà»*, Napoli, 2011, p. 60 ff. *See*, for a synoptic reading of the common law approach to property law, *ex multis*, B.C. Field, *The Evolution of Property Rights*, in *Kyklos*, 42, 1989, p. 319 ff.; and, in this context, for a view particularly favourable to identifying ownership with the concept of exclusivity, T.W. Merrill, *Property and the Right to Exclude*, in *Neb. Law Rev.*, 77, 1998, p. 730 ff., where the author speaks of this trait as a *condicio sine qua non* of ownership; *contra*, for a more diluted view, S. Balganesh, *Demystifying the Right to Exclude: Of Property, Inviolability, and Automatic Injunctions*, in *Harv. J. Law Pub. Pol.*, 31, 2008, p. 593 ff.; H.E. Smith, *Property as the Law of Things*, in *Harv. Law Rev.*, 125, 2012, p. 1691 ff.

143 *See*, on the subject, P. Grossi, *Il dominio e le cose. Percezioni medievali e moderne dei diritti reali*, cit., p. 609 ff.

144 The classic reference is to goods such as parks, public roads, aqueducts, etc.

145 C.B. MacPherson, *Democratic Theory. Essays in Retrieval*, Oxford, 1973, p. 120 ff., ove l'A., a p. 125, evidenzia che, se non si procedesse in questa ottica duale, la *common property* «[. . .] drops virtually out of sight», and, at p. 131, emphasizes the desirability of recovering property rights

It should be added, then, that the right of ownership, like other rights *in rem*, in regulating, on the one hand, the relations existing between the owner and property, and, on the other, the relations the owner has with other subjects by virtue of his position, is characterized by a particular sensitivity to changing historical conditions, which, due to the emergence of new needs and interests, reverberates on its formal scheme.[146]

There is no doubt, in fact, that the right not to be excluded, as another profile but joint to the right to be included, takes on increasing weight in an increasingly digitized world, where technological development, progressively pervading the life of the individual, amplifies the possibility of use and exploitation of both physical goods, within the limits of their materiality, and non-physical goods, beyond all geographical and chronological limits (multiple and simultaneous access and use).

Therefore, historical evolution and economic development exert a profound impact on the traditional physiognomy of the institution, which, thanks to the recovery of the factual datum,[147] adapts to the changes to which the legal system is continually subject, so much so that the exclusivity of the right traditionally recognized for the scarcity of the good that is its object,[148] would also be confirmed for intangible goods, despite their acknowledged copiousness and possibility of non-rival use.[149]

---

also «[. . .] as an individual right not to be excluded from the use or benefit of the accumulated productive resources of the whole society». See, for more on the concept of inclusivity, *infra* Chapter 3, § 3.

146 Cfr. A. de Tocqueville, *Souvenirs*, Paris, 1942, p. 32, where, in an icastic manner, the author describes the impact of property law regulation on society, noting how «Bientôt ce sera entre ceux qui possèdent et ceux qui ne possèdent pas que s'établira la lutte politique; le grand champ de bataille sera la propriété».

147 Cfr. K. Olivecrona, *Il diritto come fatto*, milano, 1967, *passim*.

148 For all, S. Rodotà, *Il terribile diritto*, cit., p. 469 ff.

149 *See*, on this point, among others, C.B. MacPherson, *Democratic Theory. Essays in Retrieval*, cit., p. 139 ff., according to whom, when one has the possibility of satisfying one's material needs and desires, the organization of human relations with a view to excluding others from the enjoyment of a *res* begins to no longer make sense, to the benefit of a co-participative logic that gives due prominence to the enjoyment of immateriality; A. Iannarelli, *"Proprietà", "immateriale", "atipicità: i nuovi scenari di tutela*, in *Diritti esclusivi e nuovi beni immateriali*, a cura di G. Resta, Torino, 2010, p. 97 ff.; U. Mattei, *Beni comuni. Un manifesto*, Roma-Bari, 2011, p. 94 e 95, where the author affirms that «[. . .] al di là dei suggestivi paralleli teorici, per cui tanto la proprietà privata delle idee quanto quella di un fondo sarebbero caratterizzate dagli stessi aspetti di "esclusione" di chi non sia autorizzato dal titolare rispettivamente ad accedervi o a farne uso, le analogie sembrano fermarsi un livello di astrazione inadatto alla pratica del diritto. Sebbene anche in ambito fondiario [. . .] il processo di mercificazione abbia ottenuto i suoi effetti, la terra è una risorsa strutturalmente limitata, non riproducibile e tendenzialmente unica, e quindi la proprietà fondiaria è scarsa in natura. Questo aspetto fondamentale non è vero» (*author's note*, "beyond the suggestive theoretical parallels, whereby both the private ownership of ideas and that of a fund would be characterised by the same aspects of *exclusion* of those who are not authorised by the owner respectively to access or make use of it, the analogies seem to stop at a level of abstraction unsuitable for the practice of law. Although even in the realm of land [. . .] the process of commodification has achieved its effects, land is a structurally limited, non-reproducible and tendentially unique resource, and thus land ownership is scarce in nature. This fundamental aspect is not true") per i beni immateriali «[D]i fronte a risorse che in natura non sono scarse il diritto di proprietà svolge cioè la funzione

In this perspective, then, it is the classic typicality of real rights, which with respect to tangible goods finds justification in the legislative will to assign the faculty to exploit limited goods to certain subjects in order to regulate, at the same time, their use and avoid situations of conflict between several holders,[150] that could be repeated, on a dissimilar basis, with respect to intangible goods.[151]

If this were the case, in fact, one would grasp the differing will to delimit *ex lege* the exploitation of specific categories of goods of an informative[152] and highly inclusive nature that *ex se* are abundant or unlimited in nature,[153] because they are easily reproducible, easily subject to legal circulation and potentially susceptible to multiple enjoyment.

If, in effect, according to Article 832 of the Italian Civil Code two rights would be associated with property, that of "disposing of" and that of "enjoying," to be exercised within the limits and with observance of the duties provided for by the

---

di renderle artificialmente tali (a fine di trarne profitto), mentre per quelle che sono già scarse la proprietà privata, limitandone l'accesso, potrebbe tutt'al più limitarne il consumo, almeno stando all'insegnamento della *tragedia dei comuni*» (*author's note*, for intangible goods "[W]hen faced with resources that are not scarce in nature, the right to property performs the function of artificially making them so (in order to make a profit), while for those that are already scarce, private property, by limiting access to them, could at most limit their consumption, at least according to the teaching of the tragedy of the commons").

150 Y.C. Chang, H.E. Smith, *The Numerus Clausus Principle, Property Customs, and the Emergency of New Property Forms*, in *Iowa Law Rev.*, 100, 2014, p. 2275 ff.

151 *See* B. Rudden, *Economic Theory v. Property Law: The Numerus Clausus Problem*, in *Oxford Essays Jurisprud.*, III, 1987, p. 239 ff.; M.A. Heller, *The Boundaries of Private Property*, in *Yale Law J.*, 108, 1999, p. 1176 ff.; T.W. Merrill, H.A. Smith, *Optimal Standardization in the Law of Property: The Numerus Clausus Principle*, in *Yale Law J.*, 110, 2000, p. 1 ff.; H. Hansmann, R. Kraakman, *Property, Contract, and Verification: The Numerus Clausus Problem and the Divisibility of Rights*, in *J. Legal Stud.*, 31, 2002, p. 373 ff., where the authors, on p. 374, justify the typicality found with respect to rights *in rem*, unlike with respect to contracts, because «(1) Property rights differ from contract rights by being "good against all the world." (2) Both the common law and the civil law limit property rights to a small number (*numerus clausus*) of well-defined types. (3) These limits serve to reduce the information-processing costs of potential purchasers of property rights in understanding precisely what they are buying and of potential tortfeasors in understanding with which property rights they must not interfere. (4) More precisely, there is an "optimal standardization" of property rights, with the appropriate number of alternative forms being determined by a trade-off between the utility of having more forms and the confusion that more forms would engender»; S. Rodotà, *Il terribile diritto*, cit., p. 258 ff.; E. Ramaekers, B. Akkermans, *European-Autonomous Property Rights: Does the EU Operate Its Own Numerus Clausus?*, in *Eur. Rev. Priv. Law*, 27(4), 2019, p. 753 ff.

152 *See* H. Hansmann, R. Kraakman, *Property, Contract, and Verification: The Numerus Clausus Problem and the Divisibility of Rights*, cit., p. 380, where the authors, taking up the theory developed by Merrill and Smith, point out that «By limiting property rights to a finite set of standard forms, they claim, the law reduces the "information-processing costs" of all persons who seek to acquire property rights. Given such limits, a potential purchaser of an asset need only determine which of the various standard packages of rights is being offered to him. He need not also incur the costs of determining whether some other, nonstandard package of rights is being offered him, nor need he incur the "measurement costs" of ascertaining attributes of nonstandard rights that are hard to discern».

153 *See*, in this regard, S. Rodotà, *Il terribile diritto*, cit., esp. p. 448 ff.; D. Kelly, *The Right to Include*, in *Emory Law J.*, 63, 2014, p. 857 ff.; M. Ferrari, *Proprietà e diritto ad essere inclusi*, in *Riv. crit. dir. priv.*, 4, 2016, p. 525 ff.

legal system to which Article 42 of the Constitution refers, according to the classical view, in reality, these two subjective situations can be easily brought back to a broader concept of enjoyment in the full sense, which goes both in the sense of using, exploiting and profiting from the property and in the sense of modifying its productive organization (so-called *ius abutendi*).[154]

Therefore, since enjoyment thus understood embraces all forms of exploitation of the asset,[155] it can still characterize the right of ownership when it only has as its object certain faculties of enjoyment (so-called fractional rights), derivable from the regulatory system and variously limited.

With regard to absoluteness, then, the 18th-century philosophical-political approach found in the first bourgeois codes,[156] according to which the right of ownership consists in a legal claim recognized by the legal system in favour of the owner that is protected against any form of unauthorized interference, finds, in the national legal system, a reason for dilution in Article 42, paragraph 2, of the Italian Constitution, which not only provides limits to the absoluteness of the dominical position,[157] but also introduces a general ordering principle on which the entire institution of ownership is structured.[158]

154 M. Costantino, *Il diritto di proprietà*, in *Tratt. di diritto privato. Proprietà. I*, Torino, 1982, p. 261.

155 L. Stiegel, *An Overview of Elder Financial Exploitation*, in *Generations*, 36(2), 2012, p. 73 ff., where the author, at p. 73, affirms that «[V]ulnerability to financial exploitation increases as financial capacity decreases. Diminished capacity leads to bad decisions and an inability to detect or prevent exploitation, and a need for assistance with financial management that exposes an impaired person to "helpers" who can easily commit exploitation. Exploitation takes myriad forms; it is defined and addressed by diverse laws, disciplines, and systems, and it is not well researched. It is imperative that aging services and allied professionals who work with older persons lacking financial capacity learn how to prevent, detect, and remedy exploitation, and to collaborate with each other to achieve those goals».

156 *See* P. Grossi, *Il dominio e le cose. Percezioni medievali e moderne dei diritti reali*, Milano, 1992, p. 603 ff.; G. Alpa, *La cultura delle regole*, Roma-Bari, 2000, p. 53 ff.; P. Grossi, *L'Europa del diritto*, Roma-Bari, 2007, p. 113 ff.

157 The social function of property, expressed in Article 42 Italian Constitution, represents, in fact, through the reference to the reservation of the law, a catalyst for the needs to improve the conditions of citizens and as a balancing instrument between the protection of proprietary interests and the pursuit of non-individualistic purposes of collective well-being. *See*, for a view of the social function of property as a profile immanent to the institution and consequent to its flexible and adaptive character to the historical evolution of human society, S. Rodotà, *Note critiche in tema di proprietà*, cit., p. 1297 ff.; P. Perlingieri, *Introduzione alla problematica della «proprietà»*, cit., p. 61 ff., where the author, at p. 61, underlines that «[. . .] il proprietario allo stato attuale, non ha più poteri illimitati [. . .]. Insistere [. . .] sulla caratteristica della "illimitatezza" della proprietà significa per lo meno fare un'affermazione anacronistica. È possibile, al contrario, sostenere che oggi la proprietà è una situazione giuridica soggettiva estremamente limitata: c'è un ritorno – dal punto di vista dommatico, teorico, costruttivo – non tanto a quella concezione romana del diritto di proprietà come individuale, unica illimitata, bensì al periodo intermedio, limitatamente all'aspetto della pluralità dei domini, della pluralità dei possessi: ogni forma di diritto reale tende ad assumere una sua autonomia» (*author's note*, "the owner in his present state no longer has unlimited powers [. . .]. To insist [. . .] on the characteristic of the "unlimitedness" of property is at least to make an anachronistic statement. It is possible, on the contrary, to maintain that property today is an extremely limited subjective legal situation: there is a return – from the dommatic, theoretical, constructive point of view – not so much to the Roman conception of property law as individual, uniquely unlimited, but rather to the intermediate period, limited to the aspect of the plurality of domains, of the plurality of possessions: every form of real right tends to assume its own autonomy"); S. Rodotà, *Il terribile diritto*, cit., p. 241 ff.

158 Cfr. M. Costantino, *op. ult. cit.*, p. 251; S. Rodotà, *Il terribile diritto*, cit., p. 273 ff.; A. Iannarelli, *"Proprietà", "immateriale", "atipicità": i nuovi scenari di tutela*, in *Diritti esclusivi e nuovi*

Lastly, it can be schematically observed how perpetuity, as a typical feature of property,[159] recalls the same Romanistic origins to which this right is linked in the contemporary civil law approach, which, in addition to differing in this respect with respect to the typical structure assumed by property in common law,[160] raises the tricky question of the configurability and admissibility in the national legal system of temporary forms of property.[161]

The assumptions developed so far could, then, be extended to digital goods, which are identified with intangible goods by sharing, in addition to not being fully corporeal, the subjective situation of belonging to which they may constitute the object.[162]

The latter, in fact, once recognized by the legal system of reference, is part of a process of valorization of digital content under the triple profile of dissemination, protection and remuneration, thus not being able to exempt itself from the modern schemes of both private legal circulation and production and fruition proper to the exercise of business activities pursuant to Article 41 of the Italian Constitution.[163]

---

beni immateriali, a cura di G. Resta, Torino, 2011, p. 183, where the author considers that the trait of absoluteness tralatially referred to the right to property is only rhetorical and evocative in character.

159 S. Harding, *Perpetual Property*, in *Fla. L. Rev.*, 61, 2009, p. 285 ff., where the author, at p. 286, affirms that «Like the *numerus clausus* principle, these temporal limitations have been relatively tenacious, limiting the longevity and remote vesting of property interests for much of the recent history of the common law of property. The most infamous and controversial of these limitations is the somewhat quirky rule against perpetuities. But recently, many of these limitations have begun to disappear. In several discrete but significant areas of property law, temporal limitations are expanding beyond recognition or are disappearing altogether, giving rise to more enduring and, in some cases, more fragmented property interests. So while limitations on the forms of property interests remain relatively stable, limitations on the duration of some property interests are disappearing, giving rise to a growing number of perpetual property interests».

160 *See*, on the Anglo-Saxon concept of property, A. Gambaro, *La proprietà nel* common law *anglo-americano*, in *Property, Propriété, Eigentum*, Padova, 1992, p. 15 ff.; L. Moccia, *Il modello inglese di proprietà*, in *Diritto privato comparato*, a cura di L. Moccia, G. Alpa, D. Corapi, V. Zeno-Zencovich, J.M. Bonell, Roma-Bari, 2009, p. 43 ff.

161 *See*, for a comparative examination of the concept of property, C. van der Merwe, A.-L. Verbeke, *Time-Limited Interests in Land*, Cambridge, 2012, *passim*. Cfr., sul concetto di proprietà temporanea, *ex multis*, N. Di Prisco, *La proprietà temporanea*, Napoli, 1979; F. Santoro-Passarelli, voce *Proprietà*, cit., p. 660; A. De Cupis, *Pienezza e perpetuità della proprietà*, in *Riv. dir. civ.*, I, 1982, p. 165 ff.; R. Caterina, *I diritti sulle cose limitati nel tempo*, Milano, 2000.

162 *See*, in this regard, D. Quah, *Digital Goods and the New Economy*, in *CEP Discussion Paper*, 563, 2002, p. 1 ff., where the author, at p. 1, affirms that «Digital goods are bitstrings, sequences of 0s and 1s, that have economic value. They are distinguished from other goods by five characteristics: digital goods are nonrival, infinitely expansible, discrete, aspatial, and recombinant. The New Economy is one where the economics of digital goods importantly influence aggregate economic performance. This Article considers such influences not by hypothesizing ad hoc inefficiencies that the New Economy can purport to resolve, but instead by beginning from an Arrow-Debreu perspective and asking how digital goods affect outcomes. This approach sheds light on why property rights on digital goods differ from property rights in general, guaranteeing neither appropriate incentives nor social efficiency; provides further insight into why Open Source Software is a successful model of innovation and development in digital goods industries; and helps explain how geographical clustering matters».

163 *See*, on Article 41 of the Italian Constitution, *ex multis*, F. Galgano, *Art. 41*, in *Commentario della Costituzione. Art. 41–44. Rapporti economici. II*, a cura di G. Branca, Bologna-Roma, 1982, p. 1

Thus, the configuration of a market of digital goods, also carried out from an entrepreneurial viewpoint, finds a balance in the required social utility, to which Article 41, paragraph 2, of the Constitution refers, which postulates the carrying out of business activities according to logic that conforms to the social objectives referable to the right to property and such as not to be detrimental to the security, freedom and human dignity of all the economic operators involved in it.[164]

In the light of the overall legal framework described so far, the problem thus arises of assessing whether the subjective situations involving digital assets configure an authentic right of ownership that, however, behaves differently from what is found in the presence of a traditional ownership structure,[165] or whether rather a more limited and circumscribed situation is to be hypothesized because it can be likened to a mere right of use.[166]

---

ff.; G. Oppo, *L'iniziativa economica*, in *Riv. dir. civ.*, I, 1988, p. 309 ff.; G. Amato, *Il mercato nella costituzione*, in *Quad. cost.*, 1992, p. 7 ff.

164 *See*, for a reflection on the development of the networked market and its impact with respect to proprietary logics, U. Mattei, *Beni comuni. Un manifesto*, Roma-Bari, 2012, p. 95, where the author observes that «[. . .] se è vero che occorrono sempre recinzioni per far nascere un mercato, quelle necessarie di fronte all'informazione e alla conoscenza devono essere particolarmente pervasive. Infatti, il potenziale acquirente di un'informazione, a differenza di quello di un qualsiasi oggetto materiale, difficilmente potrà sapere quale valore essa avrà per lui senza prima conoscerla. Ovviamente il potenziale venditore non sarà disposto a far conoscere l'informazione prima di venderla, perché questo equivarrebbe a regalarla. Di qui i problemi particolarissimi che sorgono nell'utilizzare la logica della proprietà privata in materia di informazione e la particolare virulenza che i grandi latifondisti intellettuali (case discografiche ed editrici, *big pharma*, proprietari dei grandi loghi) utilizzano per difendere i propri recinti. Questi problemi in realtà derivano dal fatto che informazioni e conoscenza crescono quantitativamente e qualitativamente con la condivisione (perché hanno natura di beni comuni relazionali), ma la condivisione non genera profitti [. . .]» (*author's note*, "If it is true that fences are always needed to create a market, those needed in the face of information and knowledge must be particularly pervasive. Indeed, the potential buyer of information, unlike the buyer of any material object, is unlikely to know what value it will have for him without first knowing it. Obviously, the potential seller will not be willing to make the information known before selling it, because that would be tantamount to giving it away. Hence the very particular problems that arise in using the logic of private property in the field of information and the particular virulence that the big intellectual landowners – record and publishing companies, big pharma, owners of the big logos – use to defend their fences. These problems actually stem from the fact that information and knowledge grow quantitatively and qualitatively with sharing – because they are relational commons – but sharing does not generate profits").

165 A. Perzanowski, J. Schultz, *The End of Ownership: Personal Property in the Digital Economy*, Boston, MA, 2016, *passim*.

166 *See*, for further details, A.A. Alchian, H. Demsetz, *The Property Right Paradigm*, in *J. Econ. His.*, 33(1), 1973, p. 16 ff., where the authors, at p. 18, affirm that «There are two important questions that can be asked about the structure of property rights in a society. The first asks which property rights exist. There may exist a particular right of use in a society that did not exist earlier or that does not exist in other societies. For example, early in the history of radio, users of frequencies did not own the right to prevent members of the community from broadcasting on these same radio frequencies. Any person who wished to could broadcast on any frequency, and that is still true today for certain bands of radio frequencies. The right to offer heroin for sale on the open market does not exist in the United States although it may in other countries. The right to advocate particular political doctrines exists in greater degree in the United States than in Russia. (It should be noted that the right to advocate is a right to use resources, for no advocacy could take place

Certainly, the right that can be hypothesized must be schematically interpreted in relation to the area in which it arises and is exercised, the conditions under which it operates, its ownership, the objective of protection that is intended to be pursued and the relative exceptions, its transferability, its attitude with respect to similar subjective situations present in other legal systems, and, lastly, the way in which its existence and operation can be justified.

The elective area of exercise of this right is the digital world, which is characterized by a series of information encoded in specific characters (so-called bits) that are used irrespective of the particular contents represented therein.[167]

Apart from the legal protection of the person who develops, entrepreneurially or otherwise, the digital content,[168] for which one could move along the lines drawn, for example, by the legislation currently in force in Germany for the protection of photographers[169] and producers of sound recordings,[170] the interest here is to be

---

without the use of a place and other facilities.) The second question calls attention to the fact that the identity of right owners may vary. Perhaps the most important ownership distinction is between state (public) ownership and private ownership. An easement right may be owned by the state or by an individual. The right to deliver first class mail is owned by the state, whereas the right to board troops without permission is not. Needless to say, the classification of social systems according to the degree of centralization of control is closely related to the degree to which property rights are owned exclusively by the state».

167 A. Perzanowski, J. Schultz, *The End of Ownership: Personal Property in the Digital Economy*, cit., esp. p. 139 ff.

168 The creation of data is either through automated processes of calculation, through purely ingenious activity or through mere computer computation.

169 *See* § 72 *Urheberrechtsgesetz* (*UrhG*) of 1965 or *German Copyright and Related Rights Act*, as amended in December 2016, according to which «(1) The provisions of Part 1 applicable to photographic works shall apply mutatis mutandis to photographs and products manufactured in a similar manner to photographs. (2) The photographer shall be entitled to exercise the right according to subsection (1). (3) The right according to subsection (1) shall expire 50 years after the photograph was released or, if its communication to the public occurred prior to that date, 50 years thereafter, although the right shall already expire 50 years after production if the photograph was not released or legally communicated to the public within this period. The period shall be calculated according to section 69».

170 See § 85 *Urheberrechtsgesetz* (*UrhG*) of 1965 or *German Copyright and Related Rights Act*, as amended in December 2016, according to which «(1) The producer of an audio recording has the exclusive right to reproduce, distribute and to make available to the public the audio recording. If the audio recording was produced in an enterprise, the owner of the enterprise shall be deemed to be the producer. The right shall not accrue on account of a reproduction of an audio recording. (2) The right shall be transferable. The producer of an audio recording may grant to another the right to use the audio recording in a particular manner or in any manner of use to which he is entitled. Section 31 and sections 33 and 38 shall apply mutatis mutandis. (3) The right shall expire 70 years after release of the audio recording. If the audio recording was not released within 70 years of production, but was used legally for communication to the public, the right shall expire 50 years after the latter. If the audio recording has not been released or legally used for communication to the public during that period, the right shall expire 50 years after production of the audio recording. The period shall be calculated in accordance with section 69. (4) Section 10 (1) and section 27 (2) and (3), as well as the provisions set out in Chapter 6 of Part 1 shall apply mutatis mutandis». Tale disposto va letto in combinazione con l'art. 2(d) *WIPO Performances and Phonograms Treaty* (*WPPT*) del 1996, secondo cui «For the purposes of this Treaty: [. . .] *(d)* "producer of a phonogram" means the person, or the legal entity, who or which takes the initiative and has the

directed to the subjective position of the user of the digital good both in relation to the creator-provider of the latter and in relation to other users.

Thus, one should assess the applicability to the digital *res* of the traditional approach that links ownership of the asset to the person who is economically responsible for its creation,[171] in order to consider the possible extensibility-transferability of the proprietary position to the different subject who is entitled to access and use the digital asset.

Protection, then, should concern both the legal position of the owner and that of the mere user, and special attention should be paid to the same time limits to which protection should be subject, without, among other things, neglecting the public interest profiles involved.

One could, in fact, envisage either a short-term protection, given the speed and ease of circulation and use of digital content, or a long-term one, given in any case the potential involvement of proprietary positions.

On the other hand, the problem of the transferability of the subjective situation of a digital asset arises, especially since the development of a fair and efficient digital market is one of the main objectives to which various legal systems have recently devoted themselves, as is well demonstrated, by way of example, by the Community system with the *Digital Single Market Strategy*.[172]

In this respect, the alternative is created between an approach based on the legal concept of ownership and an approach that looks, instead, to the practical concept of use-accessibility.[173]

Lastly, a final consideration should be made of the interaction that the right on the digital asset may have with other rights already existing and created on the basis of the allocation of the *res*, especially with reference, on the one hand, to the position of the creator of the digital asset, and, on the other, to other possible users of the same, it being understood that the possible right of the so-called contents producer cannot, in any case, compromise the protection to be recognized to the user.

An answer to the complex question now outlined cannot disregard how, from a traditional perspective, the recognition of a genuine right of ownership over an asset can only stimulate legal circulation, economic traffic and the creation of new markets, so as to also promote the growth and technological innovation necessary to make marketable, and moreover at low cost, even non-material assets.

---

responsibility for the first fixation of the sounds of a performance or other sounds, or the representations of sounds».

171 The approach envisaged is to be found, for example, in both Article 949 Italian Civil Code on specification and § 950 BGB on the acquisition of ownership of the new tangible good in favour of the person who has developed it by processing or transforming one or more substances.

172 Cfr. European Commission, *A Digital Single Market Strategy for Europe – COM(2015) 192 Final*, cit., p. 1 ff.

173 With regard to the provision of services, different solutions can be configured in contractual terms, ranging from the provision of two different fees, one higher in the case of the actual transfer of the right (owner) and the other lower in the opposite case, to the lease contract, where the economic operator identifies himself with the lessee, or the rental contract, where the economic operator identifies himself with the owner.

This function could evidently refer to digital goods, which, thanks to technological developments, could be realized and transferred in an increasingly economical and efficient manner, so much so that their potential development could be inferred both if they were brought back to a proprietary logic and if such a scheme were dispensed with.

With the diffusion of higher and more efficient technologies, in fact, digital *res* are increasingly read as authentic marketable goods capable of being subjected to proprietary schemes, and from this point of view the law takes on a double guise, because it is perceived, on the one hand, as a limitation to the free circulation of digital content,[174] and on the other, as a tool that facilitates this circulation.[175]

The tendency that arises is, therefore, to allow for the ever-increasing and efficient development of a legal framework that, operating in a digital economy, is able to ensure appropriate and functional models for digitality.

The development of a clear legal framework for digital assets, then, requires consideration of the subjective positions it touches, so as to assess whether or not the relevant concepts should include ownership of the digital asset and, consequently, identify who the original owner is.

However, the question that remains and requires a solution is to assess whether or not digital assets, when freed from ownership patterns, can be the subject of free legal circulation, albeit in the clear knowledge that different solutions could be devised and adopted, in this regard, depending on the specific type of *res* considered.[176]

6 Evolving Perspectives on Goods' Ownership in the Digital Era

If, as already noted,[177] over the years technological development has profoundly conditioned human behaviour, especially through information and communication technologies (ICTs), more recently, two circumstances have occurred that can be considered as factors that have profoundly affected certain social configurations.

The first condition came about when a complex of tools, channels and equipment gave birth to information technologies, i.e. that set of means capable of creating

174 The stimulus that law gives to legal traffic cannot but be perceived as an essential moment for the success of the *Digital Single Market*, whose philosophy is in the sense of breaking down trade barriers that may result from regulatory law.

175 Such an effect stems from the legal regulation and the establishment of clear "rules of the game," well centred on the contractual and proprietary scheme, which are designed to create a market for intangible goods through the transfer of rights.

176 It is possible to think, for instance, to the right of ownership concerning data, which, due to the potentially high number of owners, could represent an inadequate legal solution, unlike the free flow that, on the contrary, could present itself as a circulation instrument much more suited to the type of object, also because, otherwise, each new right would operate in a cumulative manner to other existing rights. *See*, for more on the subject, OECD, *Data-Driven Innovation – Big Data for Growth and Well-Being*, Paris, 2015, p. 186 ff., where, at p. 195, it is stated that «[. . .] property rights may not be the optimal solutions in the case of data».

177 *See supra* esp. Introduction.

a flow of information capable of having a genuine impact on various economic, political and cultural activities. At this moment, the resource that society as a whole has disposed of and enjoyed has been identified with information itself.[178]

The second condition occurred, on the other hand, when the new digital ecosystem began to rely on information and communication technologies, so that the huge flow of information that had been created, from being one-way, became interactive, thanks to an extensive recourse to sharing and collaboration mechanisms, which was capable of transforming not only information but the very way in which it interacted into a fruitful commodity of exchange.[179]

Thus, there has been a profound change in human behaviour that has noticeably affected the way we communicate, operate in the economy and make law.

Digitalization has strengthened interaction in multiple aspects of human life to such an extent that the traditional world of exchanges has revealed all its limits when it had to cope, with the structures it already possessed, with the exponential increase in the possibilities of acquiring and exercising rights deriving from a human activity carried out in a digital environment:[180] the classic structure in which legal circulation had hitherto taken place appeared incapable of guaranteeing protections commensurate with the scope and speed that the new markets and new economic operators required.

If digital networks, the various forms of technological cooperation and the philosophy of sharing have increasingly come to characterize a different world, which has opened up to new opportunities for the use of electronic content, the legal framework that had hitherto governed the same interests and the same economic instances has been progressively paralysed in both its operational effectiveness and its regulatory capacity.[181]

178 *See*, on the innovative concept of *information society*, F. Machlup, *The Production and Distribution of Knowledge in the United States*, Princeton, NJ, 1962, p. 8 ff.; Y. Masuda, *The Information Society as Post-Industrial Society*, Washington, DC, 1981, esp. p. 49 ff.; F. Webster, *Theories of the Information Society*, Abingdon and New York, NY, 2014, p. 24 ff.; F. Machlup, *Knowledge: Its Creation, Distribution, and Economic Significance, Volume I*, Princeton, NJ, 2016, esp. p. 27 ff.

179 M. Castells, *La sociedad red: una visión global*, Madrid, 2006, *passim*.

180 P. Seele, I. Lock, *The Game-Changing Potential of Digitalization for Sustainability: Possibilities, Perils, and Pathways*, in *Sustain. Sci.*, 12, 2017, p. 183 ff., where the authors, at p. 185, state that «[. . .] we may conclude that in leveraging the transformative potential of both sustainability and digitalization we are still right at the beginning on all levels, be it technologically, conceptually, politically, or scientifically».

181 A. Bennich, *The Digital Imperative: Institutional Pressures to Digitalise*, in *Technol. Soc.*, 76, 2024, p. 1 ff., where the author, at p. 1, considers the presence of a "digital imperative" that causes a pressure to digitalize towards the organizations. Therefore, although other studies often emphasize market pressures to digitalize, the author focuses on institutional pressures exerted on organizations that lack competitive pressures. According to institutional theory, which considers the social embeddedness of organizations, social expectations and approval can shape the way organizations respond to technological change. Therefore, analysing digitalization within the water sector, where the perceived benefits of digital technologies are advocated under the label of "digital water," the author shows that there are isomorphic processes in place through which the idea of digital water is legitimized. Hence, water utilities

An example, among others, of this phenomenon, which has a multi-level impact, is Directive 2014/26/EU[182] which, in regulating both the collective management of copyright and related rights and the granting of multi-territorial licences for rights on musical works for online use in the internal market, seeks, on the one hand, to grasp the strengths and weaknesses of the existing legal model of digital management of rights inherent to protected human creations and, on the other, to improve it, foreseeing the possible direction in which it is moving.

In this way, the EU regulator has addressed significant profiles related to the renewed need for transparency and accountability that multi-territorial licences bring with them, solving the related critical issues and envisaging the adoption of a new regulatory framework.

In these terms, we thus briefly anticipate a discourse which, taken up and explored in greater depth in the pages that follow,[183] will attempt to grasp the characteristic traits of the environment in which digital technologies are interrelated and, in this way, to investigate the incidence that, firstly, information and, then, interconnection have as highly significant social expressions.[184]

In the dimension considered, then, these institutions present themselves both as the result of a logic of sharing and as the outcome that the creation and introduction of digital technologies determine, in a distorting manner, on the most varied aspects of everyday life: interrelated and collaborative technologies are capable of radiating effects such as to be perceived as legally relevant circumstances that contribute to the emergence of specific legal devices.

Thus, it appears necessary to grasp the reasons, structures, operational mechanisms and channels that favour the shift in human behaviour towards two clear directions: on the one hand, there is a profound change in the way the new social architecture interacts, communicates, requests, produces and distributes information and, at the same time, affects politics and the economy as well as other general

---

are under institutional pressures to digitalize which, in turn, can influence how they respond to digitalization.

182 *See Directive 2014/26/EU of the European Parliament and of the Council of 26 February 2014 on Collective Management of Copyright and Related Rights and Multi-Territorial Licensing of Rights in Musical Works for Online Use in the Internal Market*, in *OJ L*, 84, 20 March 2014, p. 72 ff.

183 *See infra* Chapter 3.

184 The collaborative mechanisms, made possible by the strengthening of social interaction, represent a passage of evident legal-economic importance, as Directive 2014/26/EU well demonstrates through the Collective Management Organizations (CMOs) and their relationship with the authors they represent. In this regard, it is interesting to observe how, due to the essentially intermediation-oriented nature of the activity carried out by CMOs, the consideration of the relationship of these organizations with consumers, who should be the final users of the service they provide, does not appear secondary. Hence the centrality of issues related to transparency, accountability and possible alternatives to multi-territory licences, and how these issues can be framed in the light of the objectives and aims pursued by Directive No. 26 of 2014.

aspects; and, on the other hand, there is a legal-normative impact linked to the broad possibilities of sharing and collaboration that technologies express in artistic, scientific and literary creations.[185]

Ultimately, as already noted,[186] it is always the notion of property that is exposed to economic-cultural and legal influences that can affect its actual scope, especially in terms of belonging-accessibility-usability.

185 *See*, for a deeper view of social architecture also in the area of human resources management, G.O. Oparaocha, *Towards Building Internal Social Network Architecture That Drives Innovation: A Social Exchange Theory Perspective*, in *J. Knowl. Manag.*, 20(3), 2016, p. 534 ff., where the author, at p. 549, affirms that «in our view, the concept of exchange in an organizational context can be guided by reciprocity, contractual obligations or a hybrid mix of both and so on [. . .]. As we emphasized earlier, exchange orientations are the bedrock for almost every societal interaction. Therefore, in organizational settings, each specific exchange orientation have fundamental significance and implications for the type(s) of resources that are shared, cognitive norms guiding behavioral inclinations and an individual's willingness to participate in, and/or the actual reception to the offerings in, an exchange interaction [. . .]. Thus, we contend that the HRM function have a key role in setting an organizational architecture that facilitates either reciprocal or contractual exchange orientations. This is a key resource for information exchange and sharing of knowledge that could lead to both greater innovations and better competitive advantage or promote NIHS within the geographically dispersed organization. We now discuss the implications of our propositions and conclusions».

186 *See supra* Introduction and preceding sections in this chapter.

3 Navigating Property Dynamics in the Digital Sphere

Striking a Balance Between Access and Inclusiveness Within a Shifting Paradigm

1 The Influence of the Digital Age on Property Rights Logic

The reference to the concept of access and related issues[1] is not a typical feature of the digital age,[2] since these issues already emerged when the first electronic devices, such as the telephone, radio and television, appeared.[3]

However, until a few decades ago, these issues were mainly concerned with material aspects, such as the affordability of electronic devices or the availability of computer services, revealing a limited and limiting approach.[4]

1 *See*, for further details, K.J. Vandevelde, *The New Property of the Nineteenth Century: The Development of the Modern Concept of Property*, in *Buffalo Law Rev.*, 29, 1980, p. 325 ff.; J.C. Ribot, N.L. Peluso, *A Theory of Access*, in *Rural Sociol.*, 68(2), 2003, p. 153 ff., where the author, describing the term "access" as frequently used by property and natural resource analysts without adequate definition, elaborates a concept of access and examines a broad set of factors that differentiate access from property. Therefore, access is considered as «the *ability* to derive benefits from things», broadening from property's classical definition as «the *right* to benefit from things». Access, following this definition, is more akin to "a bundle of powers" than to property's notion of a "bundle of rights." As a consequence, the used formulation includes a wider range of social relationships that constrain or enable benefits from resource use than property relations alone. Using this framing, the author suggests a method of access analysis for identifying the constellations of means, relations, and processes that enable various actors to derive benefits from resources; H.E. Smith, *On the Economy of Concepts in Property*, in *U. Pa. L. Rev.*, 2012, 160(7), p. 2097 ff.; E.R. Claeys, *Property, Concepts, and Functions*, in *Boston College Law Rev.*, 60(1), 2019, p. 3 ff.

2 *See* R.P. Merges, *The Concept of Property in the Digital Era*, in *Houston Law Rev.*, 45(4), 2008, p. 1239 ff.

3 Early diatribes on how best to guarantee generalized access to the use of telephone or broadcasting technologies emerged periodically throughout the 20th century.

4 *See* L.S. Underkuffler, *On Property: An Essay*, in *Yale Law J.*, 100(1), 1990, p. 127 ff., where the author affirms, at p. 128, that «[T]he concept of property is powerful. It has a peculiar hold on the human imagination and a particularly fundamental place in our constitutional structure. For the Founding generation and later constitutional interpreters, property has been more than simply an imaginative or symbolic concept: it has been the medium through which struggles between individual and collective goals have been refracted. Protection of individual property rights has cut across all parts of the political spectrum and has advanced radically different visions of the values to be protected in American society. What is property? The importance of this concept is matched by the difficulty of its definition. Felix Cohen has written that any useful definition of property "must reflect the fact that property merges by imperceptible degrees into government, contract, force, and value." Another commentator has written that "what is property may depend upon the action that is

DOI: 10.4324/9781003424413-4

And yet, the dynamics currently being recorded on the subject are marking a serious change of pace: hitherto, the idea of access has especially referred to problems constructed in a circumscribed manner and linked in particular to the availability of new technologies, but nowadays the questions that relate to it are touching much deeper sides of human existence and the way in which the relationship between *homo atque res* might be structured in the 21st century.[5]

---

dependent upon the answer."». Therefore the author argues that «[. . .] contemporary attempts by scholars to reconstruct the historical understanding of property also fail to overcome this incoherence. Both efforts – which reflect what I shall call an "absolute approach" – fail because they are based upon the same unarticulated assumptions: that property is objectively definable or identifiable, apart from social context; and that it represents and protects the sphere of legitimate, absolute individual autonomy. The contemporary impulse toward equating the sphere of absolute individual autonomy with the concept of property is, in fact, a radical narrowing of the historical understanding of property. During the American Founding Era, property included not only external objects and people's relationships to them, but also all of those human rights, liberties, powers, and immunities that are important for human well-being, including: freedom of expression, freedom of conscience, freedom from bodily harm, and free and equal opportunities to use personal faculties. From an analysis of the particular rights, liberties, powers and immunities contained within this broader conception» the author argues that «[. . .] property, in the historical view, did not represent the autonomous sphere of the individual to be asserted against the collective; rather, it embodied and reflected the inherent tension between the individual and the collective. This tension – now seen as something external to the concept of property – was in fact internal to it. Reclaiming this conception – [. . .] "comprehensive approach" – provides an analytic framework that lends important insights into the historical and jurisprudential treatment of the concept of property. [. . .] Adoption of the comprehensive approach would force courts to face explicitly the real policy issues involved in cases decided under the takings and due process clauses, rather than resolving them silently and obliquely through artificial manipulation of technical definitions of property. This framework also makes explicit the role that an assumed, absolute conception of property has had in the choice of the type of protection given to interests threatened under the takings clause, and in the calculation of compensation when the latter is imposed».

5 *See*, for further details on the notion of "digital era," J. Shepherd, *What Is the Digital Era?*, in *Social and Economic Transformation in the Digital Era*, edited by G. Doukidis, N. Mylonopoulos, N. Pouloudi, Hershey, PA, 2004, p. 1 ff., affirms that «[W]hile there are many useful ways of describing and discussing the Digital Era, explanations of its existence are lacking. The Digital Era is characterized by technology which increases the speed and breadth of knowledge turnover within the economy and society. Evolutionary theory, as an explanation of the system we live in, states that sustainability relies on knowledge turnover. In parts of the system which are relatively stable, knowledge turnover is low, and new variation, when produced, is rarely retained. In other, less stable parts of the system, faster knowledge turnover is advantageous as new knowledge is produced more frequently allowing for adaptation to the changing surrounding environment. Mixing and matching rates of knowledge turnover makes for a dynamic but ever-lasting world. The Digital Era can be seen as the development of an evolutionary system in which knowledge turnover is not only very high, but also increasingly out of the control of humans, making it a time in which our lives become more difficult to manage. For example, in the second generation Internet, "the semantic web," functionality, which understands meaning, replaces the search function of unknowingly matching words, which often have multiple meanings. In time, within this version of the Internet, software agents will exchange knowledge without human intervention. Equally, our understanding of the knowledge embedded within the human genome about how we relate to the world, generated in association with technology and freely available on the Internet, raises questions about our assumptions of control. Do we know enough about our future to change our genome? Can we control such changes and their diffusion? The social and economic implications of the Digital Era are huge and will increase as technological functionality

This theme is therefore taking on a very different guise, involving more significant and, for this reason, complex and articulated traits, since the digital revolution, with its aptitude and, at the same time, capacity to channel heterogeneous forms of communication and dissemination of goods into an integrated network, has made the fruition of digitality an indispensable element for survival in an increasingly connected world.[6]

It is no coincidence that today's world has technologies that have made and continue to make available in digital form all sorts of data, information and works, which can then be disseminated through branched digital networks.[7]

If, therefore, physical transfer represents the traditional form of distribution of material *res*, electronic transmission in digital networks follows different paths, since all data and instructions, processed through a computer,[8] are reproduced in its RAM, i.e. in its memory, for a certain period of time.

What is more, with the transmission of documents or, more generally, digital data via the Internet, numerous copies of a temporary nature are reproduced not only in the RAM of the sender's computer, but also in that of the Internet service provider (ISP), in numerous routers operating on the Internet, in the recipient's service provider's computer, and in that of the recipient himself.

Although, then, RAM constitutes a volatile memory, numerous judgments have qualified the reproductions contained therein as real copies, so much so that any dissemination of data carried out with the aid of electronic devices implies the necessary making of duplicates.[9]

What, then, are the consequences of living in a world that is continuously connected and where physical transfers are increasingly accompanied by a dematerialized circulation of goods? Where the material availability of a *res*, as an expression of the tangible property over which it is exercised, becomes less and less relevant compared to a generic possibility of use? Where does digitality become more and more relevant in legal-economic life? Where does immateriality become a marketable good in itself? Where one and the same good is broken down and polarized into a plurality of absolutely identical goods that can be used in a qualitatively and quantitatively similar way to the presumed original by an indistinct number of owners? Where does a physical dimension give way to one that exceeds the boundaries of space and time, disrupting the very way of conceiving the use of a good?

---

becomes more knowledge-based, our everyday lives and understanding of ourselves become more linked to it, and it takes on a "life" of its own. Understanding the Digital Era in terms of evolution will help ensure we build sustainable socio-economic relationships both with technology and with the advanced knowledge that technology helps us create».

6 P. Damaskopoulos, *Network Topology of the New Economy: Organizational Passages from Knowledge to Innovation*, in *Social and Economic Transformation in the Digital Era*, cit., p. 220 ff.

7 *See*, for further details, *supra* Chapter 1, § 1.

8 A computer, for example, allows software applications to be run, the web to be surfed and information to be displayed without necessarily having to be downloaded to the hard drive.

9 *See*, for all, *MAI System Corp. v. Peak Computer, Inc.*, 991 F.2d 511 (9th Cir. 1993), *cert. dismissed*, 114 S. Ct. 671 (1994), where this type of reasoning is conducted in light of the US Copyright Act. *See*, for more details, *infra* Chapter 4, § 3.

More specifically, the issue at stake is no longer simply the profile of access physically and materially understood, but extends to the whole economic and especially legal world that is linked to this concept, especially, as already mentioned,[10] in terms of ownership of the asset that is digitally used.[11]

It is precisely the increasingly pervasive character that digitality is taking on in contemporary life, which means that the profiles linked to access and its implications tend to become some of the most significant in the years to come, linking to them a substantial part of human existence.

In fact, it is a question of grasping the actual scope of the concept of access,[12] which is not to be understood in a narrow and material sense because it is linked to the mere use of technologies, but in an extended and immaterial sense because it is linked to its very teleological scope.

Ultimately, it must be assessed whether, in a digitized reality, the same proprietary logic based on a distinction of spheres of ownership and use that is based on "one's own" and "others" can still be fully suited to construct the legal-economic relations of individuals, or whether, on the contrary such an approach, aimed at defining the fundamental nature of the human being and his position within the organized society of which he is a part, should be placed in a different overall framework, so as to be more capable of grasping the typicalities that the current reality or a part of it is able to express in the contemporary world.

10 *See supra* esp. Introduction and Chapter 2.

11 *See* R.P. Merges, *To Waive and Waive Not: Property and Flexibility in the Digital Era*, 2011, available at SSRN 1854731, where the author states that «[E]ven in an era when creative works can sometimes be made collectively, and where copying and modifying existing works is often easy, individual ownership of discrete creative works still makes sense. Individual creative effort is still the crucial ingredient for many high quality works, and the control conferred by ownership is often the most efficient, and even more frequently the most fair, social arrangement. Even so, a common argument against property rights in the digital era is that they come with a heavy transactional burden. The need to clear permission to use digital works is said to impede the potential of high velocity distribution models and participatory creative efforts. There are, broadly speaking, three solutions to the problem. First, society can cut back on the number of property rights, or rework the structure of rights with an eye toward transactional efficiencies. Second, right holders or society in general can invest in rights clearance mechanisms that make it easier for users and consumers of rights-protected works to transact more efficiently. Third, legal rules can be tailored to make it easier for right holders to commit to a binding non-enforcement of their rights». Therefore, the author explores in some depth this third option, beginning by describing how waiver contributes to the supple texture of property rights, making it easy for individuals to exercise choices after rights have been granted. This represents a cornerstone feature of property rights, and one of their chief advantages over other entitlements and incentive regimes. Next, the author shows «[. . .] how waiver fits with other basic features of property rights» and he argues that «[. . .] waiver can be thought of as an aspect of the structure of rights, as well as a (particularly simple) rights clearance mechanism». Finally, he describes «[. . .] some simple ideas that could clarify knotty issues surrounding legal requirements for waiver of intellectual property rights. The most important are: 1) binding, easily verified waiver mechanisms that are "good against the world"; and 2) scope of waiver rules that make it simple for right holders to selectively waive rights, for example, permitting some uses and not others». The author, then concludes «with a call for more attention to the waiver strategy as a way of retaining our traditional commitment to property while easing the transactional burden that property rights entail».

12 *See supra* Introduction.

If past epochs have been characterized in their economic-legal dimension by proprietary approaches based on material relations and exchanges, perhaps the present and future epochs will be influenced by new digital technologies not only in the way interchanges operate but also in the way ownership of goods is conceived.[13]

The digital world thus represents not just a place read and perceived in traditional space-time terms, but a "territory" in which millions of users operate favoured by a reality that goes beyond the materiality of space and time to access an immaterial *quid novi*.[14]

It brings with it both an innovative toolbox to draw upon in the attempt to grasp the contemporary unfolding of human existence, and a complex of new conceptual contributions in the light of which to try to frame the new juridical-economic cosmos in which the man of the present and future is called to live.

13 *See*, for further details, S. Reis, *Toward a Digital Transfer Doctrine – the First Sale Doctrine in the Digital Era*, in *Northwest. Univ. Law Rev*., 109, 2014, p. 173 ff., where the author, at pp. 175 and 176, states that «[I]n copyright law, the first sale doctrine allows a customer who owns a copyrighted work to lend, sell, or give away the item to someone else. As a result, it serves as a significant limitation on copyright holders' rights. When someone purchases a physical book from the bookstore, she becomes the owner of that copy. Under the first sale doctrine, she may sell that copy to a used bookstore, donate it to the library, or give it away to a friend. In contrast, when someone purchases a Kindle e-book from Amazon or a song or movie from the iTunes store, she cannot resell or transfer any of these digital files to anyone else because she only became a "licensee" of the digital content rather than an "owner" of it. When a customer is merely a licensee of a copy of a copyrighted work, the first sale doctrine does not apply because there was no initial "sale." [. . .] The *Kirtsaeng* and *ReDigi* decisions give copyright holders an incentive to favor distributing their media to consumers in digital formats rather than in physical formats. Most importantly, copyright holders can exert a significant degree of control over digital content because customers are not legally authorized to resell it if they buy it from the major digital retailers such as Amazon or Apple because both companies impose licensing agreements on the content they sell. For instance, John Wiley & Sons, the publisher in Kirtsaeng, cannot prevent people from importing the publisher's textbooks from foreign countries where they are sold at lower prices and reselling them to customers in the United States. But John Wiley & Sons can exert a great deal of control over textbooks sold as e-books through the Kindle store because no purchaser of one of their textbooks as an e-book would be able to legally resell it or transfer it to someone else.

14 S. Reis, *Toward a Digital Transfer Doctrine-the First Sale Doctrine in the Digital Era*, cit., pp. 175 and 176, where the author affirm that «[R]ecently, the Supreme Court ruled in *Kirtsaeng v. John Wiley & Sons, Inc.* that the first sale doctrine does not have geographic restrictions. The ruling favored a student who had invoked the first sale doctrine as an affirmative defense against a publisher that was the copyright holder of the textbooks at issue. Because the decision reaffirmed the significance of the first sale doctrine in copyright law, many scholars and practicing attorneys viewed this ruling as a consumer-friendly decision. But two weeks later, copyright holders were the ones rejoicing instead of consumers. The US District Court for the Southern District of New York limited the scope of the first sale doctrine in *Capitol Records, LLC v. ReDigi Inc.* by holding that the doctrine did not apply to digital music files – specifically, MP3 files purchased from iTunes. *ReDigi* calls into question the actual effect *Kirtsaeng* will have in a culture where digital content is becoming increasingly popular. Although *Kirtsaeng* reinforced the importance of the first sale doctrine by holding that the doctrine is not subject to geographic limitations, its focus was on physical textbooks and not on digital content. *ReDigi* focus, however, was on the application of the first sale doctrine to MP3 files purchased from iTunes, and the district court explicitly limited the doctrine's scope by stating that customers were not entitled to resell their digital music files to others. In the year following *ReDigi*, no other cases were decided in federal courts regarding the first sale doctrine's application to copyrighted works in digital formats».

The gradual but inexorable affirmation of a digital revolution, the existence of a global economic network, and the presence of an a-spatial and a-temporal reality in which to establish legal-economic interrelationships, represent so many phenomena that always present in the background a direct or indirect reference to access and possible sharing.

On the other hand, can it be considered that the subject-good relationships established in the digital sphere are entirely comparable to traditional ones, to the extent that they can replace their scope and significance?

What is certain is that the traditional way and the digital way represent two distinct ways through which the man-thing binomial can be realized, because their assumptions, implementation tools and reference values are different, resulting in a basic irreconcilability that is difficult to recompose in a homogenizing analogy.

Their glue is undoubtedly represented by the common notions that derive from reciprocal obligations and faculties and common goals, but the differences are evident and unbridgeable when we move on to consider the modalities through which they find expression and realization, since, on the one hand, relationships based on materiality live in a symbiotic manner with finiteness, while, on the other, relationships based on immateriality present themselves as potentially separated from any kind of physical boundary.

Certainly, with the advance of digitality, the relevance of traditional relationships as set on a physical-material plane is reduced as much as the sap of materiality necessary in the human-*res* relationship to ensure the full and exclusive enjoyment of the good: space and time from primary factors of reality become profiles of secondary value.

The crucial question that seems to emerge is, therefore, linked to the exact nature and consistency of access as a concept that can affect the notion of ownership, conditioning its actual value.

In fact, and as already noted,[15] if in the past, according to a traditional sentiment, the notion of property was typically read in the light of exclusivity,[16] since this trait

15 *See supra* esp. Chapter 2, § 4.

16 In civil law systems, where the trait of exclusivity is generally presented as one of the fundamental elements of property along with individuality, the notion of ownership hinges on the absolute character of the right, deriving from this that the owner, in addition to enjoying all the utilities of the property that is its object, has the faculty to exclude any other individual from the benefits that can be derived from the *res*. A similar approach is also found in common law systems, where the majority orientation is to consider the right of exclusion as an essential element of the right to property, albeit tempered by numerous exceptions. *See*, with reference to *civil law, ex multis*, R.J. Pothier, *Traité du droit de domaine de propriété*, in *Œuvres de Pothier. IX*, Paris, 1846, p. 197, ove l'A. afferma che «[. . .] il est de l'essence de ce droit, que deux personnes ne puissent avoir chacune pour le total le domaine de propriété d'une même chose»; P. Perlingieri, *Introduzione alla problematica della «proprietà»*, cit., p. 60, where the author points out that the «[. . .] caratteristica che solitamente si attribuisce al diritto di proprietà, nella scía della tradizione romanistica, cioè la "esclusività" almeno tendenziale del godimento del proprietario, non deve ritenersi essenziale ed assoluta [. . .]. Se poi si vuole intendere per esclusività qualcosa di diverso dall'esclusività del godimento, e cioè il fatto che ogni situazione giuridica soggettiva spetta o appartiene a un titolare e quindi a costui in sostanza spetta esclusivamente quella situazione giuridica soggettiva, se in altre parole nell'esclusività si vuol sottolineare quel legame tra la situazione giuridica soggettiva e il suo titolare, in sostanza

was perceived as a useful tool to manage the allocation of resources and stimulate the production of new goods, today it should rather be enriched by the opposite attribute of inclusiveness, to be understood as a legal characteristic capable of ensuring a nature of the right predisposed to both participation and extension.

Taking the necessary in-depth analysis further,[17] it can already be observed now that to speak of inclusive property appears, however, anomalous, especially from the point of view of recognizing an effective legal value to this concept, because, in a classical perspective, exclusivity is considered a typical and essential element of this right.[18]

---

questa non sarà piú una caratteristica peculiare del diritto di proprietà, ma costituirà una delle caratteristiche tipiche delle situazioni giuridiche soggettive, giacche le situazioni giuridiche soggettive non possono che spettare a determinati soggetti. Quando la titolarità appartiene o spetta ad uno solo, è evidente che la situazione giuridica soggettiva è di esclusiva spettanza o appartenenza di un determinato soggetto» (*author's note*, "characteristic that is usually attributed to the right of property, in the wake of the Romanistic tradition, i.e. the at least tendential 'exclusiveness' of the owner's enjoyment, must not be considered essential and absolute [. . .]. If exclusivity is to be understood as something different from the exclusivity of enjoyment, i.e. the fact that every subjective legal situation belongs or belongs to a holder and therefore the holder is essentially exclusively entitled to that subjective legal situation, if in other words exclusivity is to emphasise that link between the subjective legal situation and its holder, in essence this will no longer be a special characteristic of the right of property, but will constitute one of the typical characteristics of subjective legal situations, since subjective legal situations can only belong to certain subjects. When ownership belongs or pertains to only one, it is evident that the subjective legal situation is the exclusive right or belonging of a given subject"); F. De Martino, *Beni in generale*, in *Commentario del codice civile*, a cura di A. Scialoja e G. Branca, Bologna-Roma, 1976, p. 146, where the author, identifying exclusivity with the absoluteness of the right, states that «[. . .] il proprietario ha diritto che tutti i terzi si astengano da qualsiasi invasione nella sfera del suo diritto [. . .]. Il suo diritto cioè opera *erga omnes*» (*author's note*, "the owner is entitled to have all third parties refrain from any invasion of the sphere of his right [. . .]. That is, his right operates *erga omnes*"); F.A. Hayek, *Law, Legislation, and Liberty. I*, London and Chicago, IL, 1973, p. 107, where the author considers that property rights were essentially perceived as a legal and social set of «expectations [. . .] designating [. . .] ranges of objects over which only particular individuals are allowed to dispose and from the control of which others are excluded»; M. Xifaras, *La propriété. Etudes de philosophie du droit*, Paris, 2004, p. 145 ff. *See*, with reference to *common law*, T.W. Merrill, *Property and the Right to Exclude*, in *Neb. Law Rev.*, 77, 1998, p. 730 ff., according to who exclusivity is the *condicio sine qua non* of ownership; J.E. Penner, *The Idea of Property in Law*, Oxford, 1997, p. 68, where the author states that «[T]he right to property is a right to exclude others from things which is grounded by the interest we have in the use of things»; *contra*, S. Balganesh, *Demystifying the Right to Exclude: Of Property, Inviolability, and Automatic Injunctions*, in *Harv. J. Law Poli.*, 31, 2008, p. 593 ff.

17 *See infra* § 3.

18 According to Article 832 of the Italian Civil Code, in fact, «Il proprietario ha diritto di godere e di disporre delle cose in modo pieno ed esclusivo, entro i limiti e con l'osservanza degli obblighi stabiliti dall'ordinamento giuridico» (*author's note*, "The owner has the right to enjoy and dispose of things in a full and exclusive manner, within the limits and in compliance with the obligations established by the legal system"). *See*, anyway, L. Barassi, *La proprietà*, Milano, 1941, p. 49, where the author, in footnote 23, states that exclusivity has neither autonomous nor «[. . .] è qualità a sua volta assoluta» (*author's note*, "it is itself absolute quality"); and then, the lucid and far-sighted observations of S. Pugliatti, *La proprietà nel nuovo diritto*, cit., p. 136, where the author affirms that «[. . .] non è [. . .] il caso di dare troppa importanza al carattere della esclusività (come aspetto autonomo che possa farsi valere come specifico ai fini della definizione della proprietà [. . .]. Insistendo, invece, sulla pienezza del godimento, l'esclusività si può considerare come elemento

While much can certainly be derived from a structuring of exchanges that takes full advantage of the potential offered by digitality and the network, it is also true that it is necessary to assess the so-called legal drawbacks that would arise to the legal circulation and ownership of goods as a result of these profound changes.

An age centred on access therefore forces one to ask what impact it has on the foundations of reciprocal relations, because, ultimately, this concept touches as much on the type as on the level of socio-political and economic-legal participation.[19]

---

complementare o inscindibile aspetto di quella pienezza. Così la formula della legge dirà che il diritto di proprietà e caratterizzato dalla sua totalità potenziale, dalla sua tendenza ad espandersi indefinitamente, sì che non può dirsi un diritto assoluto ed illimitato, ma sì un diritto assorbente ed al quale non si possano predeterminare limiti fissi e certi una volta per tutte [. . .]. Anzi non si può predeterminare il limite unico che ne circoscriva rigidamente l'ambito. Si possono, invece [. . .] determinare limiti particolari a tutela di definiti interessi. Questa capacità di espansione, questa tendenza al totale assorbimento di tutte le possibilità di utilizzazione della cosa, costituiscono, positivamente (la sostanza del diritto di proprietà; e i limiti specifici operano dall'esterno, si direbbe negativamente, ad ostacolarne in direzioni e in zone determinate l'espansione. E il tipico riflesso del carattere che si e messo in evidenza è la c.d. elasticità (del dominio, qualità per cui il diritto di proprietà, ed esso soltanto, qualunque sia il carico di pesi, oneri, limiti che lo gravino, tende sempre a liberarsi di essi e ad espandersi: ad acquistare, cioè anzi a riacquistare la massima estensione» (*author's note*, "it is [. . .] not the case that too much importance should be attached to the character of exclusivity (as an autonomous aspect that can be asserted as specific for the purposes of defining property [. . .]. Instead, by insisting on the fullness of enjoyment, exclusivity can be considered as a complementary or inseparable aspect of that fullness. Thus the formula of the law will say that the right to property is characterised by its potential totality, by its tendency to expand indefinitely, so that it cannot be said to be an absolute and unlimited right, but rather an absorbing right to which fixed and certain limits cannot be predetermined once and for all [. . .]. On the contrary, one cannot predetermine a single limit that rigidly circumscribes its scope. Instead, [. . .] particular limits can be determined to protect defined interests. This capacity for expansion, this tendency to the total absorption of all the possibilities of use of the thing, constitutes, positively (the substance of the right of ownership; and the specific limits operate from the outside, one would say negatively, to hinder its expansion in determined directions and areas. And the typical reflection of the character that has been highlighted is the so-called elasticity (of dominion, a quality whereby the right of ownership, and it alone, whatever the burden of burdens, burdens, limits that weigh it down, always tends to free itself of them and expand: to acquire, that is to say, to reacquire the maximum extension").

19 H. Dagan, *Inside Property*, in *Univ. Toronto Law J.*, 63(1), 2013, p. 1 ff., where the author, taking seriously the complexity and heterogeneity of property law, claims that a proper conception of property must account for both governance and inclusion. Indeed, neglecting governance obscures the significance of the internal life of property, which is often structured by sophisticated mechanisms aiming to facilitate various forms of interpersonal relationships in ways that no contractual arrangement can. On the other hand, ignoring inclusion improperly marginalizes non-owners' rights to entry in categories of cases where inclusion is an indispensable feature of the property institution under examination. Anyway, looking inside property in these two senses requires abandoning the conception of property as an exclusive right and substituting for it a pluralist conception. Therefore, property should be understood as an "umbrella" for a limited and standardized set of institutions, which serve as important default frameworks of interpersonal interaction regarding various types of resources. At its best, the plurality of property configurations – the different contents of owners' rights in these different property institutions – enables property law to vindicate differing balances among the different values that property can serve, according to the type of social relationship and the nature of the resource at stake. The pluralist conception of property, therefore, not only fits property law better; it is also the only understanding of property suitably attending to and facilitating the individuality enhancing role of multiplicity, which is indispensable for meaningful autonomy.

And it is not just a question of grasping who has access to what, but rather what kinds of relations with things access can achieve and realize.

In other words, it is necessary to assess whether the changes taking place are bringing about a shift from a traditional to an innovative logic of ownership in the wake of a new way of operating exchanges, a transition from an economic-spatial dimension because it is geographical to an a-spatial dimension because it is digital, and a profound change in the circulation of goods, which from being purely material becomes increasingly purely immaterial.[20]

On the answer given to this fundamental question may depend the very conformation that will be given to the (juridical) man-thing cosmos of the centuries to follow.

2 Access: A Mere Descriptive Term or a Novel Technical-Legal Manifestation of Ownership?

Until the advent of digitalization and the widespread dissemination and utilization of the potential of the Internet, people's greatest concern was with ownership, which, as the ultimate form in which the physical world is acquired, processed and transformed into a good, essentially becomes a way of (physically and legally) changing natural reality and dividing it between one's own and others.[21]

The focus of individuals has thus always been on the best and most efficient mechanism to accumulate (material) capital, to produce physical goods and services, and to distribute ownership.[22]

20 *See*, in this perspective, L.S. Underkuffler, *On Property: An Essay*, cit., p. 142 ff., where the author suggests the idea that there is intrinsic value in rethinking the concept itself. The concept of property has powerful, rhetorical force, because it is not incidental to our lives or to our legal system, but it is of central, almost emotional importance. Therefore, although contemporary approaches proceed from a vision of property as that which protects and separates the individual from the collective sphere, by viewing the collective context as necessary for the definition and exercise of individual rights, the comprehensive approach forces to rethink the image of the relationships between individuals and the collectives of which they are parts. It can lead to a different concept of individual well-being and autonomy: one that recognizes the individual's need for freedom as well as the need for the development and expression of that freedom in the context of relatedness to others.

21 T. Veblen, *The Beginnings of Ownership*, in *Am. J. Soc.*, 4(3), 1898, p. 352 ff., where the author, at p. 354, states that «[T]he view that ownership is an outgrowth of the customary consumption of such things as weapons and ornaments by individuals is well supported by appearances and has also the qualified sanction of the natural rights preconception. The usages of all known primitive tribes seem at first sight to bear out this view. In all communities the individual members exercise a more or less unrestrained right of use and abuse over their weapons, if they have any, as well as over many articles of ornament, clothing, and the toilet. In the eyes of the modern economist this usage would count as ownership. So that, if the question is construed to be simply a question of material fact, as to the earliest emergence of usages which would in the latter-day classification be brought under the head of ownership, then it would have to be said that ownership must have begun with the conversion of these articles to individual use. But the question will have to be answered in the contrary sense if we shift our ground to the point of view of the primitive men whose institutions are under review. The point in question is the origin of the institution of ownership, as it first takes shape in the habits of thought of the early barbarian. The question concerns the derivation of the idea of ownership or property».

22 *See*, for further details, T.J. Brailsford, B.R. Oliver, S.L. Pua, *On the Relation Between Ownership Structure and Capital Structure*, in *Accoun. Fin.*, 42(1), 2002, p. 1 ff.; R. Boodhoo, *Capital Structure and Ownership Structure: A Review of Literature*, in *J. Online Edu.*, 2009, p. 1 ff.; J. Pindado,

In a pre-digital age, the control of natural resources and, consequently, of labour, conditioned, on an economic level, the way of allocating property, and, on a sociological level, the way of dividing the community into social classes.

Now that the world is digital, it is immateriality that takes over and dictates its own rhythms, without space or time, both in the distribution of wealth, which is progressively being identified with a knowledge composed of information and data, and in the creation of an increasingly liquid society because it is rapidly decomposed and recomposed, in a continuous, fluid and volatile manner.[23]

However, the foregoing assumptions should not be slavishly read either in the sense of considering that issues inherent in the content of property cannot have any bearing on the formal definition of the subjective situation involved,[24] or in the sense of accepting the idea that the discrepancies perceptible in property law are inherent in the diversity of socio-economic content, but that, as such, are never likely to affect the legal structure of property.[25]

If, in fact, the first modus operandi implies an aprioristic definition of property that implicitly recalls a basic value, the second, by emphasizing in an almost unilateral manner the aptitude of legal schemes to include in them situations that have undergone modifications with respect to those originally envisaged, so crystallizes the nexus between legal structure and social reality as to create an irremediable reciprocal disagreement.[26]

It follows, therefore, that the analysis of the content of the subjective situation takes on even greater significance when it comes into contact with reality, because such an in-depth analysis should facilitate the differentiation of the various positions inherent in the right referred to.[27]

From this point of view, property becomes the expression of a multiplicity of situations which, while representing the starting point for appropriate differentiations,

---

C. De La Torre, *Capital Structure: New Evidence From the Ownership Structure*, in *Int. Rev. Fin.*, 11(2), 2011, p. 213 ff., where the authors provide theory and empirical evidence supporting a complementary perspective on capital structure based on corporate ownership structure. According to the classic ownership view, capital structure is partly determined by the incentives and the goals of those who are in control of the firm. As a consequence of managerial entrenchment and rent expropriation phenomena, self-interested agents (entrenched managers and controlling owners) chose the capital structure most appropriate for their own best interest. Additionally, the authors find evidence of an interaction effect between managerial ownership and ownership concentration, in particular, the larger debt increments promoted by outside owners when managers are entrenched.

23 Z. Bauman, *Liquid Modernity*, Cambridge, 2000, p. 5 ff.

24 *See*, in this sense, for all, J. Dabin, *Le droit subjectif*, Paris, 1952, p. 231.

25 *See*, in this sense, *ex multis*, F. De Martino, *Della proprietà*, in *Commentario del codice civile*, a cura di A. Scialoja e G. Branca, Bologna-Roma, 1957, p. 125.

26 *See* S. Rodotà, *Il terribile diritto*, cit., p. 253.

27 *See* S. Rodotà, *Il terribile diritto*, cit., where the author, in confirmation of this assumption, refers to the wording of the German (Article 14 GG) and Italian (Article 42 Const.) constitutional texts, which, having overcome the conception of the external limit, imply that the determination of the content of property becomes «[. . .] l'unica determinante anche al fine di risolvere le questioni in tema di interventi legislativi sul regime di appartenenza dei beni» (*author's note*, "the only determinant also for the purpose of resolving questions regarding legislative interventions on the property ownership regime").

must not, however, lead to a fragmentation[28] of the situation that has been classically framed in a granitic *unicum*, but to the simple realization that the phenomenon of property ownership can also take on new characteristics.[29]

If by belonging is meant those subjective positions in which the holder of the right is placed by the legal system in the condition of directly satisfying his own interest in one or more assets, without the collaboration of other determined subjects being required, two different criteria can be grasped to which the legal system can resort to define the attribution of legal powers attached to the *res*.

In fact, considering that the favoured subject is the protected subject, his identification can be made either through the recognition of the effects of a *de facto* relationship that takes place between subject and property, so as to ensure protection of the situation that is actually present (so-called *de facto* or possessory situations), or through the attribution of positions of belonging that resort to formal procedures by which a title is conferred that can also be transmitted to other subjects through the application of certain rules (so-called situations of law).[30]

28 *See*, for an pragmatic application of the concept of fragmentation to ownership, N. Schulz, F. Parisi, B. Depoorter, *Fragmentation in Property: Towards a General Model*, in *J. Instit. Theor. Econ. (JITE)/Zeitschrift für die gesamte Staatswissenschaft*, 2002, p. 594 ff., where the authors develop a general model of anticommons fragmentation in property. Therefore, via several related examples, they consider the *equilibria* obtained under different scenarios and the various illustrations are utilized to develop a model of fragmented property. The model reveals that the private incentives of excluders do not capture the external effects of their individual decisions. The developed model, which allows the authors to explore some important implications for the institutional responses to issues of property fragmentation, suggests that the results of underutilization of joint property increase monotonically in both (i) the extent of fragmentation and (ii) the forgone synergies and complementarities between the property fragments.

29 *See*, on the concept of belonging, P. Perlingieri, *Introduzione alla problematica della "proprietà,"* cit., p. 105 ff., where the author, after distinguishing also chronologically between membership and the existence of the subjective legal situation, states, at p. 106, with reference to the subjective legal situation and the entitlement thereto, that «[. . .] si tratta di due nozioni diverse, in quanto la titolarità consiste nel legame tra la situazione giuridica soggettiva ed il soggetto, legame che se è attuale, rispetto ad una situazione soggettiva finale, si esprime appunto in termini di appartenenza. L'appartenenza si può definire appunto come una forma di titolarità (della situazione giuridica soggettiva). Questo consente anche di comprendere che talune situazioni giuridiche soggettive, che pure esistono, non hanno medio tempore alcun titolare; cioè, in termini di appartenenza, si può dire che non appartengono ancora ad un soggetto determinato» (*author's note*, "these are two different notions, since ownership consists in the link between the subjective legal situation and the subject, a link that if it is current, with respect to a final subjective situation, is expressed precisely in terms of belonging. Belonging can be defined precisely as a form of ownership – of the subjective legal situation. This also makes it possible to understand that certain subjective legal situations, although they exist, do not have any holder in the medium term; that is, in terms of belonging, it can be said that they do not yet belong to a determined subject"). *See*, for a traditional sociological insight, V. Kruse, *The Right of Property*, Oxford, 1939, *passim*; H. Westermann, *Sachenrecht*, Karlsruhe, 1960, p. 113 ff.

30 *See*, in this sense, A. Gambaro, *La proprietà*, cit., p. 2 ff., where the author, at p. 3, states that «[L]e posizioni di appartenenza si delineano quando la protezione che l'ordinamento assegna ai titolari sia duratura nel tempo. In questo caso occorre anche stabilire le regole di circolazione delle titolarità per far fronte a tutti gli accadimenti della vita dei soggetti resi titolari della posizione di appartenenza,

Well then, the consideration of the obligations or limitations weighing on ownership, on the one hand, and on belonging, on the other, does not affect ownership so profoundly as to undermine its integral fullness, but represents the foundation from which the elaboration of new systematic criteria takes its cue, which, also in the light of the (social) function of this right,[31] allow for a new interpretation of other real rights, such as, for example, usufruct and emphyteusis.

Having thus broadened the horizon of enquiry to include real schemes other than those traditionally accepted, and turned our gaze to the enterprise[32] and, above all, to intangible goods, we come to embrace all those borderline situations that in any case add to the nuance of obligatory traits and material apprehension the traits of the proprietary phenomenon, so that we can almost speak of graduated forms of belonging.[33]

The current proprietary phenomenon, in essence, manifests the evident tendency to expand its objective profile, which, penetrating the digital world, stimulates the change of many traditional traits of the right of ownership, expressing, in this way, the capacity to encompass within itself, attracting other rights.

---

e, infine, poiché l'ordinamento deve essere effettivo per essere legittimo, deve istituire un sistema di protezione delle posizioni di appartenenza che ha attribuito; il che comporta anche l'istituzione di un insieme di rimedi specifici che il titolare della posizione può attivare ogni volta che sia spogliato di essa o turbato nel suo esercizio» (*author's note*, "[T]he positions of belonging are delineated when the protection that the order assigns to the holders is lasting in time. In this case, it is also necessary to establish the rules of circulation of the entitlements in order to cope with all the events in the life of the subjects made holders of the position of belonging, and, finally, since the system must be effective in order to be legitimate, it must establish a system of protection of the positions of belonging that it has attributed; which also entails the establishment of a set of specific remedies that the holder of the position can activate whenever he is dispossessed of it or disturbed in its exercise").

31 *See*, for a careful examination of the evolution of the social function of property over the last century, C. Salvi, *Teologie della proprietà privata*, cit., p. 82 ff. *See*, in general, for a view of the concept of social function, seen as too vague, G. Branca, F. De Martino, *Della proprietà. III*, Bologna-Roma, 1951, p. 118 ff.; seen as contradictory, S. Pugliatti, *La proprietà nel nuovo diritto*, cit., p. 141 ff.; seen as too focused on the thing in a collectivistic dimension rather than on an individual one, E. Betti, *Problemi proposti dallo sviluppo del capitalismo e della tecnica di guerra. II*, in *Studi in onore di Antonio Cicu*, Milano, 1951, p. 591 ff.; G. Cottino, *Le convenzioni di voto nelle società commerciali*, Milano, 1958, p. 96 ff.; seen as contrary to the same proprietary logic, G. Branca, *Sul possesso dell'azienda*, in *Foro it.*, I, 1958, c. 702 ff.; seen as instrumental only to the realization of a public interest, A.M. Sandulli, *Spunti per lo studio dei beni privati d'interesse pubblico*, in *Diritto dell'economia*, 1956, p. 56 ff.; seen as inherent in the ownership structure itself, U. Natoli, *Limiti costituzionali dell'autonomia privata nel rapporto di lavoro*, Milano, 1955, p. 89 ff. Cfr., in general on the subject, most recently, F. Macario e M.N. Miletti (a cura di), *La funzione sociale del diritto privato tra XX e XXI secolo*, Roma, 2017.

32 *See*, for a classic perspective directed at the combination of the legal *datum* with the economic *datum*, especially integrated by the company or joint-stock company, *ex aliis*, A.A. Berle Jr., G.C. Means, *The Modern Corporation and Private Property*, New York, NY, 1932, *passim*; L. Mengoni, *Recenti mutamenti nella struttura e nella gerarchia dell'impresa*, in *Rivista delle società*, 1958, p. 706 ff.

33 Consider, in this sense, the «gradazioni dell'appartenenza» (*author's note*, "gradations of belonging") referred to D. Barbero, *Sistema istituzionale del diritto privato italiano. I*, Torino, 1958, p. 705. *See*, for an extensive examination of the phenomenon of belonging, U. Breccia, *I quarant'anni del libro terzo del Codice civile*, in *Rivista del critica del diritto privato*, 1983, p. 352 ff.

The law, thus, would only be responding to the demands coming from historical reality, giving voice and recognition to new situations that, also from the point of view of belonging, seem capable of expressing a legal concept of property, which, like that of common law,[34] appears more contiguous to its socio-economic dimension.[35]

These broad study perspectives, in an attempt to grasp the new scope of traditional juridical categories, make it possible to overcome the artificial relations created between Roman law and modern dogmatics in order to grasp the juridical scheme of property in the fullness of its historicity: the jurist of every age must endeavour to identify the actual content of a juridical concept that, while remaining unchanged in its *nomen*, may have undergone profound changes that have altered its way of being at different levels.[36]

Certainly, even in an age as fertile with rapid innovations as the digital age, the search for new qualifications for atavistic institutions runs the risk, in some cases, of appearing purely nominalistic and, in fact, sterile of effective results, but at the same time, there must be an awareness that insisting on conceptual forms that are by now obsolete and no longer in line with factual reality runs the risk, likewise, of falling into the trap of a mere fluctuation of content that would translate, in essence, into affirming the lack of legal transformation of what has, however, already changed factually.[37]

34 W. Friedmann, *Law in a Changing Society*, London, 1959, p. 66 ff.

35 *See* L.S. Underkuffler, *On Property: An Essay*, cit, p. 128, where the author states that «[T]he concept of property is powerful. It has a peculiar hold on the human imagination and a particularly fundamental place in our constitutional structure. For the Founding generation and later constitutional interpreters, property has been more than simply an imaginative or symbolic concept: it has been the medium through which struggles between individual and collective goals have been refracted. Protection of individual property rights has cut across all parts of the political spectrum and has advanced radically different visions of the values to be protected in American society».

36 *See* G. Branca, *Sul possesso dell'azienda*, in *Foro italiano*, I, 1958, c. 702, where the author invites us not to accept the categories as they come to us tralatically, so that we can eventually «[. . .] creare altre qualifiche e non allargare smisuratamente gli schemi che ci vengono dal diritto romano» (*author's note*, "create other qualifications and not overstretch the schemes that come to us from Roman law").

37 *See*, for the emphasis to be placed on the factual and factual profile, G. Capograssi, Agricoltura, diritto, *proprietà*, in *Rivista di diritto agrario*, I, 1952, p. 271 ff.; T. Ascarelli, *Per uno studio della realtà giuridica effettuale*, in *Dir. dell'econonomia*, 1956, p. 775 ff.; R. Nicolò, *Riflessioni sul tema dell'impresa e su talune esigenze di una moderna dottrina del diritto civile*, in *Riv. di diritto commerciale*, I, 1956, p. 177 ff., where the author, at p. 179, criticizes the civil law doctrine of his time by noting that «[. . .] il mancato rinnovamento dei vecchi schemi che avrebbe permesso di colmare lo yhatus tra le categorie concettuali, fondamentalmente elaborate dalla pandettistica e ancora oggi in grande onore e la nuova realtà, non più comparabile per la sua eterogeneità di presupposti, di strumenti e di fini, con quella che aveva formato l'oggetto del diritto romano comune e della dottrina pandettistica» (*author's note*, "[. . .] the failure to renew the old schemes, which would have made it possible to bridge the yhatus between the conceptual categories, fundamentally elaborated by Pandettism and still in great honour today, and the new reality, no longer comparable in its heterogeneity of presuppositions, instruments and ends, with that which had formed the object of common Roman law and of the Pandettist doctrine"); S. Rodotà, *Il terribile diritto*, cit., p. 258, where the author points out that successful investigations «[. . .] condotte in vista dell'interesse regolato e tenendo presente qual e l'attività che il proprietario può svolgere, [. . .] conducono al discoprimento di vere e proprie diversità strutturali [. . .]» (*author's note*, "conducted in view of the regulated

The apparent disarticulation of legal figures constantly perceived in their monolithic nature, consequent to the prominence attributed first to new profiles of belonging and then to access, embodies one of the most relevant nodes that the contemporary private individual is called upon to resolve: while maintaining the character of realty, are we faced with innovative forms of property centred on a graduation of apprehension and a different way of using the property, or with new real rights that undermine the very *numerus clausus* of realty as traditionally conceived?[38,39]

While adherence to the classic *numerus clausus* approach may affect, by limiting it, the will of private individuals, it cannot also affect the activity of the legislator,[40] the fact remains that the concept of access may remain linked to a merely practical-commercial sphere, thus assuming a mainly descriptive value of the modalities by which it is possible to make use of a specific digital asset, or it may depart from such a scope to assume a more stringent and purely legal meaning

---

interest and bearing in mind what activity the owner may carry out, [. . .] lead to the discovery of real structural diversity").

38 *See*, for further details on the *numerus clausus* of rights *in rem*, L. Barassi, *I diritti reali nel nuovo codice civile*, Milano, 1943, p. 38 ff.; G. Balladore Pallieri, *Diritto soggettivo e diritto reale*, in *Jus*, 1952, p. 15 ff.; M. Allara, *Le nozioni fondamentali del diritto civile. I*, Torino, 1958, p. 625 ff. See, on the distinction between typicality and closed number of rights *in rem*, for all, M. Giorgianni, *Contributo alla teoria dei diritti di godimento su cosa altrui. I*, Milano, 1940, p. 169 ff.; S. Ginossar, *Droit réel, propriété et créance*, Paris, 1960, p. 146 ff.; A. Guarnieri, *Diritti reali e diritti di credito: valore attuale di una distinzione*, in *Trattato dei diritti reali. I. Proprietà e possesso*, diretto da A. Gambaro, U. Morello, Padova, 1979, p. 29 ff.; M. Comporti, *Tipicità dei diritti reali e figure di nuova emergenza*, in *Studi in onore di Cesare Massimo Bianca. II*, Milano, 2006, p. 771 ff.; S. van Erp, *A Numerus Quasi-Clausus of Property Rights as a Constitutive Element of a Future European Property Law?*, in *Elect. J. Comp. Law*, 7, 2003, p. 3 ff.; da ultimo, G. Resta, *Nuovi beni immateriali e* numerus clausus *dei diritti esclusivi*, in *Diritti esclusivi e nuovi beni immateriali*, Torino, 2010, p. 21 f., where the author points out, at p. 23, that «[. . .] nel modello affermatosi con la rivoluzione francese, il *numerus clausus* era inteso come un principio di ordine pubblico, in quanto rappresentava un baluardo istituzionale contro i rischi di smembramento della proprietà e di proliferazione di diritti reali atipici» (*author's note*, "that in the model established with the French Revolution, the numerus clausus was understood as a principle of public order, as it represented an institutional bulwark against the risks of dismemberment of property and the proliferation of atypical real rights").

39 *See*, for a "defence" of the classical concept of ownership, which is achieved through an attempt to reconcile the reaction to fragmentation with the simultaneous approximation of other situations considered substantially different to ownership, Salv. Romano, *Sulla nozione di proprietà*, in *Rivista trimestrale di diritto civile*, 1960, p. 337 ff., where the author, at p. 344, defines property rights as the «[. . .] stato di soggezione di una *res* alla potestà di autonomia privata e, più precisamente, alla sfera di questa costituita dai poteri dispositivi di alienazione e acquisto, nonché costitutivi di rapporti reali e obbligatori. Più semplicemente e obiettivando la formula di Erwin Seidl, proprietà è situazione reale di disponibilità nell'ambito dell'autonomia privata o pubblica» (*author's note*, "state of subjection of a res to the power of private autonomy and, more precisely, to the sphere of this constituted by the dispositive powers of alienation and acquisition, as well as constitutive of real and obligatory relations. More simply and objectivising Erwin Seidl's formula, property is a real situation of availability in the sphere of private or public autonomy").

40 *See*, in this regard, S. Rodotà, *Il terribile diritto*, cit., p. 259, where the author notes that «il compito del legislatore non va confuso con quello dell'interprete, al quale soltanto spetta di indicare il "segno" da usare per la normativa riassunta a mezzo di esso» (*author's note*, "the legislator's task is not to be confused with that of the interpreter, whose sole task is to indicate the *sign* to be used for the legislation summarized through it").

because it aims at describing a mode of use and enjoyment of the asset that is an alternative/integration with respect to the ownership linked to the traditional logic of ownership. Certainly, beyond the opportunity and difficulty – which cannot be addressed here – that a definition of property that is homogenized or differentiated from the Bartolian definition encounters,[41] it appears clear, on the one hand, the non-univocal use of the term "property" and, on the other, the impossibility of an abstract and rigorous enunciation, unless it is limited to referring to one or some of the situations it is called upon to indicate.[42]

Wanting to reason in terms of a simple systematic framework, this realistic acknowledgment of the barriers to an exhaustive – but how effectively useful? – a definitive reconstruction of the phenomenon of ownership, can only be translated into the mere observation that a notion of property rights, with the ensuing

41 *See* Bartoli a Saxoferrato, *Commentaria in primam Digesti Novi partem*, Venetiis, 1615, f. 84, according to who the classic definition «Quid ergo est dominium? [. . .] est ius de re corporali perfecte disponendi nisi lex prohibehatur [. . .] de re corporali dixi ad differentiam incorporalium, in quibus non cadit dominium proprie». *See*, for further details, P. Grossi, *Il dominio e le cose. Percezioni medievali e moderne dei diritti reali*, Milano, 1992, p. 87, where the author, at p. 89, explains that «[*D*]*ominium* è una nozione relativa, cioè con molteplici significati nell'universo del diritto. Può essere la categoria larghissima, fin troppo larga, di cui Bartolo ha discorso prima, e qui trovan posto il pieno dominio, la nuda proprietà, l'usufrutto, l'uso quindi anche tutte le titolarità di *iura in re*, tutte le situazioni per cui posso dire: (ego habeo dominium illius iuris). Può essere anche la *species* dominio pieno, dominio pieno di una cosa. A seconda che si assuma nella prima o nella seconda accezione, l'usufrutto si atteggerà diversamente come *pars*: nella prima accezione, considerato nella sua veste autonoma di usufrutto formale, di servitù, di proprietà del diritto di usufrutto, sarà *species* di un *genus* e si porrà come *pars praedicamentalis*, nella seconda, considerato come usufrutto causale e articolazione interna al *dominium*, sarà parte di un tutto e si porrà come *pars integralis*» (*author's note*, "*Dominium* is a relative notion, that is, with multiple meanings in the universe of law. It can be the very wide category, far too wide, of which Bartolus spoke earlier, and here we find full dominion, bare ownership, usufruct, use, therefore also all the titularities of *iura in re*, all the situations whereby I can say: (*ego habeo dominium illius iuris*). It can also be the species *dominio pieno*, full dominion of a thing. Depending on whether it is assumed in the first or second meaning, the usufruct will behave differently as pars: in the first meaning, considered in its autonomous guise of formal usufruct, of servitude, of ownership of the right of usufruct, it will be a species of a genus and will stand as *pars praedicaxmentalis*, in the second, considered as causal usufruct and internal articulation of the dominium, it will be part of a whole and will stand as *pars integralis*"), and, again, at p. 91, «[I]l *dominium* autentico non può non essere *dominium rei corporalis*, non può non essere l'approccio-confronto fra uomo e cosmo, soggetto e cosa. Prima ancora che un dato tecnico è questa una acquisizione antropologica tenacemente abbarbicata alla coscienza giuridica dell'Ottocento secondo un filo conduttore che va dalle costruzioni classiche al BGB» (*author's note*, "The authentic dominium cannot but be dominium rei corporalis, it cannot but be the approach-confrontation between man and cosmos, subject and thing. Even before being a technical fact, this is an anthropological acquisition tenaciously rooted in the legal consciousness of the 19th century according to a thread that runs from classical constructions to the BGB").

42 *See*, S. Rodotà, *Il terribile diritto*, cit., p. 379, according to who «[B]isogna, allora, tener conto del fatto che la molteplicità degli statuti, il loro differenziarsi, è il risultato di un intreccio di tre ordini di fattori, rispettivamente rinvenibili negli elementi caratterizzanti la descrizione classica della situazione proprietaria, e dunque nel soggetto, nell'oggetto, nel contenuto» (*author's note*, "Before, it must be borne in mind that the multiplicity of statutes, their differentiation, is the result of an interweaving of three orders of factors, respectively traceable in the elements characterising the classical description of the proprietary situation, and thus in the subject, the object, and the content").

statements on the subject of modes of acquisition, enjoyment and limits on its exercise, translates, in an essentially logical manner, into leaving the situation referable to the owner entirely to the legislator.[43]

Although it is certainly not possible to undertake a reconnaissance, even a summary one, of the special Italian and European legislation, in order to grasp the characteristics that a property "normative reading" comes to assume,[44] it is sufficient to observe that, beyond ethical justifications or economic arguments, it cannot realistically be considered that there is only one concept of property in the national legal system, because it cannot but give way to the presence of a plurality of its statutes.[45]

43 *See* L.S. Underkuffler, *On Property: An Essay*, cit., pp. 131–133, where the author observes that «Richard Epstein, in *Takings: Private Property and the Power of Eminent Domain*, sets forth a conception of property that he attributes to Locke and the American Founders. Under this view, property is a simple concept: it is the individual's right to unfettered possession, disposition, and use of corporeal and incorporeal objects. Any governmental action that limits these rights, as historically defined, is a prima facie "taking" under the Fifth Amendment. If the taking is a justified exercise of the police power, no compensation is due; if it is not, it can only be done for another legitimate public use, and only with the payment of compensation. Under this analysis, all governmental attempts to redistribute income through modification of common law liability rules, taxes, and other regulations are takings. To the extent that such governmental transfers do not equally benefit the parties from whom they are taken and to whom they are given, they are unconstitutional. [. . .] The Supreme Court's formulations, and the historical portrayals above, all rest on the assumptions that property is something that is objectively definable or identifiable, apart from social context, and that it represents and protects the sphere of legitimate, absolute individual autonomy. The thrust of such conceptions of property is the identification of what the individual's autonomous sphere should be, based upon the recognition and protection of individual interests alone. If individual interests fall within the layperson's "ordinary understanding," are "reasonable," serve a valid economic function, or concern the possession, use or disposition of corporeal or incorporeal objects, then they are property; the consideration of collective interests is a distinctly separate and second-order matter. When this absolute approach to property is combined with seemingly absolute constitutional guarantees, a difficult problem is presented. Property rights, like all individual rights, are rarely absolute in any society. If property is that which objectively describes the individual's autonomous sphere, how can the protection of property under the takings and due process clauses be reconciled with conflicting social goals? Must we choose between the artificial manipulation of a purportedly absolute conception (with resulting intellectual incoherence) and the endorsement of radical individualism if we are to retain any fidelity to historical or intuitive understandings?»

44 *See*, on this profile, the enlightening words of F. Vassalli, *Motivi e caratteri della codificazione civile*, in *Studi giuridici. II*, 2, Milano, 1960, p. 614 ff., where the author, at pp. 622, 623 and 632, affirms that «[N]el nuovo quadro della politica economica il diritto patrimoniale dei privati assume una funzione del tutto complementare rispetto al regolamento amministrativo. [. . .] Il diritto soggettivo figura ancora nel codice: [. . .] ma lo spirito della legge è mutato. [. . .] Le norme del codice, malgrado il prestigio della presentazione, sono più spesso – e soprattutto quelle che hanno attinenza con l'attività economica – delle norme complementari [. . .]. Carattere del nuovo codice [è, *a.d.r.*] una permeazione del medesimo, non nello spirito generale – il che è di tutti i tempi ma nelle singole sue statuizioni, della ragione del pubblico interesse, così come inteso e governato dal pubblico potere» (*author's note*, "[I]n the new framework of economic policy the patrimonial right of private individuals assumes an entirely complementary function with respect to administrative regulation [. . .] The subjective right still appears in the code: [. . .] but the spirit of the law has changed [. . .] The norms of the code, despite the prestige of the presentation, are more often – and above all those that have a bearing on economic activity – complementary norms [. . .]. Character of the new code [is, ed.] a permeation of the same, not in the general spirit – which is of all times – but in its individual statutes, of the reason of the public interest, as understood and governed by the public power").

45 *See*, in doctrine, S. Pugliatti, *La proprietà nel nuovo diritto*, Milano, 1964, p. 145 ff.; and, in jurisprudence, Italian Cort. cost., n. 55 e 56 del 1968, in *Giur. cost.*, 1968, p. 838 ff.

This is the result of an undeniable process that, over time, while preserving the ownership scheme, has, in fact, deeply altered it, dissolving the old unitary category through its gradual stratification: recourse has been had to the ownership scheme whenever it could be used to support situations that, justified from a realistic point of view, required, in the social perception, a strong protection equal to that recognized to the right to property.[46]

It follows, then, the need to grasp the actual relationship that exists between the different property statutes and the attempt, at least theoretically, to maintain a unitary notion, not only from a linguistic but also from a conceptual point of view,[47] in the full awareness that, in the current phase, two different dimensions coexist, the unitary and the multidimensional, whose reciprocal distancing becomes concretely stronger in a digitized age capable of detaching itself from space-time limits.

And a similar assumption appears valid even if one admits that this problem is not current and momentary,[48] but is rooted in a historical-tralatial perspective that an apparent unitary surface has been flanked by the actual perception of profoundly different sector disciplines, the undoubted existence of which makes one doubt how the very formation of a consolidated unitary orientation on the concept of property was possible.[49]

In essence, and to draw the initial threads of the discourse, it seems beyond doubt to affirm that ownership is configured, without doubt, as a scheme which, in order to be grasped in a valence that reflects and recognizes the interests actually at stake, must be framed in the perspective of a profound relativity that is capable of underlining its polysense value.[50]

Thus, if the importance of the concept in the correct understanding of an institute is undeniable, it is also undeniable that this truth shall not lead to overlook the

46 Consider, in this respect, what happened, for example, with the company. *See*, for more details, R. Nicolò, *Riflessioni sul tema dell'impresa e su talune esigenze di una moderna dottrina del diritto civile*, in *Rivista del diritto civile*, I, 1956, p. 181 ff.; S. Cassese, *Dalla proprietà all'impresa: i beni privati destinati dallo Stato alla produzione*, in *Politica del diritto*, 1975, p, 609 ff.

47 The possible shift from single and unique property to properties differentiated in their concrete scope implies that, in any case, one must continue to give due prominence to norms, conceptual schemes, and ordinary notions based on the features of a property right that remain identical in their profound essence and continue to be valid, but in different terms.

48 *See*, for an initial breakdown of the unitary concept of property, O. von Gierge, *Die soziale Aufgabe des Privatrechts*, Berlin, 1889, *passim*; L. Duguit, *Traité de droit constitutionnel. II*, Paris, 1923, p. 210 ff. *See*, on the plasticity of property law, L. Jossernad, *Cours de droit civil positif français. I*, Paris, 1938, p. 839. *See*, on the original idea of "several properties" instead of a unitary ownership scheme borrowed from French codification and pandering, F. Vassalli, *Per una definizione legislativa del diritto di proprietà*, in *Studi giuridici. III*, Milano, 1960, p. 331, «[S]embra corrispondente allo stato attuale delle leggi, le quali hanno disciplinato in vario modo i poteri del proprietario, riconoscere che non vi è una sola proprietà, che vi sono piuttosto delle proprietà, in quanto l'interesse pubblico è che l'appropriazione dei beni comporti statuti diversi in armonia con gli scopi perseguiti, i quali variano assai» (*author's note*, "It corresponds to the current state of the laws, which have regulated the powers of the owner in various ways, to recognise that there is not just one property, that there are rather properties, since the public interest is that the appropriation of property should entail different statuses in harmony with the aims pursued, which vary greatly"); S. Pugliatti, *La proprietà nel nuovo diritto*, cit., p. 148 ff.

49 *See*, for further details, S. Rodotà, *Il terribile diritto*, cit., p. 127 ff.

50 *See*, for all, A. Gambaro, Jus edificandi *e disciplina civilistica della proprietà*, Milano, 1975, p. 345.

peculiarities of a legal scheme: the model must be relativized in its actual scope in order to become one of the factors to be considered in an investigation that relates to the period or sector considered.[51]

It appears, however, relevant to note that even an analysis so set out would be of little value if it led to the mere proliferation of notions of property by reason of individual statutes of reference. It follows that, in full respect of the field of investigation of the present work and giving due prominence to the direct observation of reality, it would be more useful to grasp the constituent elements of the legal scheme of property in the current system of digitalization, emphasizing its unity, albeit multifaceted, without however arriving at the unidimensional crystallization of its legal structure.[52]

In essence, property in general (general concept), and digital property in particular (sector concept), must be seen as the fruit of a process that through the historical overlapping of different levels has reached the contemporary era with characteristic traits that nonetheless allow for its tracing back to a specific scheme that, despite its flexibility and fragmentary nature, is capable of describing the different types of relationships that bind man to thing.[53]

Nonetheless, the awareness of the specificities of the environment under consideration, i.e. the digital world, would impose avoiding that the peculiar traits of the proprietary scheme operating therein can be extended to "all" properties: a given conceptual framework should not be read as a single conceptual model that can be extended to every similar situation.[54]

51 J. Gerring, *What Makes a Concept Good? A Criterial Framework for Understanding Concept Formation in the Social Sciences*, in *Polity*, 31(3), 1999, p. 357 ff., where the author, at p. 357, affirms that «[G]oodness in concept formation, I argue, cannot be reduced to "clarity," to empirical or theoretical relevance, to a set of rules, or to the methodology particular to a given study. Rather, I argue that conceptual adequacy should be perceived as an attempt to respond to a standard set of criteria, whose demands are felt in the formation and use of all social science concepts: (1) familiarity, (2) resonance, (3) parsimony, (4) coherence, (5) differentiation, (6) depth, (7) theoretical utility, and (8) field utility».

52 S. Rodotà, *Il terribile diritto*, cit., p. 57, where the author warns that «[L]a mancata considerazione dell'"ambiente" in cui uno specifico statuto proprietario vive [. . .] può indurre ad elevare tale statuto a modello di un più generale ordinamento dei beni, proiettando le conclusioni tratte dall'analisi di "una" proprietà su "tutte" le proprietà, così ricalcando proprio lo schema (e il vizio) d'origine della definizione unitaria (in cui [. . .] sostanzialmente si rispecchiano i caratteri tipici della disciplina della proprietà terriera». (*author's note*, "The failure to take into account the *environment* in which a specific proprietary statute lives [. . .] may lead to elevating that statute to a model of a more general order of property, projecting the conclusions drawn from the analysis of *one* property onto *all* property, thus tracing precisely the scheme (and flaw) of the origin of the unitary definition – in which [. . .] the typical features of the discipline of land ownership are substantially reflected").

53 *See*, on the concept of disruptive innovation and technologies, C. Hopp, D. Antons, J. Kaminski, T. Oliver Salge, *Disruptive Innovation: Conceptual Foundations, Empirical Evidence, and Research Opportunities in the Digital Age*, in *J. Prod. Innov. Manag.*, 35(3), 2018, p. 446 ff.

54 Cfr. S. Rodotà, *Il terribile diritto*, cit., p. 57, according to whom «[I]n definitiva, tutte le indagini tendenti a sostituire ad un riferimento concettuale unico una molteplicità di assunzioni concrete [. . .] devono decifrare una dialettica complessa: se non possono trascurare il fatto che, per un periodo sufficientemente lungo e rappresentativo, proprio il concetto "astratto" ha costituito il "reale" punto d'avvio di operazioni legislative, giurisprudenziali e scientifiche [. . .], neppure possono rinunciare, già nella prospettiva storica e non solo ricostruendo i lineamenti dell'ordinamento vigente, a misurare la rilevanza effettiva dei singoli statuti» (*author's note*, "In short, all investigations tending to replace a single conceptual reference with a multiplicity of concrete assumptions [. . .] must decipher a complex dialectic:

This would lead to the development of a conceptualism no longer statically steeped in dogmatism (formalistic abstraction), because it is entangled in the coils of abstract and immutable definitions, but dynamically oriented towards enhancing the flow of time and its impact on legal institutions and capable of achieving an inclusive elasticity of property law (factual effectiveness).[55]

3 Inclusivity: A Feature of Contemporary Property Models?

It is well known, on the one hand, that the proprietary model has classically represented a strong protection scheme, operating as a reference for elaborating the very notion of subjective right or being linked to the due process of law, so as to be extended to situations considered relatable or superior in socio-economic relevance to the proprietary scheme, and, on the other hand, that proprietary protection has been placed to protect resources that were becoming progressively scarce, so as to pose the problem of how and how much access to them and how and how much to enjoy them.[56]

On closer inspection, however, such an approach, especially in its latest implications, turns out to be only partial and not fully exhaustive when it refers to goods that, by their nature and intrinsic character, are not subject to the schemes of materiality and thus the limitation of resources, but are theoretically reproducible without limits, as evidently happens for immaterial *res*, first and foremost the digital ones.

Therefore, the classic proprietary discipline appears to run up against the very physical characteristics of these goods and fails to express exhaustively the relationship between interests and the subjects that make themselves bearers of them, on the one hand, and goods, on the other, since it is forced, in fact, to select the holders of these situations with individualistic criteria that discount the orientations proper to the model of (more or less) solitary property generally adopted by the various legal systems.[57]

It would seem, therefore, that in the field of intangible assets, recourse to the proprietary scheme, as traditionally understood, could only take place at the cost

---

if they cannot overlook the fact that, for a sufficiently long and representative period, the very *abstract* concept has constituted the 'real' starting point of legislative, jurisprudential and scientific operations [. . .], neither can they renounce, already in the historical perspective and not only by reconstructing the lineaments of the existing legal system, to measure the actual relevance of individual statutes").

55 P. Grossi, *Il dominio e le cose. Percezioni medievali e moderne dei diritti reali*, Milano, 1992, p. 605, where the author, referring in particular to Pugliatti's masterly and innovative work on the unhinging of property, affirms that «[L]o storico non può che sentirsi a suo agio dinnanzi a questa estrazione della proprietà dal suo secolare recinto sacrale, a questa sua immersione nel profano delle cose costringendola a fare i conti, ormai al di fuori dello scrigno protettivo del soggetto, con le crudezze dei fatti naturali ed economici. È l'invito a relativizzare nozione e istituto che egli può pienamente e senza timore raccogliere come messaggio di questo fertile ripensamento teorico, che vuole essere soprattutto profanazione di un simulacro e recupero alla storia d'un modello assoluto» (*author's note*, "The historian cannot but feel at ease with this extraction of property from its age-old sacred enclosure, with this immersion in the profane of things, forcing it to come to terms, now outside the protective casket of the subject, with the crudeness of natural and economic facts. It is the invitation to relativise notion and institute that he can fully and fearlessly take up as the message of this fertile theoretical rethinking, which aims above all to be the profanation of a simulacrum and the recovery to history of an absolute model").

56 *See supra* esp. Chapter 2, § 4.

57 *See* P. Barcellona, *L'individualismo proprietario*, Torino, 1978, p. 78 ff.

of an evident distortion of the real situation: a conflict between the reference legal logic, i.e. the proprietary root, and the reality of the interests involved in the transaction, i.e. the non-proprietary ground, would be evident.[58]

In fact, according to the traditional understanding, the right of exclusion is connected to the individuality of the right of ownership: since the owner can exclude any other subject from the utilities and enjoyment of the resources he owns, he is the only one who can benefit from them.

This sentiment implies that the exclusivity of property would refer to the uniqueness of the owner-subject with respect to a *res* perceived in its entirety, such that, in general, no sharing of the fruits generated by the *res* that is its object would be allowed.

In the same perspective, then, if the exclusivity could be perceived as an implication of the absoluteness of the property that characterizes the relationship that may exist between the owner and third parties, at a closer look, these are two distinct profiles, since, on the one hand, the first tends to describe the relationship existing between a bundle of (absolute) faculties and the other subjects of the legal system, which are consequently excluded from the enjoyment of any utility absolute right more, while the second tends to consider the entirety of the right that the owner has towards the property in relation to others.[59]

The technique of the proprietary type, attributing to the exclusive dominion of a subject an asset that can potentially be enjoyed without its detriment by an indeterminable and indeterminable collectivity, may appear socially less acceptable and practically more difficult to structure when dealing with intangible assets.[60]

Prima facie, and in a purely theoretical line, intangible goods, in general, and digital goods, in particular, do not pose those problems *ex rerum natura* that, instead, are found in physical goods, for which it is unthinkable that a generalized ownership could be dispersed in innumerable rivulets of which each could represent an autonomous portion to be enjoyed and, thus, an individualistic interest to be protected.[61]

58 *See*, for further consideration, D. Messinetti, *Oggettività giuridica delle cose incorporali*, Milano, 1970, esp. p. 205 ff.

59 *See*, *ex multis*, A. Gambaro, *La proprietà*, cit. p. 215 ff.

60 *See* H. Dagan, *The Social Responsibility of Ownership*, in *Cornell Law Rev*., 92, 2006, p. 1255 ff.; A. Dorfman, *The Normativity of the Private Ownership Form*, in *Mod. Law Rev*., 75(6), 2012, p. 981 ff., where the author starts his analysis moving from one of the most acute charges against private property, according to which ownership generates a trespassory duty of exclusion that far exceeds the requirements of a commitment to values such as freedom and well-being, and accordingly there exists an analytical mismatch between the form of protecting ownership and the functions that this protection may serve. Therefore the author develops a novel account of ownership's normativity, maintaining that, apart from the functions it may render to external values, the form of ownership is in itself a source of value, in virtue of the society it may engender between free and equal persons. As a consequence, any gap between the form and the function of ownership need not plague private ownership, because the functions of ownership do not exhaust the explanation of its good. The formal core of private property is a distinctively social one, even in the most isolated case of trespass to property.

61 *See*, in this perspective, *ex aliis*, L. Katz, *Exclusion and Exclusivity in Property Law*, in *Univ. Toronto Law J*., 58, 2008, p. 275 ff., where the author, at p. 277, affirms that «[. . .] ownership, like sovereignty, is an exclusive position that does not depend for its exclusivity on the right to exclude others from the object of the right».

It is precisely the structural characteristics of this type of resource that do not set insurmountable limits to its fragmentation and ensure a basic usability that, without a doubt, can be ensured, to the same degree and in the same way, to an indistinct conglomeration of users who are the bearers of their own interests.[62]

Indeed, intellectual property itself, beyond the aspects inherent to its mere economic exploitation, reveals *ex se* a scenario whose profiles of exclusion and inclusion are closely intertwined.

Exclusivity implies that, once one has authorized the use and enjoyment of the resource one owns,[63] one can include other subjects, even in copious numbers, in the benefits linked to the availability of the asset, since the products of the intellect can be enjoyed in a multiple and non-antagonistic manner.[64]

In general, in fact, if thanks, for example, to lease, rent or commodate, the owner of a tangible asset can admit only a limited number of individuals to the enjoyment of the effects that are connected to the ownership of the *res*, on the other hand, a potentially indefinite number of persons could be legitimized to exploit an intellectual work or an invention, since the benefits that one of them derives from the asset do not invalidate or reduce those of another.

On the other hand, however, the discipline of intellectual works presents numerous boundaries inherent to its very nature, and within which both public and private interests must be harmonized – as, for example, is the case with the regime of exceptions[65] – that prevent the occurrence of full and perfect exclusivity.[66]

62 *See*, also for a comparative point of view, R. Lubens, *The Social Obligation of Property Ownership: A Comparison of German and US Law*, in *Ariz. J. Intern. Comp. Law*, 24, 2007, p. 389 ff.

63 *See*, in this regard, G. Giannelli, *Open Source e diritti morali*, in *Open Source*, a cura di M. Bertani, Milano, 2005, p. 201, where the author, with specific reference to the copyleft's phenomenon, states that «[. . .] il meccanismo adoperato è pur sempre fondato [. . .] sull'utilizzo di una serie di prerogative del diritto d'autore» (*author's note*, "[. . .] the mechanism used is still based [. . .] on the use of a series of copyright prerogatives"), hence «[. . .] il sistema di licenze non comporta o non dovrebbe comportare abdicazione dai diritti morali che restano pur sempre in capo all'autore; cioè il diritto alla paternità ed all'integrità dell'opera, il diritto a pubblicare l'opera o a mantenerla inedita, il diritto al ritiro dell'opera dal commercio; pacificamente considerati diritti irrinunciabili, imprescrittibili e intrasmissibili e, come tali, non oggetto di negoziazione» (*author's note*, "the licensing system does not entail or should not entail the abdication of moral rights that still remain with the author, i.e. the right to the paternity and integrity of the work, the right to publish the work or to keep it unpublished, the right to withdraw the work from the market; peacefully considered inalienable, imprescriptible and intransmissible rights and, as such, not subject to negotiation"). *See*, for further details on the copyleft's scheme, *infra* Chapter 4.

64 If the owner of a flat can, for physical reasons, rent it out to a limited number of persons, a potentially unlimited group of persons could be legitimized, on the other hand, to exploit an intellectual work because the advantage of one would not compromise the advantage of the other.

65 Consider, for example, of the privileges attached to copyright, private use, time restrictions attached to the exploitation of intellectual property, fair use.

66 If this assumption is not entirely applicable to trademarks, since the owner generally does not grant a licence to use them to others, and to patents, the exploitation of which is legitimized exclusively by the owner, the same cannot be said for other intellectual creations, such as, for example, musical pieces that can never be listened to or distributed without the author's authorization, or patents on computer components that are generally never licensed to those who actually manufacture them.

More concretely, then, what should be meant by inclusiveness, and hence, conversely, exclusiveness?

The concept of inclusive property is certainly not new to Anglo-Saxon doctrine, which has elaborated it since the 1970s,[67] and was then embraced with particular impetus, among others, by Italian scholars who have linked to it the idea of a property regime that should allow more subjects access to a similar resource,[68] so that any limitations to the exercise of the right to property have been reinterpreted from the viewpoint of inclusiveness.[69]

67 *See* C.B. Macpherson, *Liberal Democracy and Property*, in *Property, Mainstream and Critical Positions*, edited by C.B. Macpherson, Oxford, 1978, p. 201, where the author states that «[P]roperty [. . .] need not to be confined, as liberal theory has confined it, to a right to exclude others from the use or benefit of some thing, but may equally be an individual right not to be excluded by others from the use or benefit of some thing». More recently, however, the notion of inclusiveness or inclusive property has also been referred to intellectual property. *See*, in this sense, P. Drahos, *A Defence of Intellectual Commons*, in *Consumer Policy Rev.*, 3, 1996, p. 2 ff.; R.P. Merges, *Justifying Intellectual Property*, Cambridge, MA, 2011, p. 295 ff., where the author, referring especially to informal modes of inclusion, such as, for instance, non-enforcement, states, at p. 295, that «[A]ttending to the post-grant stage in the life of a typical property right (including especially most IP rights) reveals all sorts of ways that the supposedly exclusive right of property is actually bound up with various forms of inclusion», and, at p. 296, that «[P]roperty is in this sense a two-way door: we can enter the word of property, but private actors can choose to leave it if and when they wish . . . it is completely at odds with the superficial emphasis on property as a right to exclude. The ability to easily include is an important flip side to the grant of property rights». Merges mainly refers to *informal* modes of inclusion (see further), such as non-enforcement (see p. 295); S. Dusollier, *The Commons as a Reverse Intellectual Property – From Exclusivity to Inclusivity*, in *Concepts of Property in Intellectual Property*, edited by H. Howe and J. Griffiths, Cambridge, 2013, p. 258 ff.; G. Van Overwalle, *Inventing Inclusive Patents. From Old to New Open Innovation*, in *Kritika: Essays on Intellectual Property. 1*, edited by P. Drahos, G. Ghidini and H. Ullrich, Cheltenham, 2015, p. 206 ff., where the author, with reference to the so-called inclusive patent, states, at p. 206 and p. 208, that «[T]he inclusive patent is perceived as a one-sided right geared to include rather than to exclude others, and encompasses as an attribute the right to enforce sharing behaviour and take non-sharing users to court. [. . .] Rather than offering a right to exclude, the "inclusive patent" encompasses the right to include: it empowers the owner to include others, to control licensing conditions and to enforce alignment with the open source like commitments».

68 *See*, for all, S. Rodotà, *Il terribile diritto*, cit., esp. p. 39 ff., where the author states that «[I]l discorso sull'esclusione viene tramutato [. . .] in quello sull'accessibilità. Si tratta, in tal modo, di ripartire da una diversa "base" per ricostruire i tratti e la legittimazione di una nuova situazione proprietaria. E si rileva come una incontestata utilizzazione delle tecniche proprietarie possa essere rinvenuta in due direzioni: tutela offerta ad interessi che, nella scala dei valori socialmente rilevanti, si sono affiancati o hanno sopravanzato quelli proprietari; garanzia di situazioni legate al soddisfacimento delle esigenze e dei bisogni essenziali dell'individuo» ("The discourse on exclusion is transformed [. . .] into that on accessibility. In this way, it is a question of starting from a different *base* in order to reconstruct the features and legitimation of a new proprietary situation. And it is noted how an undisputed use of proprietary techniques can be found in two directions: protection offered to interests that, in the scale of socially relevant values, have flanked or surpassed proprietary ones; guarantee of situations linked to the satisfaction of the essential needs and requirements of the individual"); and, lastly, M. Ferrari, *Proprietà e diritto ad essere inclusi*, in *Rivista critica di diritto privato*, 4, 2016, p. 525 ff.

69 Such an approach must be traced back to Article 42 of the Italian Constitution, which, by providing that «[L]a proprietà privata è riconosciuta e garantita dalla legge, che ne determina i modi di acquisto, di godimento e i limiti allo scopo di assicurarne la funzione sociale e di renderla accessibile a tutti» (*author's note*, "Private property is recognized and guaranteed by the law, which

Thus, inclusiveness is considered the result not only of the possibility of including others in the benefits that can be drawn from the property of others, but more generically, as a trait characterizing situations in which several persons are legitimized to make use of an asset, in a collective and shared manner and without the possibility of excluding others from that utility.

In essence, inclusivity, as a trait clearly opposed to exclusivity, which is essentially the right to enjoy the good in an individual manner and without intrusion by third parties, is presented as the absence of the power to exclude others: the inclusive and collective traits would represent the two dimensions and the two indicators of inclusivity that would be manifested both in the inclusion in the use of the *res* and in the commonality of use.

According to a traditional approach, in effect, the lack of exclusivity in the exercise of the right, can be made to descend either from the absence of an authentic right of ownership[70] or, on the contrary, from the presence of a right of ownership lacking the character of exclusivity.[71]

The question that now arises is to assess whether inclusiveness, to be referred to all those situations in which the enjoyment of a resource, whether tangible or intangible, is shared, individually or collectively, by a certain number of subjects, without any of them having the power to exclude the others from such advantageous use, translates into the absolute lack of ownership or into a different attitude of the right of ownership.

In other words, going along with a classical view, it could be assumed that since exclusivity is the essential trait of property, inclusiveness is a trait, albeit not essential, either of some forms of property or of some non-property situations.

Adopting, however, a different approach that enhances the new patterns that the subject-thing relationship seems to assume, especially in the new digital world, inclusivity would fall within the logic of ownership and would be placed within it as an expression of the different gradation that exclusivity can assume.

determines the ways in which it may be acquired, enjoyed and its limits in order to ensure its social function and to make it accessible to all"), allows, in essence, even non-owning individuals to be recipients of the proprietary regime.

70 Consider the public domain which can affect the area of intellectual property. In this case, one is in the presence of intellectual works or inventions that are not protected by copyright or patent law, or are no longer protected by patent law due to the expiry of the term of legal protection, and which, consequently, can be freely used, without requesting prior licences or authorizations or paying any remuneration. Therefore, the privileges linked to the exclusivity of the right are removed by allowing anyone to make use of the good that falls under the public domain and enjoy it by having common and equal ownership.

71 Consider the exceptions that apply to copyright or copyleft licences. With particular reference to the latter case, in fact, the owner renounces the exclusive nature of the right in order to guarantee others ample freedom of use, thus creating a double defect of exclusivity: on the one hand, the owner of the copyright renounces its exclusivity and, on the other, allows third party-licensees to make non-exclusive use of the asset (work or invention) that is its object. The copyleft license differs, therefore, from the classic licence linked to copyright because, in the former, it is available to any potential user and guarantees similar rights to each, whereas, in the latter, the license refers to a specific and determined user.

In essence, precisely because of the in reality only theoretical character of full exclusivity, the right to property could be read as the fruit of profiles that contextually favour exclusion and inclusion,[72] with all the consequences that this assumption could entail on the regime concretely applicable to concrete cases.

In the perspective described above, however, two aspects must be kept in mind with reference to digital or more generically digital goods, since it could be noted, on the one hand, that the elaborations developed in a proprietary key impose, in any case, forms of balancing of interests among the potential users of the intangible *res* considered, and, on the other hand, that the sublimation of defences of a proprietary type could lead to the strengthening of the position of those subjects who more than others, in practice, behave as owners of the asset in question, generating a contradiction between the centrality of proprietary protection and the selection of interests theoretically referable to it.[73]

Nonetheless, the situation described here would present peculiar traits resulting from the possibility of not finding interests in reciprocal contrast even though burdened by the same asset, inasmuch as immateriality allows, in power, an analogous opportunity and intensity of enjoyment of the *res* by an indistinct plurality of subjects, without this necessarily translating into mutual prejudice or mutual limitation.

It is, therefore, in a renewed perspective that takes into account the appropriate diversity of both the assets and the interests at stake, that the distinctive traits of the ownership of digital assets must be grasped, while being aware of the proper role played by classical schemes for the correct framing of the new situations of interest, value and discipline.[74]

In fact, only in the *modus operandi* now outlined would it be possible to adopt a line of enquiry capable of grasping the various interests involved and, in the name of polysemy and polycentrism, to verify in their perspective the actual scope of the proprietary schemes:[75] it is necessary to analyse reality in order to find the actual

72 *See*, in this sense, D. Kelly, *The Right to Include*, in *Emory Law J.*, 63, 2014, p. 857 ff., according to whom the power of exclusion, which is so profoundly inherent in the right of ownership, concerns both the right to exclude and the right to include, so that certain costs and benefits are linked to one or the other of the proprietary situation, as determined by the *voluntas domini* or the *voluntas legis*. So much so that any such inclusion is traced back to the will of the owner.

73 This distinction would realize a contrast between "good" and "bad" property, which has played such a large part in the progressive creation of instruments of proprietary protection appropriate to the guarantee requirements of the former.

74 It should be noted that such an attitude must not, however, lead to the extremes of either a necessarily revolutionary approach or a slavish adherence to traditional systematics, because the polestar must continue to be the correct perception of real situations.

75 *See* S. Rodotà, *Il terribile diritto*, cit., p. 451, where the author, with reference to an enquiry approach based on the opposition exclusion-inclusion, states that recourse to the inclusive model «[P]er il giurista, [. . .] si converte in domande concrete intorno alla possibilità di conformare alcuni almeno tra gli statuti proprietari in modo tale da renderli disponibili proprio all'inclusione di soggetti e interessi diversi da quelli del titolare del diritto di proprietà» (*author's note*, "[P]er the jurist, [. . .] converts into concrete questions about the possibility of conforming some at least of the

legal background that represents the indispensable prerequisite for giving a correct collocation to the proprietary institution itself.

It follows that, going beyond formulas that are empty because they are abstract in their formalism, one would follow reconstructive paths that would lead one to consider the complex dialectic that exists between the unitary concept and the theories of "plus" and "new" property – of which we have tried to highlight some essential profiles – so as to overcome, through the realist instance, a unitary and formal notion of property, through its decomposition into the multiplicity of statutes referable to the various categories of property, to then recompose it in the light of the existing link between economic expectations and property protection.[76]

The different protection needs expressed by the owners of the goods and underlying the reformed proprietary notion would not, however, overshadow that new unifying element which, at a substantial level, is translated into the natural aptitude of each good to be the object of enjoyment and economic exploitation.

The paths thus open to the interpreter could lead either to a re-dimensioning of the systematic incidence of property or to its valorization, but always with a view to an opportune recovery of the realistic scope of the theory of property or of the new property, and not of aprioristic framings that would end up immolating factual reality on the altar of an immediate repetition and reproduction of the proprietary modules that would disregard giving correct consideration to the different legal sectors and to the different categories of goods.[77]

If set out in the terms described, the discourse thus appears functional to encompassing an increasing number of hypotheses, which the digital age reveals, if the asset presents a contextual and shared use and, in this way, expresses its own utility and protection needs.

---

property statutes in such a way as to make them available precisely to the inclusion of subjects and interests other than those of the owner of the property right").

76 *See*, classically, Italian Cort. cost., n. 55 del 1968, cit., p. 838 ff.

77 *See*, for a broaden approach to an effective analysis of ideas and concepts, Q. Skinner, *Meaning and Understanding in the History of Ideas*, in *History Theory*, 8(1), 1969, p. 3 ff., where the author, at p. 50, states that «[. . .] the critique I have mounted already serves to suggest a much more obvious and less remote point about the philosophical value of studying the history of ideas. On the one hand, it has [. . .] become clear that any attempt to justify the study of the subject in terms of the "perennial problems" and "universal truths" to be learned from the classic texts must amount to the purchase of justification at the expense of making the subject itself foolishly and needlessly naive. Any statement, [. . .], is inescapably the embodiment of a particular intention, on a particular occasion, addressed to the solution of a particular problem, and thus specific to its situation in a way that it can only be naive to try to transcend. The vital implication here is not merely that the classic texts cannot be concerned with our questions and answers, but only with their own. There is also the further implication that – to revive Collingwood's way of putting it – there simply are no perennial problems in philosophy: there are only individual answers to individual questions, with as many different answers as there are questions, and as many different questions as there are questioners. There is in consequence simply no hope of seeking the point of studying the history of ideas in the attempt to learn directly from the classic authors by focusing on their attempted answers to supposedly timeless questions».

4 The Subtle Erosion of Ownership Rights: Property Status as a Cluster of Powers or Entitlements

The perception of the right to property in the "disintegrating" perspective of the plurality of ownership statuses and inclusion stimulates a renewed consideration of property and its regimes of ownership, which leads one to consider the relationship existing between the multiplicity of regimes and the potential permanence of common rules[78] in the light of a different way of using-possessing.[79]

Therefore, a revisitation of the ownership model, which is also aimed at reflecting the characteristics of the digital world, leads to a particular adaptation of multiple ownerships which, as a consequence, does not lead to a mere crisis of the atavistic ownership scheme, but to its extension beyond the limits tralatically assigned to it.

In other words, the realist dissolution that would unveil the powers in which this right expresses itself and its defence of economic utilities, and then move into the potential and specific protection of these utilities to be traced back to the classical scheme of ownership, would affect property.

The result would thus be a greater penetration of property not only in the place traditionally assigned to it, the centre of the legal system, thanks to the privilege classically granted to domination, but more widely wherever there might be economic utilities to be protected.

The paradox is thus realized, because the disintegration of the granitic proprietary scheme is not accompanied by the dissolution of the centrality of property in and of itself considered, but by a substantial strengthening of it that finds its origin in a greater pervasiveness, which, without translating itself into the necessary split between property and control[80] or between property and freedom,[81] entails the establishment of a less intense bond with the *res* (so-called realist centrism) and a stronger bond with economic utility (so-called economic centrism).

78 *See*, for more details, F. Romano, *Diritto e obbligo nella teoria del diritto reale*, Napoli, 1967, *passim*, where the author argues that the changes that deeply affect society and reverberate on property do not necessarily entail the disruption of the same concept and ownership model; S. Rodotà, *Il terribile diritto*, cit., p. 449, wherein the author, in the face of the theoretical upheavals that have from time to time affected the very concept of property, warns against the easy alteration of the logic of ownership, stating that «[Q]ueste sono descrizioni di una società che muta nelle sue componenti e nei suoi rapporti, non una dimostrazione persuasiva del fatto che nuove componenti e nuovi rapporti sono sottoposti a logiche regolative diverse da quelle del passato» (*author's note*, "These are descriptions of a society that is changing in its components and relations, not a persuasive demonstration of the fact that new components and new relations are subject to regulatory logics different from those of the past").

79 *See* P. Grossi, *Un altro modo di possedere*, Milano, 1977, *passim*, where the author focuses on the collective profiles of property and delves into the concept of ownership from a historical and philosophical perspective, exploring the various ways in which people have understood and practiced ownership throughout different periods of history. The author examines the evolution of ownership and property rights, considering social, cultural, and legal dimensions and offers a thought-provoking analysis of the complex relationship between individuals and the things they own, shedding light on the multifaceted nature of possession.

80 *See* F. Galgano, *Proprietà e controllo della ricchezza: storia di un problema*, in *Quaderni fiorentini per la storia del pensiero giuridico moderno*, V–VI, Milano, 1978, p. 681 ff.

81 *See* L. Mengoni, *Proprietà e libertà*, in *Rivista critica di diritto privato*, 1989, p. 427 ff.

In this way, the exclusion-inclusion opposition and the problem of the content of property re-emerges, in a version aimed at re-evaluating the quasi-availability of the proprietary substance and the importance attributable to multiple interests that have the property as their point of reference and incidence.

Of primary importance is the way in which the possible arrangements of interests and the distribution of powers inherent in the use of the property can be realized,[82] for the concrete development of which the reference to the bundle of rights of Hohfeldian memory appears of great importance,[83] underlying which is both the idea of the "decomposability" of the granitic totem of classical property and the idea of the substantial availability of the individual rights that make up the bundle, without necessarily annulling the reference to the proprietary scheme.[84]

In essence, the concept of a bundle of rights allows the interpreter to better understand the real scope of property which, in this way, would see unveiled a

82 Cfr. P. Perlingieri, *Introduzione alla problematica della «proprietà»*, cit., pp. 113 and 114, where the author observes that «[S]i afferma – sulla scía della dottrina tradizionale – che la proprietà è la massima gradazione di appartenenza, volendo sottolineare che la proprietà, rispetto a tutte le altre situazioni soggettive reali, è quella situazione giuridica che dal punto di vista quantitativo maggiormente appartiene al suo titolare. Qui dunque la titolarità incide sul contenuto della situazione giuridica, sulla sua estensione sí da diventarne anche l'aspetto caratterizzante, l'aspetto qualitativo. A nostro parere, invece, il contenuto del diritto non è collegato alla titolarità di un soggetto [. . .]: non si può dire cioè che se un bene appartiene quantitativamente di più ad un soggetto questi ne é proprietario, mentre se gli appartiene quantitativamente di meno ne è soltanto creditore. Invero la situazione giuridica soggettiva appartiene *tout-court*, senza differenze quantitative, non essendo l'appartenenza niente altro che titolarità attuale di una situazione giuridica soggettiva; ed il problema della gradazione dell'appartenenza di una determinata situazione giuridica soggettiva ad un soggetto è un problema mal posto perché delle due l'una: o una situazione giuridica soggettiva appartiene ad un soggetto e dunque quel soggetto ne è titolare o quella situazione giuridica soggettiva non appartiene a quel soggetto, e dunque quel soggetto ha verso quella situazione una spettanza – ed è titolare in termini di potenzialità – o non è affatto titolare di quella situazione» (*author's note*, "It is affirmed – in the wake of traditional doctrine – that ownership is the highest gradation of belonging, wanting to emphasise that property, with respect to all other real subjective situations, is that legal situation that from a quantitative point of view belongs most to its owner. Here, therefore, ownership affects the content of the legal situation, its extension to such an extent that it also becomes its characterising aspect, its qualitative aspect. In our view, on the other hand, the content of the right is not linked to the ownership of a subject [. . .]: that is, it cannot be said that if a good quantitatively belongs more to a subject he is its owner, whereas if it belongs quantitatively less to him he is merely its creditor. Indeed the subjective legal situation belongs *tout-court*, without quantitative differences, belonging being nothing other than the actual ownership of a subjective legal situation; and the problem of the gradation of the ownership of a given subjective legal situation to a subject is an ill posed problem because there are two things: either a subjective legal situation belongs to a subject and therefore that subject is the owner of it or that subjective legal situation does not belong to that subject, and therefore that subject has a claim to that situation – and is the owner in terms of potential – or he is not the owner of that situation at all").

83 *See* Chapter 2, § 4.

84 *See* B. Ackerman, *Private Property and the Constitution*, New Haven, CT and London, 1977, p. 26, where the author affirms that «[I]nstead of defining the relationship between a person and "his" things, property law discusses the relationships that arise *between people* with respect to things. More precisely, the law of property considers the way rights to use things may be parceled out amongst a host of competing resource users».

unitary nature that is only nominalistic and formalistic,[85] where instead the real disarticulation of the institution should be grasped in the actual and concrete development of the subjective situation as it manifests itself specifically.[86]

In other words, it is beyond mere profiles of form that the idea of the "disjointedness" of the notion of property finds a correct methodological basis which, by enhancing reality, aims at reconstructing legal concepts in the light of their attitude in the factual world.[87]

If, then, the reading of property law through the lens of the bundle of rights aims at underlining the different and variegated way in which the proprietary model can position itself towards the resource that constitutes its object, one can easily understand the difference that exists between this approach and the only apparently adjacent notion of elasticity of the dominical situation, from which derives the possibility of the property right to extend or contract in its scope, by reason of the possible relationship established with other and conflicting subjective situations that could burden the same *res*.[88]

85 *See* P. Grossi, *Il dominio e le cose. Percezioni medievali e moderne dei diritti reali*, cit., p. 626, where the author notes that «[. . .] nell'universo giuridico, le forme sono spesso soltanto le punte emergenti di un gigantesco edificio sommerso, un edificio costruito si valori e che a quei valori chiede innanzi tutto il suo essere diritto, regola osservata e rispettata perché aderente alle scaturigini più vive d'un costume, di credenze religiose, di certezze sociali. Solo tutto questo può spiegare il cospicuo ritardo della costruzione giuridica d'una nuova proprietà [. . .]. I valori sono, certo, storicamente variabili, ma la loro e variazione lenta, faticosa, non indolore; e il loro prodotto [. . .] continua a vivere quasi oltre la sua vita naturale; serpeggiando fra le strutture e arrivando perfino a condizionarne il divenire, ma soprattutto annidandosi nelle coscienze» (*author's note*, "In the juridical universe, forms are often only the emerging tips of a gigantic submerged edifice, an edifice built on values and that from those values demands first and foremost its being law, a rule observed and respected because it adheres to the liveliest springs of a custom, of religious beliefs, of social certainties. This alone can explain the conspicuous delay in the legal construction of a new property [. . .]. Values are, of course, historically variable, but their variation is slow, laborious, and not painless; and their product [. . .] continues to live almost beyond its natural life; meandering through structures and even conditioning their future, but above all nesting in the consciences of the people").

86 *See*, in this sense, *ex multis*, N. Irti, *Proprietà fondiaria, contratto e impresa*, in *Quadrimestre*, 1988, p. 30, where the author affirms that «[. . .] il mito della proprietà come unità è definitivamente caduto» (*author's note*, "the myth of property as a unit has definitively fallen"); P. Rescigno, voce *Proprietà (dir. priv.)*, in *Enciclopedia del diritto*, XXXVII, Milano, 1998, p. 267, where the author states that «[. . .] l'analisi della concreta esperienza suggerisce al giurista [. . .] di dissolvere l'unità concettuale dell'istituto della proprietà» ("the analysis of concrete experience suggests to the jurist [. . .] to dissolve the conceptual unity of the institution of property"). *See*, for further references, Chapter 1, § 2.

87 *See* S. Pugliatti, *La proprietà nel nuovo diritto*, cit., p. 146, where the author emphasizes that «[. . .] il procedimento astrattivo, che tende alla costruzione del concetto, non deve oltrepassare quel segno oltre il quale il concetto perde ogni contatto con la realtà». (*author's note*, "the abstract procedure, which tends towards the construction of the concept, must not go beyond that mark beyond which the concept loses all contact with reality").

88 *See*, on this profile, S. Rodotà, *Il terribile diritto*, cit., according to whom the idea of multiple properties allows the overcoming of an abstract notion in favour of an analytical and realistic approach thanks to «[. . .] materiali normativi diversi, in cui più direttamente si riflettono e si riconoscono gli interessi concretamente in gioco [. . .]. Attraverso il riconoscimento della effettiva funzione storica dei diversi elementi costitutivi del sistema giuridico della proprietà [. . .] possono emergere le finalità perseguite con i diversi statuti e il progetto sociale d'insieme [. . .] non più cristallizzato intorno

Elasticity, in fact, must be perceived as an instrument to which the legal system resorts in order to prevent a defined series of powers and prerogatives from being effectively exercised over a property,[89] because only by operating in this way does the legal system prevent a situation characterized by the non-referability of property rights over a property from resulting in a potential loss that, at the same time, benefits no one.[90]

Given its potential extension, the system identifies property as a point of reference for allocating extinguished ownership, and the requirement of elasticity is invoked as an aid to the rules of attribution of assets without a proprietor, as well as a causative moment of the polarization towards the two guises, formal and substantial, that the proprietary situation may assume.[91]

In the light of the considerations made so far, two different paths present themselves before the jurist, one of which is aimed at considering the market, whose inspiring and driving forces would be reflected in the legal structures, and the other is aimed at giving an account of the use that is made of the legal instruments because they contain a value judgment that must be rediscovered and reconsidered.[92]

---

ad un'unica nozione, formalmente unitaria, ma ricavato dall'osservazione diretta di una realtà non più rinsecchita in poche formule dottrinarie» (*author's note*, "different normative materials, in which the interests concretely at stake are more directly reflected and recognized [. . .]. Through the recognition of the actual historical function of the various constituent elements of the legal system of property [. . .] the aims pursued with the various statutes and the overall social project [. . .] can emerge [. . .] no longer crystallized around a single notion, formally unitary, but derived from the direct observation of a reality no longer dried up in a few doctrinaire formulas").

89 *See*, on this profile, V.A. Mikryukov, *On the Property of Elasticity of the Right of Ownership in Case of Its Limitation and Encumbrance*, in *Perm U. Herald Jurid. Sci.*, 14, 2011, p. 100 ff., where the author considers ownership as a passive right by nature that does not constitute a third-party civil right related to the owner's assets, while all encumbrance is active by nature and does constitute a civil right. The author, therefore, demonstrates specific practical differences between limiting and encumbering manifestations of elasticity of the owner's legal rights and observes that when encumbrance exits the owner's legal rights are not invalidated but merely reassigned to other persons, and are then restored to the original owner after the encumbrance is discontinued. The latter feature contrasts sharply with restricted legal ownership rights that exist only as a potential, and reemerge as soon as the limitation is lifted. The author explains the different consequences triggered by destruction of an asset when the respective ownership right is limited or encumbered. The implicitly paid nature of encumbrance is understood to be the special distinctive manifestation of elasticity of the encumbered ownership right. Finally, the author states that differences between the mechanism through which limitations and encumbrances affect the content of the ownership right – and these differences are found through examination of elasticity as an attribute that is highly typical for the ownership right – demonstrate the vital theoretical and practical need to refrain from and prevent confusion of such notions as "encumbrance" and "limitation" in legislative proceedings, legal enforcement, and science research.

90 *See* H. Demsetz, *Some Aspects of Property Rights*, in *J. Law Econ.*, 9, 1966, p. 61 ff. A. Gambaro, *La proprietà*, cit., p. 232.

91 *See* L. De Alessi, *The Economics of Property Rights: A Review of the Evidence*, in *Res. Law Econ.*, 2, 1980, p. 1 ff.; Y. Barzel, *Economic Analysis of Property Rights*, Cambridge, 1997, p. 85 ff.; S. Pugliatti, *La proprietà nel nuovo diritto*, cit., p. 234.

92 *See* H. Demsetz, *The Exchange and Enforcement of Property Rights*, in *J. Law Econ.*, 7, 1964, p. 11 ff. S. Rodotà, *Il terribile diritto*, cit., p. 452 ff.; A.M. Kim, *A Market Without the "Right" Property Rights*, in *Econ. Trans.*, 12(2), 2004, p. 275 ff.

In both cases, the focal point of distinction would, however, be the nature of the *res* considered, since for digital goods one could not repeat those limiting considerations that the physicality associated with material goods would inevitably bring with it.

If, in fact, with regard to material goods one would return to an inevitable weighting and valorization of the utilities that have already been considered, in this paragraph, in order to untie the knot of the redistribution of resources and relative powers among the various subjects involved, the same approach could not be applied to digital goods due to their theoretical reproducibility *ad libitum* and inexhaustibility that would make the proposed allocative needs disappear as a defining momentum of the bundle of concretely explainable powers.

Once, then, with particular reference to digitality, the possible redistributive conflict has been eliminated, with the consequent explication of all its resolving effects on the correlated conflict inherent in the limits of appropriation, the potential conflict on the modalities of utilization of goods by the subjects to whom they have been legitimately attributed should also be revisited in a different perspective, with respect to which the compatibility between conflicting categories of interests in relation to property should be resolved in the dimension of both the attitude of the content of the right and the responsibilities, towards third parties, connected to the exercise of proprietary powers.[93]

And here, again, an important contribution that the jurist could benefit from in a simplifying perspective, would be to link it to the logic of access to digital goods, which, although to be traced back to a circulatory model of exploitation centred on the free use of the contractual instrument,[94] would not, however, be understood as an aptitude to take possession of the resource in an exclusive manner, but should be understood in an open and inclusive sense, and such as to allow the identification of forms of broad enjoyment that could allow mechanisms precisely of inclusion of interests and, at the same time, of enjoyment not subject to spatial and temporal limits.[95]

With a view to considering in more detail the impact that the characteristics referable to digital goods have on the concept of property, it is now necessary to look more concretely at copyleft in order to grasp the qualifying intent connected to the underlying subjective situation, without neglecting the digital single

93 *See*, for further details, M. Hildebrandt, Properties, Property and Appropriateness of Information, in Info*rmation, Freedom and Property*, Abingdon, 2016, p. 34 ff.

94 See, for more details, G.D. Libecap, *Contracting for Property Rights*, in *Property Rights: Cooperation, Conflict, and Law*, edited by T.L. Anderson, F.S. McChesney, Princeton, NJ, 2003, p. 142 ff.

95 *See*, in this view, already F. Vassalli, *Per una definizione legislativa del diritto di proprietà*, in *La concezione fascista della proprietà privata*, Roma, s.a., p. 103, where the author states that «[. . .] i poteri attribuiti al proprietario, e in generale la disciplina giuridica della proprietà, sono diversi a seconda dei beni che formano oggetto del diritto. Sembra corrispondente allo stato attuale delle leggi, [. . .] riconoscere che non vi è una sola proprietà, che vi sono piuttosto delle proprietà in quanto l'interesse pubblico è che l'appropriazione dei beni comporti statuti diversi in armonia cin gli scopi perseguiti, i quali variano assai» (*author's note*, "the powers attributed to the owner, and in general the legal regulation of property, are different depending on the property that is the subject of the right. It seems to correspond to the current state of the law, [. . .] to recognise that there is not a single property, that there are rather properties inasmuch as the public interest is that the appropriation of property should entail different statutes in harmony with the aims pursued, which vary widely").

market, as a strategy adopted by the European Commission to ensure access to online activities,[96] in compliance with the limits of fair competition, consumer and data protection,[97] and to remove the obstacles that can be connected to copyright deriving from geographical barriers.[98]

96 *See*, for further details, D. Broussolle, *A Note on Services in the European Union Regulations: Is Online Digital Content a Service?*, in *Laboratoire de Recherche en Gestion et Economie (LaRGE), Université de Strasbourg*, 7, 2016, p. 1 ff., where the author at first examines the European Union's regulations concerning the distinction between goods and services. He shows that it is essentially based on the opposition between materiality and immateriality, and also points out that the wording of the main article on services in the Treaty (TFEU) tends to introduce confusion. Secondly, the author sets out the new economic approach to services, which is particularly well suited to the knowledge economy, and then he shows that the *Digital Single Market Strategy* faces problems caused by the use of an outdated definition of service. The difficulties concern, on the one side, the VAT rate applicable to intangible goods, considered by the EU to be services (e.g. digital books as opposed to tangible books), and on the other, the directives and communications that deal with the supply of digital content. This concept, invented in particular to circumvent the outdated concept of service, leads to overcome legal treatment and the development of unjustified contractual idiosyncrasies. Adopting the new economic approach to the service would make it possible to resolve these problems and encourage the development of the digital economy.

97 *See, ex multis*, J. Hojnik, *Technology Neutral EU Law: Digital Goods Within the Traditional Goods/Services Distinction*, in *Int. J. Law Inform. Tech.*, 25(1), 2017, p. 63 ff., where the author, at p. 63, affirms that «The European Commission has defined the completion of the Digital Single Market as one of its 10 political priorities. A Digital Single Market is, according to the 2015 Commission's Communication, "one in which the free movement of persons, services and capital is ensured and where the individuals and businesses can seamlessly access and exercise online activities under conditions of fair competition, and a high level of consumer and personal data protection, irrespective of their nationality or place of residence." This should ensure that Europe maintains its position as "a world leader in the digital economy, helping European companies to grow globally." A well-functioning Digital Single Market should make online access to goods and services easier and, therefore boost the traditional free movement of goods and services. It will also increase the digital skills and learning of European citizens so they can use digital transactions to their personal benefit – as consumers, patients and public administration clients. At the centre of the Digital Single Market are digital goods, a broad and rapidly expanding term in view of the variety of "goods" actually covered, referring to all goods that are stored, delivered and used in its electronic format, such as smartphone applications, digital music and books, computer design files for 3D printed products, for instance houses, medical devices and food. As such digital goods may be distinguished from physical (or analogue) goods that refer to material things with physical dimensions, but also from services that were traditionally considered as something that cannot be stored nor owned. Therefore, digital goods bring a broad range of legal challenges in respect of whether they should legally be treated as physical goods or as services – or, alternatively, as a *sui generis* concept and what consequences this would bring – *inter alia* in the field of copyright, taxation and consumer protection law».

98 *See* J. Hojnik, *Technology Neutral EU Law: Digital Goods Within the Traditional Goods/Services Distinction*, in *Int. J. Law Inform. Tech.*, cit., p. 63 ff., where the author addresses the growing number of requests made by both governmental and non-governmental organizations urging the EU institutions to establish consistent legal guidelines for the treatment of digital and physical goods. The author examines the existing criteria used to distinguish between goods and services in the field of marketing and evaluates the significance placed on the tangibility and marketability of goods by the Court of Justice of the European Union. Based on this analysis, she explores the potential implications of considering digital goods to be equivalent to physical goods in various areas of law. Finally, the author highlights the crucial legal implications of categorizing digital goods in fields such as copyright, taxation, and consumer protection; I. Graef, *Rethinking the Essential Facilities Doctrine for the EU Digital Economy*, in *Revue Juridique Themis*, 53, 2019, p. 33 ff.; L. Cabral, J. Haucap, G. Parker, G. Petropoulos, T.M. Valletti, M.W. Van Alstyne, *The EU Digital Markets Act:*

A Report from a Panel of Economic Experts, in *The EU Digital Markets Act*, edited by Cabral, L. Cabral, J. Haucap, G. Parker, G. Petropoulos, T.M. Valletti, M.W. Van Alstyne, Luxembourg, 2021, where the authors observes that in recent years, numerous reports have emphasized the dominant market position of prominent online platforms that function as intermediaries between businesses and consumers, highlighting the challenge faced by traditional competition policy tools in effectively addressing anti-competitive practices within these platforms. In response to this concern, the European Commission has recently unveiled a proposal known as the Digital Markets Act (DMA), aimed at supplementing existing competition policy tools with *ex ante* obligations for platforms. The authors endorse the principles embodied in the DMA, which include the identification of large gatekeeper platforms and the introduction of a set of *ex ante* obligations that these platforms must adhere to. They acknowledge the precarious task of striking an equilibrium between the advantages derived from network effects associated with large platforms and the potential detrimental effects stemming from anti-competitive conduct and winner-takes-all dynamics prevalent in online services. While some instances of anti-competitive behaviour are well-known from traditional competition cases, data-driven multi-sided platforms have devised novel methods of engaging in tying, bundling, and self-preferencing, presenting new challenges for regulators. The authors delve into these behaviours within specific contexts, such as online advertising and mobile ecosystems, exploring avenues for leveraging valuable platform-generated data for pro-competitive purposes and the broader societal benefit. An ongoing issue in the effective implementation of the DMA obligations pertains to information asymmetry between platforms and regulators. It is imperative to address this matter to ensure the obligations are implemented successfully and to uphold a higher standard of fairness in the equitable distribution of the social value generated by these prominent platforms.

4 Copyleft as a Paradigm of Shifting in Property Conceptualization?

1 Manifestations of Digital Liberty and the Emergence of the Sharing Culture

If the possessive individualism of the 17th and 18th centuries,[1] which picking up the erosive criticism of previous theological strands, interpreting the sense of cultural upheavals and making the design of emerging classes its own gives rise to a new anthropological model capable of conditioning,[2] under the banner of a property founded on freedom, the way of conceiving the relationship between man and good, freedom is once again found as a founding value in an era of profound technological development.

As already noted, in fact, the digital world does not reveal a scarcity in nature of its goods, which, unlike material goods, are difficult to exclude and non-rivalrous.[3]

1 *See*, for further details, C.B. Macpherson, *The Political Theory of Possessive Individualism: Hobbes to Locke*, Oxford, 1962, where the author argues that the chief difficulty of the notion of individualism that underpins classical liberalism lies in what he calls its «possessive quality», and therefore «its conception of the individual as essentially the proprietor of his own person or capacities, owing nothing to society for them» (p. 3). Under such a conception, (i) the essence of humanity becomes freedom from dependence on the wills of others, (ii) society is little more than a system of economic relations, and (iii) political society becomes a means of safeguarding private property and the system of economic relations rooted in property.

2 R.C. Grady, *Workplace Democracy and Possessive Individualism*, in *J. Pol.*, 52(1), 1990, p. 146 ff.; P. Grossi, *Il dominio e le cose. Percezioni medievali e moderne dei diritti reali*, cit., p. 627; T.W. Greene, *Three Ideologies of Individualism: Toward Assimilating a Theory of Individualisms and Their Consequences*, in *Crit. Soc.*, 34(1), 2008, p. 117 ff.; N. Abercrombie, S. Hill, B.S. Turner, *Sovereign Individuals of Capitalism*, Abingdon, 2015, p. 1 ff.; D.W. Bromley, *Possessive Individualism: A Crisis of Capitalism*, Oxford, 2019, *passim*.

3 Cfr. P.A. David, *Intellectual Property Institutions and the Panda's Thumb*, in *Global Dimensions of Intellectual Property Rights in Science and Technology*, edited by M.B. Wallerstein, M.E. Mogee and R.A. Schoen, Washington, DC, 1993, p. 26, ove l'A., facendo generale riferimento alle idee, afferma che «[I]f nature has made any one thing less susceptible than all others of exclusive property, it is the action of the thinking power called an idea, which an individual may exclusively possess as long as he keeps it to himself; but the moment it is divulged, it forces itself into the possession of every one, and the receiver cannot dispossess himself of it. Its peculiar character, too, is that no one possesses the less, because every other possesses the whole of it [. . .]. That idea should freely spread from one to another over the globe, for the moral and mutual instruction of

DOI: 10.4324/9781003424413-5

Then there is a further aspect that pertains more to competition, given that the fixed costs for the production of original digital goods can also be very high, where the marginal costs of reproduction and distribution are usually low, as a result of which, anyone can reproduce and distribute digital goods at low costs without having to face the huge expenses incurred by the initial producer.

In this context, any user of digital goods can *de facto* turn into a dangerous competitor of the original producer, resulting in a typical case of market failure.

If, therefore, the State did not intervene to correct this discrepancy,[4] the market would present obvious difficulties in its functioning, which could be accompanied by an insufficient production of the technological goods most exposed to these risks, such as, for example, computer programmes or software.[5]

---

man, and improvement of his condition, seems to have been peculiarly and benevolently designed by nature, when she made them, like fire, expansible over all space, without lessening their density in any point, and like the air in which we breathe, move, and have our physical being, incapable of confinement or exclusive appropriation».

4 *See*, for further information, M.A. Lemley, *Antitrust and the Internet Standardization Problem*, in *Conn. Law Rev*., 28, 1995, p. 1041 ff.; R.C. Picker, *Copyright as Entry Policy: The Case of Digital Distribution*, in *Antitrust Bulletin*, 47(2–3), 2002, p. 423 ff.; H.A. Shelanski, *Information, Innovation, and Competition Policy for the Internet*, in *Univ. Penn. Law. Rev*., 161, 2012, p. 1663 ff.

5 A software is composed of a series of mathematical calculation procedures, codes, diagrams and/or algorithms, substantiating itself in a set of instructions given to the computer to enable it to perform certain functional operations to achieve given results. These instructions are concretized in the so-called object code (elaborated by the machine) which represents, in essence, the translation into the so-called machine language of an earlier expression of the idea underlying the intellectual creation in a language characterized by a considerable technicality, which however does not make it incomprehensible to man, the so-called source code or programme (elaborated by man). In Italy, significant questions have been raised on the type of protection to be granted to software and on the adequacy of copyright law to ensure protection for computer programmes, especially with reference to the object code. More specifically, initially, the applicability to software of either the protection envisaged by copyright law or the protection envisaged for industrial patents was debated, also in light of the accepted understanding that rights on industrial inventions arise at the moment the patent is obtained, whereas copyrights on intellectual works arise at the very moment the work is created. Observing that software takes the form of impulses that take on an expressive form that is difficult to bring back to the traditional idea of a protected literary work, some authors have found a problem of communicative capacity that makes the programme incompatible with the logic of the legislation on the protection of intellectual works provided for by Articles 1 and 2 of Law no. 633 of 1941. In fact, precisely by emphasizing the technical nature of programs and their purpose directed to the operation of the machine and not to the communication of ideas and feelings to others, it was held that software could not be classified as intellectual works. Currently, the majority doctrinal orientation is in the sense of considering software as an asset belonging to the category of intangible goods, and this has caused a shift in its analysis towards the field of copyright. *See*, among the authors who have supported the qualification of software as a work of the intellect, G. Santini, *La tutela giuridica della programmazione elettronica*, in *Giurisprudenza italiana*, IV, 1968, p. 225 ff.; G. Galtieri, *Note sulla proteggibilità dei programmi*, in *Diritto di autore*, 1971, p. 425 ff.; G. Sena, *Software: problemi di definizione e di protezione giuridica*, in *Rivista di diritto industriale*, II, 1983, p. 479 ff.; C. Ciampi, *La proteggibilità dei programmi elettronici e dei relativi manuali applicativi quali opere dell'ingegno di carattere creativo*, in *Diritto dell'informazione e dell'informatica*, 1985, p. 258 ff.; e, *contra*, E. Luzzato, *Una norma di legge francese da non imitare (a proposito*

Thus, the provision of (intellectual) property rights conceptually responds precisely to the need to ensure the development of a digital market that can certainly respond to the need for innovation and at the same time protection, but without neglecting the peculiarities that characterize the digital world itself.

In the age of digitalization, the need to ensure due freedom for the conception, development and dissemination of the most diverse technological solutions is felt with particular urgency, without this precluding, at the same time, the protection needs of the owners of technological assets, also for the obvious economic reasons involved.

It follows, then, that there are two factors that interpenetrate the digital ecosystem and present themselves in theoretical conflict: on the one hand, an instance of protection, and on the other, an instance of sharing.

---

della brevettabilità o meno dei programmi o serie di istruzioni per lo svolgimento delle operazioni dei calcolatori elettronici), in *Rivista di diritto industriale*, I, 1968, p. 297 ff.; E. Luzzato, *La crisi del software*, in *Problemi attuali del diritto industriale*, Milano, 1977, p. 719 ff.; G. Ghidini, *I programmi per computers fra brevetto e diritto d'autore*, in *Giurisprudenza commerciale*, I, 1984, p. 251 ff.; R. Borruso, *L'Algoritmo per computer e la sua brevettabilità*, in *Diritto dell'informazione e dell'informatica*, 1987, p. 75 ff.; G. Floridia, *La protezione del software nel sistema delle esclusive sulle creazioni intellettuali*, in *Diritto dell'informazione e dell'informatica*, 1989, p. 71 ff.; G. Guglielmetti, *L'invenzione di software*, Milano, 1997, p. 214 ff.; M. Bertani, *Open source ed elaborazione del software proprietario*, in *Open source*, cit., p. 116 ff., where the author speaks, on the one hand, of the source code as an expressive form belonging to the areas of human knowledge in which intellectual creativity cannot substantially express itself, and, on the other, of the object code as exceptionally protectable by copyright. The impossibility of recognizing patent protection for software is, in any case, reinforced by the express prohibition contained in Article 12 of Royal Decree no. 1127 of 1939, containing the *Testo delle disposizioni legislative in materia di brevetti per invenzioni industriali*, as amended by Presidential Decree No. 338 of 1979. *See*, on the impracticability of software patent protection, S. Pastore, *Il cammino della tutela giuridica del software, opera dell'ingegno di carattere creativo*, in *Diritto d'Autore*, 1987, p. 177, where the author underlines that «[. . .] la disciplina del diritto d'autore non subordina la protezione all'adempimento di alcuna formalità di deposito o di registrazione; con la tutela del diritto d'autore il software consegue una protezione erga omnes; la proteggibilità del software attraverso il diritto d'autore è più ampia di quella brevettuale, anche dal punto di vista quantitativo, oltre che qualitativo, in quanto può riguardare qualsiasi tipo di programma e concernere sia il programma che le istruzioni; la tutela del diritto d'autore è meno rigorosa di quella brevettuale, richiedendo, anche sul piano tecnico, un accenno modesto di originalità personale; la tutela attraverso il diritto d'autore, infine, comporta il riconoscimento dei vari diritti esclusivi previsti dal legislatore in capo al titolare dell'opera dell'ingegno» (*author's note*, "the discipline of copyright does not make protection conditional on the fulfilment of any filing or registration formalities; with copyright protection, software obtains erga omnes protection; the protectability of software through copyright is broader than that of patents, also from a quantitative point of view, as well as qualitative, since it can concern any type of program and concern both the program and the instructions; copyright protection is less rigorous than patent protection, requiring, even on a technical level, a modest hint of personal originality; finally, copyright protection entails the recognition of the various exclusive rights provided by the legislature to the owner of the original work"). *See*, for further details, G. Alpa, *La tutela giuridica del software*, Milano, 1984, *passim*; S. Gatti, voce *Software*, in *Enciclopedia del Diritto*, XLII, Milano, 1990, p. 1208 ff.; L. Bosotti, G. Jacobacci, *I brevetti. La valorizzazione dell'innovazione d'impresa*, Torino, 1993, *passim*.

As to the first profile, in fact, the wide legal circulation that digitality ensures raises questions as to whether or not it satisfies the need to protect the (moral) right to the recognition of the authorship of the work and the right to the integrity of the work as the power to prevent its modification or transformation.

As for the second profile, the regime of free sharing of changes made to the original programme, which represents so much of the free/open source culture, seems to evoke the regime of free uses, which will be explored further below.[6] Now let it suffice to anticipate that this regime, while reflecting the idea of sharing a creative result that is also the basis of free/open sources, is in derogation of the regulations on copyright, while the rationale of the latter can make use of the copyright itself although in an anti-protectionist perspective.

According to article 64-*bis* of Law no. 633 of 1941 (copyright law), in fact, the author may exercise the right to "reproduce, permanently or temporarily, totally or partially, the computer program by any means or in any form," even if limited to loading or display, except for the possibility of the user to reproduce the program for use, pursuant to article 64-*ter* of Law no. 633 of 1941, or to decompile it in order to allow its interoperability with other programs, pursuant to Article 64-*quater* of Law no. 633 of 1941.

According to some authors,[7] the particularly broad wording used by the legislator in the regulation just described, would highlight the attempt, on the one hand, to go beyond the more limited concept of multiplication in copies of the work, to which Article 13 of Law no. 633 of 1941 explicitly refers, and, on the other hand, to make the work more accessible to the public, and on the other hand again, to consider unlawful any processing having as its object software which, not resulting in a reproduction, transformation, adaptation or modification of the program carried out or authorized by the author, reveals an appreciable creative content.

It would therefore follow that the creative elaboration would be subject to copyright protection only if it is carried out without prejudicing the existing rights in the original work, hence the necessary prior consent of the owner of the copyright on the latter.

However, it must not be forgotten that one of the peculiarities of software is its tendentially non-final character, which derives from its possibility of being reworked, updated and modified, even in such terms as to lose all contact with

6 *See*, on the subject, M. Di Rienzo, *L'organizzazione dei mondi open source: profili soggettivi*, in *AIDA*, 2004, § 4 ff. *See infra* §§ 3 and 4.

7 *See*, on the subject of free uses, in general, T. Ascarelli, *Teoria della concorrenza e dei beni immateriali*, cit., p. 741 ff.; P. Greco, P. Vercellone, *I diritti sulle opere dell'ingegno*, in *Trattato di diritto civile italiano*, Torino, 1974, p. 164 ff.; e con particolare riferimento al *software*, P. Auteri, *Diritto d'autore*, in *Diritto industriale. Proprietà intellettuale e concorrenza*, a cura di P. Auteri, G. Floridia, V. Mangini, G. Olivieri, M. Ricolfi, R. Romano, P. Spada, Torino, 2001, p. 574 ff.; N. Abriani, *Le utilizzazioni libere nelle società dell'informazione: considerazioni generali*, in *AIDA*, 2002, p. 98 ff.

the original work.[8] In general terms, then, a derivative work is protected if it is in itself original with respect to the original work, provided that the two conditions are met: it must be clearly traceable to the original work and the author of the original work must authorize the author of the derivative work to exercise the rights related to it.[9]

In fact, according to the common understanding, any updating or improvement of the programme would be subject to the exclusivity reserved to the owner of the copyright.[10]

But can a proprietary scheme that gives due prominence to the peculiarities of digitality be an instrument to be called upon to safeguard the coexistence of this apparent contrast?

Certainly, there are many needs to be met in addressing this primary question, but a correct answer cannot disregard the solicitations that permeate the digital world and that translate into the culture of sharing, mentioned several times in the preceding pages.

In this sense, the so-called openness, understood as openness and confrontation, is configured as a mental attitude of dissemination, change and propensity towards the future and the new technology, with a view to accentuating the circulation of tools strongly aimed at innovation – without, however, neglecting the due protection requirements of the sector's operators.[11]

8 In the latter eventuality, this could create problems of compatibility both with the discipline envisaged by Article 4 of Law no. 633 of 1941 and with the special protection of the author. *See*, in this regard, A. Calisse, *Opera derivata e diritti d'autore con riferimento alla protezione del software*, in *Rivista di diritto industriale*, II, 1988, p. 290 ff.

9 *See* P. Greco, P. Vercellone, *I diritti sulle opere dell'ingegno*, cit., p. 83 ff.; L.C. Ubertazzi, *Spunti sulla comunione di diritti d'autore*, in *AIDA*, 2003, p. 514 ff.

10 *See* A. Calisse, *Opera derivata e diritti d'autore con riferimento alla protezione del* software, cit., p. 290 ff.; A. Musso, *Elaborazioni creative del software e programmi derivati*, in *La legge sul* software. *Commentario sistematico*, a cura di L.C. Ubertazzi, Milano, 1994, p. 47 ff.; P. Auteri, *Internet e il contenuto del diritto d'autore*, in *AIDA*, 1996, p. 86 ff.; L. Nivarra, *Le opere multimediali su Internet*, ibidem, p. 141 ff.; V. Ricciuto, *Internet,* l*'opera multimediale e il contenuto dei diritti connessi*, ibidem, p. 101 ff.; G. Giannelli, *Open source e diritti morali*, in *Open Source*, a cura di M. Bertani, Milano, 2005, p. 206 ff.

11 *See*, on this topic, G. De Michelis, *Aperto molteplice continuo. Gli artefatti alla fine del Novecento*, Milano, 1998, p. 52, where the author observes that «[L']apertura è una qualità importante degli artefatti se si vuole che essi siano usabili in contesti sociali ad alta visibilità, come sono quelli che sempre più frequentemente si presentano ai nostri giorni. [. . .] Un artefatto può essere aperto in molti modi diversi e da molti punti di vista. In primo luogo esso può essere aperto, dal punto di vista del numero di utenti che ammette, se non esclude nessuno, se non richiede procedure complesse per accedervi, se imparare ad usarlo è facile. In secondo luogo, dal punto di vista della sua capacità di combinarsi con altri artefatti, se esso si integra negli ambienti in cui viene situato, se si può comporre con altri artefatti per dare vita a nuovi artefatti più complessi. In terzo luogo, dal punto di vista delle modalità di uso, se offre ai suoi utenti ampi margini di liberta d'uso che ne possono fare, se offre loro la possibilità di inventarsi il loro modo di usarlo» (*author's note*, "[Openness] is an important quality of artefacts if they are to be usable in high-visibility social contexts, such as those that increasingly arise in our time. [. . .] An artefact can be open in many different ways and from many perspectives. Firstly, it can be open, from the point of view of the number of users it admits, if

This ideational-creative model, which presents itself as one of the traits characterizing digital culture, has found particular affirmation in the development of information technologies, where the sensitivity towards forms of freedom from the imposition of legal barriers that prevent an openness towards the dissemination and use of technology has assumed significant importance.[12]

A case in point, in this regard, is software[13] which, in its being a typical intellectual creation, reflects a stratified and multifaceted legal protection that stems from the tendency to extend the classical protection models of industrial law[14] – copyright and patent law[15,16] which then gave way to a gradual framing in "broad-meshed"

---

it does not exclude anyone, if it does not require complex procedures to access it, if learning to use it is easy. Secondly, from the point of view of its ability to combine with other artefacts, if it integrates into the environments in which it is located, if it can be composed with other artefacts to give rise to new, more complex artefacts. Thirdly, from the point of view of the way it is used, if it offers its users wide margins of freedom in the use they can make of it, if it offers them the possibility of inventing their own way of using it"). *See*, in the EU context, *Directive 2013/37/EU of the European Parliament and of the Council of 26 June 2013 Amending Directive 2003/98/EC on the Re-use of Public Sector Information*, in *OJ L*, 175, 27 June 2013, p. 1 ff.

12 Cfr. S. Aliprandi, *Apriti standard! Interoperabilità e formati aperti per l'innovazione tecnologica*, cit., p. 14, where the author affirms that «[. . .] libertà dai vicoli giuridici della cosiddetta proprietà intellettuale, libertà dalle ottiche prettamente economiche che svilivano il software da oggetto di innovazione tecnologica a prodotto commerciale, libertà dalle valutazioni meramente strategiche delle aziende produttrici che andavano a scapito di una virtuosa condivisione delle conoscenze informatiche» (*author's note*, "freedom from the legal entanglements of so-called intellectual property, freedom from purely economic perspectives that debased software from an object of technological innovation to a commercial product, freedom from the purely strategic evaluations of manufacturing companies that were to the detriment of a virtuous sharing of IT knowledge").

13 In software matters, it is significant to distinguish between private or customized software and commercial software, where the former is software developed for an individual user, especially an organization or company, that uses it and does not distribute it to the public in the form of executables or source code, and the latter is software developed by a company for profit.

14 The US Congress, thanks to the Software Copyright Act 1980, was the first to outline the principles that extended the discipline of copyright to computer programmes, and which were then the inspiration for the main technologically advanced countries, such as Australia in 1984 or Italy in 1992 implementing the *Council Directive 91/250/EEC of 14 May 1991 on the Legal Protection of Computer Programs*. *See*, for more details, G. Pascuzzi, R. Caso, *I diritti sulle opere digitali. Copyright statunitense e diritto d'autore italiano*, Milano, 2002, *passim*; T. Synodinou, *Directive 91/250/EEC on Software Copyright Protection: Computer Programs Created by Employees*, 2023, available at https://ssrn.com/abstract=4630857 or https://doi.org/10.2139/ssrn.4630857.

15 At first, then, software, thanks to its classification in the category of inventions endowed with industrial character, was considered to be subject to the disciplinary regime of the patent, even though it lacked the materiality that some authors consider indispensable for recognizing patent protection.

16 The tendency of software manufacturers was thus to start marketing programmes covered by copyright and accompanied by user licences, i.e. the indication of a series of limitations that had to be respected by the user of the work. To this legal limitation, a technical limitation was then added, consisting in the distribution of software in the form of binary code and, therefore, without its source code, so as to prevent its use going beyond the permitted uses through the use of codes that could only be read by computers.

forms of protection, such as free/open software[17] with copyleft effect,[18] which have

17 It is to the United States that one has to look to trace the origins of the first copyleft licence, the General Public License (GNU), in 1989, from which the whole free software phenomenon has grown. It is, however, only in recent years that this phenomenon has taken on a certain legal-economic importance. Proof of this is the fact that it was only in 2004 that the first European pronouncement was made, that of the Munich court, which, on the action of the open source project netfilter/iptables, obliged a networking company, Sitecom, to respect the GPL licence attached to the software it used and implemented. In accordance with the founding principles of the GPL, Sitecom was therefore obliged to publish under the GPL – and with disclosure of the source code – the software it was associating with the wireless network routers it marketed, since this software was itself based on the source developed by the netfilter/iptables open source project and protected by the GPL. *See*, District Court of Munich, *Welte v. Sitecom Deutschland GmbH*, 19 May 2004, case 21 O 6123/04, available at www.jbb.de/leadmin/download/judgment_dc_munich_gpl.pdf. Three levels of copyleft software can then be identified, varying according to the protection afforded to the work that is its object: strong copyleft, weak copyleft, and no copyleft. *See infra* § 2.

18 According to the majority orientation followed by the jurists who have dealt with the copyleft argument, these licences must be qualified as contracts, in which the licensor manifests the will to distribute his work according to the terms of the licence when he attaches it to the work, and the licensee manifests the will to accept the terms of the licence through a demeanour that unequivocally expresses his adherent will. The contractual nature of copyleft would be, inter alia, demonstrated by some open content licences that self-qualify in these terms (i.e. Creative Commons licences). If from the contractual nature of copyleft licences their general collocation within the legal system, at least in Italy, descends, since they are expressive forms of the autonomy sanctioned by Article 1322 of the Italian Civil Code, the question they raise rather concerns their compatibility with the limits and schemes within which private individuals can regulate their relationships: are the clauses contained in copyleft licences valid and effective in light of, for example, the discipline of vexatious clauses? Certainly, in the absence of a general discipline that defines in detail the operative modalities of such licences, it is the contract that must be referred to. *See*, in general on the subject of the legal qualification of copyleft licences, M. Bertani, *Guida alle licenze di software libero e open source*, Milano, 2004, *passim*; V. Zeno-Zencovich, P. Sammarco, *Sistema e archetipi delle licenze open source*, Milano, 2004, *passim*. A very different problem, which can only be mentioned here due to its complexity, is the application of copyleft in Italy, where the Italian Society of Authors and Publishers (SIAE), in its capacity as an associative body responsible *ex lege* for the collective management of intellectual property rights, in fact exercises an authentic monopolistic function that finds its legitimacy in Article 180, paragraph 1, of Law no. 633 of 1941 (copyright law), according to which «L'attività di intermediario, comunque attuata, sotto ogni forma diretta o indiretta di intervento, mediazione, mandato, rappresentanza ed anche di cessione per l'esercizio dei diritti di rappresentazione, di esecuzione, di recitazione, di radiodiffusione ivi compresa la comunicazione al pubblico via satellite e di riproduzione meccanica e cinematografica di opere tutelate, è riservata in via esclusiva alla Società italiana degli autori ed editori (SIAE)» (*author's note*, "The activity of intermediary, howsoever carried out, under any direct or indirect form of intervention, mediation, mandate, representation and also assignment for the exercise of rights of representation, performance, recitation, broadcasting including communication to the public via satellite and of mechanical and cinematographic reproduction of protected works, is exclusively reserved to the Italian Society of Authors and Publishers (SIAE)"). On closer inspection, however, since the subject matter in these pages focuses essentially on the incidence that the circulation of F/OSS software with non-copyleft effect exerts on the proprietary logic, the question of the harmonization of copyleft with the activity of the SIAE, although of certain relevance, fades in the general economy of the discourse. *See*, on the copyleft-SIAE relationship, S. Aliprandi, *Teoria e pratica del Copyleft*, cit., p. 44 ff., where the author, at p. 44, after emphasizing the exclusive nature of Siae's activity, emphasizes that it is «[. . .] facile intuire come

essentially inverted the same operating methods as copyright.[19]

In fact, referring to the following pages for further details, it suffices here to observe that whereas copyright is based on user licences that channel the exploitation of the work within certain tracks desired and fixed by its creator, copyleft is centred on the idea of "no rights reserved" or "no rights reserved" that does not limit but liberates the use of the good,[20] without however reaching the extremes of public domain or public domain.[21]

Compared to the latter, in fact, which would seem to be free from any link with a proprietary scheme, copyleft, even in the milder configuration of non-copyleft, still preserves a relationship between the licensor-author and the licensee-user which, even if configured differently, due to its greater or lesser intensity, would still seem to be referable to the proprietary scheme and the adaptations that digitality allows.

In essence, the framing of the subject-digital asset relationship also passes through the recovery of the role of copyright with respect to the circulation of digital content, given that the latter may lose its character of incentive to creative production, which is classically attributed to it thanks to the exclusive right to the

---

una simile impostazione difficilmente possa convivere con la scelta di rilasciare opere in regime di copyleft. È vero che gli autori sono liberi di scegliere di non usufruire dei servizi di tutela offerti dalla Siae e a maggior ragione di non associarsi all'ente. Ma è anche vero che attualmente in Italia e solo la Siae ad avere i mezzi per garantire certi servizi determinanti relativi alla distribuzione e allo sfruttamento economico di opere dell'ingegno [. . .]. Da ciò deriva che: primo, vista la situazione di monopolio l'autore che voglia avvantaggiarsi di tali servizi non può far altro che affidare la gestione dei diritti sulla sua opera alla Siae; secondo, vista l'impostazione esclusiva, l'autore che effettuasse questa scelta perderebbe la possibilità di promuovere e diffondere la propria opera attraverso altri canali, compresa la possibilità di applicazione di una licenza copyleft» (*author's note*, "It is easy to see how such an approach can hardly coexist with the choice to release works under the copyleft regime. It is true that authors are free to choose not to take advantage of the protection services offered by SIAE, and all the more so not to join the organisation. But it is also true that currently in Italy, it is only SIAE that has the means to guarantee certain decisive services relating to the distribution and economic exploitation of intellectual works [. . .]. It follows from this that: firstly, given the monopoly situation, an author wishing to take advantage of such services has no choice but to entrust the management of the rights to his work to SIAE; secondly, given the exclusive approach, an author making this choice would lose the possibility of promoting and disseminating his work through other channels, including the possibility of applying a copyleft licence").

19 *See* R. Stallman, *GNU Manifesto*, in *Dr. Dobb's Journ. of Software Tools*, 3, 1985, p. 32, where the author, in describing the GNU General Public Licence (GNU GPL or simply GPL) as a strong copyleft licence for free software, states that «GNU is not in the public domain. Everyone will be permitted to modify and redistribute GNU, but no distributor will be allowed to restrict its further redistribution. That is to say, proprietary modifications will not be allowed. I want to make sure that all versions of GNU remain free».

20 As for private software, we are faced with a free program in the borderline case in which its sole user enjoys full freedom over it, but if he distributes copies to others without assigning similar freedom to them, these copies will not constitute free software. As for commercial software, it is usually proprietary, but there is no lack of cases of commercial free software, just as there is no lack of cases of non-free non-commercial software.

21 The term *public domain* generally refers to the set of works or information that, once the period of legal protection has expired, may be freely used, without the need to obtain any prior authorization or to pay a fee.

proceeds of the intellectual work, to enhance the presence of a right to the use of a work on a public network in the absence of a physical support:[22] the original subjective situation is influenced by the access to and distribution of content of a creative nature, which still – it should be pointed out – does not represent the totality of digital content.

Depending on the case, the author finds himself in the condition of being able to profoundly influence distribution, having total access to the distribution tools and becoming an integral part of a market process fully aimed at the production and circulation of a digital work, even without a physical support, and therefore usable with the multiple distribution possibilities enjoyed by intangible goods.

Therefore, underlying the idea of openness, which appears to be a fundamental ethical value in technological development, is that same idea of sharing that has given rise to the emerging culture of the sharing economy.[23]

22 More specifically, there are digital works that do not present a correspondent in material form (so-called digital works *sensu stricto*) and digital works that represent the digital reproduction of works that are also available in traditional formats (so-called digital works *sensu lato*). *See*, for more details, V. Falce, *La modernizzazione del diritto d'autore*, Torino, 2012, p. 45 ff., where the author frames the protection of property in the light of the form, digital or otherwise, that it takes; E. Prosperetti, *L'opera digitale tra regole e mercato*, cit., p. 10 ff., where the author, on p. 10, emphasizes that «[A]ttraverso le reti telematiche vi sono molteplici tecniche per attingere e contribuire materiale digitale in molteplici formati; le norme che dovrebbero regolare e presiedere i meccanismi di circolazione digitale contengono principi di amplissimo respiro che, tuttavia, trovano ancora applicazione in base a meccanismi, tempistiche e criteri giurisdizionali concepiti quando la distribuzione digitale non era possibile e perciò difficilmente applicabili alla circolazione digitale in mancanza di idonei criteri di collegamento. [. . .] Sono pertanto necessari adeguamenti e riforme per consentire ai principi del diritto d'autore di trovare effettività nel quadro della società dell'informazione e della distribuzione digitale» (*author's note*, "Through telematic networks there are multiple techniques to retrieve and contribute digital material in multiple formats; the rules that should regulate and preside over the mechanisms of digital circulation contain very wide-ranging principles that, however, are still applied on the basis of mechanisms, timeframes and jurisdictional criteria conceived when digital distribution was not possible and therefore difficult to apply to digital circulation in the absence of appropriate connecting criteria. [. . .] Adjustments and reforms are therefore necessary to allow the principles of copyright law to be effective in the context of the information society and digital distribution").

23 The sharing economy is also referred to as collaborative economy, peer-production economy or peer-to-peer economy. *See* Y. Benkler, *The Wealth of Networks: How Social Production Transforms Market and Freedom*, New Haven, CT and London, 2006, esp. p. 59 ff.; D. Tapscott, A.D. Williams, *Wikinomics: How Mass Collaboration Changes Everything*, London, 2008, *passim*; R. Botsman, R. Rogers, *What's Mine Is Yours: The Rise of Collaborative Consumption*, New York, NY, 2010, *passim*; R.J. May, M.J. Horney, *The Sharing Economy: A Positive Vision for the Future*, in *Perspectives from FSF Scholars*, 1, 2014, p. 8, where the authors point out that «[O]n line applications offer a new, additional means of enabling trust, thereby facilitating trading and sharing in a way that creates new consumer choices and positively impacts the economy»; V. Comito, *La sharing economy. Dai rischi incombenti alle opportunità possibili*, Roma, 2016, p. 9 ff., where the author, at pp. 9 and 10, states that «[L]a crescente affermazione della cosiddetta "economia della condivisione" (*sharing economy*), fenomeno che tende a diffondersi sempre di più in tutto il mondo e a interessare un numero crescente di settori, pone dei temi di tutto rilievo all'analisi economica, sociale, politica. Tanto più che tale fenomeno si sta svolgendo nel quadro di un più generale e progressivo processo di digitalizzazione dell'economia; esso, dopo lo sviluppo dell'internet "tradizionale," vede anche, tra l'altro, l'affermazione dell'"internet delle cose" e una nuova fase

The latter, which, among other things, has contributed to correcting market imperfections without the need to resort to traditional forms of economic regulation,[24] can be read as a space in which networks of people dedicated to distribution intersect, allowing them, in return for economic benefits, to exchange goods or services that would otherwise be underused.[25]

---

di un rinnovato attivismo della robotica e dell'intelligenza artificiale (quest'ultima costituendo per molti "l'avvenire dell'informatica"), mentre si affacciano il *cloud computing* e il *big data*, la realtà virtuale e quella aumentata, la stampa in tre dimensioni, ecc., sulla base anche di nuove e più avanzate premesse tecnologiche ed economiche per il settore. Tali fenomeni, soprattutto se considerati insieme, fanno pensare che siano in atto delle trasformazioni molto importanti a livello planetario, [. . .] trasformazioni indotte dall'innovazione tecnologica, ma mosse poi indirettamente da alcuni problemi di fondo dello sviluppo capitalistico contemporaneo. Naturalmente, almeno in parte, la direzione futura di tali trasformazioni dipenderà da come la politica, i movimenti sociali, il sistema delle imprese si porranno di fronte ad esse» (*author's note*, "[T]he growing affirmation of the so-called *sharing economy*, a phenomenon that is tending to spread more and more throughout the world and to affect an increasing number of sectors, poses major issues for economic, social and political analysis. All the more so since this phenomenon is taking place within the framework of a more general and progressive process of digitisation of the economy. After the development of the "traditional" internet, it is also seeing, among other things, the affirmation of the *internet of things* and a new phase of renewed activism of robotics and artificial intelligence (the latter constituting for many the *future of information technology*), while cloud computing and big data, virtual and augmented reality, three-dimensional printing, etc. are appearing, also on the basis of new and more advanced technologies, such as the Internet, which is becoming more and more widespread all over the world and is affecting a growing number of sectors, also based on new and more advanced technological and economic premises for the sector. These phenomena, especially when taken together, suggest that some very important transformations are taking place on a planetary level, [. . .] transformations induced by technological innovation, but then driven indirectly by some basic problems of contemporary capitalist development. Of course, at least in part, the future direction of these transformations will depend on how politics, social movements, and the business system deal with them").

24 *See*, on the typical modes of operation of regulation, G.A. Akerlof, *The Market for "Lemons": Quality Uncertainty and the Market Mechanism*, in *Q. J. Econ.*, 3, 1970, p. 488 ff.; A.E. Kahn, *The Economics of Regulation: Principles and Institutions*, Boston, MA, 1971; M. Steckbeck, P.J. Boettke, *Turning Lemons into Lemonade: Entrepreneurial Solutions in Adverse Selection Problems in E-Commerce*, in *Markets, Information and Communication: Austrian Perspectives on the Internet Economy*, edited by J. Bimer and P. Garrouste, London, 2003, p. 218 ff., where the authors, at p. 222, observe that «[M]arket processes emerge from a series of trial and error experimentations, derived from a progression of finding a more efficient means of facilitating exchange».

25 The sharing economy generates revenue especially because it gives individuals the opportunity to make fruitful use of certain goods (e.g. flats, cars), which would otherwise represent dead capital; because, by putting different buyers and sellers in direct contact, it makes supply and demand more competitive and specialized; because it allows general savings on exchanges by reducing their costs and expanding their range of uses, because it allows a general saving on exchanges by reducing their costs and broadening their commercial purposes; because it significantly reduces the problem of information asymmetries that normally exist between producer and consumer by collecting and making public their observations; because by amplifying and exploiting the potential of a free market, it avoids the distortions created by the phenomenon of "regulatory capture," which occurs when an authority, instead of operating independently and autonomously, panders to the dominant commercial or special interests in the industry or sector being regulated. *See* C. Koopman, M. Mitchell, A. Thierer, *The Sharing Economy and Consumer Protection Regulation: The Case for Policy Change*, in *J. Bus. Entrep. Law*, 2, 2015, p. 531 ff.

The potential demonstrated by the sharing economy can certainly contribute to improving the conditions of market participants by offering more innovation, more choice, more convenience in prices, and more differentiation of services, but none of this would be possible without the Internet and the technologies that have profoundly contributed to opening up markets towards innovation and competition.[26]

More specifically, technology has enabled a wider range and more extensive usability of goods and services, because the facilitation of the development and dissemination of innovations, which is inherent to the digital world, has enabled new operators to guarantee a better choice of products and a greater possibility of solving problems that before, in the absence of a valid technological contribution, were considered unsolvable.[27] It has also broadened the range and quality of information on goods and services, allowing economic operators to take advantage of it to conduct their business in a more conscious and functional manner in the search for the most appropriate solutions, while at the same time lowering the costs associated with commercial exchanges.[28] Finally, it has facilitated the formation in the digital ecosystem

26 A reflection of the culture of sharing can be seen in the open source movement which, assuming philosophical prominence, aims to achieve an innovative and more open conception of life through the sharing of knowledge. *See infra* § 2.

27 *See* A. Thierer, *Permissionless Innovation: The Continuing Case for Comprehensive Technological Freedom*, Arlington, VA, 2014, p. 1 ff.; H. Chesbrough, M. Van Alstyne, *Permissionless Innovation*, in *Comm. ACM*, 58(8), 2015, p. 24 ff.; T. Dotson, *Technological Determinism and Permissionless Innovation as Technocratic Governing Mentalities: Psychocultural Barriers to the Democratization of Technology*, in *Engag. Sci. Technol. Soc.*, 1, 2015, p. 98 ff.; and, with a specific reference to the blockchain phenomenon, E.C. Alp, *Towards General-Purpose Decentralized Computing with Permissionless Extensibility* (No. 8858), Lausanne, 2024, where the author, considering smart contracts as the most promising foundations for applications of the blockchain technology, observes that, although smart contracts are expected to serve as the backbone of the next-generation web, they have several limitations that hinder their widespread adoption, namely limited computational functionality, restricted programmability, and lack of data confidentiality. Moreover, addressing these challenges manually in application-specific ways requires a lot of developer effort and time due to the monolithic architecture of smart contracts. In this dissertation, we start over with a novel architecture for building and deploying general-purpose decentralized programs. To this end the author first proposes a new architecture that replaces the monolithic execution model of smart contracts with a modular one to support a rich set of functionality, which can be easily and permissionlessly extended at any time. Second, to support the efficient deterministic execution required by computationally advanced smart contracts, the author builds a deterministic sandbox with floating-point arithmetic support that brings safe and deterministic execution together with general-purpose programming without having to sacrifice performance. Finally, the author combines threshold cryptography and blockchain technology to build a framework that enables mutually distrustful parties to share their confidential data in a fully auditable, transparent and decentralized manner. Through prototyping and evaluation using real-world applications, the author tries to demonstrate that it is possible and feasibly practical to build a decentralized computing platform that can support general-purpose computations.

28 *See* C. Shirky, *Here Comes Everybody: The Power of Organizing Without Organizations*, London, 2008, p. 47 ff., where the author mentions, at p. 54, a set of activities allowed by "social tools" that are relevant «[. . .] because the desire to be part of a group that shares, cooperates, or acts in concert is a basic human instinct that has always been constrained by transaction costs»; J. Salgado-Criado, C. Mataix-Aldeanueva, S. Nardini, C. López-Pablos, M. Balestrini, C.S. Rosales-Torres, *How Should We Govern Digital Innovation? A Venture Capital Perspective*, in *Technol. Forecast. Soc. Change*, 200, 2024, p. 1 ff., where the authors observe how ethical and governance issues regarding digital innovations developments like artificial intelligence have attracted abundant debate and research. Indeed, many perspectives – societal, engineering, research, management

of a vast and efficient mechanism of comments and opinions that allows users to have greater awareness and confidence in the economic transactions conducted.[29]

In essence, the sharing economy, with the philosophy of sharing that underlies it, represents an instrument that has so far proved capable of guaranteeing greater effectiveness, greater price competitiveness, and higher quality of goods and services,[30] without it proving necessary to call upon public regulation, competition between enterprises, and brand trust to ensure greater market efficiency and greater user protection, as, on the other hand, proved necessary in the pre-Internet era.

---

and policymaking – have been extensively analysed in an attempt to understand the role of the different stakeholders in minimizing risks and amplifying opportunities. Interestingly, however, the investment community has been scarcely studied, despite the critical role of financing in technology innovation. Therefore, the authors attempt to characterize investors' perceptions around the concept of digital innovation governance. They present insights derived from qualitative research using constructivist grounded theory, based on a series of interviews to numerous venture capital investment managers. As a consequence, analysis of the data collected suggests several categories of important factors regarding how venture capital managers engage in Digital Innovation Governance (DIG): legitimacy of involvement, opportunity of conducting and capability to lead DIG initiatives in the invested startups. The author offers a structured inventory of venture capital manager insights and perceptions on innovation governance. According to their research, venture capital managers, and investors in general, find themselves capable of and see opportunities and relevance in effectively fostering a digital innovation governance that takes into account the potential risks of artificial intelligence and identifies business and societal opportunities.

29 Cfr. D.D. Friedman, *Future Imperfect: Technology and Freedom in an Uncertain World*, Cambridge, 2008, p. 100, where the author observes that «[. . .] reputational enforcement works by spreading true information about bad behaviour. People who receive that information modify their actions accordingly, which imposes costs on those who have behaved badly»; A. Hearn, *Structuring Feeling: Web 2.0, Online Ranking and Rating, and the Digital "Reputation" Economy*, in *Ephemera: Theory & Politics in Organization*, 2010, p. 10 ff.; C. Dellarocas, *The Reputation Society: How Online Opinions Are Reshaping the Offline World*, Boston, MA, 2011, p. 3 ff., where the author, at p. 3, underlines that «[R]eputation systems are arguably the unsung heroes of the social web. In some form or another, they are an integral part of most of today's social web applications», and, at p. 4, explains that «[R]eputation is a summary of one's relevant past actions within the context of a specific community, presented in a manner that can help other community members make decisions with respect to whether and how to relate to that individual (and/or to the individual's works). Accordingly, a reputation system is an information system that mediates and facilitates the process of assessing reputations within the context of a specific community»; N.A. Draper, *The Identity Trade: Selling Privacy and Reputation Online*, New York, NY, 2019, *passim*; S. Hinduja, *The Importance of Your Digital Reputation*, in *Cyberbullying Research Center*, 2023, available at https://cyberbullying.org/the-importance-of-your-digital-reputation; J. Marx, F. Brünker, M. Mirbabaie, S. Stieglitz, *Digital Activism on Social Media: The Role of Brand Ambassadors and Corporate Reputation Management*, in *Proceedings of the 57th Hawaii International Conference on System Sciences*, Honolulu, HI, 2024, p. 7205 ff., where the authors stress how social media constitute an important arena for public debates and steady interchange of issues relevant to society. To boost their reputation, commercial organizations also engage in political, social, or environmental debates on social media. To engage in this type of digital activism, organizations increasingly utilize the social media profiles of executive employees and other brand ambassadors. However, the relationship between brand ambassadors' digital activism and corporate reputation is only vaguely understood. The results of a qualitative inquiry suggest that digital activism via brand ambassadors can be risky (e.g., creating additional surface for firestorms, financial loss) and rewarding (e.g., emitting authenticity, employing "megaphones" for industry change) at the same time. The paper informs both scholarship and practitioners about strategic trade-offs that need to be considered when employing brand ambassadors for digital activism.

30 Cfr. J. Owyang, *People Are Sharing in the Collaborative Economy for Convenience and Price*, in *Web-Strategic.com*, 2014, available at www.web-strategist.com/blog/2014/03/24/people-are-sharing-in-the-collaborative-economy-for-convenience-and-price/.

As will be seen below,[31] current technology allows the rights holder to modulate and remodulate access to the digital asset in real time according to logics and modalities that were previously unthinkable and unrealizable, so that the original owner of the digital asset and its user find themselves in a position of substantial equivalence in the exercise of rights over it.

While it is not possible in these pages to delve into such a complex and meaningful issue as that of the culture of sharing, it seems appropriate to observe how the last decade has witnessed the greatest expansion of relations characterized by interdependence and interconnection that humanity has ever known, thanks, on the one hand, to so-called interoperability[32] and, on the other, to so-called permissionless innovation.[33]

The digital world, in fact, operating through open platforms and benefiting from ever deeper interactions between different information systems ("interoperability"), has experienced the development of new models of commerce and the offer of new services, without this generally being accompanied by the prior and necessary request for specific authorizing measures by national public authorities.

From this point of view, there is justification for the close link that is increasingly emerging between interoperability and the use of internationally shared standards,

31 *See infra* in this chapter.

32 The term "interoperability" refers to the general ability of information systems and their supporting mechanisms to enable the exchange of data and ensure the sharing of information and knowledge. In other words, interoperability refers, on the one hand, to the interaction between different software applications, and, on the other, to the exchange and re-use of information that can take place even between non-homogeneous information systems, all channeled towards ensuring real competition between market players. *See*, on this point, European Commission, *New European Interoperability Framework. Promoting Seamless Services and Data Flows for European Public Administrations*, 2017, available at https://ec.europa.eu/isa2/sites/isa/files/eif_brochure_final.pdf, p. 5, where, at § 1.1.1, one defines interoperability as «[. . .] the ability of interact towards mutually beneficial goals, involving the sharing of information and knowledge between these organisations, through the business processes they support, by means of the exchange of data between their ICT systems», and, in § 3, *infra*, the different levels are distinguished (*legal interoperability, organisational interoperability, semantic interoperability e technical interoperability*). *See*, on the topic, S. Aliprandi, *Apriti standard! Interoperabilità e formati aperti per l'innovazione tecnologica*, cit., p. 16 ff., where the author, at p. 17, notes, recalling the Microsoft case, that «[P]ensiamo al caso più lampante di un'azienda di dimensione globale che produce il più diffuso e, servendosi degli strumenti classici del diritto industriale (segreto industriale, copyright, brevetto), non consente ad altre aziende di conoscere le informazioni necessarie per realizzare gli applicativi che funzionino correttamente su quel sistema operativo. In questo modo la stessa azienda può accaparrarsi anche il mercato degli applicativi, forte del vantaggio competitivo derivante dalla disponibilità interna di quelle informazioni. Comportamenti simili dovrebbero essere (e per fortuna sono) monitorati e opportunamente sanzionati dalle autorità antitrust» (*author's note*, "If we consider the most glaring case of a company of global dimension that produces the most widely used and, using the classic tools of industrial law [industrial secret, copyright, patent], does not allow other companies to know the information needed to make applications that work properly on that operating system. In this way, the same company can also corner the market for applications, on the strength of the competitive advantage deriving from the internal availability of that information. Similar behaviours should be [and fortunately are] monitored and appropriately sanctioned by the antitrust authorities"). *See infra* in this section.

33 With the syntagma "permissionless innovation," we wish to refer to that systematic approach that allows subjects to develop and use new devices and services, and thus to operate freely in the experimentation of new technologies and business models, without requiring the prior and necessary consent of specific public bodies in charge of exercising, in this sense, a permissive-authorizing activity. *See*, for more details, A. Thierer, *Permissionless Innovation. The Continuing Case for Comprehensive Technological Freedom*, cit., p. 2 ff. *See infra* in this section.

which leads to the growing use of uniform open or open source schemes that find their own legitimacy ensured by their effective dissemination.

Let us add, then, the fruitful and continuous search for innovation that, carried out on several levels and profiles and stimulated by a human creativity that has been able to move, without any particular constraints, under the banner of its own curiosity and its own desire to innovate, has found comfort in a freedom that has provided stimulus and contributed to the success of digitality and to the development of current economic approaches ("permissionless innovation").

Thus, we return to that starting value, freedom, which is the foundation of openness itself and which leads to the liberation from traditional technological and legal barriers, and which translates into a profile that is not so much ethical as technical, the manifestation of which is, among others, the so-called open source[34] from which

34 In computer science, the term *open source* is used to indicate software whose authors make the source code public, i.e. the text of an algorithm of a programme realized in a programming language that is included in a source file, favouring its diffusion and free study and allowing independent programmers, by means of user licences, to modify and extend it. In this regard, the Open Source Definition (OSD) is of particular importance. Elaborated by Perens, it represents a sort of decalogue intended to help the user agent correctly understand the value to be attributed to this concept. *See* B. Perens, *The Open Source Definition*, in *Open Sources: Voices from the Open Source Revolution*, 1, 1999, p. 171 ff.; M. Bertani, *Guida alle licenze di software libero e open source*, cit., *passim*; V. Zeno-Zencovich, P. Sammarco, *Sistema e archetipi delle licenze open source*, cit., *passim*; A. Florio, *Il problema della qualificazione giuridica delle licenze software free ed open source*, in *dirittodellinformatica.it*, 2009, available at www.dirittodellinformatica.it/diritto-autore/copyright-focus/qualificazione-giuridica-licenze-software-free-open-source.html; D. Riehle, *The Future of the Open Source Definition*, in *Computer*, 56(12), 2023, p. 95 ff. where the author, aware of the fact that many forces pull to change the definitions of what free and open source software are, describes the way these forces are built and speculates what the future will hold in store for the definition of open source software, and concludes, at p. 99, that «[T]he vendor-owned open source firms will not succeed in weakening the open source definition. I expect them to move on and utilize secondary devices to bestow goodwill onto their products. An obvious choice for a secondary device is open source foundations. I expect real or fake foundations with the goal of channeling goodwill and marketing attention to the products of the commercial firms backing them. The open source world at large would be well advised to come up with their own commercial open source foundation. The essence of the foundation would be to provide independent specifications and certifications of good behavior. Certification marks could be acquired (and lost) by vendors who seek such certifications to win user trust. This way, open source would keep its sterling reputation». *See*, with reference to the open hardware, the J.R. Ackermann, *Toward Open Source Hardware*, in *U. Dayton L. Rev.*, 34(2), 2009, p. 183 ff., where the author, at pp. 183 and 184, affirms that «[O]pen Source Software, that is, software distributed and licensed in a way that allows users to modify and further distribute its source code, has become an accepted part of the computer world. Most people involved in computer law today are familiar with the community-oriented philosophy behind Open Source Software licenses such as the Free Software Foundation's General Public License. The purpose of such licenses is to ensure that software users retain the freedoms described in the Free Software definition, in particular, they seek to ensure that Free Software cannot be "taken proprietary" by its incorporation into programs whose source code is not made available. At its most fundamental, the goal of licenses like the GPL is to foster a community where those who benefit from the work of others in turn contribute their improvements to that community. A similar movement, inspired by many of the same concerns that drove those software developers, has taken shape among people involved in electronic hardware design efforts on a collaborative basis: the idea of Open Source Hardware. Many people believe that the "build it yourself" days of electronics are over because of both the extreme complexity and the extreme miniaturization of modem technology. Some of us have a mental picture of old-time radio hobbyists, often ham radio operators, hunched over a smoking soldering iron in a basement workshop, building a radio from plans in a magazine – Open Source Hardware in an earlier form – and assume that those days are gone forever. Two facts undercut this assumption.

the idea of free software[35] and the copyleft solution, which we will discuss further on, originate.

First, software programs now available at affordable prices or for free (in fact, some are GPL licensed) allow the design of complex circuits and printed circuit board layouts. Second, an industry has grown up around low-volume production of printed circuit boards. One can email the output files created by one of those design programs to a company which will use the files to make printed circuit boards in a short time for a low cost. For example, one company will make three customized circuit boards for approximately fifty dollars and ship them within a day or two of receiving a customer's data files. As a result, a number of individuals and groups now create sophisticated electronic designs for their own use, and, driven by some of the same motivations that drive Open Source Software developers, often want to make these designs available to others. One of the same concerns that drove the creation of the Open Source Software community is now plaguing these hardware developers. They want to make their designs available to the public, but they do not want those designs co-opted by parties unwilling to contribute back to the community. A group of these developers in the ham radio community asked the author of this article to create an Open Source Hardware license that implements a Free and Open Source philosophy in the same way that the GNU General Public License does for software. This effort led to the present article that will first describe the process of developing an electronic product based on a printed circuit board and describe how that process differs from software development. Second, it will describe the legal implications of the hardware development process. Finally, this article will describe an attempt to reconcile the legal and practical implications of applying an Open Source philosophy to hardware development, which culminated in the TAPR Open Hardware License and the Noncommercial Hardware License».

35 W. Scacchi, Free/Open Source Software Development. In *Proceedings of the 6th Joint Meeting of the European Software Engineering Conference and the ACM SIGSOFT Symposium on the Foundations of Software Engineering*, Irvine, CA, 2007, p. 459 ff., where the author, at p. 459, explains what is FOSS/D affirming that «Free (as in freedom/liberty) software and open source software are often treated as the same thing. However, there are differences between them with regards to the licenses assigned to the respective software. Free software generally appears licensed with the GNU General Public License (GPL), while OSS may use either the GPL or some other license that allows for the integration of software that may not be free software. Free software can be seen as a social movement, whereas OSS is just a software development methodology, according to free software advocates like Richard M. Stallman and the Free Software Foundation. The hallmark of free software and most OSS is that the source code is available for remote access, open to study and modification, and available for redistribution to other with few constraints, except the right to insure these freedoms. OSS sometimes adds or removes similar freedoms or copyright privileges depending on which OSS copyright and end-user license agreement is associated with a particular OSS code base. More simply, free software is always available as OSS, but OSS is not always free software. FOSS developers are typically also end-users of the FOSS they develop, and other end-users often participate in and contribute to FOSSD efforts. There is also widespread recognition that FOSSD projects can produce high quality and sustainable software systems that can be used by thousands to millions of end-users. Subsequently, what is known about SE processes may not be equally applicable to FOSSD processes without some explicit rationale or empirical justification. Thus, it is appropriate to review what is known about FOSSD»; F. Martini, *Open Source, pubblica amministrazione e libero mercato concorrenziale*, in *Il diritto dell'economia*, 3–4, 2009, p. 676 ff., ove l'A., a p. 686, sottolinea la importanza del *free software* nell'incentivare il progresso tecnologico tanto da sostituirsi progressivamente «[. . .] alla standardizzazione fino ad oggi generata dai modelli di diffusione del software proprietario che hanno fortemente ristretto la concorrenza sui mercati sfruttando il diritto di proprietà intellettuale in chiave protezionistica. La libera disponibilità del programma modificabile e utilizzabile da chiunque incentiva i produttori di programmi ad interagire e a migliorare il prodotto, può essere uno strumento di differenziazione delle imprese e, in ultima analisi, può svolgere un'importante funzione pro-concorrenziale» (*author's note*, "standardisation to date generated by proprietary software dissemination models that have severely restricted competition in the markets by exploiting intellectual property rights in a protectionist manner. The free availability of the program modifiable and usable by anyone incentivises programme producers to interact and improve the product, can be a tool for differentiating companies and, ultimately, can play an important pro-competitive function to the standardisation hitherto generated by the models of diffusion of proprietary software that have strongly restricted competition in the markets by exploiting intellectual property rights in a protectionist key").

The correct framing of copyleft cannot, moreover, disregard the consideration of net neutrality as a broad principle deeply inherent to the concept of open source and, more in general, to the very architecture of digital networks: the network of which the digital ecosystem is composed and articulated must be governed by a logic that, on the one hand, does not discriminate against the system's operators, and, on the other, acts under the banner of third party status with respect to the type of information circulating therein.[36]

Therefore, the objective to which net neutrality aspires is to avoid disparities both in the fruition of the various services and network contents by the user and in the circulation of ideas, data, and information, so as to favour a sharing that can be to the benefit of the network's multidimensionality and of the parity of technologies.

At a closer look, therefore, neutrality is related, in a more limited perspective, to the concept of interoperability, because it aims at guaranteeing both the pluralism of those who develop technologies and the freedom of choice of those who use them,[37] and, in a broader perspective, to the culture of sharing, because it advocates and promotes an authentic idea of sharing based on non-discrimination.

36 *See*, however, K. Bode, *The AT&T-Time Warner Merger and the End of Net Neutrality Are a Nightmare Combination for Consumer*, in *Motherboard*, June 18, 2018, available at https://motherboard.vice.com/en_us/article/zm88zw/att-time-warner-merger-net-neutrality, where the author, recalling the ruling by US District Court Judge Richard Leon allowing *AT&T* to purchase *Time Warner* because «[. . .] the government failed to meet the burden of proving that the deal would severely harm the company's competitors», fears the risk of creating a media conglomerate with *CNN*, *HBO* and *TBS*, which risks putting an end to net neutrality, with consequent damage especially to consumers and their independence. *See*, further, *supra* Chapter 1, § 1.

37 I. de Sola Pool, *Technologies of Freedom*, London and Cambridge, MA, 1983, p. 226 ff.; K.B. Murray, G. Häubl, *Freedom of Choice, Ease of Use, and the Formation of Interface Preferences*, in *MIS Quart.*, 2011, p. 955 ff.; M. Klesel, S. Haag, F.M. Oschinsky, K. Ortbach, *Freedom of Technology Choice: An Experimental Evaluation*, in *Fortieth International Conference on Information Systems*, Munich, 2019, p. 1 ff., where the authors, at pp. 1 and 2, underline that «[I]n today's digital age, users have a multiplicity of technological alternatives to choose from to perform tasks. For example, when checking email or playing a mobile game, we can choose from a number of tablet devices, including the Apple iPad, the Samsung Galaxy Note, or the Microsoft Surface. While users commonly choose from those options to perform tasks in their personal lives, the degree to which organizations grant users the freedom to choose from alternative technologies is often limited. Some organizations orientate themselves toward higher degrees of freedom of technology choice and allow their employees to bring along their own personal devices or apps. In doing so, they define particular bring-your-own-device (BYOD) policies (Gregory et al. 2018). However, there are also many organizations that mandate the use of specific technologies [. . .]. This mandate can also be a subject of explicit policies. Nevertheless, it is oftentimes only implicit. The implications of restricting users' freedom of technology choice is well recognized in research on shadow information technology (IT). Studies show that more than 80% of users who are restricted in their technology choice by organizational policies start to ignore those restrictions and select and use their preferred technology at work [. . .]. While employees may have the chance to use technologies that are better aligned with their idiosyncratic preferences [. . .], which reduces their levels of frustration, the outcome may also risk organizational digital assets, including sensitive data [. . .]. Therefore, limiting employees' freedom to choose their preferred technologies minimizes the likelihood that individuals can use the technologies they feel confident with, and increases the risk of shadow IT use in organizations. With the millennial generation entering the workforce, the trend toward a technologically advanced workplace accelerates [. . .]. For this group, individually chosen technologies are very important

Copyleft responds precisely to the desire to ensure broad freedom of use for others, and thus stands as a vivid example of a different way of conceiving the logic of ownership, no longer based on the classic and hegemonic exclusivist approach.

Copyleft, in fact, can be synoptically described as a way in which copyright can be exercised by exploiting its basic principles not to control the circulation of the work, but precisely to establish a broad model of circulation, which is opposed to the proprietary scheme as traditionally perceived.

Therefore, precisely because a licence based on the principles of copyleft can ensure that the maximum number of proprietary rights are transferred in perpetuity to the users of the work,[38] also allowing them to substantially modify it, it can be said that the very concept of copyleft is based on that of freedom, to be read also as the faculty to improve the programme and distribute the improvements, so that the community can benefit from them.[39]

2 Advancements in Information Technology and the Diverse Landscape of Copyleft: Bridging Free and Non-Free Software

The rights that intellectual property, by its very nature and function, generally guarantees, can sometimes be exercised to degrade the exclusivity of the right of ownership and to confer, at the same time, to third parties the advantages that are linked to proprietary situations.[40]

Copyleft, as a scheme that stands as an alternative way of managing copyright, should be brought back to this perspective because, although firmly based on the latter, it differs profoundly from it by not following the normal practice that sees

---

and have a great influence on their choice of employer. This underpins the relevance of properly managing users' freedom of technology choice, or the lack thereof, in organizational contexts». Therefore, the authors' target is to better understand the role of freedom of technology choice, or the lack thereof, as a contextual variable by investigating its causal effect on users' technology-related perceptions and behaviours. Indeed, the results of a lab experiment provide initial evidence that freedom of technology choice has a significant influence on key IS variables. In particular, participants' cognitions of the usefulness and ease of use of the technology, their emotions regarding the satisfaction with and enjoyment of the technology, and their task performance are substantially lower when their freedom of technology choice is constrained. *See*, always on this topic, D.W. Allen, C. Berg, S. Davidson, *The New Technologies of Freedom*. American Institute for Economic Research, Great Barrington, MA, 2020; Á. Fernández-Baldor, A. Boni, A. Hueso, *Technologies for Freedom: Una visión de la tecnología para el desarrollo humano*, in *Stud. Appl. Econ.*, 30(3), 2012, p. 971 ff.; S. Dorrestijn, P.P. Verbeek, *Technology, Wellbeing, and Freedom: The Legacy of Utopian Design*, in *Int. J. Des.*, 7(3), 2013, p. 45 ff.

38 According to the principle of contractual autonomy, the author of a work is free to draw up the document specifying the conditions of its distribution.

39 S. Williams, *Free as in Freedom (2.0): Richard Stallman and the Free Software Revolution*, Boston, MA, 2010, p. 59 ff., where the author, quoting Stallman's thought, points out that the rights attached to computer copyleft consist of four fundamental freedoms: the freedom to run the programme for any purpose (or freedom 0), the freedom to study the programme and modify it (or freedom 1), the freedom to redistribute copies of the programme so as to help others (or freedom 2), and the freedom to modify the programme and publicly distribute its improvements (or freedom 3).

40 It seems fair to note that other examples in this perspective, in addition to copyleft, are, for example, the public domain, participatory housing, open collaborative creation, or collective rights management. *See*, for more details, Chapter 3, § 3.

ownership transferred, in whole or in part, in compliance with specific temporal and subjective standards.[41]

The examination of the impact that copyleft can have on copyright and even more generally on the logic of ownership, cannot, however, overlook some fundamental, albeit synthetic, clarifications on substantial concepts such as copyright and user licence.

In practice, the first term can be elementarily described as the indication of who is the owner of the copyright on a work, such as software, whose creative work is protected through rules that attribute various subjective situations that can be enforced against third parties (heteronomy); the second term can be seen as the set of all the rules that the author himself establishes for the distribution and use of his work (autonomy).

Therefore, the licence of use has practically no value if the copyright is not also present, i.e. if the subject or subjects who own the rights to the work that is the subject of the licence are not present, since only they can act to ensure compliance with the terms of the licence.

In fact, a work of others cannot be legitimately exploited at will without the consent of its author, unless there is no copyright and the work is not explicitly distributed in the public domain or public domain,[42] or there is no licence to use it, or the terms of use are not indicated,[43] or there is both copyright and a licence to use it, but the user-distributor unlawfully fails to respect the latter.

Copyleft, then, constitutes a general scheme whose actual use is subordinate to the use of specific terms, the tenor of which can also be very different depending on the hypotheses practically considered.[44]

If, in fact, copyright confers on the author of a work or an invention the right to exercise, on an exclusive basis, the faculties connected to it and that the author himself, in compliance with the existing legal framework, will be free to define the *ante* and *quomodo* of the possible transfer to others, copyleft presents itself as a means by which the owner of the copyright frees himself of the exclusive rights to the benefit of other subjects who will acquire the faculties connected to the use of those works and inventions.[45]

41 *See* Article 19 of Law no. 633 of 1941, *Protection of Copyright and Other Rights Related to Its Exercise*, according to which «I diritti esclusivi previsti dagli articoli precedenti sono fra loro indipendenti. L'esercizio di uno di essi non esclude l'esercizio esclusivo di ciascuno degli altri diritti. Essi hanno per oggetto l'opera nel suo insieme ed in ciascuna delle sue parti» (*author's note*, "The exclusive rights provided for in the preceding articles are independent of each other. The exercise of one of them does not exclude the exclusive exercise of each of the other rights. They shall cover the work as a whole and each of its parts").

42 In this regard, it is worth pointing out, on the one hand, that even if the work is completely anonymous, the author is well entitled to claim rights over it, and, on the other hand, that copyrights represent subjective situations whose effectiveness varies depending on the specific cases considered, so that when the copyright expires, the work can be used by everyone by falling into the public domain.

43 In this case, in fact, full reference must be made to copyright law, which will also operate in a supplementary key.

44 *See infra* in this chapter for the problem of diversification and proliferation of licences.

45 More precisely, the copyright holder indicates to the public which rights it intends to keep for itself and which rights it intends to divest itself of.

Thus, copyleft can be differentiated, because it is capable of creating independent legal situations precisely because of the high rate of freedom of use that, in essence, can be recognized to the user, and that can even transform him into the owner of the derivative work if the weaker copyleft schemes are used.

In fact, one can identify different degrees or intensity of the impact that copyleft can exert on the derived work, the intensity of which can range from the extremes of non-copyleft, where the work in question can not only be used but also modified and relicensed without the results of these changes having to be subject to the extremes of the original license, to those of strong copyleft, where the effects of the license tend to extend as far as possible to any derived work, passing through the balanced compromise of weak copyleft, which lies between the two positions described above.[46]

In essence, it is precisely the characteristics that accompany the copyleft scheme with the consequent possibility left to the licensor-author to affect the position of the licensee-user and the derivative works that make it possible both to establish a profound relationship between copyleft and proprietary logic, and to experiment in this sphere with the assumptions on how a different way of conceiving a property right steeped in digitality can be conceived.

Certainly, the possible configuration of the copyleft system is closely linked to the technological developments that have taken place over the last few decades, thanks to the general spread of information technology and the consequent digitality that has been able to reconfigure the positions of subjects operating in the world of creativity and communication.[47]

Although based in the American legal system, the ecosystem in which copyleft moves is *per se* digital and closely linked to the Internet,[48] so much so that it has

46 To stay with the IT theme that is of most interest here, it can be observed that the weak copyleft operates not at the software or programme level, but at the file level, so that if a programmer modifies the copylefted file, the extremes of this licence must still apply. If, however, the source code of that file is combined with that of other source code to create an object file that encompasses them and represents a broader work, the resulting object file, although incorporating the code envisaged by the copyleft licence, does not have to be released under the conditions envisaged in the original copyleft licence, and the resulting product may also be subject to a proprietary licence.

47 *See*, on this point, S. Aliprandi, *Teoria e pratica del Copyleft. Guida all'uso delle licenze opencontent*, Santa Giustina, 2006, p. 14, where the author observes that «[F]ino a qualche decennio fa era impossibile ad esempio pensare che un autore scrivesse un libro e che fosse lui stesso a diffonderlo al pubblico. Era necessaria l'intermediazione di un soggetto professionale (come l'editore) che si occupasse di supervisionare la redazione dell'opera, di finanziare la realizzazione di copie cartacee della stessa e di mettere tali beni materiali a disposizione del pubblico e quindi sul mercato. Ora non e più così. [. . .] Di conseguenza è anche prevedibile che sia l'autore stesso a voler decidere direttamente come gestire i diritti che la legge gli conferisce sull'opera» (*author's note*, "[F]or a few decades ago it was impossible, for example, to think of an author writing a book and disseminating it to the public. It was necessary the intermediation of a professional subject (such as the publisher) who would supervise the writing of the work, finance the production of hard copies of it and make these material goods available to the public and thus on the market. This is no longer the case. [. . .] Consequently, it is also foreseeable that it is the author himself who wants to decide directly how to manage the rights that the law confers on him over the work"). *See*, for more details, *supra* esp. Chapter 1 and Chapter 2, § 1.

48 *See*, for further details, R. Caso, *Il (declino del) diritto d'autore nell'era digitale: dalle misure tecnologiche di protezione al "Digital Rights Management,"* in *Foro it.*, II, 2004, c. 610 ff.; G.

been profoundly influenced by the globalization of markets more than by the international conventions[49] that have tried to prepare adequate harmonization tools for industrial law.[50]

Therefore, it becomes necessary to specify, albeit with the brevity that these pages impose, the way in which copyleft can behave with respect to the digital good that most appears to be the result of the digital cosmos: software.

In this respect, it is necessary to start from the fundamental bipartition between free software and non-free software,[51] which leads us to trace back to the first syntagma the idea that software is distributed in such a way that anyone has permission to use it, make copies of it, and distribute it, whether or not they have modified it, free of charge or not,[52] and, by negation, to the second syntagma, the idea that

---

Pascuzzi, *Il diritto dell'era digitale. Tecnologie informatiche e regole privatistiche*, Bologna, 2016, *passim*; A. Khang, V. Abdullayev, V. Hahanov, V. Shah, (edited by), *Advanced IoT Technologies and Applications in the Industry 4.0 Digital Economy*, Boca Raton, FL, 2024, *passim*.

49 One thinks, on the one hand, of the existence of the World Intellectual Property Organization (WIPO) with worldwide jurisdiction in the protection of intellectual property, and, on the other hand, *ex aliis*, of the Paris Convention for the Protection of Industrial Property of 1883, the Berne Convention for the Protection of Literary and Artistic Works of 1886, the Rome Convention for the Protection of Performers, Producers of Phonograms and Broadcasting Organisations, and the Agreements on Trade Related Aspects of Intellectual Property Rights or TRIPs of 1994.

50 Broadly speaking, it should be noted that, in addition to the specific regulatory differentiations obviously present in the various legal systems with regard to intellectual property, there is a substantial difference between two generally assimilated concepts, reflecting the heterogeneous approaches of origin (common law and civil law): copyright and copyright. The concept of copyright, typical of Anglo-Saxon legal systems, has the main purpose of stimulating the economic sector of culture, resulting, on the one hand, in its function of *erga omnes* protection of the economic interest of the entrepreneur who invests in the commercialization of the work, and, on the other, in its spectrum of action aimed at any work that can be exchanged, regardless of its traits of originality and creativity. The copyright, of continental matrix, which in Italy is acquired by simply creating the work (Article 2576 of the Italian Civil Code and Article 106 of Law no. 633 of 1941) and simply showing that you have a copy (Article 8 of Law no. 633 of 1941), is more properly addressed to the author who, even after having assigned the patrimonial rights over it, can still continue to control it thanks to a set of faculties that is enriched, compared to the purely patrimonial one, by personal profiles pertaining to the author himself (e.g. protection of honour, protection of reputation). *See*, for more details, R. Caso, *L'evoluzione del Copyright statunitense e del diritto d'autore italiano*, in *I diritti sulle opere digitali. Copyright statunitense e diritto d'autore italiano*, a cura di R. Caso e G. Pascuzzi, Padova, 2002, p. 21 ff.; R. Romano, P. Spada, *Il diritto industriale. Parte generale*, in *Diritto industriale. Proprietà intellettuale e concorrenza*, a cura di P. Auteri, G. Floridia, V.M. Mangini, G. Olivieri, M. Ricolfi, R. Romano e P. Spada, Torino, 2016, p. 26 ff.

51 *See*, for a general view, R. Stallman, *Viewpoint Why "Open Source" Misses the Point of Free Software*, in *Comm. ACM*, 52(6), 2009, p. 31 ff.; Id., *Why Free Software Is More Important Now Than Ever Before*, in *For Free Information and Open Internet*, 11, 2014, p, 57 ff.

52 In the latter regard, it should be pointed out that while the trial version of a complete GNU system dates back to 1996 and includes the kernel, GNU Hurd, developed since 1990, it is since 2001 that the system (with GNU Hurd) has started to operate reliably. However, since the Hurd is not very widespread, as it still lacks some important functionalities, the GNU/Linux system, i.e. a derivation of the GNU system that uses Linux as the kernel instead of the GNU Hurd, started to be very successful from the 1990s onwards. *See*, for further details, M. Mustonen, *Copyleft – the Economics of Linux and Other Open Source Software*, in *Inf. Econ. Pol.*, 15(1), 2003, p. 99 ff., where the author observes that an astonishing phenomenon is the rise of a large population of programmers

software incorporates any program that is not free software, so that its use, redistribution or modification is prohibited, or requires prior authorization from its author, or is subject to constraints that severely limit these activities (so-called proprietary software[53]).[54]

More specifically, the attitude of openness and sharing, which has gradually asserted itself in the IT world, has its roots, at first, in the Free Software movement, which started in 1984, thanks to the work of Richard M. Stallman, creator of the GNU/Linux GNU. Stallman, creator of GNU's Not Unix (GNU),[55] then consolidated with the establishment of the Free Software Foundation,[56] and later in the Open Source movement, which started in February 1998 with the foundation of the Open Source Initiative, by Bruce Perens and Eric S. Raymond, whose goal is to promote open source software.[57]

---

who, seemingly against economic logic, develop and distribute software that is copylefted: freely available but licensed. He suggests that the occupational choices of programmers based on reputation incentives determine the qualities of programs. A monopolist has to take into account the free software in the consumer market. When software implementation costs are low, the monopolist accepts the copyleft program in the market. The author explains the simultaneous existence of commercial and copylefted programs, like Windows and Linux, and also why commercial alternatives to copyleft programs may not exist.

53 *See*, further, *infra* in this section.

54 With more specific reference to copyleft, it is customary to distinguish between "complete" copyleft, which occurs when all parts of a work (except the licence itself) can be modified by subsequent authors, and "partial" copyleft, which occurs when only some parts of the creation are excluded from unrestricted modification or are otherwise not fully subject to all copylefting principles. In this last regard, it should be noted that many partial (or not complete) copyleft licences are presented as share-alike licences, which impose sharing only under the same terms as the original work, so that any freedom granted in relation to the latter or its copies remains unchanged in any derivative work. It follows, therefore, that each copyleft complete licence is *per se* a share alike licence, but not vice versa. It is customary to say, in this regard, that if the motto referring to copyright is "all rights are reserved" and the motto referring to full copyleft is "all rights are reversed," share-alike licences are rather qualified by the words "some rights are reserved." As a rule, the dissemination of Creative Commons licences (a non-profit organization based in Mountain View whose aim is to expand the range of works available for public sharing and use in a legal manner, and whose most common expression is licences labelled "approved for free cultural works") is a vivid example of share-alike licences.

55 *See*, for clarification on GNU and its nature as a complete Unix-like operating system using only free software, *infra*.

56 *See*, for more details, *supra* § 1 and *infra* in this section.

57 The Open Source Initiative (OSI) only seeks to establish the method of distribution of software, without, however, guaranteeing the freedoms necessary for its qualification as free: software that is open source is not necessarily free software, and therefore the latter cannot contain all open source software. In practice, the activity of the *OSI* – which, on the basis of a possible application, tries to establish whether a licence is open source or not – is characterized by a recent tendency to reduce the proliferation of licences through a more stringent application of the criteria for their approval. On closer inspection, indeed, although the term open source was coined in an attempt to remove ambiguity from the concept of free software, the result has not been entirely achieved. Since, however, very little software is recognized by the OSI that is not also free software, the term free and open source software or FOSS is often used (examples of FOSS are the Apache licence, the MIT licence and the BSD licence). In any case, it should be noted that the philosophy of the open source movement is inspired by the open content movement, which envisages not the free availability of a software source code, but of any kind of creative work, or content (*i.e.* text, images, video and

Since free software and open source software have common aspects, it can happen that, in some cases, a piece of software complies with both definitions, as well as that a programme belongs only to one or the other category,[58] thus making it complex to determine, in general, whether a licence is attributable to free software and/or open source software.[59]

In fact, although their synonymic use is common, the syntagma free software and open source have a profoundly different valence, which sees in the first concept the more general description of the freedoms applied to a work, always from the perspective of the consultability and modifiability of the source code, but with a special accentuation of the ethical profile underlying it, and in the second the exclusive valorization of the freedom to use the source code of a work, regardless of any value reference and from a maximum technical-legal point of view: free software indicates that programme whose licence meets the requirements of a definition that is mainly based on ethical concepts (value meaning), such as the possibility of studying, of helping others, of favouring information technology, while open source software identifies that programme that is based on respect for the Open Source Definition,[60] whose criteria, purely legal, must be met for a licence to be considered effectively free (technical meaning).

Thus, the term *open source* is characterized by a partially different meaning from that of free software, because it does not include certain types of open source licences that, in practice, are too restrictive to be considered effectively and fully free.

music), which, published under a free licence, can be freely copied and modified by anyone who wants to. Wikipedia is a clear example of the fruits of this movement.

58 It should be noted that if a piece of software is free or open source at the time of its creation, it may later change its status, because the rules that allow it to qualify under the terms of the free-side licence may be transformed, and a licence that was free under the previous rules may no longer be free under the new ones. In any case, and merely by way of example, all software issued under the NASA Open Source Agreement licence is not free software because it is open source.

59 On the other hand, there are various and diverse ways that can be followed to make a programme free, since, as they say in the IT world, free software is a matter of true freedom and not of price. Therefore, free software should not be confused with freeware, i.e. the free use of programmes, where free simply means free, because the latter, strictly speaking, does not imply the four freedoms that must necessarily characterize free software. On closer inspection, on the other hand, proprietary software companies use the term free software to refer to profiles that, in the end, are inherent in the price, since they want to indicate either the possibility of obtaining a copy of the binary free of charge, or the possibility that a copy is included in the computer being purchased. So, in order to clear up this possible confusion, it seems appropriate to note that if a software company claims to produce free software, its user licences should be checked to see if users can actually enjoy the freedoms that free software in the technical sense attributes. If this is the case, it is about considering the actual free software, otherwise, if only price profiles are considered, it is simply about freeware.

60 The Open Source Definition is the definition of an open source licence drafted by the Open Source Initiative on the basis of the Debian Free Software Guidelines, i.e. a set of principles developed and endorsed by the creators and supporters of the Debian project (a multi-architecture computer operating system composed entirely of free software) to define their conception of free software. More in detail, the creators of the Debian system have elaborated ten principles, to which the relative licences must be inspired, which can be grasped and summarized as free redistribution, the inclusion of source code, the possibility of developing derivative works, the integrity of the author's source code, and the absence of discrimination towards persons, groups or fields of use.

In essence, software is free when, in compliance with the freedoms sanctioned by Stallman,[61] its source code is available and possibly included in a (free) operating system such as GNU or in free versions of the GNU/Linux system, while software is open source when its source code is still open to development by contributions from everyone (so-called open development), but beyond compliance with certain ethical profiles.

If, then, almost all free software is open source software, the reverse is not true, and the difference is purely technical-legal, so that one can distinguish the former with or without copyleft.[62]

In this respect, we should point out the public domain[63] software, which, being copyright-free software,[64] constitutes a special case of free software without copyleft, so that some copies or modified versions may not be free at all, but covered, in turn, by restrictions on their dissemination or use.

Not all free software is in the public domain, because it can happen that the author chooses to exercise his rights to apply a free licence that allows everyone to use the software without any restrictions, just as it can also happen that a program is in the public domain although the source code is not available. Even in that eventuality, the program cannot be classified as free, because the very prerequisite of access to the source code is lacking.

On the other hand, if software with copyleft is free or open when the conditions for its distribution require that all copies of each version be distributed under the same conditions,[65] free software without copyleft allows, in addition to the redistribution and modification of the program, the addition of further restrictions.

61 *See supra* notes 19 and 35.

62 *See*, for further information, *infra* § 4.

63 The syntagma "public domain" is sometimes used in a vague sense to mean free or freely available, but, upon closer inspection, the public domain has a clear legal significance that means precisely "copyright free."

64 According to the Berne Convention for the Protection of Literary and Artistic Works, adopted in Berne in 1886 and ratified by Italy on 20 June 1978 with ratification of Law no. 399 of 1978, which establishes for the first time the mutual recognition of copyright, any written work, thus including computer programs, is automatically covered by copyright. It follows that if the author wants to place a programme he has made in the public domain, he must specifically disavow the copyright, otherwise the latter will also apply to the work in question.

65 By way of example, it can be observed how copyleft licences generally prevent redistributors from restricting the circulation of software already in place and require that the source code be made available, thus preventing, under certain conditions deemed acceptable, the programme and its derivatives from being made proprietary. In this sense, a classic is represented by the GNU Project, whose General Public License (GNU GPL), representing a specific set of distribution terms to copyleft a programme, ensures that almost all written software is copylefted, so as to guarantee every user the freedoms inherent in the concept of free software. More specifically, the GNU system is a complete Unix-type operating system, i.e. composed of many programmes (both the official GNU packages and many others, such as the X Window System and TeX, which are not GNU software), totally free and in development since 1984. It is precisely its Unix nature that allows the GNU system to operate not as a static set of programs, as users and distributors can choose different software according to their needs and preferences, resulting in a result that is always a variant of the GNU system. Since GNU aims to be free, every single component of the GNU system must be free software, although not necessarily copylefted: any type of free software is legally appropriate to be included if

In this latter regard, in fact, it is noted that if a program is open, but not copylefted, some copies or modified versions may not be free at all, since a software company may well compile the program, whether or not making variations, and distribute the executable file as a proprietary software product.[66]

One also speaks, in this case, of software with a permissive licence, since almost all uses of the source code are permitted, such as the distribution of proprietary executables with or without modifications to the original code.

On the other hand, the so-called freeware, which consists of (proprietary) software packages that can be used and redistributed free of charge, but not modified, because its source code is not available to users, and the so-called shareware,[67] which consists of software that, while allowing copies of the programme to be redistributed, requires users to pay for the licence to use it.[68]

Basically, if the main categories of free software licences can be traced back to two, copyleft and non-copyleft,[69] it is mainly to the latter that we need to look in these pages to analyse the impact that digitality has on proprietary logics.

---

it contributes to achieving the technical goals that have been set. In fact, while some GNU software is developed by Free Software Foundation (FSF) staff, most of it results from the work of volunteers, which can be copyrighted either by the FSF or by those who wrote it. More specifically, if subsequent programmers have transferred the copyright to the FSF, the programme becomes GNU software with the FSF's copyright and the FSF's ability to enforce the licence; if, on the other hand, they have chosen to keep the copyright for themselves, they will have to enforce the licence themselves. Therefore, it is incorrect to assume that free software and GPL-covered software are synonymous.

66 An exemplary case in this sense is the X Window System. The X Consortium, in fact, created the X11 program by stipulating distribution terms, then tended to be followed by subsequent developers, which made it non-copylefted free software. The consequence was, on the one hand, that the version aligned with the distribution terms indicated *ab origine* certainly constituted free software, and, on the other, that the copy, with or without modifications, that deviated from the original line lost the traits of openness to take on proprietary ones. In fact, with regard to workstations and graphics cards for personal computers, whose non-free versions are the only ones operational, X11 has become non-free software, and this has been possible precisely because the developers of X11, operating on the basis of a non-free licence, have been able to take advantage of the complete management of the source code.

67 Shareware cannot be classified either as free software or as software that is semi-free or that allows modification and non-commercial redistribution, because, on the one hand, it is absolutely impossible to modify the program because, in most cases, shareware software does not have source code available, and, on the other hand, it is not distributed with the authorization to copy and install it without paying a licence fee, not even by those who use it for non-profit purposes.

68 L. Takeyama, *The Shareware Industry: Some Stylized Facts and Estimates of Rates of Return*, in *Econ. Innov. New Technol.*, 3(2), 1994, p. 161 ff.; W. Hui, B. Yoo, K.Y. Tam, *Economics of Shareware: How Do Uncertainty and Piracy Affect Shareware Quality and Brand Premium?*, in *Decis. Support Syst.*, 44(3), 2008, 580 ff., where the authors show how increased network speed has opened up new opportunities for developers to distribute their products as shareware through the Internet. The authors therefore analyse the interrelationships among key issues that are central to the software industry, including uncertainty, piracy, shareware quality and full version price. They show that customers' aversion to uncertainty of software quality tends to increase shareware quality while piracy tends to decrease it. Counter-intuitively, the perceived quality of the full version software or the trust towards the software developer does not affect the full version price and the profit of the firm when piracy is prevalent.

69 As we have seen, if copyleft licences, such as the GNU GPL, require that derivative versions of the original program be left free or open, non-copyleft licences move in the opposite direction,

3 Exploring Non-Copyleft Software and Its "Anti"-Copyright Attributes: Transcending the First Sale Doctrine and the Fair Use Doctrine

Resorting to a classic toolkit, one could describe the operation of copyleft, especially in its variant of non-copyleft, as antithetical to traditional copyright, because if the latter concerns one or more determined or determinable subjects, the former presents only one determined subject.[70] Therefore, the licensor, who, in general, coincides with the author of the work, who, in his capacity as the owner of the fruit of his genius, decides to apply a copyleft licence to it, where, on the other hand, there is a subject that is very difficult to determine, which, for the sake of simplification could be qualified as a licensee, since it corresponds to any subject making use of the work in question.[71]

On closer inspection, however, the latter does not stand as a simple licensee-user, who, in the scheme commonly followed in the management of copyright, is a subject bound by the terms of the licence (the so-called disclaimer)[72] with which the licensor-author can limit the exclusivity of his ownership.

Indeed, in the weakest version of copyleft, that of non-copyleft, the licensee-user can not only become part of the distribution mechanism of the work,[73]

---

even admitting the possibility of derivative programs becoming subject to a proprietary licence. It is therefore considered that the former are preferable when the author is motivated by the intention of ensuring a secure margin of freedom and usability for all future and subsequent users, and that the latter are more appropriate when the upstream programmer wishes to allow users to manage the licence autonomously and unconditionally, even transforming its nature, but always preserving the possibility of the software being kept free as it was originally.

70 These are, in essence, figures that stand alongside the author, such as, for example, the publisher or producer.

71 I.V. Heffan, *Copyleft: Licensing Collaborative Works in the Digital Age*, in *Stan. L. Rev.*, 49, 1996, p. 1487 ff.; D.M. Kennedy, *A Primer on Open Source Licensing Legal Issues: Copyright, Copyleft and Copyfuture*, in *St. Louis U. Pub. Law Rev.*, 20, 2001, p. 345 ff.; R. Sen, C. Subramaniam, M.L. Nelson, *Open Source Software Licenses: Strong-Copyleft, Non-Copyleft, or Somewhere in Between?*, in *Decis. Support Syst.*, 52(1), 2011, p. 199 ff., where the authors underline that studies on open source software (OSS) have shown that the license under which an OSS is released has an impact on the success or failure of the software. The authors therefore develop a model based on the relationship between an OSS developer's utility, the effort that goes into developing an OSS, his attitude towards the freedom to choose an OSS license, and the choice of OSS license. They find that the larger the effort to develop OSS, the more is the likelihood that the OSS license would be free from restrictions. Interestingly, the result holds even when all OSS developers prefer restrictive licenses or less-restrictive license. The results suggest that least restrictive or non-copyleft license will dominate other types of OSS license when a large effort is required to develop derivative software. On the other hand, most restrictive or strong copyleft licenses will be the dominant license when minimal effort is required to develop the original OSS and the derivative software.

72 The disclaimer – which is composed of a copyright note with which the owner identifies the rights on the work and the date of their acquisition and the copyright note that identifies the license that the author has decided to apply – consists of a text with which the licensee/user is made aware of the main data on the work, and performs a dual and contextual function, since, from an informative point of view, it identifies the limits of the license referred to, and, from a legal point of view, it identifies the applicable discipline for the correct use of the good.

73 Distribution here means the assembly of software that originates from different sources and is carried out by an operator who chooses a specific content and configuration of the software (normally, a version of Linux, a certain amount of software from the GNU project, a package management

but even affect it, modifying and possibly improving it, and becoming a true author capable of enforcing *erga omnes* the rights he has acquired and decided to protect.

In the most extreme cases of copyleft, one can thus hypothesize that the author has the possibility of leaving the software in a regime, if not in the public domain, of non-exclusivity, so that anyone, if they so wish, is legitimized to act as owner.

The user, in fact, by encrypting the source and disowning its public provenance, could even attribute to himself exclusive rights of protection, commercializing the programme in the version he has modified, and transforming it, in essence, into a true proprietary software.

The non-copyleft therefore allows one to go far beyond the openings granted by the ordinary configuration of copyright, thanks to both the principle of exhaustion or *first sale doctrine*[74] and the *fair use doctrine*.[75]

More specifically, this doctrine causes the author to see some of the rights usually granted to him exclusively compressed: once a specific work is put on the market, the person who owns one or more intellectual property rights over it loses some of the faculties inherent in it.

However, this principle, with the obvious restrictions it entails, is effective only if the marketing of the good is carried out directly by the owner of the right, or following his specific instructions if it is done with his consent (i.e. through a licensee).

It should be emphasized, however, that despite the operation of the principle of exhaustion, the owner of the intellectual property right is not completely deprived of all the faculties connected to his position as author, which he will continue to protect *erga omnes*.

On closer inspection, in fact, the first sale doctrine is limited only to the distribution rights of which the author is the original owner, not allowing the purchaser of

---

system for updating and installing additional components, applications, etc.), compiles the software from source and distributes it as a stand-alone product. Since some basic programmes, such as GNU/Linux, have a particular relevance, each distribution is different from the others, but also similar to the others. Think of the user who creates a link for the distribution of a digital good, such as free software or open source.

74 The principle of exhaustion or first sale doctrine, which consists, in essence, of a limitation affecting the copyright holder's right of distribution, found its first affirmation in the 19th-century US system, originating from a jurisprudential orientation prohibiting obstacles to the free alienation of tangible goods.

75 The origins of fair use lead back to the United Kingdom and the *Cary v. Kearsley* ruling (170 Eng. Rep. 679 [1802]), where a right to «fairly adopt part of the work of another» to prevent placing undue constraints on scientific dissemination. It was, however, US Supreme Court Justice Joseph Story, who, in *Folsom v. Marsh* (9 F. Cas. 342 [C.C.D. Mass. 1841]), laid the foundations for a modern definition of the doctrine, indicating its main distinctive features, which were then taken up and codified in the US Copyright Act of 1976 with the addition of the «purpose and character of the use» (17 U.S. Code § 107[1]). More specifically, Story, starting from the generic need to provide for exceptions to copyright, identified a number of factors that, in his view, could help in grasping whether or not a particular use was fair, stating that «[W]e must often, in deciding questions of this sort, look to the nature and objects of the selections made, the quantity and value of the materials used, and the degree in which the use may prejudice the sale, or diminish the profits, or supersede the objects, of the original work».

the single copy, which is the fruit of the intellectual work and covered by copyright, to make a copy and disseminate it freely.[76]

Exhaustion, then, only concerns certain faculties that can no longer be exercised after the first transfer of a specific good, understood as a *specimen* that is the fruit of the creative activity of a subject, actually placed on the market.[77] By way of example, therefore, once a person has acquired ownership of a copy of a book, he may well sell it, rent it, or donate it, without having to ask permission from the owner of the industrial property right or pay the relevant royalties to him.

The exercise of these privileges by the buyer is, however, subordinate to the legitimate acquisition of ownership, and not mere possession, of the specific copy, to which, by way of example, the author might expressly attach an authorization to print further copies for dissemination or the law might allow non-authors to make legitimate copies.

The principle of exhaustion, therefore, seeks to balance two relevant but antinomian interests inherent in any legal system: on the one hand, the tendency to ensure the exclusivity of intellectual property rights, and on the other, the free circulation of goods and services. Given its relevance, then, it is not surprising that it has been expressly affirmed both in the Community legal system and in the national legal systems or those of other countries.

As for the more specific profile of its applicability to the digital world, the first sale doctrine, as classically conceived, would not appear reconcilable *sic et simpliciter* with the alienation of copies of digital works:[78] in this eventuality there would not be a real transfer because the recipient would only receive the new copy of a work that, in its original version, remains at the full disposal of the sender, unless it has been definitively deleted.[79]

76 R. Colby, *The First Sale Doctrine: The Defense That Never Was?* in *J. Copyright Soc. USA*, 32, 1984, p. 77 ff.; R.A. Reese, *First Sale Doctrine in the Era of Digital Networks*, in *Boston College Law Rev.*, 44, 2002, p. 577 ff.; S. Reis, *Toward a Digital Transfer Doctrine – The First Sale Doctrine in the Digital Era*, in *Northwest. Univ. Law Rev.*, 109, 2014, p. 173 ff.

77 See, for further details, Y. Even, *Appropriability, First Sale & Exhaustion*, 2008, p. 1 ff., available at https://ssrn.com/abstract=1274822; P. Mezei, *Digital First Sale Doctrine Ante Portas: Exhaustion in the Online Environment*, in *J. Intell. Prop. Info. Tech. Elec. Com. L.*, 6, 2015, p. 23 ff.; R. Nimmer, *The Interesting Case of Licensing, First Sale and Exhaustion*, in *Unif. Commer. Code Law J.*, 47, 2017, p. 231 ff.; L. Determann, *Digital Exhaustion*, in *Berkeley Tech. Law J.*, 33(1), 2018, p. 185 ff.

78 In the United States, for example, it is peacefully assumed that the first sale doctrine does not apply to the transfer of e-books and that, consequently, they cannot be lent freely and indefinitely after their purchase. E-book publishers, however, have developed a business model that focuses on the subscription of the text licence, so that they can limit both the number of times an e-book can circulate and the time frame in which it can be considered part of a library's collection before the licence expires and the e-book is no longer available to them. *See*, on this topic, M. Chiarizio, *An American Tragedy: E-Books, Licenses, and the End of Public Lending Libraries?*, in *Vanderbilt Law Rev.*, 2, 2013, p. 615 ff.

79 *See*, in this regard, the exemplary case *Capitol Records, LLC v. ReDigi, Inc.*, 934 F. Supp. 2d 640 (S.D.N.Y. 2013), where Judge Richard J. Sullivan, in an alleged copyright infringement case involving digital music transferred online, ruled in favour of the plaintiff (Capitol Records), stating that the transfer of digital data from one storage medium to another constitutes copyright infringement:

Merely mentioning the problem, which, by necessity, is briefly alluded to below, there arises, then, the need to verify whether the first sale doctrine can be readapted to the digital age to reflect its specific characteristics.[80]

Indeed, the extension of the principle of exhaustion to digital goods could reverberate on the market for original works with a much greater intensity than in the case of the transfer of physical copies, since, on the one hand, physical works are subject to a continuous process of material degradation, whereas digital works are potentially never subject to such degradation, and, on the other hand, works in digital format can be reproduced perfectly and disseminated everywhere without any particular difficulty.

At community level, the first sale doctrine has found recognition in the discipline of trademarks, thanks to Article 7, Exhaustion of the Rights Conferred by a Trade Mark, of Directive 2008/95/EC of the European Parliament and of the Council of 22 October 2008 to approximate the laws of the Member States relating to trade marks,[81] and, in the discipline of copyright, thanks to Article 4, Distribution Eight, of Directive 2001/29/EC of the European Parliament and of the Council of 22 May 2001 on the harmonisation of certain aspects of copyright and related rights in the information society (EUCD),[82] which was strongly inspired by the WIPO Copyright Treaty[83] and the WIPO Performances and Phonograms Treaty.[84]

---

the music copy at issue constituted an unauthorized reproduction, and therefore could not benefit from the protection of the first sale doctrine.

80 *See*, further, The Berkman Center for Internet & Society at Harvard Law School, *iTunes: How Copyright, Contract, and Technology Shape the Business of Digital Media – A Case Study*, in *Berkman Publication Series*, 7, 2004, p. 55 ff.

81 According to Article 7 of the Directive 2008/95/EC, «1. The trade mark shall not entitle the proprietor to prohibit its use in relation to goods which have been put on the market in the Community under that trade mark by the proprietor or with his consent. 2. Paragraph 1 shall not apply where there exist legitimate reasons for the proprietor to oppose further commercialisation of the goods, especially where the condition of the goods is changed or impaired after they have been put on the market».

82 In this regard, an important principle is affirmed by recital 31 of Directive 2001/29/EC, according to which «[. . .] a fair balance of rights and interests between [. . .] different categories of rightholders and users of protected subject-matter must be safeguarded», which is then taken up and specified by the following Article 4, according to which «1. Member States shall provide for authors, in respect of the original of their works or of copies thereof, the exclusive right to authorise or prohibit any form of distribution to the public by sale or otherwise. The distribution right shall not be exhausted within the Community in respect of the original or copies of the work, except where the first sale or other transfer of ownership in the Community of that object is made by the right holder or with his consent».

83 As is well known, this is the World Intellectual Property Organization (WIPO), one of the specialized agencies of the United Nations, established in 1967 to promote creative activity and the protection of intellectual property worldwide.

84 The WIPO Copyright Treaty (WCT) and the WIPO Performances and Phonograms Treaty (WPPT), unlike, for example, the US system – as the Digital Millennium Copyright Act (DMCA) Section 104 Report well demonstrates – clearly distinguish between what is provided for tangible copies of works, in respect of which they sanction a distribution right, and what is provided for intangible copies, in respect of which they sanction an exclusive right of transmission or right of making available to the public. Indeed, if Article 6(1) WCT («authors of literary and artistic works shall enjoy the exclusive right of authorising the making available to the public of the original and

More specifically, in the Community context, with reference to both tangible and intangible works, the principle of exhaustion of rights applies.

With regard to the former, in fact, under Article 4 of Directive 2001/29/EC, tangible copies of a work, made by incorporating them in media that allow direct or indirect use thanks to the aid of specific technical instruments, will no longer be subject to the author's control over the subsequent transfers of ownership, once the right holder has placed them in the Community distribution circuit, either in person or with his consent.

Therefore, the distribution right is exhausted with the first act of sale or other transfer of ownership, and subsequent acts by which that particular copy of the work is transferred will no longer be subject to the prior authorization of the original right holder.

---

copies of their works through sale or other transfer of ownership») and Article 8(1) («Performers shall enjoy the exclusive right of authorizing the making available to the public of the original and copies of their performances fixed in phonograms through sale or other transfer of ownership») and 12(1) WPPT («Producers of phonograms shall enjoy the exclusive right of authorizing the making available to the public of the original and copies of their phonograms through sale or other transfer of ownership») provide for exclusive rights in the distribution of tangible goods, Article 8 WCT («[. . .], authors of literary and artistic works shall enjoy the exclusive right of authorising any communication to the public of their works, by wire or wireless means, including the making available to the public of their works in such a way that members of the public may access these works from a place and at a time individually chosen by them») and Article 10 («Performers shall enjoy the exclusive right of authorizing the making available to the public of their performances fixed in phonograms, by wire or wireless means, in such a way that members of the public may access them from a place and at a time individually chosen by them») and 14 WPPT («Producers of phonograms shall enjoy the exclusive right of authorizing the making available to the public of their phonograms, by wire or wireless means, in such a way that members of the public may access them from a place and at a time individually chosen by them») grant a separate exclusive right for the transmission of intangible works in digital networks, such as the Internet, for dissemination to the public. The WIPO treaties, therefore, mention and recognize the principle of exhaustion only in the context of distribution rights, given that Article 6(2) WCT («Nothing in this Treaty shall affect the freedom of Contracting Parties to determine the conditions, if any, under which the exhaustion of the right in paragraph (1) applies after the first sale or other transfer of ownership of the original or a copy of the work with the authorisation of the author») and Article 8(2) («Nothing in this Treaty shall affect the freedom of Contracting Parties to determine the conditions, if any, under which the exhaustion of the right in paragraph (1) applies after the first sale or other transfer of ownership of the original or a copy of the fixed performance with the authorization of the performer») and 12(2) WPPT («Nothing in this Treaty shall affect the freedom of Contracting Parties to determine the conditions, if any, under which the exhaustion of the right in paragraph (1) applies after the first sale or other transfer of ownership of the original or a copy of the phonogram with the authorization of the producer of the phonogram») provide, without however requiring it, that the Contracting Parties limit the distribution right by resorting either to the principle of exhaustion that applies after the first sale or to any other form of authorization for the transfer of ownership of the original work or a copy thereof. In other words, it is left to the national systems adhering to these treaties to decide whether, and under what conditions, the described limitations should apply to the right of distribution of tangible goods. Consequently, since the WIPO treaties do not regulate a similar right governing the availability of intangible copies, theoretically, the first sale doctrine to be applied to digital works would not seem to be derivable directly from international copyright law.

As regards the latter, and in particular software, by virtue of Article 4(2)[85] of Directive 2009/24/EU on the legal protection of computer programs, when the author has sold the copy of a program for the first time he exhausts his right to its further dissemination, since he can no longer control its further distribution or prohibit its resale.

The same principle also applies when the work has been made available by downloading via the Internet, given the equivalence that the European Court of Justice (ECJ) makes between the sale of a program conducted in those terms and the sale of a computer program on CD-ROM or DVD.[86]

In fact, in *UsedSoft GmbH v. Oracle International Corp.* of 3 July 2012, the European Court of Justice, ruling on the preliminary question of the interpretation of Articles 4(2) and 5(1) of Directive 2009/24/EC, affirmed the principle that licensing and downloading are inseparable, thus abolishing the distinction, formed in practice, between the sale of software on a physical medium and the sale of client/server software.[87]

In this judgment, in fact, it is stated that "[. . .] first, [. . .] it does not appear from Article 4(2) of Directive 2009/24 that the exhaustion of the right of distribution of copies of computer programs mentioned in that provision is limited to copies of programmes on a material medium such as a CD ROM or DVD. On the contrary, that provision, by referring without further specification to the "sale [. . .] of a copy of a program," makes no distinction according to the tangible or intangible form of

85 According to Article 4, para. 2, of Directive 2009/24/EU, «The first sale in the Community of a copy of a program by the rightholder or with his consent shall exhaust the distribution right within the Community of that copy, with the exception of the right to control further rental of the program or a copy thereof».

86 Indeed, it is worth noting how, over time and with the evolution of technology, even resuming a trite distinction made between *corpus mystichum* and *corpus mechanicum*, the distinction between the informative-expressive content, on which the author does not hold exclusive rights, and the internal and external form of the work, which, on the contrary, are included in such exclusivity, has been accentuated. If, in fact, the adjective "immaterial" has been incorrectly linked to industrial or intellectual works and the *res* subject to intellectual property rights have been generically qualified as "immaterial goods," on closer inspection, these works include a component, the *corpus mysticum*, which cannot be traced back to materiality since it is normally associated with a support or means of dissemination, the *corpus mechanicum*. It is, therefore, the latter that plays the role of a good that, in factual and legal terms, stands as an object of exchange, unlike the right to the work that remains non-transferable and reverts to the author as soon as the physical good perishes. *See*, on this subject, L.C. Ubertazzi, voce *Diritto d'autore*, in *Dig. Disc. Priv., Sez. comm.*, IV, Torino, 1989, p. 366 ff.; E. Prosperetti, L'*opera digitale. Tra regole e mercato*, 2013, Torino, p. 12, where the author, with specific reference to digital works, states that they lack the *corpus mechanicum* «[. . .] ed è il solo *corpus mysticum* a circolare in forma digitale sulle reti telematiche e ad essere fruito. La memorizzazione o riproduzione su un *corpus mechanicum* (supporto) è del tutto eventuale o riveste, in ogni caso, carattere effimero e temporaneo: essa non e in alcun modo un fatto essenziale in quanto l'opera rimane completa e fruibile già nel suo formato digitale privo di supporto» (*author's note*, "and is the only corpus mysticum to circulate in digital form on telematic networks and be enjoyed. The storage or reproduction on a corpus mechanicum (support) is entirely possible or, in any case, has an ephemeral and temporary character: it is in no way an essential fact since the work remains complete and usable already in its unsupported digital format").

87 The sale of software operated on a client/server basis consists of the sale of a programme on a non-tangible medium involving the connection of a client computer to a server computer for the use of a given service.

the copy in question [*author's note, see* § 55]. [. . .] from an economic point of view, the sale of a computer program on CD ROM or DVD and the sale of a program by downloading from the internet are similar. The on-line transmission method is the functional equivalent of the supply of a material medium. Interpreting Article 4(2) of Directive 2009/24 in the light of the principle of equal treatment confirms that the exhaustion of the distribution right under that provision takes effect after the first sale in the European Union of a copy of a computer program by the copyright holder or with his consent, regardless of whether the sale relates to a tangible or an intangible copy of the program" (*author's note, see* § 61).[88]

More specifically, the possibility of reselling a piece of software even if downloaded directly from the Internet has been upheld, resulting in the application of the first sale doctrine, when the program was originally sold to a user for use for an indefinite period of time.

In such a case, in fact, a genuine property right would flow from the transfer, which would preclude a software programmer from preventing its subsequent transfer by any of its rightful owners.

In this regard, the ECJ has merely pointed out that, although it is difficult to put into practice the clause preventing the previous owner from making legitimate use of the licensed software after it has been resold, this should not hinder the subsequent alienation of the program and the consequent application of the first sale doctrine, since similar problems, which in any case do not prevent the peaceful application of this principle, may also be encountered when software is installed on a physical support.

It should also be noted that, although the orientation pronounced by the ECJ finds, as a matter of course, explicit and direct application in the European Union, there are no theoretical impediments to its possible extension to the North American system.

In Italy, the principle is provided for in the field of intellectual property by Article 17 of the Italian Law no. 633 of 1941,[89] in the field of copyright on successive

88 European Court of Justice, Judgment of the Court (Grand Chamber), 3 July 2012, *UsedSoft GmbH v. Oracle International Corp.*, C 128/11.

89 According to Article 17 of Italian Law no. 633 of 1941, «1. Il diritto esclusivo di distribuzione ha per oggetto la messa in commercio o in circolazione, o comunque a disposizione, del pubblico, con qualsiasi mezzo ed a qualsiasi titolo, dell'originale dell'opera o degli esemplari di essa e comprende, altresì, il diritto esclusivo di introdurre nel territorio degli Stati della Comunità europea, a fini di distribuzione, le riproduzioni fatte negli stati extracomunitari. 2. Il diritto di distribuzione dell'originale o di copie dell'opera non si esaurisce nella Comunità europea, se non nel caso in cui la prima vendita o il primo atto di trasferimento della proprietà nella Comunità sia effettuato dal titolare del diritto o con il suo consenso. 3. Quanto disposto dal comma 2 non si applica alla messa a disposizione del pubblico di opere in modo che ciascuno possa avervi accesso dal luogo e nel momento scelti individualmente, anche nel caso in cui sia consentita la realizzazione di copie dell'opera. 4. Ai fini dell'esaurimento di cui al comma 2, non costituisce esercizio del diritto esclusivo di distribuzione la consegna gratuita di esemplari delle opere, effettuata o consentita dal titolare a fini promozionali, ovvero di insegnamento o di ricerca scientifica» (*author's note*, "1. The exclusive distribution right has as its object the placing on the market or in circulation, or in any case at the disposal, of the public, by any means and for any reason, of the original of the work or copies thereof and also includes the exclusive right to introduce into the territory of the States of the European Community, for distribution purposes, reproductions made in non-Community countries. 2.

sales of works of art by Article 144 of the same law,[90] and in the field of industrial property by Article 5 of the Italian Industrial Property Code (Legislative Decree No. 30 of 10 February 2005).[91]

Given the impossibility here of analysing the disciplines in the various countries where the first sale doctrine is applied,[92] allow me to briefly recall only the

---

The right of distribution of the original or copies of the work shall not be exhausted in the European Community unless the first sale or the first act of transfer of ownership within the Community is made by the rightholder or with his consent. 3. Paragraph 2 shall not apply to the making available to the public of works in such a way that members of the public may access them from a place and at a time individually chosen by them, including where the making of copies of the work is permitted. 4. For the purposes of the exhaustion referred to in paragraph 2, the distribution of copies of the works free of charge made or permitted by the rightholder for promotional, teaching or scientific research purposes shall not constitute an exercise of the exclusive right of distribution").

90 According to Article 144 of Italian Law no. 633 of 1941, «1. Gli autori delle opere d'arte e di manoscritti hanno diritto ad un compenso sul prezzo di ogni vendita successiva alla prima cessione delle opere stesse da parte dell'autore. 2. Ai fini del primo comma si intende come vendita successiva quella comunque effettuata che comporta l'intervento, in qualità di venditori, acquirenti o intermediari, di soggetti che operano professionalmente nel mercato dell'arte, come le case d'asta, le gallerie d'arte e, in generale, qualsiasi commerciante di opere d'arte. 3. Il diritto di cui al comma 1 non si applica alle vendite quando il venditore abbia acquistato l'opera direttamente dall'autore meno di tre anni prima di tali vendite e il prezzo di vendita non sia superiore a 10.000,00 euro. La vendita si presume effettuata oltre i tre anni dall'acquisto salva prova contraria fornita dal venditore» (*author's note*, "1. authors of works of art and manuscripts are entitled to a remuneration on the price of any sale subsequent to the first transfer of such works by the author. 2. For the purposes of subsection (1), a subsequent sale shall be understood as any sale involving the intervention, as sellers, buyers or intermediaries, of persons professionally operating in the art market, such as auction houses, art galleries and, in general, any dealer in works of article 3. The right referred to in paragraph 1 shall not apply to sales when the seller has acquired the work directly from the author less than three years before such sales and the sale price does not exceed 10,000.00 euros. The sale shall be presumed to have taken place more than three years after the purchase unless the seller proves otherwise").

91 According to Article 5 of the Italian Industrial Property Code, «1. Le facoltà esclusive attribuite dal presente codice al titolare di un diritto di proprietà industriale si esauriscono una volta che i prodotti protetti da un diritto di proprietà industriale siano stati messi in commercio dal titolare o con il suo consenso nel territorio dello Stato o nel territorio di uno Stato membro della Comunità europea o dello Spazio economico europeo. 2. Questa limitazione dei poteri del titolare tuttavia non si applica quando sussistano motivi legittimi perché il titolare stesso si opponga all'ulteriore commercializzazione dei prodotti, in particolare quando lo stato di questi è modificato o alterato dopo la loro immissione in commercio» (*author's note*, "1. The exclusive powers conferred by this Code on the holder of an industrial property right shall end once the products protected by an industrial property right have been put on the market by the holder or with his consent within the territory of the State or within the territory of a Member State of the European Community or the European Economic Area. 2. This limitation of the proprietor's powers shall not, however, apply where there are legitimate reasons for the proprietor to oppose further commercialisation of the products, in particular where the condition of the products is changed or altered after they have been put on the market").

92 In the EU context, it is worth noting that in Germany, for example, the *Gesetz zur Regelung des Urheberrechts in der Informationsgesellschaft* (Law on the Regulation of Copyright in the Information Society), in Article 15, differentiates between rights that are exclusively attributable to the author of tangible works, which also include reproduction and distribution, and the right to realize intangible works intended for the public, and, in Article 17(2), codifies the principle of exhaustion, in harmony with the EUCD and the WIPO treaties. In the United Kingdom, Sec. 56 of the Copyright, Designs, and Patents Act of 1988 (CDPA), substantially implementing the EUCD, deals with the

experience gained in the United States, as the country in which this principle was first affirmed, where the US Copyright Act, in the same way as the first sale doctrine, has been adopted by the United States. The Copyright Act, like § 109(a),[93] gives the author the right "to distribute copies or phonorecords of the copyrighted work to the public by sale or other transfer of ownership, or by rental, lease, or lending" (17 U.S. Code § 106(3), Exclusive Rights in Copyrighted Works).

In this light, the first sale doctrine, as codified, allows only the resale of the particular and specific copy of the work of which the purchaser has become the material owner, without, however, extending to other rights exclusively referable to the author, such as the right to develop derivative works.

Moreover, it is normatively limited to specific categories of goods that may be covered by copyright, such as software, and to certain types of transfers, such as rentals.

In this regard, it suffices to observe that in the perspective of digitality, and therefore of the possibility that the same goods can be enjoyed analogously and indistinctly by millions of persons at the same time, it is the very notion of enjoyment in the strict sense, according to which the immediacy between the good and the person

transfer of works in electronic format, applying «(1) [. . .] where a copy of a work in electronic form has been purchased on terms which, expressly or impliedly or by virtue of any rule of law, allow the purchaser to copy the work, or to adapt it or make copies of an adaptation, in connection with his use of it», and providing, in this regard, that «(2) If there are no express terms – (a) prohibiting the transfer of the copy by the purchaser, imposing obligations which continue after a transfer, prohibiting the assignment of any licence or terminating any licence on a transfer, or (b) providing for the terms on which a transferee may do the things which the purchaser was permitted to do, anything which the purchaser was permitted to do may also be done without infringement of copyright by a transferee; but any copy, adaptation or copy of an adaptation made by the purchaser which is not also transferred shall be treated as an infringing copy for all purposes after the transfer. (3) The same applies where the original purchased copy is no longer usable and what is transferred is a further copy used in its place. (4) The above provisions also apply on a subsequent transfer, with the substitution for references in subsection (2) to the purchaser of references to the subsequent transferor». In Japan, for example, the Copyright Law, in the wake of the WIPO treaties, distinguishes the distribution right for tangible goods from the right of making available to public (Article 26, according to which «(1) The author of a cinematographic work shall have the exclusive rights to distribute copies of his work. (2) The author of a work reproduced in a cinematographic work shall have the exclusive right to distribute copies of his work») or transmission (Article 23, according to which «(1) The author shall have the exclusive right to make the public transmission of his work [including the making transmittable of his work in the case of the interactive transmission]. (2) The author shall have the exclusive right to communicate publicly, by means of a receiving apparatus, his work of which the public transmission has been made») for digital works, guaranteeing the author the exclusive right of distribution. *See*, for more details on the application of the exhaustion principle in the Japanese system, T. Doi, *The Territorial Principle of Patent Protection and Conflict of Laws: A Review of Japanese Court Decisions*, in *Fordham Int. Law J.*, 26, 2003, p. 386 ff.

93 According to 17 U.S. Code § 109(a), Limitations on Exclusive Rights: Effect of Transfer of Particular Copy or Phonorecord, «Notwithstanding the provisions of section 106(3), the owner of a particular copy or phonorecord lawfully made under this title, or any person authorized by such owner, is entitled, without the authority of the copyright owner, to sell or otherwise dispose of the possession of that copy or phonorecord.».

performing the act of negotiated or material disposition is essential,[94] that finds new light and breadth, and in this way also affects the very principles of effectiveness.

But with what consequences?

Certainly, the first sale doctrine operates an exception to the right of distribution of which the author would theoretically be the exclusive owner, but not to his right of reproduction.

The electronic transfer of a digital good operated through a computer network would generally not be covered by the principle of exhaustion, because, even if the reproduction were temporary, copyright infringements could occur, as we have already seen,[95] leading to the liability of the person who has committed them.

Consequently, the person who has legitimately paid for and downloaded software from a virtual shop cannot easily resell and transmit it via the web, since such transmission would consist in a reproduction of the digital structure of the programme in the RAM of his computer, in that of the other computers involved in the communication that belongs to the same network, and, finally, in that of the recipient's computer.

As an alternative to the transfer via the Internet, the same person could copy the software onto a material support, such as a CD, and then send it to its assignee.

But even in this case, unless expressly authorized by the author, numerous (illegal) copies of the same computer programme would be made.[96]

And even if one were to assume that the original copy would be deleted by the first purchaser after reproduction on a CD, the situation would not change, since the user would not be transferring the specific copy of the program he has purchased, but a duplication of it (copy of the copy), thus violating what the first sale doctrine traditionally requires.

94 *See*, for further details, B. Kim, *Understanding Key Factors of Users' Intentions to Repurchase and Recommend Digital Items in Social Virtual Worlds*, in *Cyberpsychol. Behav. Soc. Netw.*, 15(10), 2012, p. 543 ff.; E.K. Karpunina, S.N. Yashin, A.S. Molchan, E.V. Lisova, E.A. Derkacheva, *The Price of Pleasure: The Challenges and Threats of the Digital Economy*, in *Digital Future Economic Growth, Social Adaptation, and Technological Perspectives*, Cham, 2020, p. 363 ff., where the authors attempt to study the concept "pleasure" from the standpoint of different scientific schools and through the prism of the Utility Theory. They analyse the factors determining the possibility of obtaining pleasure by a person, and determine the effects of the digital economy (the attention of the target audience rather than the product or service itself, becomes a scarce resource; network effect, consisting in an increase in the number of connections; the change the relationship between different types of transaction costs) that will transform the classical model of the process of choice and consumption of goods and increase the importance of "pleasure." Thus, they evaluate how services and information technologies cover the process of human labor, the sphere of education and leisure, daily life and communication, as well as improve the process of choice and consumption of goods and create conditions for maximizing pleasure and reducing discomfort. Finally, the authors observe that despite the obvious advantages of modern digital technologies and the expansion of the range of opportunities for pleasure, there are information, economic and psychological threats and dangers.

95 *See supra* Chapter 3, § 1.

96 In fact, there would be one copy in the RAM memory of the computer of the party wishing to transfer the software back by copying it onto a CD, another in the same CD, yet another in the memory of the computer of the assignee when it intends to reproduce the CD in order to use the program contained therein.

However, the scenario would seem to change if one were to operate only on a material level, and thus the person who had purchased in a real shop a programme contained in a DVD would then proceed to resell that specific material support,[97] thus conforming to the principle of exhaustion.[98]

Just as the first sale doctrine, in order to balance the protection of the author with public access to the fruit of his genius, aims at tempering the exclusive right that he can claim in the distribution of his work, the fair use doctrine,[99] in order to balance property with intellectual freedom,[100] operates as an exception to the rule of proprietary exclusivity (so-called monopoly rights or rights of exploitation) monopoly rights or property rights) that confers benefits on the owner and, at the same time, imposes costs on the community, allowing the user to make use, in a reasonable manner, of the copyrighted material without requiring the author's prior consent.[101]

Therefore, the justification for the use of this doctrine is to be found in the so-called transformative use that may concern a work subject to copyright, because

97 B. Kim, *Understanding Key Factors of Users' Intentions to Repurchase and Recommend Digital Items in Social Virtual Worlds*, in *Cyberpsychol. Behav. Soc. Netw.*, 15(10), 2012, p. 543 ff.; J. Hamari, L. Keronen, *Why Do People Buy Virtual Goods: A Meta-Analysis*, in *Comp. Human Behav.*, 71, 2017, p. 59 ff.; O. Atasoy, C.K. Morewedge, *Digital Goods Are Valued Less Than Physical Goods*, in *J. Consum. Res.*, 44(6), 2018, p. 1343 ff., where the author notes that digital goods are, in many cases, substantive innovations relative to their physical counterparts. Yet, in five experiments, people ascribed less value to digital than to physical versions of the same good. Research participants paid more for, were willing to pay more for, and were more likely to purchase physical goods than equivalent digital goods, including souvenir photographs, books (fiction and nonfiction), and films. Participants valued physical goods more than digital goods whether their value was elicited in an incentive compatible pay-what-you-want paradigm, with willingness to pay, or with purchase intention. It is not a case that greater capacity for physical than digital goods to garner an association with the self (i.e., psychological ownership) underlies the greater value ascribed to physical goods. Differences in psychological ownership for physical and digital goods mediated the difference in their value, and indeed, experimentally manipulating antecedents and consequents of psychological ownership (i.e., expected ownership, identity relevance, perceived control) bounded this effect, and moderated the mediating role of psychological ownership. The assumptions of the author show how features of objects influence their capacity to garner psychological ownership before they are acquired, and provide theoretical and practical insights for the marketing, psychology, and economics of digital and physical goods.

98 *See*, however, for further reflections, *infra* in this section.

99 The reasons by which the fair use doctrine is usually justified, not only in the United States but internationally, are well expressed in *Iowa State University Research Foundation, Inc. v. American Broadcasting Companies, Inc.*, 621 F.2d 60 (2nd Cir. 1980), where it was held that fair use «[. . .] permits courts to avoid rigid application of the copyright statute when, on occasion, it would stifle the very creativity which the law is designed to foster».

100 G. Pascuzzi, R. Caso, *I diritti sulle opere digitali: Copyright statunitense e diritto d'autore italiano*, Padova, 2002, p. 24, where the authors affirm that «[N]el momento della nascita dei moderni sistemi di tutela giuridica delle opere dell'ingegno, il diritto di esclusiva appariva come lo strumento giuridico migliore per la costruzione di un mercato della creatività» (*author's note*, "At the time of the emergence of modern systems of legal protection of intellectual works, exclusive rights appeared to be the best legal instrument for building a market for creativity").

101 *Rosemont Enters., Inc. v. Random House, Inc.*, 366 F.2d 306 (2nd Cir. 1966), where fair use is described as a where fair use is described as a «[. . .] privilege in others than the owner of a copyright to use the copyrighted material in a responsible manner without his consent, notwithstanding the monopoly granted to the owner».

it adds "something new, with a further purpose of different character, altering the first with new expression, meaning, or message,"[102] because it benefits "the public beyond that produced by the first author's work,"[103] and because it balances the collective interest in freely accessing and modifying copyrighted works with the goal of stimulating creativity.[104]

Although the actual scope of fair use rights may differ widely from country to country, according to a classic approach, the principle allows copyrighted material to be used for informational, critical or teaching purposes.

At the EU level, it is commonly believed that the fair use doctrine was essentially introduced by Directive 2001/29/EC (EUCD), whereby no Member State may provide for exceptions to copyright that go beyond those specifically mentioned in Article 5.[105]

102 *Campbell v. Acuff-Rose Music*, 510 U.S. 579 (1994).

103 *Sony Corp. of America v. Universal City Studios, Inc.*, 464 U.S. 478 (1984), also known as the *Betamax Case*.

104 *See*, in defence of the fair use doctrine, also *Warner Bros. Entertainment, Inc. and J.K. Rowling v. RDR Books*, 575 F. Supp. 2d 513 (S.D.N.Y. 2008), where rules to avoid copyright infringement of literary works are identified. *See*, in general on fair use, *ex multis*, W.J. Gordon, *Fair Use as Market Failure: A Structural and Economic Analysis of the "Betamax" Case and Its Predecessors*, in *Columbia Law Rev.*, 82, 1982, p. 1600 ff.; P. Level, *Toward a Fair Use Standard*, in *Harv. Law Rev.*, 103, 1990, p. 1105 ff.; B. Depoorter, F. Parisi, *Fair Use and Copyright Protection: A Price Theory Explanation*, in *Int. Rev. Law Econ.*, 4, 2002, p. 453 ff.; and P. Samuelson, *Unbundling Fair Uses*, in *Fordham Law Rev.*, 77, 2009, p. 2538 ff.

105 According to Article 5 of Directive 2001/29/EC (EUCD), «1. Temporary acts of reproduction referred to in Article 2, which are transient or incidental [and] an integral and essential part of a technological process and whose sole purpose is to enable: (a) a transmission in a network between third parties by an intermediary, or (b) a lawful use of a work or other subject-matter to be made, and which have no independent economic significance, shall be exempted from the reproduction right provided for in Article 2. 2. Member States may provide for exceptions or limitations to the reproduction right provided for in Article 2 in the following cases: (a) in respect of reproductions on paper or any similar medium, effected by the use of any kind of photographic technique or by some other process having similar effects, with the exception of sheet music, provided that the rightholders receive fair compensation; (b) in respect of reproductions on any medium made by a natural person for private use and for ends that are neither directly nor indirectly commercial, on condition that the rightholders receive fair compensation which takes account of the application or non-application of technological measures referred to in Article 6 to the work or subject-matter concerned; (c) in respect of specific acts of reproduction made by publicly accessible libraries, educational establishments or museums, or by archives, which are not for direct or indirect economic or commercial advantage; (d) in respect of ephemeral recordings of works made by broadcasting organisations by means of their own facilities and for their own broadcasts; the preservation of these recordings in official archives may, on the grounds of their exceptional documentary character, be permitted; (e) in respect of reproductions of broadcasts made by social institutions pursuing non-commercial purposes, such as hospitals or prisons, on condition that the rightholders receive fair compensation. 3. Member States may provide for exceptions or limitations to the rights provided for in Articles 2 and 3 in the following cases: (a) use for the sole purpose of illustration for teaching or scientific research, as long as the source, including the author's name, is indicated, unless this turns out to be impossible and to the extent justified by the non-commercial purpose to be achieved; (b) uses, for the benefit of people with a disability, which are directly related to the disability and of a non-commercial nature, to the extent required by the specific disability; (c) reproduction by the press, communication to the public or making available of published articles on current economic,

Their provision within individual national legal systems is, however, merely optional, with the exception of the provision under Article 5(1) EUCD, which concerns transient copies that represent "an integral and essential part of a technological process" intended to allow either their transmission on a network operated by third parties or their lawful use.

In doing so, the intention was to prevent Internet service providers (ISPs), operators using routers and other subjects involved in the transmission of data from being held liable because reproductions pass through their equipment and, in this way, allowing users to use software that requires to be temporarily reproduced on the RAM of their computers for their use.

In this regard, however, mention must be made of the restrictions that seem to emerge from the Directive (EU) 2019/790 of the European Parliament and of the Council of 17 April 2019 on Copyright and Related Rights in the Digital Single Market and Amending Directives 96/9/EC and 2001/29/EC,[106] which, in an

political or religious topics or of broadcast works or other subject-matter of the same character, in cases where such use is not expressly reserved, and as long as the source, including the author's name, is indicated, or use of works or other subject-matter in connection with the reporting of current events, to the extent justified by the informatory purpose and as long as the source, including the author's name, is indicated, unless this turns out to be impossible; (d) quotations for purposes such as criticism or review, provided that they relate to a work or other subject-matter which has already been lawfully made available to the public, that, unless this turns out to be impossible, the source, including the author's name, is indicated, and that their use is in accordance with fair practice, and to the extent required by the specific purpose; (e) use for the purposes of public security or to ensure the proper performance or reporting of administrative, parliamentary or judicial proceedings; (f) use of political speeches as well as extracts of public lectures or similar works or subject-matter to the extent justified by the informatory purpose and provided that the source, including the author's name, is indicated, except where this turns out to be impossible; (g) use during religious celebrations or official celebrations organised by a public authority; (h) use of works, such as works of architecture or sculpture, made to be located permanently in public places; (i) incidental inclusion of a work or other subject-matter in other material; (j) use for the purpose of advertising the public exhibition or sale of artistic works, to the extent necessary to promote the event, excluding any other commercial use; (k) use for the purpose of caricature, parody or pastiche; (l) use in connection with the demonstration or repair of equipment; (m) use of an artistic work in the form of a building or a drawing or plan of a building for the purposes of reconstructing the building; (n) use by communication or making available, for the purpose of research or private study, to individual members of the public by dedicated terminals on the premises of establishments referred to in paragraph 2(c) of works and other subject-matter not subject to purchase or licensing terms which are contained in their collections; (o) use in certain other cases of minor importance where exceptions or limitations already exist under national law, provided that they only concern analogue uses and do not affect the free circulation of goods and services within the Community, without prejudice to the other exceptions and limitations contained in this Article 4. Where the Member States may provide for an exception or limitation to the right of reproduction pursuant to paragraphs 2 and 3, they may provide similarly for an exception or limitation to the right of distribution as referred to in Article 4 to the extent justified by the purpose of the authorised act of reproduction. 5. The exceptions and limitations provided for in paragraphs 1, 2, 3 and 4 shall only be applied in certain special cases which do not conflict with a normal exploitation of the work or other subject-matter and do not unreasonably prejudice the legitimate interests of the rightholder».

106 The Directive on Copyright in the Digital Single Market, or Directive 2019/790, is an EU directive that aims to harmonize the EU copyright framework in the context of digital technologies and in particular the Internet. It is the result of a process started since 2015.

attempt to harmonize copyright protection and, at the same time, strengthen it at EU level, also seems to affect the so-called digital and sharing rights[107] referred to in Article 17.[108]

Although, then, this is not the most appropriate place to go into such complex thematic profiles in depth, it is however interesting to note, especially with reference to the topic dealt with here, how, at least in its original wording, the proposal leads to a dichotomous attitude: on the one hand, it undoubtedly aims at increasing copyright protection against possible infringements perpetrated in the fluid digital world, but, on the other hand, it inevitably has repercussions on innovation and Community competition in the open source field.

In the intentions of the Community legislator, the proposal would lead online platforms hosting creative content made by others, without, however, paying them any remuneration, to respect copyright, but, in reality, the regulation could also go beyond its intended purposes.

In this sense, what stands out in particular is Article 11,[109] which, according to its detractors, would foresee the introduction of a so-called link tax, i.e. the prospect

107 In this regard, one must, however, consider the restrictions that seemed already to emerge from the *Proposal for a Directive of the European Parliament and of the Council on Copyright in the Digital Single Market* – COM(2016)593, which, in the intentions of the EU legislator, sought to respond to the new challenges posed by the digital world, since, as stated in point 1 of the Explanatory Memorandum, «1. [. . .] The evolution of digital technologies has changed the way works and other protected subject-matter are created, produced, distributed and exploited. New uses have emerged as well as new actors and new business models. In the digital environment, cross-border uses have also intensified and new opportunities for consumers to access copyright-protected content have materialised. Even though the objectives and principles laid down by the EU copyright framework remain sound, there is a need to adapt it to these new realities». In tal senso, specie l'art. 1, operando sulla sostanza della EUCD, prevede che «1. Member States shall provide for an exception to the rights provided for in Article 2 of Directive 2001/29/EC, Articles 5(a) and 7(1) of Directive 96/9/EC and Article 11(1) of this Directive for reproductions and extractions made by research organisations in order to carry out text and data mining of works or other subject-matter to which they have lawful access for the purposes of scientific research. [. . .] 3. Rightholders shall be allowed to apply measures to ensure the security and integrity of the networks and databases where the works or other subject-matter are hosted. Such measures shall not go beyond what is necessary to achieve that objective. 4. Member States shall encourage rightholders and research organisations to define commonly-agreed best practices concerning the application of the measures referred to in paragraph 3».

108 It follows, in fact, from Article 17 of the Directive, the exclusion from the scope of application of the directive of providers of content-sharing services, i.e. online encyclopedias acting on a non-profit basis, non-profit containers of educational and scientific material, open source software development platforms, providers of Internet access services, providers of cloud services that allow users to upload content, and platforms for online purchases.

109 According to Article 15, Protection of Press Publications Concerning Digital Uses, «1. Member States shall provide publishers of press publications established in a Member State with the rights provided for in Article 2 and Article 3(2) of Directive 2001/29/EC for the online use of their press publications by information society service providers. The rights provided for in the first subparagraph shall not apply to private or non-commercial uses of press publications by individual users. The protection granted under the first subparagraph shall not apply to acts of hyperlinking. The rights provided for in the first subparagraph shall not apply in respect of the use of individual words or very short extracts of a press publication. 2. The rights provided for

of a sum that publishers would be entitled to receive for the publication by digital platforms of a link to one of their articles, incorporating an excerpt or summary of the content.

Thus, copyright would be extended to so-called snippets, i.e. previews of articles consisting of title, image and summary, automatically developed by social networks and news aggregators when they publish a link.

This provision which, *prima facie*, appears unexceptionable, could, in substance, give rise to problems, because the publisher could be deprived of effective market power if it is not put in a position to benefit from the use of an aggregator.[110]

If, therefore, the downsizing of aggregators could be detrimental to the individual publisher, who, should he or she not be able to deal with a platform provider, could find it difficult to make use of search engines or search engines, at the same time, publishers could benefit from a right that would be contextually almost unwaivable but also unbalanced.

In order to protect individual publishers, in fact, the reform would presuppose the existence of contractual agreements between them and the pre-eminent platforms,[111] without, however, granting them sufficient resources to negotiate on an equal footing with the latter, and, by doing so, inducing them more and more

in paragraph 1 shall leave intact and shall in no way affect any rights provided for in Union law to authors and other rightholders, in respect of the works and other subject matter incorporated in a press publication. The rights provided for in paragraph 1 shall not be invoked against those authors and other rightholders and, in particular, shall not deprive them of their right to exploit their works and other subject matter independently from the press publication in which they are incorporated. When a work or other subject matter is incorporated in a press publication on the basis of a non-exclusive licence, the rights provided for in paragraph 1 shall not be invoked to prohibit the use by other authorised users. The rights provided for in paragraph 1 shall not be invoked to prohibit the use of works or other subject matter for which protection has expired. 3. Articles 5 to 8 of Directive 2001/29/EC, Directive 2012/28/EU and Directive (EU) 2017/1564 of the European Parliament of the Council (19) shall apply mutatis mutandis in respect of the rights provided for in paragraph 1 of this Article 4. The rights provided for in paragraph 1 shall expire two years after the press publication is published. That term shall be calculated from 1 January of the year following the date on which that press publication is published. Paragraph 1 shall not apply to press publications first published before 6 June 2019. 5. Member States shall provide that authors of works incorporated in a press publication receive an appropriate share of the revenues that press publishers receive for the use of their press publications by information society service providers».

110 In the IT world, the term *aggregator* refers to a software or web application that searches for information or content (even excerpts and snippets) on the web and then recompiles and republishes it in aggregated form to be better enjoyed. One of the main types of aggregator is the so-called aggregator or feed reader, consisting of a software or web application that collects content from the web, such as, for instance, news headlines, blogs, podcasts, and video blogs in a single space, for easy consultation. The function of aggregators is, then, to reduce the time and energy needed to regularly follow the updates of a website and, at the same time, to allow the creation of an individual information space.

111 In this regard, one can observe the centrality that, in this perspective, would assume both the management of the contractual relationships between providers and publishers, and the identification of mechanisms aimed at ensuring the transparency of the content of these contracts, since, to a certain extent, they could also present a discriminatory character with respect to the rights holders due to the different importance that some publishers may have compared to others.

to take on an associative dimension that would allow them to adequately represent them and ensure equal means and conditions between publishers and providers.

Article 17 of the Directive,[112] on the other hand, aims to regulate *ab origine* the relationship between the rights holder and the platform operator in order to protect

112 According to Article 17, Use of Protected Content by Online Content-Sharing Service Providers, «1. Member States shall provide that an online content-sharing service provider performs an act of communication to the public or an act of making available to the public for the purposes of this Directive when it gives the public access to copyright-protected works or other protected subject matter uploaded by its users. An online content-sharing service provider shall therefore obtain an authorisation from the rightholders referred to in Article 3(1) and (2) of Directive 2001/29/EC, for instance by concluding a licensing agreement, in order to communicate to the public or make available to the public works or other subject matter. 2. Member States shall provide that, where an online content-sharing service provider obtains an authorisation, for instance by concluding a licensing agreement, that authorisation shall also cover acts carried out by users of the services falling within the scope of Article 3 of Directive 2001/29/EC when they are not acting on a commercial basis or where their activity does not generate significant revenues. 3. When an online content-sharing service provider performs an act of communication to the public or an act of making available to the public under the conditions laid down in this Directive, the limitation of liability established in Article 14(1) of Directive 2000/31/EC shall not apply to the situations covered by this Article. The first subparagraph of this paragraph shall not affect the possible application of Article 14(1) of Directive 2000/31/EC to those service providers for purposes falling outside the scope of this Directive. 4. If no authorisation is granted, online content-sharing service providers shall be liable for unauthorised acts of communication to the public, including making available to the public, of copyright-protected works and other subject matter, unless the service providers demonstrate that they have: (a) made best efforts to obtain an authorisation, and (b) made, in accordance with high industry standards of professional diligence, best efforts to ensure the unavailability of specific works and other subject matter for which the rightholders have provided the service providers with the relevant and necessary information; and in any event (c) acted expeditiously, upon receiving a sufficiently substantiated notice from the rightholders, to disable access to, or to remove from their websites, the notified works or other subject matter, and made best efforts to prevent their future uploads in accordance with point (b). 5. In determining whether the service provider has complied with its obligations under paragraph 4, and in light of the principle of proportionality, the following elements, among others, shall be taken into account: (a) the type, the audience and the size of the service and the type of works or other subject matter uploaded by the users of the service; and (b) the availability of suitable and effective means and their cost for service providers. 6. Member States shall provide that, in respect of new online content-sharing service providers the services of which have been available to the public in the Union for less than three years and which have an annual turnover below EUR 10 million, calculated in accordance with Commission Recommendation 2003/361/EC ([20]), the conditions under the liability regime set out in paragraph 4 are limited to compliance with point (a) of paragraph 4 and to acting expeditiously, upon receiving a sufficiently substantiated notice, to disable access to the notified works or other subject matter or to remove those works or other subject matter from their websites. Where the average number of monthly unique visitors of such service providers exceeds 5 million, calculated on the basis of the previous calendar year, they shall also demonstrate that they have made best efforts to prevent further uploads of the notified works and other subject matter for which the rightholders have provided relevant and necessary information. 7. The cooperation between online content-sharing service providers and rightholders shall not result in the prevention of the availability of works or other subject matter uploaded by users, which do not infringe copyright and related rights, including where such works or other subject matter are covered by an exception or limitation. Member States shall ensure that users in each Member State are able to rely on any of the following existing exceptions or limitations when uploading and making available content generated by users on online content-sharing services: (a) quotation, criticism, review;

the former in the event that individual users publish online content protected by third party copyright.

If, then, Article 11 would sanction a sort of presumption of unlawfulness of all content to which a given copyright is attached that the rights holder has not communicated to the platform, Article 15 would require all digital platforms to monitor content that users have put online to prevent copyright infringement.

In essence, the proposal, seen in critical terms, would imply, for example, that open source coding and exchange platforms could be required to act in advance to prevent copyright-protected material from being exchanged without a prior and specific licence, but doing so could make the whole process of sharing computer data slower and more complex even if it did not touch copyrighted aspects; that the information shared by so-called whistleblowers could be shared with other platforms without a prior licence; that the information shared by users could be shared with other platforms without a prior and specific licence; that the information shared by whistleblowers could be shared with other platforms without a prior

---

(b) use for the purpose of caricature, parody or pastiche. 8. The application of this Article shall not lead to any general monitoring obligation. Member States shall provide that online content-sharing service providers provide rightholders, at their request, with adequate information on the functioning of their practices with regard to the cooperation referred to in paragraph 4 and, where licensing agreements are concluded between service providers and rightholders, information on the use of content covered by the agreements. 9. Member States shall provide that online content-sharing service providers put in place an effective and expeditious complaint and redress mechanism that is available to users of their services in the event of disputes over the disabling of access to, or the removal of, works or other subject matter uploaded by them. Where rightholders request to have access to their specific works or other subject matter disabled or to have those works or other subject matter removed, they shall duly justify the reasons for their requests. Complaints submitted under the mechanism provided for in the first subparagraph shall be processed without undue delay, and decisions to disable access to or remove uploaded content shall be subject to human review. Member States shall also ensure that out-of-court redress mechanisms are available for the settlement of disputes. Such mechanisms shall enable disputes to be settled impartially and shall not deprive the user of the legal protection afforded by national law, without prejudice to the rights of users to have recourse to efficient judicial remedies. In particular, Member States shall ensure that users have access to a court or another relevant judicial authority to assert the use of an exception or limitation to copyright and related rights. This Directive shall in no way affect legitimate uses, such as uses under exceptions or limitations provided for in Union law, and shall not lead to any identification of individual users nor to the processing of personal data, except in accordance with Directive 2002/58/EC and Regulation (EU) 2016/679. Online content-sharing service providers shall inform their users in their terms and conditions that they can use works and other subject matter under exceptions or limitations to copyright and related rights provided for in Union law. 10. As of 6 June 2019 the Commission, in cooperation with the Member States, shall organise stakeholder dialogues to discuss best practices for cooperation between online content-sharing service providers and rightholders. The Commission shall, in consultation with online content-sharing service providers, rightholders, users' organisations and other relevant stakeholders, and taking into account the results of the stakeholder dialogues, issue guidance on the application of this Article, in particular regarding the cooperation referred to in paragraph 4. When discussing best practices, special account shall be taken, among other things, of the need to balance fundamental rights and of the use of exceptions and limitations. For the purpose of the stakeholder dialogues, users' organisations shall have access to adequate information from online content-sharing service providers on the functioning of their practices with regard to paragraph 4».

licence; and that the information shared with other platforms could be shared with other platforms without a prior and specific licence. The information shared by the so-called whistleblowers on secure sites could be monitored, if not even blocked, in the event of the emergence of copyright-conflicting profiles; furthermore, access to databases could be made more difficult when it relates to data even indirectly tangential to copyright.

As far as Italy is concerned, it is undisputed that a substantial reproduction of the US fair use doctrine found affirmation with the implementation of the already known Directive 2001/29/EC, first, by Legislative decree no. 68 of 2003, which led to the amendment of article 70 of the copyright law (Italian Law no. 633 of 1941),[113] and, then, with Italian Law no. 2 of 2008 (Provisions Concerning the Italian Society of Authors and Publishers), which, again with a view to implementing the directive in question, extended the scope of application of the same Article 70 thanks to the introduction of paragraph 1-*bis*.[114]

In light of the aforementioned regulatory references, which are to be interpreted in such a way as to take technological progress into account, it follows that the possibility of overcoming, thanks to fair use, the stringent limits set by copyright is subordinated to the existence of specific purposes of use of the described material,[115]

113 In the wording resulting from the entry into force of Legislative Decree no. 68 of 2003, Article 70 of Italian Law no. 633 of 1941 provides that «Il riassunto, la citazione o la riproduzione di brani o di parti di opera e la loro comunicazione al pubblico sono liberi se effettuati per uso di critica o di discussione, nei limiti giustificati da tali fini e purché non costituiscano concorrenza all'utilizzazione economica dell'opera; se effettuati a fini di insegnamento o di ricerca scientifica l'utilizzo deve inoltre avvenire per finalità illustrative e per fini non commerciali. Nelle antologie ad uso scolastico la riproduzione non può superare la misura determinata dal regolamento, il quale fissa la modalità per la determinazione dell'equo compenso. Il riassunto, la citazione o la riproduzione debbono essere sempre accompagnati dalla menzione del titolo dell'opera, dei nomi dell'autore, dell'editore e, se si tratti di traduzione, del traduttore, qualora tali indicazioni figurino sull'opera riprodotta» (*author's note*, "The summary, quotation or reproduction of passages or parts of works and their communication to the public are free if carried out for the purpose of criticism or discussion, within the limits justified by such purposes and provided that they do not constitute competition with the economic use of working and debating, within the limits justified by these purposes and provided that they do not constitute competition for the economic use of the work; if carried out for teaching or scientific research purposes, the use must also be for illustrative and non-commercial purposes").

114 According to Article 70(1-*bis*) of Italian Law no. 633 of 1941, «È consentita la libera pubblicazione attraverso la rete internet, a titolo gratuito, di immagini e musiche a bassa risoluzione o degradate, per uso didattico o scientifico e solo nel caso in cui tale utilizzo non sia a scopo di lucro. Con decreto del Ministro per i beni e le attività culturali, sentiti il Ministro della pubblica istruzione e il Ministro dell'università e della ricerca, previo parere delle Commissioni parlamentari competenti, sono definiti i limiti all'uso didattico o scientifico di cui al presente comma» (*author's note*, "The free publication via the Internet of low-resolution or degraded images and music for educational or scientific use is allowed, free of charge, and only where such use is not for profit. By decree of the Minister for Cultural Assets and Activities, after consulting the Minister for Education and the Minister for Universities and Research, and after receiving the opinion of the competent parliamentary committees, the limits to the didactic or scientific use referred to in this paragraph shall be defined").

115 The permitted purposes are criticism, discussion, teaching or scientific research.

to the autonomy of the purposes of the work developed with respect to the purposes pursued by the work cited,[116] to the partial and not full use of the work to the extent justified by the purposes exhaustively indicated, to the non-competitive use of the work with respect to that set by the rights holder,[117] and, lastly, to the clear indication of the use for which it is intended.[118]

In addition to the limits described in Article 70 of the Copyright Act, there is also the need to positively pass the so-called three step test,[119] provided for by numerous international conventions, such as the Berne Convention (Article 9, § 2),[120] the WIPO treaties (Article 10 WCT[121] and Article 16 WPPT[122]), and TRIPs (Article 13),[123] as well as by the Copyright Act (Article 13), and the recital 44 of

116 In particular, the use permitted under fair use must not lead to the creation of a substitute for the work cited or its derivative uses.

117 It is understood that the work developed through fair use must not be of such economic significance as to be detrimental to the economic interests of the author or his successors in title, or, better still, must not be for profit and must not contain elements that may place it in competition with the work from which it originates.

118 For example, the title of the work from which the quotation is taken, the name of the author and the publisher must be indicated.

119 The so-called three-step test, which was originally provided for in the Berne Convention as revised in 1967 and is applied only in the cases expressly provided for, requires a three-step test to which the conformity of the exceptions and limitations considered is subordinated. Indeed, on one hand, whoever distributes the program with proprietary licenses benefits from copyright protection by reserving the right to copy, modify, and distribute the software, thus securing economic benefits. On the other hand, distributing the program under a free license with copyright permission ensures that the freedoms granted remain available for subsequent users, and any modifications and improvements made to the program are accessible to the entire community. Only by proceeding to the effective recovery of this balancing act can the legitimate interests of producers of intellectual works, users of these works, and society in general be recomposed.

120 According to Article 9(2) of the Berne Convention, «It shall be a matter for legislation in the countries of the Union to permit the reproduction of such works in certain special cases, provided that such reproduction does not conflict with a normal exploitation of the work and does not unreasonably prejudice the legitimate interests of the author».

121 According to Article 10 WCT, Limitations and Exceptions, «(1) Contracting Parties may, in their national legislation, provide for limitations of or exceptions to the rights granted to authors of literary and artistic works under this Treaty in certain special cases that do not conflict with a normal exploitation of the work and do not unreasonably prejudice the legitimate interests of the author. (2) Contracting Parties shall, when applying the Berne Convention, confine any limitations of or exceptions to rights provided for therein to certain special cases that do not conflict with a normal».

122 According to Article 16 WPPT, Limitations and Exceptions, «(1) Contracting Parties may, in their national legislation, provide for the same kinds of limitations or exceptions with regard to the protection of performers and producers of phonograms as they provide for, in their national legislation, in connection with the protection of copyright in literary and artistic works. (2) Contracting Parties shall confine any limitations of or exceptions to rights provided for in this Treaty to certain special cases which do not conflict with a normal exploitation of the performance or phonogram and do not unreasonably prejudice the legitimate interests of the performer or of the producer of the phonogram».

123 According to Article 13 TRIPs, Limitations and Exceptions, «Members shall confine limitations or exceptions to exclusive rights to certain special cases which do not conflict with a normal

Directive 2001/29/EU:[124] the exceptions and limitations can only be applied in specific and determined cases (first step), which, in any case, must not be in contrast with the normal exploitation of the work (second step), and must not cause unjustified prejudice to the right holders (third step).

In essence, then, and taking into account the due distinctions,[125] the application of the fair use doctrine follows in Italy as in the European Union the same application conditions that were established *ab initio* in the US system, and which are sanctioned by 17 U.S. Code § 107.[126]

According to the provision in question, therefore, fair use must be identified, case by case, in light of the four criteria, not decisive, that it itself sanctions, and which are identified with "[. . .] (1) the purpose and character of the use, including whether such use is of a commercial nature or is for nonprofit educational purposes; (2) the nature of the copyrighted work; (3) the amount and substantiality of the portion used in relation to the copyrighted work as a whole; and (4) the effect of the use upon the potential market for or value of the copyrighted work."

The judge who is called upon to pronounce on the possible case of *fair use* must certainly consider the parameters that the rule *ex* 17 U.S. Code § 107, referring in

---

exploitation of the work and do not unreasonably prejudice the legitimate interests of the right holder».

124 According to recital 44 of the Directive 2001/29/EU, «When applying the exceptions and limitations provided for in this Directive, they should be exercised in accordance with international obligations. Such exceptions and limitations may not be applied in a way which prejudices the legitimate interests of the rightholder or which conflicts with the normal exploitation of his work or other subject-matter. The provision of such exceptions or limitations by Member States should, in particular, duly reflect the increased economic impact that such exceptions or limitations may have in the context of the new electronic environment. Therefore, the scope of certain exceptions or limitations may have to be even more limited when it comes to certain new uses of copyright works and other subject-matter».

125 If, in fact, in civil law countries, such as Italy, France and Germany, exceptions to copyright are specifically indicated that integrate as many cases of fair use doctrine, in common law countries, such as Canada and the United Kingdom, fair dealing is invoked with regard to specific activities such as communication and parody. *See*, for Italy, Article 70 of the Copyright Act; for France, Article L122-5 *Code de la propriété intellectuelle*; for Germany, §§ 45–53 *Gesetz über Urheberrecht und verwandte Schutzrechte* (*Urheberrechtsgesetz* or *UrhG*); for Canada, § 29 Copyright Act (1985) (R.S.C., 1985, ch. C-42) (Can.); and, for the United Kingdom, §§ 29–30 UK Copyright, Designs and Patents Act 1988 (*CDPA*). *See*, for further discussion of the Italian system, *supra* in this section.

126 According to 17 U.S. Code § 107(1)–(4), Limitations on Exclusive Rights: Fair Use, «Notwithstanding the provisions of sections 106 and 106A, the fair use of a copyrighted work, including such use by reproduction in copies or phonorecords or by any other means specified by that section, for purposes such as criticism, comment, news reporting, teaching (including multiple copies for classroom use), scholarship, or research, is not an infringement of copyright. In determining whether the use made of a work in any particular case is a fair use the factors to be considered shall include: (1) the purpose and character of the use, including whether such use is of a commercial nature or is for nonprofit educational purposes; (2) the nature of the copyrighted work; (3) the amount and substantiality of the portion used in relation to the copyrighted work as a whole; and (4) the effect of the use upon the potential market for or value of the copyrighted work. The fact that a work is unpublished shall not itself bar a finding of fair use if such finding is made upon consideration of all the above factors».

substance to the case *Folsom v. Marsh*,[127] indicates, and thus weigh them and relate them to the purposes of copyright,[128] albeit in the knowledge that the list provided by the provision[129] is not exhaustive[130] but merely illustrative as it allows – as usually happens in the US system – the reference to the jurisprudential data that may have already matured on similar facts.[131]

In this way, the centrality of the fair use internal balancing clause is grasped as a principle that, thanks to a casuistic method, becomes indispensable for the reconstruction of an application scheme that is as consistent as possible with the function conventionally attributed to copyright, as an instrument aimed at ensuring

127 *Folsom v. Marsh*, 9 F. Cas. 342 (C.C.D. Mass. 1841). *See*, for further details, *supra* note 75.

128 *Campbell v. Acuff-Rose Music, Inc.*, 510 U.S. 569 (1994), where the US Supreme Court, in upholding the possibility of bringing parody under the concept of fair use, expressly states at p. 575 the need for a fair use assessment «in the light of the purposes of copyright».

129 Consider, in fact, how 17 U.S. Code § 107 recognizes fair use in cases «[. . .] such as criticism, comment, news reporting, teaching (including multiple copies for classroom use), scholarship, or research [. . .]».

130 In fact, it can be observed how the US courts, on the one hand, have brought back to fair use the quotation of documents in a newspaper article, and, on the other hand, have denied such classification where the part quoted was much more than a mere excerpt or was equivalent to most of the original and, in this way, could damage the market of the original work by reducing its revenue. *See*, e.g., in the first sense, *Religious Technology Center v. Lerma*, 897 F. Supp. 260 (E.D. Va. 1995); and, in the second, *Love v. Kwitny*, 706 F. Supp. 1123 (S.D.N.Y. 1989). It should be noted, however, that US case law has shown a more tolerant attitude when the second work makes non-commercial use of the first, as is well illustrated, for example, by the well-known *Betamax Case* (*Sony Corporation of America v. Universal City Studios*, Inc., 464 U.S. 417, 450–451 [1984]), where it was held that «[T]he purpose of copyright is to create incentives for creative effort. Even copying for noncommercial purposes may impair the copyright holder's ability to obtain the rewards that Congress intended him to have. But a use that has no demonstrable effect upon the potential market for, or the value of, the copyrighted work need not be prohibited in order to protect the author's incentive to create. The prohibition of such non-commercial uses would merely inhibit access to ideas without any countervailing benefit. Although every commercial use of copyrighted material is presumptively an unfair exploitation of the monopoly privilege that belongs to the owner of the copyright, non-commercial uses are a different matter. [. . .] challenge to a noncommercial use of a copyrighted work requires». In the same vein, US courts do not require that the market to which the work whose fair use is at issue potentially relates actually already exists, as is well shown in *American Geophysical Union v. Texaco* (60 F.3d 913 [2nd Cir. 1995]), upholding the relevance of the «[. . .] impact on potential licensing revenues for traditional, reasonable, likely developed market», and *A&M Records, Inc. v. Napster, Inc. Napster, Inc.* (239 F.3d 1004 [9th Cir. 2001]), which states that «[. . .] lack of harm to an established market cannot deprive the copyright holder of the right to develop alternative markets for the work».

131 When the court finds itself assessing a specific hypothesis that does not fit perfectly with the exemplifications indicated by law, it must consider to what extent the second work is merely a substitute for the first or whether it confers on the latter a different and additional quid. See, in this sense, also *Campbell v. Acuff-Rose Music, Inc.*, 510 U.S. 575 (1994). *See*, e.g., *Grand Upright Music, Ltd v. Warner Bros. Records, Inc.*, 780 F. Supp. 182 (S.D.N.Y. 1991), where the sampling of music recordings in another recording intended for commercial use was held not to be fair use, or *Dr. Seuss Enterprises, L.P. v. Penguin Books USA, Inc.*, 109 F.3d 1394 (9th Cir. 1997), where, on the one hand, satire or appropriation of remarks about society at large is not considered an expression of fair use, and, on the other hand, parodies commenting on the original and copying no more than is strictly necessary are.

the simultaneous purposes of effectiveness of protection and the functions of dissemination and incentive of creativity.[132]

The considerations made so far highlight both the different perspectives emphasized by the two orientations analysed and the general trend demonstrated, in general, by contemporary legal systems.

From the first point of view, if the first sale doctrine is presented as an exception to copyright that aims to balance the interests of the copyright holder with those of the community by operating on the distribution network, the fair use doctrine still affects the strict boundaries of copyright by expanding them but acting on the different front of the use and exploitation of the original work.

It is clear, then, the different extension in which the exception to copyright takes shape which, on the one hand, is integrated by the first sale doctrine given its limitation to distribution profiles, on the other hand, by the fair use doctrine given its limitation to specific use profiles, and, finally, by copyleft given its potential lack of limits to the rights that can be exercised on the original work from the point of view of distribution, use, modification and acquisition.

From the second point of view, a comparative assessment of the legal systems taken into consideration allows us to grasp, with special reference to the EU and US legal frameworks, the tendency towards a regulatory convergence that leaves, however, the peculiarities of the discipline that the two doctrines demonstrate on the front of the contract, copyright and anti-circumvention regulations as they refer to the copyright owner, the online service provider and the user.

Beyond, therefore, the full and unconditional applicability of the first sale doctrine and the fair use doctrine not only to tangible goods, but also to digital goods,[133] the different way in which these principles condition copyright, proves once again how the latter, impacted by digitality, can then affect the structure, implementation and harmonization of the same global models of conducting business and therefore, in a more or less direct manner, the concept of property and its deployment.

The bursting significance of this assumption is well grasped with particular reference to the first sale doctrine, the application of which to the digital world has

132 *See*, in this regard, P. Stevens, *The Generativity of Sony v. Universal: The Intellectual Property Legacy of Justice Stevens*, in *Fordham Law Rev.*, 74, 2006, p. 101 ff.

133 The Berkman Center for Internet & Society at Harvard Law School, *iTunes: How Copyright, Contract, and Technology Shape the Business of Digital Media – A Case Study*, cit., pp. 56 and 57, where the authors underline that «[T]he application of the first sale doctrine to digital works [. . .] is often restricted by license agreement [. . .]. The basic idea behind such licenses is to structure the "purchase" of digital content as a grant of a license instead of a sale that transfers ownership. However, in the offline context and with regard to shrink-wrap licenses, some courts have qualified such transactions as sales rather than licenses, thus preserving the applicability of the first sale doctrine, because "ownership" [. . .] is one of its prerequisites of first sale. [. . .] application [. . .] to digital work, first and foremost, is limited by the interpretation and application of copyright law. Moreover, the application of the first sale doctrine with respect to digital works is limited by restrictive contractual agreements imposed by digital content providers such as online music stores. In combination with these two constraints, a third factor limits the application of the first sale doctrine to digital works: technical protection measures and the DMCA». *See*, for more details on the subject, *supra* in this section and note 84.

already been mentioned,[134] and which is now taken up again to highlight how the affirmed referability of the principle of exhaustion to digitality is reconnected to the profound change it has imprinted on the concept of ownership.

If, in fact, the first sale doctrine is pacifically considered applicable only when a legitimate right of ownership of an asset is transferred,[135] its deemed extensibility to digital assets, such as software, rests precisely on the labile licence-sale boundary which, favoured by their extensive usability, faithful reproducibility and easy transferability, translates into full usability that conditions the scope of the ownership referable to them.

Nonetheless, and perhaps as a demonstration of the profound homogeneity of fact that characterizes two situations that are legally very distant from each other, some programmers or publishers of digital content provide *expressis verbis* in their licence agreements with the end user or end-user licence agreement (EULA)[136]

134 *See supra* in this section.

135 Consider, for example, 17 U.S. Code § 109(d), which provides for the inapplicability of the first sale doctrine where the availability of the copy derives from «by rental, lease, loan, or otherwise without acquiring ownership of it».

136 With reference to so-called proprietary software, i.e. proprietary or non-free or closed source software, which consists of a programme whose licence allows the beneficiary its use under specific conditions and prevents its modification, sharing, study, redistribution or reverse engineering, i.e. the specific analysis of its operation, of its design and development to produce one or more new programmes that have a similar functioning, if necessary improving or increasing the efficiency of the original version, without actually copying anything from it, one speaks of the end-user licence agreement (EULA) or software licence agreement to refer to that contract between licensor and licensee in which the rights of use owned by the latter are fixed. This licence may, therefore, indicate the methods of use of the copy that are permitted and that may be added to those that may be provided for *ex lege*. This type of agreement, in addition to the undoubted vexatiousness profiles that it may give rise to, has raised perplexity as to its legitimacy, with particular reference to the possible dissemination of pre-installed software by the so-called original equipment manufacturer (OEM), i.e. the company that makes equipment that will then be installed in a finished product, usually a personal computer on which the final manufacturer affixes its own brand, using integrally or almost integrally components produced by suppliers, i.e. the OEMs. Indeed, it may be the case that the user, in the presence of alternative programmes more suited to his needs and of lower or zero cost, may prefer different solutions to those essentially imposed on him by the pre-installation of a given programme on the personal computer he has purchased. In this case, the user may therefore not wish to accept the EULA associated with the pre-installed product and, consequently, activate the refund procedure. In Italy, a similar hypothesis was dealt with by the *Corte di Cassazione* with sentence No. 19161 of 2014, which confirmed both the decision taken in first instance by the *Giudice di pace* of Florence and that adopted on appeal by the Court of Florence with sentence No. 2526 of 2010, sanctioning the condemnation of *HP Italia* to reimburse the licence costs of the operating system, with the addition of accessory expenses, in favour of a purchaser who did not intend to use the Windows operating system preinstalled on his notebook. More specifically, the court of legitimacy, analysing the software licence agreement, i.e. the EULA relating to the operating system pre-installed on the computer, held that there was no negotiating link between the contract of sale of the computer and the software licence, and that the end user, who had expressed a negative intention to use the software in question when he first started the computer, was entitled to reimbursement of the portion of the price attributable to the programme in question. The *Corte di Cassazione* therefore held to be insufficient the provision of the licence according to which, in the event of its rejection of the EULA associated with the operating system, it provided for the mere full return of the machine by the user, in addition to the reimbursement of

that the digital good is the object of a licence and not of sale, so as to paralyse the operativity of the first sale doctrine.[137]

In this regard, and especially with reference to the United States, one observes the presence of numerous and heterogeneous jurisprudential orientations that attempt to address and resolve the problem of the qualification, in terms of sale-property or licence–non-property, to be conferred on the legal situations that may arise in the presence of real or facade-only end-user licence agreements.

Courts usually tend to go beyond mere appearances in cases presented to them as software-licensing agreements, ruling that there is either an actual licence or a

only the purchase costs, but with the exclusion of accessory costs. *See*, for more details, *Corte di Cassazione*, decision no. 19161 of 2014.

137 In this regard, it is worth noting the frequent use of tear-off or shrink-wrap licences (representing a typical EULA enclosed with software packaged in a plastic film, the removal of which is followed by the full effectiveness of the relevant licence), click-wrap licences (representing a common type of agreement that is mainly used on the Internet, as part of the installation process of numerous software packages, or in other situations where an agreement is required by electronic means, the mode of operation of which consists of requiring the end user to indicate his or her consent to the use of the product or service, by clicking on a dialogue box or popup displaying an "ok" or "agree," or his disagreement by clicking on "delete" or closing the dialogue box), to browse-wrap licences (which are typically used for the diffusion of content via the Internet, and which are characterized by the implicit acceptance of the licensee by providing the surfer with a link to the applicable contractual conditions), or to other types of licences used precisely to overcome the applicability of the first sale doctrine. If, for example, when downloading music in MP3 format through the Amazon.com website, the relative files cannot be resold by the recipient-plaintiff because they are expressly qualified as the object of a mere licence, the situation is different for MP3 music downloaded through the iTunes Store, for which, based on the language used by Apple in its EULAs, one could speak of an actual sale, with the consequent legitimacy of the recipient-plaintiff to resell the relative files, if the other conditions for the applicability of the first sale doctrine also exist. *See*, with reference to the shrink wrap licence, in Italian case law, *Corte di Cassazione* no. 19161 of 2014 (so-called *HP Case*); and, in the United States, *Specht v. Netscape Communications Corp.*, 306 F.3d 17 (2nd Cir. 2002), where the US Court of Appeals for the Second Circuit ruled on the binding nature of this type of licence, making its effectiveness conditional on the fact that «[R]easonably conspicuous notice of the existence of contract terms and unambiguous manifestation of assent to those terms by consumers are essential if electronic bargaining is to have integrity and credibility»; in doctrine, for all, D. Halbert, *The Open Source Alternative: Shrink-Wrap, Open Source and Copyright*, in *Murdoch Univ. Elect. J. Law*, 4, 2003, p. 1 ff. *See*, in general, on mass market licences of copyright material, D. Lindsay, *The Law and Economics of Copyright, Contract and Mass Market Licenses*, Strawberry Hills, 2002, esp. p. 70 ff.; N. Boschiero, *Le licenze F/OSS nel diritto internazionale privato: il problema delle qualificazioni*, Milano, 2004, p. 201 ff. *See*, with more specific reference to click-wrap licences, in EU case law, European Court of Justice, 21 May 2015, *El Majdoub v. CarsOnTheWeb. Deutschland GmbH, C-322/14*, where, conforming to the concept of general conditions expressed in *Regulation 44/2001/EC on jurisdiction and the recognition and enforcement of judgments in civil and commercial matters* (now, *Regulation 1215/2012/EU*), the legitimacy of click-wrap agreements is upheld in the presence of certain conditions; and, in the US case law, *Register.com, Inc. v. Verio, Inc.*, 356 F.3d 393 (2nd Cir. 2004), stating that «[E]ssentially, under a clickwrap arrangement, potential licensees are presented with the proposed license terms and forced to expressly and unambiguously manifest either assent or rejection prior to being given access to the product»; in doctrine, for all, J.A. Obar, A. Oeldorf-Hirsch, *The Clickwrap: A Political Economic Mechanism for Manufacturing Consent on Social Media*, in *Soc. Med. Soc.*, 2018, p. 1 ff. *See*, for further discussion on the subject, *infra* in this section.

genuine sale, which then allows the application of the first sale doctrine under 17 U.S. Code § 109(a).

Consequently, if the parties specify that the agreement consists only of a licence and thus manifest the will to establish a licensor-licensee relationship between them, this is not sufficient to bring the hypothesis outside the proprietary schemes necessary for the application of the principle of exhaustion, since, on the other hand, in addition to the presence of other contractual terms concretely expressive of this determination, the concrete realization of a relationship legally framed in the licence is required.[138]

138 In this regard, with reference to the EU experience, the *UsedSoft v. Oracle* case stands out, in which the European Court of Justice ruled that the sale of software, carried out by resorting either to the use of a material support or to simple downloading, entails, according to EU law, the transfer of ownership of the asset that is the subject of the sale, resulting in the application of the first sale doctrine on the basis of the overcoming of the "licensed, not sold" legal theory. *See*, for further discussion, *supra* in this paragraph. With reference, instead, to the US experience, it seems useful to mention the case *Vernor v. Autodesk, Inc.*, 2010 WL 3516435 (9th Cir. Sept. 10, 2010), in which the court affirmed the possibility of verifying whether a given software licence agreement is actually capable of creating a licence relationship with the end user through the application of a so-called three-factor test. Thus, it follows that in order to assess «[. . .] whether a software user is a licensee, rather than an owner of a copy», it is necessary «[F]irst, [. . .] consider whether the copyright owner specifies that a user is granted a licence. Second, [. . .] consider whether the copyright owner significantly restricts the user's ability to transfer the software. Finally, [. . .] consider whether the copyright owner imposes noticeable use restrictions» (*Vernor v. Autodesk, Inc.*, no. 09–35969, slip op. at 13871 and 13872). Considering, therefore, that in the *Vernor case*, the licence agreement between the parties maintained Autodesk's ownership of the software and that the user was only granted a non-exclusive licence to use it, the court found that «*Autodesk* [. . .] imposed significant transfer restrictions: it stated that the licence is nontransferable, the software could not be transferred or leased without *Autodesk*'s written consent, and the software could not be transferred outside the Western Hemisphere. The *SLA* also imposed use restrictions against the use of the software outside the Western Hemisphere and against modifying, translating, or reverse-engineering the software, removing any proprietary marks from the software or documentation, or defeating any copy protection device. Furthermore, the *SLA* provided for termination of the license upon the licensee's unauthorized copying or failure to comply with other license restrictions. Thus, because *Autodesk* reserved title to Release 14 copies and imposed significant transfer and use restrictions, we conclude that its customers are licensees of their copies of Release 14 rather than owners» (*Vernor v. Autodesk, Inc.*, no. 09–35969, slip op. at 13878). If, then, the agreement provided for restrictions on modifying, transferring, reverse-engineering the software, and removing any proprietary marks from the programme packaging or documentation, the Ninth Circuit could infer that Vernor was merely a licensee of the software developed by Autodesk, and that since he was not the owner, he could not resell it on eBay without Autodesk's consent. The Ninth Circuit itself, however, decided against applying *Vernor*'s three-factor test in *UMG v. Augusto*, 558 F. Supp. 2d 1055 (C.D. Cal. 2008), where it decided an alleged licensing agreement that, according to the plaintiff, was concluded when UMG had sent CDs, without having been requested to do so, to music critics. In fact, despite the fact that the packaging in which the promotional CDs were contained bore the statement that «[T]his *CD* is the property of the record company and is licensed to the intended recipient for personal use only. Acceptance of this *CD* shall constitute an agreement to comply with the terms of the license. Resale or transfer of possession is not allowed and may be punishable under federal and state laws», Augusto had tried to sell them on eBay. UMG then argued that the first sale doctrine did not apply, because UMG and Augusto were in a simple licensing relationship, not a sales relationship. The court then ruled, on the one hand, in favour of the applicability of the first sale doctrine when a CD was given as a gift, and, on the other hand, for

It is also in this perspective, then, that it is necessary to read the apparent anomaly that the copyleft creates with respect to the traditional structure of ownership, conferring on the user authentic active subjective situations that can be opposed to all, should problems arise relating to the distribution and use of the work, so much so that he is legitimately placed in a position to assert against those who damage him in his use the rights that the copyleft has made him the owner of.

Especially in its most attenuated version, that of non-copyleft, it allows the user not only to make use of someone else's work, but also to alter it, to freely modify[139] it and therefore appropriate it, also changing its legal circulation regime and altering, in essence, the system of cascading transmission of rights that non-copyleft licences allow: the lawful appropriation by the user of someone else's work originally determines changes in the proprietary regime that, *de facto*, interrupt the operation of the original licence or, where applicable, of derivative licences.

If, therefore, the physiology of things were to be replaced by their pathological development, there would be a need to ensure an apparatus of protections that would not only operate in favour of the owner-author, as has always happened with reference to land and intellectual property respectively, but also in favour of users, who in the new digital dynamic as the logic of copyleft well demonstrates,[140] actively become part of the same mechanisms of modification and distribution of the good and thus assume a position that, going beyond the traits of the mere user, makes them assume those that, according to a classic view, would be more properly referable, exclusively, to the owner of the good.

It is noted, however, that the problem of the proliferation of licences, whereby their greater circulation corresponds to greater difficulty in monitoring their functioning on a planetary scale,[141] represents, in its own way, a collateral effect of the autonomy of protection.

---

the non-acceptance of the terms of the licence merely because the recipient of the unsolicited CDs did not return them to the sender.

139 Freedom to modify consists in the possibility of correcting any errors found in a programme, or of making the software more efficient and functional, or of resolving any security problems. In the case of proprietary software, on the other hand, the user may, at most, ask the provider to add features and correct errors, leaving him the choice of whether or not to do so.

140 The reference is specifically to open source software (OSS) hypotheses, whose analysis has shown that the type of licence under which an OSS is placed positively or negatively influences the success of the software. *See*, in this regard, R. Sen, C. Subramaniam, M.L. Nelson, *Open Source Software Licenses: Strong-copyleft, Non-copyleft, or Somewhere in Between?*, in *Decis. Support Syst.*, 1, 2011, p. 199 ff., where the authors note a close interrelationship between the benefits that the developer of an OSS can achieve, the effort put into the development of an *OSS*, the attitude that the operator shows towards the freedom of choice of an OSS licence, and the choice of an OSS licence itself. More specifically, it has been noted that the greater the effort put into the development of an OSS, the more likely it is that the OSS licence will contain minimal restrictions. Consequently, less restrictive or non-copyleft licences would prevail when more effort would be required in the development of a derived software, while more restrictive or strong-copyleft licences would prevail when minimal effort would be required in the development of an original OSS and derived software.

141 In this perspective, the contrast between the orientation followed by the Free Software Foundation, which proposes the elaboration of a single licence model, the GNU GPL, whose legal meaning should be reproduced by other possible licence schemes, and the Open Source Initiative, which has

In fact, the freedom associated with the copyleft mechanism means that anyone is always in a position to draw up their own personal licence to suit their needs and apply it in the ways and forms most suited to their requirements.[142]

If, then, the progress of knowledge and freedom of thought lead one not to prefer and not to legitimize a single form of protection, the freedom to be able to choose the physiognomy of control that one deems most appropriate to one's needs, constitutes the prerequisite for the growth and dissemination of knowledge in the digital age, in full respect of the economic needs that are co-present and push for adequate and innovative ownership structures.

4 Community Free/Open Source Licenses and the New European Union Public License (EUPL): A Comparative Analysis

As we have seen in the previous pages,[143] the concept of free or open source is used to refer to software whose authors, beyond a more or less strong respect for specific ethical implications, make the source code public in order to allow its use, to favour free study and to allow other programmers to make modifications, extensions and possibly redistribute derivative works, thanks to the application of specific user licences.

The peculiarity of this type of licence is, therefore, the possibility granted to authors to allow others to use, copy, modify, extend, elaborate or sell software they have created, without imposing any obligation of reward on them.

Thus, in order to proceed with the distribution of free or open software, it is necessary to associate a copyright with it, and then indicate a licence for use that respects the freedoms enshrined respectively by either the free software movement (i.e. the GNU GPL) or the Open Source Initiative (i.e. the GNU Free Documentation License used by Wikipedia): the user can create his own licence or adopt an existing one and, if it respects the freedoms previously considered, proceed to distribute free or open software.

In any case, although in theory the necessary distinctions between the two concepts must be maintained, in practice software recognized as open source is often also free software, and vice versa, so that the term free and open source software (or FOSS) is often used.[144]

---

limited itself to elaborating the Open Source Definition, which acts as a decalogue to be referred to in the elaboration of a genuinely open source software, is justified.

142 *See*, on this profile, *Softman Products Co., LLC v. Adobe System, Inc.*, 171 F. Supp. 2d 1075 (C.D. Cal. 2001), where, with specific reference to the so-called shrink-wrap licences, the judge inferred the applicability of the first sale doctrine to the relevant digital goods that are the subject matter, since they would be real sales rather than genuine licences, and this by virtue of the particular way in which the terms of use are negotiated. In fact, the object of these licences is software intended for large-scale distribution, the conditions of use of which are printed on the back of the packaging containing the material support (i.e. CD or DVD) of the software, where it is specified that their acceptance by the purchaser takes place at the moment he opens the packaging. It is thus that the assignee is entitled to use the copy of the software.

143 *See supra* esp. §§ 1 and 2.

144 A. Metzger (edited by), *Free and Open Source Software (FOSS) and Other Alternative License Models. A Comparative Analysis*, New York, NY, Dordrecht, and London, 2015.

And it is this type of licence that the European Union looked to when it decided to endow the free/open source software (F/OSS) licence with a common discipline thanks to the European Union Public Licence (EUPL),[145] which, as the first European F/OSS licence, represents a unitary legal instrument that can be used by anyone, not only within the European Union, who intends to proceed with the distribution of computer programmes.[146]

The EUPL is, then, a free/open source software licence, with copyleft effect,[147] drawn up and approved by the European Commission,[148] whose purpose is to stimulate a process of promotion of the free/open source model in order to increase its

145 Interestingly, the EUPL, which was developed in 23 languages, was approved in January 2007 in the English, French and German versions, and was then translated into the other 20 official languages of the Union in 2008. The European Commission adopted an updated version of the licence, the EULP 1.1, on 9 January 2009, making it valid in all Member States, and released a new one, the EUPL 1.2, on 18 May 2017. More than 500 software solutions have thus been brought under the EUPL since 2012. *See* European Commission, *Commission Implementing Decision (EU) 2017/863 of 18 May 2017 Updating the Open Source Software Licence EUPL to Further Facilitate the Sharing and Reuse of Software Developed by Public Administrations*, in *OJ L*, 128, 19 May 2017, p. 59 ff.

146 The EUPL, which is supposed to represent the first licence issued by a supranational body, was originally conceived as a method of issuing projects developed within the framework of the IDABC (now ISA), which is a tool designed especially for the public sector. *See*, for further details, *infra* in this section.

147 In this respect, Article 5, Obligation of the Licensee, is of particular relevance, «The grant of the rights mentioned above is subject to some restrictions and obligations imposed on the Licensee. Those obligations are the following: [. . .] Copyleft clause: If the Licensee distributes or communicates copies of the Original Works or Derivative Works, this Distribution or Communication will be done under the terms of this Licence or of a later version of this Licence unless the Original Work is expressly distributed only under this version of the Licence – for example by communicating "EUPL v. 1.2 only." The Licensee (becoming Licensor) cannot offer or impose any additional terms or conditions on the Work or Derivative Work that alter or restrict the terms of the Licence. [. . .]», and, further, Article 6, Chain of Authorship, states that «The original Licensor warrants that the copyright in the Original Work granted hereunder is owned by him/her or licensed to him/her and that he/she has the power and authority to grant the Licence. Each Contributor warrants that the copyright in the modifications he/she brings to the Work are owned by him/her or licensed to him/her and that he/she has the power and authority to grant the Licence. Each time You accept the Licence, the original Licensor and subsequent Contributors grant You a licence to their contributions to the Work, under the terms of this Licence».

148 According to Article 2, Scope of the rights granted by the Licence, of EUPL v. 1.2, in fact, «The Licensor hereby grants You a worldwide, royalty-free, non-exclusive, sublicensable licence to do the following, for the duration of copyright vested in the Original Work: – use the Work in any circumstance and for all usage, – reproduce the Work, – modify the Work, and make Derivative Works based upon the Work, – communicate to the public, including the right to make available or display the Work or copies thereof to the public and perform publicly, as the case may be, the Work, – distribute the Work or copies thereof, – lend and rent the Work or copies thereof, – sublicense rights in the Work or copies thereof. Those rights can be exercised on any media, supports and formats, whether now known or later invented, as far as the applicable law permits so. In the countries where moral rights apply, the Licensor waives his right to exercise his moral right to the extent allowed by law in order to make effective the licence of the economic rights here above listed. The Licensor grants to the Licensee royalty-free, non-exclusive usage rights to any patents held by the Licensor, to the extent necessary to make use of the rights granted on the Work under this Licence».

diffusion and knowledge, in the light of a valorization of this type of software initiated by the Community institutions themselves.

It is no coincidence that, on the one hand, the European Commission distributes its management programme using this type of licence, and on the other hand, some applications developed within the framework of the Interoperable Delivery of European eGovernment Services to Public Administrations, Businesses and Citizens (IDABC)[149] programme, now ISA,[150] such as, for example, Communication and Information Resource Centre for Administrations, Businesses and Citizens (CIRCABC)[151] or EUSurvey,[152] have been subject to the EUPL for almost two decades.

But what were the reasons that led to the development of such a licence, even in the presence of an IT scenario populated by hundreds of free/open source software, such as, for example, the General Public License (GPL)?

The European Commission felt the need to develop *ex novo* a different legal instrument, such as the EUPL, due to the lack of a licence that, due to its specific

149 The Interoperable Delivery of European eGovernment Services to Public Administrations, Business and Citizens (IDABC) is a programme that seeks to take advantage of all the opportunities that information and communication technologies offer to stimulate and facilitate the cross-border delivery of public sector services to EU businesses and citizens, to improve the efficiency and collaboration between EU public administrations, and to help make Europe a more attractive place to live, work and invest. The IDABC aims to achieve its objectives not only by allocating funding for those projects that aim to align with EU policies, but also by issuing recommendations, developing solutions and providing services that enable national and EU administrations to communicate electronically in providing modern public services to EU businesses and citizens. The first IDABC software applications are: CIRCA, a groupware for document sharing, IPM and the G2G, G2C, G2B specifications of the eLink software. *See*, for more details, European Commission, *IDABC*, available at http://ec.europa.eu/idabc/en/home.html.

150 The Interoperability Solutions for (European Public) Administration (ISA) was conceived to enable easy communication of digital information across borders between public administrations in order to strengthen the reuse and exchange of existing ICT solutions. In fact, the *ISA*, which is embedded in the Directorate-General for Informatics (DIGIT), plays a very important role in promoting both the EU *Digital Agenda* and the *e-Government Action Plan*. Furthermore, the collaborative platform JoinUp, founded by ISA and operational at the end of 2011 as a replacement for the European Open Source Observatory and Repository (OSOR), offers a range of services to help e-Government practitioners share their experiences in the field of interoperability and facilitate the search, selection, re-use, development and application of FOSS and semantic interoperability-focused resources. *See* European Commission, *ISA2*, available at https://ec.europa.eu/isa2/isa2_en; Id., *State of Play of Interoperability in Europe – Report 2016*, Luxembourg, 2017, p. 7 ff.; and, for further details, L. Guibault, O. Salamanca, *Fitting the Bill: FOSS and Alternative Copyright Licenses in the Netherlands*, in *Free and Open Source Software (FOSS) and Other Alternative License Models. A Comparative Analysis*, edited by N. Dietrich, L. Guibault, T. Margoni, K. Siewicz, A. Wiebe, Göttingen, 2013, p. 314 ff.

151 The CIRCABC is an open source application used to develop a collaborative platform where communities of users can work together (so-called collaborative workspace) using the web and share information, documents and resources, so as to facilitate their distribution and management. *See*, for more details, European Commission, *CIRCAB*, available at https://circabc.europa.eu/faces/jsp/extension/wai/navigation/container.jsp.

152 EUSurvey is an online survey management system that enables the creation and publication of publicly accessible forms, such as user satisfaction surveys and public consultations. *See*, for further details, European Commission, *EUSurvey*, available at https://ec.europa.eu/eusurvey/.

characteristics, had the capacity to satisfy certain needs perceived at Community level, especially in terms of guaranteeing the uniformity of copyrights in the Member States of the European Union, while retaining compatibility with other F/OSS licences such as the GPL.

The EUPL, in fact, made it possible to respond to the need to have a licence of equal legal value in many languages throughout the entire Community area, which, using particularly effective terminology in the field of intellectual property, complied with the requirements of Community law, which allowed for a detailed and specific delimitation of responsibilities and protections precisely because it was valid in all Member States, and which did not limit itself to using the wording "to the extent allowed by the law," as is the case with most licences that are drawn up taking into account the schemes typically used in the United States.

Confirmation of the European Commission's desire to create an additional F/OSS licence in order to have a licence translated into the official languages of the European Union, and, in this way, to overcome the risks deriving from the localization of the language and the applicable law, can also be found in the possible use to which the EUPL can be put: although the potential users of software that can be traced back to the EU institutions are mainly administrations of the most diverse public sectors,[153] there is nothing to prevent this type of licence from being used more widely.[154]

The EUPL, in essence, presents itself as the first licence that is coherent with both EU law and the copyright law provided for in the individual Member States,[155] while at the same time preserving the compatibility of the patterns of other F/OSS licences.[156]

153 Despite its adaptability to any software, the EUPL was originally conceived for the distribution of software developed under the IDABC programme. Indeed, since October 2008, when OSOR came into operation, then migrated to JoinUp (January 2012), numerous software applications produced mainly by European administrations have become available under the EUPL licence. *See*, for more details, European Commission, *JoinUp. Share and Reuse Interoperability Solutions or Public Administrations, Business and Citizens*, available at https://joinup.ec.europa.eu.

154 Although the main addressee of the EUPL is the public administration of the European Union and its Member States, everyone, in fact, can use this licence.

155 In this sense, reference is also made to the so-called e-Commerce Directive (Directive 2000/31/EC) and the Computer Programs Directive (Directive 2009/24/EC). *See Directive 2000/31/EC of the European Parliament and of the Council of 8 June 2000 on Certain Legal Aspects of Information Society Services, in Particular Electronic Commerce, in the Internal Market*, in *OJ L*, 178, 17 July 2000, p. 1 ff.; *Directive 2009/24/EC of the European Parliament and of the Council of 23 April 2009 on the Legal Protection of Computer Programs*, in *OJ L*, 111, 5 May 2009, p. 16 ff.

156 The spirit of preservation that underlies the regulation of the EUPL is evident both in Article 13(2), Miscellaneous, where it states that «If any provision of the Licence is invalid or unenforceable under applicable law, this will not affect the validity or enforceability of the Licence as a whole. Such provision will be construed or reformed so as necessary to make it valid and enforceable», and in Article 5, where, in addition to a certain freedom of distribution, there is a margin of compatibility with some of the main F/OSS licences in the copyleft discipline, as is well demonstrated in the following Appendix, where it is specified that «Compatible Licences' according to Article 5 EUPL are: – GNU General Public License (GPL) v. 2, v. 3 – GNU Affero General Public License (AGPL) v. 3 – Open Software License (OSL) v. 2.1, v. 3.0 – Eclipse Public License (EPL) v. 1.0 – CeCILL v. 2.0, v. 2.1; Mozilla Public Licence (MPL) v. 2 – GNU Lesser General Public Licence

This, however, has not avoided the criticism that has been levelled in the free/open source software world at the decision to adopt a new strong copyleft licence in addition to those already in use, as the reasons for contributing to the proliferation of licences do not seem sufficient to balance the disadvantages caused by the presence of an additional F/OSS licence.

In fact, since the EUPL can be used by anyone who owns the copyright on parts of a piece of software, it could operate as an adequate instrument of legal interoperability at the trans-European level.

In this perspective, then, the EUPL would conform to the common trend, also expressed in Italian law through Articles 64-*ter* and 64-*quater* of Law no. 633 of 1941, of loosening the rigid web with which the copyright on the computer program is woven, when it is indispensable to proceed to overcome the prohibition of reproduction, without authorization, of the code of the computer program and of the translation of its form, and therefore the exclusivity of the subjective situation expressed, "to obtain the information necessary to achieve the interoperability, with other programs, of an independently created computer program," pursuant to Article 64-*quater*, § 1, of Law no. 633 of 1941.[157]

(LGPL) v. 2.1, v. 3 – Creative Commons Attribution-ShareAlike v. 3.0 Unported (CC BY-SA 3.0) for works other than software; European Union Public Licence (EUPL) v. 1.1, v. 1.2 – Québec Free and Open-Source Licence – Reciprocity (LiLiQ-R) or Strong Reciprocity (LiLiQ-R+) – The European Commission may update this Appendix to later versions of the above licences without producing a new version of the EUPL, as long as they provide the rights granted in Article 2 of this Licence and protect the covered Source Code from exclusive appropriation».

157 Interoperability is, therefore, cause to overcome the exclusive nature of the copyright on the software, without this – in full compliance with the Berne Convention on the Protection of Literary and Artistic Works ratified and made enforceable by Italian Law no. 399 of 20 June 1978 – unduly prejudicing the legitimate interests of the rights holder or being in conflict with the normal exploitation of the program (para. 4), provided that the «le seguenti condizioni: a) le predette attività siano eseguite dal licenziatario o da altri che abbia il diritto di usare una copia del programma oppure, per loro conto, da chi è autorizzato a tal fine; b) le informazioni necessarie per conseguire l'interoperabilità non siano già facilmente e rapidamente accessibili ai soggetti indicati alla lettera a); c) le predette attività siano limitate alle parti del programma originale necessarie per conseguire l'interoperabilità. 2. Le disposizioni di cui al comma 1 non consentono che le informazioni ottenute in virtù della loro applicazione: a) siano utilizzate a fini diversi dal conseguimento dell'interoperabilità del programma creato autonomamente; b) siano comunicate a terzi, fatta salva la necessità di consentire l'interoperabilità del programma creato autonomamente; c) siano utilizzate per lo sviluppo, la produzione o la commercializzazione di un programma per elaboratore sostanzialmente simile nella sua forma espressiva, o per ogni altra attività che violi il diritto di autore. 3. Le clausole contrattuali pattuite in violazione dei commi 1 e 2 sono nulle» (*author's note*, "following conditions are met: (a) the aforesaid activities are carried out by the licensee or by others having the right to use a copy of the program or, on their behalf, by those authorised to do so; (b) the information necessary to achieve interoperability is not already easily and rapidly accessible to the persons referred to in subparagraph (a); (c) the aforesaid activities are limited to the parts of the original program necessary to achieve interoperability. 2. The provisions referred to in paragraph 1 shall not permit the information obtained by virtue of their application: (a) to be used for purposes other than achieving interoperability of the independently created program; (b) to be disclosed to third parties, except to the extent necessary to achieve interoperability of the independently created program; (c) to be used for the development, production or marketing of a computer program substantially similar in its form of expression, or for any other activity which

In essence, the willingness expressed by the European Commission in developing a free software licence with copyleft effect highlights, once again, the centrality that this model has assumed and continues to assume in the IT world, but not only, as a consequence of the sharing philosophy itself.

Sharing, in fact, continues to increasingly increase its influence on social relations and thus on legal relations, impacting the very way of conceiving the ownership of *res*, no longer of a specific subject but of a plurality of subjects, who in a perspective of freedom can, however, also change, in full autonomy, its legal regime, limiting, if necessary, its use, as the weakest form of copyleft, non-copyleft, allows on the same derived goods.

5 Non-Copyleft: Navigating "Anomalous" Licensing and Substantive Ownership in the Digital Sphere

Copyleft, as is now well known, is a deeply permissive type of licence, so much so as to allow the development of derivative works whose regime of use, dissemination and modification can take on, in the case of non-copyleft, traits that are completely different from those that the licence of the original work envisaged.[158]

It is perhaps precisely because of these characteristics, which are extremely suited to valorizing shared freedom,[159] that this licence is accepted and promoted by both the free software movement and the Open Source Initiative, as is well demonstrated, on the one hand, by the fact that both the FSF and the OSI place copyleft and non-copyleft in the list of accepted licences, and on the other, by the fact that some of the software included in the GNU Project are even distributed under a non-copyleft licence.

---

infringes copyright. 3. Contract terms agreed in breach of paragraphs 1 and 2 shall be null and void").

158 Generally speaking, it has been noted that copyleft represents a model of copyright management based on a system of licences that allows the creator, in his capacity as the original owner of the rights to the work, to indicate to the users of the work how it should be used, disseminated and often also modified, while respecting certain essential conditions. In the strongest version of copyleft, users of the work are obliged, should they wish to distribute it after modifying it, to do so under the same legal regime and generally under the same licence provided *ab initio* by the author of the original work, so that he is guaranteed the possibility of providing a similar set of freedoms throughout the distribution chain and the possible development of further licences. Beyond the strictly technical-legal profiles, the term copyleft is also used to indicate a cultural orientation that aims to challenge the rigidities of copyright in its traditional setting. *See*, in the latter regard, P. Pisano, *Managing Innovation. Creare, gestire e diffondere. Innovazione nei sistemi relazionali*, Limena, 2011, p. 224 ff. *See*, for more details, *supra* § 2.

159 In this regard, it can be noted how the advantages of copyleft in the broad sense of the term are identified with its permissiveness, which manifests itself in the possibility of sublicensing, creating and distributing derivative works without any limits whatsoever, especially in the case of non-copyleft, with all the advantages this entails for programmers, also in terms of the greater difficulty of emerging potential conflicts with other copyleft or proprietary licences. However, with a view to completely promoting the philosophy of sharing, non-copyleft may be perceived negatively precisely because of the possibility it gives, in addition to the other freedoms just indicated, to subject derivative works to proprietary licences, so as to restrictively affect the full expression of the freedoms of future users.

Furthermore, the EUPL itself only nominally presents itself as a strong copyleft licence, because it is expressly compatible with weak copyleft licences,[160] and thus easily loses its strong character if it is distributed under weak copyleft terms.[161]

The profound alterations that non-copyleft imposes on the traditional set-up or modus operandi of the proprietary scheme, then, explicate their effects not only on the cascade system of proprietorships that can be constituted through derivative licences, but through it, on the scheme of protections to which the proprietary logic itself can be appealed and in which it finds manifestation.

In fact, according to the canonical vision of property, both in its dominical and immaterial declination, the legal instrumentality with which its protection is ensured is linked, on the one hand, to the exclusivity of the relationship that this right gives rise to between the owner and the *res* (character of realness), and, on the other, to the absoluteness that this subjective situation reveals in the eventual relationship that the damaged owner establishes with the damaging third party (character of opposability *erga omnes*).

More specifically, and with specific regard to copyright, to which the copyleft model under analysis is interrelated, it should be noted how – at least in Italy and unlike the US system where it originated[162] – it consists of two distinct profiles that give prominence, on the one hand, to a patrimonial aspect (patrimonial copyrights)[163] and, on the other, to a moral aspect (moral or personal copyrights).[164]

If, in fact, patrimonial rights are the exclusive rights of the author to whom they allow, pursuant to Article 12 of Italian Law no. 633 of 1941 and Article 2577 of the Italian Civil Code, the economic use of his work in any form and manner, original and derivative, and to receive the resulting remuneration; moral copyrights are the exclusive rights that the law recognizes in favor of the author to protect his personality. In the light of the above, this protection finds expression, pursuant to Articles 20–24 of Italian Law no. 633 of 1941, in the right to exploit his work, even in the presence of an anonymous and pseudonymous author, and in the right to object to

160 *See*, for the distinction between strong and weak copyleft, *supra* § 1.

161 According to Article 6(2), Chain of Authorship, in fact, «Each Contributor warrants that the copyright in the modifications he/she brings to the Work are owned by him/her or licensed to him/her and that he/she has the power and authority to grant the Licence». For the detractors of this flexibility inherent in the EUPL, this profile could facilitate the confusion of programmers and copyright holders, since they could find themselves the recipients of different legal effects than those expected, if they were mistakenly convinced of a substantial de facto equivalence between GPL and EUPL licences.

162 US copyright law, in fact, focuses more on enhancing economic rights than moral or personal copyright.

163 More specifically, the patrimonial copyrights provided for by Italian Law no. 633 of 1941 include the right to elaborate and modify the work (Articles 4 and 18), the right of publication (Article 12), the reproduction right (Articles 13, 68 and 71-*sexies*), the transcription right (Article 14), the right of public performance, representation or recitation (Article 15), the right of communication to the public (Article 16), the rental right and lending right (Article 18-*bis*), the resale right (Article 144).

164 More specifically, the author's moral rights envisaged by Italian Law no. 633 of 1941 include the right to the integrity of the work (Articles 2 and 22), the right to authorship of the work (Articles 20 and 21), the right to unpublished works (Articles 24 and 112) and the right of repentance (Articles 142 and 143).

defamations or mutilations of the work that may harm the author's honor and reputation, and, pursuant to Articles 142 and 143 of Italian Law no. 633 of 1941, in the right to withdraw the work from the market for serious reasons that may include both ethical, intellectual, political and religious reasons and a contrast of the work with the author's changed personality.

Moreover, both the patrimonial rights under Article 19 of Italian Law no. 633 of 1941 and the moral rights are independent of each other, because the exercise of one of them does not exclude the exclusive exercise of each of the other's rights, and therefore they may be exercised either severally or jointly, just as they may be exercised over the work in its entirety or over each of its parts.

However, unlike patrimonial rights, which have a time limit, in that they last for the author's entire life and until the 70th year after his death, pursuant to Article 25 of the Copyright Law, they are renounceable and can be assigned to third parties, pursuant to Article 107 of the Italian Copyright Law and Article 2581 of the Italian Civil Code, moral rights, which are exercisable when their infringement may cause harm to the honour or reputation of the author, are inalienable, imprescriptible and unwaivable, hence the possibility of exercising them irrespective of the ownership of the patrimonial rights deriving from the creation of the work, even when the latter have been assigned to third parties.

It follows, then, that moral rights, although, like patrimonial rights, arise in the author's hands *ex lege* as soon as the work is created, are the only ones to be perceived, in the common mind, as non-transferable, thus impacting on the same protection that can be granted to them that reaches, through them, the work as originally created and conceived.

In civil law legal systems, where this dichotomous approach exists, the problem then arises of assessing what are the consequences of the author maintaining control over the work, which he cannot get rid of even when he has decided to assign the rights of economic exploitation,[165] as happens, for example, in the case of open content software with non-copyleft effect.[166]

The issue is of primary importance not only for the practical implications connected to it, but also for the theoretical implications arising from the need to harmonize the possibility of perpetual control over the work with its subjection to a

165 The moral rights of the author are unlimited in time, so that after the author's death they may be claimed by his spouse, descendants and ascendants. If public purposes so require, then the relevant action may be brought by the President of the Council of Ministers.

166 It seems appropriate to note that, although under the law on copyright, in addition to the moral rights to the work (authorship, etc.), the rights inherent in its economic exploitation should also apply, in the field of information technology, this provision does not operate automatically, software and databases being an exception. In fact, under Article 12-*bis*, it is provided that «Salvo patto contrario, il datore di lavoro è titolare del diritto esclusivo di utilizzazione economica del programma per elaboratore o della banca di dati creati dal lavoratore dipendente nell'esecuzione delle sue mansioni o su istruzioni impartite dallo stesso datore di lavoro» (*author's note*, "Unless otherwise agreed, the employer shall be the owner of the exclusive right to the economic use of the computer program or database created by the employee in the performance of his duties or upon instructions given by the same employer").

non-copyleft model, which theoretically renders the object of the creative activity so free in its fruition as to allow for a radical change in its own regime.[167]

In fact, when reasoning in these terms, one's thoughts go not only to the necessary articulations, patrimonial and moral,[168] in which copyright is articulated, but much further to the instruments of protection that the subject who has become owner must be recognized.

More specifically, with regard to the right to claim the paternity of the work,[169] if no particular theoretical problems seem to arise, considering that most of the licences currently in circulation envisage clauses requiring the authors of the original work to be disclosed, in practical terms the question becomes more complicated in the case of works, such as computer programmes, which, by their very nature, lend themselves to being modified, integrated and improved by new authors, if the relative licence allows it, as happens for F/OSS software with non-copyleft effect.

This eventuality may arise especially with reference to software that is particularly widespread or in whose original creation or derived modification an indefinite group of developers have participated, which may also lead to the case in which the individual contributions are so reciprocally integrated as to be inseparable from the work as a whole: the problem that arises in such an eventuality is to distinguish the contributions made by each programmer, in order to guarantee the legitimate exercise of the moral rights of the author that are connected thereto.

Although it is of particular moment to note that the problem, on the resolution of which depends the right to take legal action against possible infringement, must always be resolved in the light of the licence on whose clear and unequivocal indication of the authors the correct operation of the copyleft itself is entrusted, it finds a different solution depending on whether one is in the presence of copyleft or non-copyleft software: in the first hypothesis it is necessary to refer to all existing F/OSS licences (original and derivative), whereas in the second hypothesis it is necessary to consider not only the F/OSS licences, but also any proprietary licences that may have subsequently come into being, with the consequent emergence, in the latter eventuality, of both the moral and patrimonial profiles interconnected with the copyright that may have been infringed.

It can be seen, then, how precisely with particular reference to free/open content programmes subject to non-copyleft, due to their full modifiability by subsequent

167 In this regard, it should be noted that such a problem arises from the fact that in the United States, the context in which copyleft originated, the distinction between patrimonial rights and moral rights of the author is not perceived, and, consequently, the assignment of the rights of economic exploitation of the work acts on the entire subjective situation, i.e. also on that which, from a civil law perspective, makes up the moral part of the right.

168 *See infra* in this section.

169 The importance of identifying the author of the work also lies in the fact that, in the traditional scheme, it is the licensor-author who has the legitimacy to sue to assert the prejudice resulting from the feared infringement.

users, it is important that the relative licence indicates in as much detail as possible which parts have been modified and who the author is.

Traits of compatibility between the unwaivability of the moral copyright, pursuant to Article 22(1) of Italian Law no. 633 of 1941, and the non-copyleft model, which are even more complex than those just highlighted for the right to the authorship of the work, are found for the right to the integrity of the work, i.e. the right to object to deformations or mutilations of the work that may result in prejudice to the latter or to the author's reputation.

Even more so, the framework envisaged finds an articulation in the presence of a non-copyleft software scheme that, by its very nature, tends to be applied globally and directly, as well as used freely and simultaneously by an indistinct congeries of users who are potential authors of derivative proprietary programmes, with the consequent loss of the possibility of ascertaining and monitoring the changes made to the work that is subject to it.

In this regard, at least with regard to the Italian legal system, Article 22 of Italian Law no. 633 of 1941 is of help, which, by allowing a partial and tacit derogation to the principle of inalienability where the author has "known and accepted the modifications of his work," entails the loss of the right to "act to prevent their execution or to request their suppression."

The recourse *ab origine* to the non-copyleft scheme, with the consequences that derive therefrom in terms of freedom to modify even the legal title to use the work, highlights the clear willingness of the first author to accept, in a more or less tacit manner, deformations or mutilations that the various users may make during the use of the good.

A similar argument must be made about the right of repentance, with respect to which Article 142 of Italian Law no. 633 of 1941, while reaffirming, in § 2, the personality and non-transferability, states, in paragraph 1, the author's right, "if serious moral reasons exist, [. . .] to withdraw the work from the market, except for the obligation to indemnify those who have acquired the rights to reproduce, disseminate, perform, represent or distribute the work."

Well then, in the presence of a non-copyleft software intended *ex se* for a global and indistinct diffusion, the problem arises both of identifying all the licensees of the work to whom the licensor's will to exercise his right of repentance must be communicated, as is found in cases of copyright and strong or weak copyleft, but also, and above all, to determine who are the users who, following the transformation of the software into a proprietary one due to the legitimate modifications made to it, have become subjects in turn entitled to withdraw the work from the market for serious moral reasons in their capacity as actual author-owners.

Now, beyond the aforementioned issues that, on a practical level, are certainly relevant, in the dynamics of the present work it is significant to note how these concrete implications are revealing of the bursting impact that the non-copyleft model, specifically, and digitality, in general, exert on the classic proprietary model.

Beyond the specific legal qualification of copyleft licences in general,[170] one thus notes the presence of a mechanism that allows the configuration of a structure that alters the traditional proprietary approach: the development of open content software with a non-copyleft effect allows the affirmation of a logic that, in addition to determining the overcoming of absoluteness and exclusivity as paradigms proper to traditional property rights, allows simple users to even transform the very title on which the availability of the digital asset used (the computer programme) is based, which from legitimizing a position of mere free usability can lead, by reason of the modifications made to the programme and without the prior authorization of the developer, to an authentic ownership over it that manifests itself in the conversion of the software originally F/OSS into a proprietary one, with all that this entails with regard to the exercise of both the patrimonial and moral rights of copyright.

And this also goes beyond the classic reference to computer interoperability which, as we have seen,[171] presents itself as a legitimizing factor for the possible modification of the computer programme by the user, without prior authorization by the programmer-author: non-copyleft software, in addition to being characterized by a free modifiability that does not find necessary justification in interoperability, does not, by its very nature, assume the features of the share-alike scheme.[172]

In short, the prospect of a new way of conceiving ownership, at least of digital goods, seems to be progressively favoured, on the one hand, by the phenomenon of free and open source software, which, by guaranteeing freedom of access to and modification of the source code, has been able to open up new horizons for innovation and redistribution, to the extent of encouraging the development of a large number of computer programmes of remarkable quality and constantly updated, and, on the other hand, by the copyleft phenomenon which, thanks to its function of facilitating the conquest of a widespread interest in the access and usability of knowledge, represents the legal instrument that, more than any other, has allowed the author to define the modalities of distribution of his work and to clarify the degree of freedom to be granted to its final user.

6 The Demise of the Proprietary Monolith and the Rise of Proprietary Digitality: A Prophesied Tale of Conclusion?

The analysis conducted so far highlights the need for a study of property that does not stop at the appearances that tradition has wanted to create around it, because reasoning that is limited to the recognition of abstract terms could prove misleading, especially in the complex economic-legal reality that appears daily.

170 *See*, in this regard, S. Aliprandi, *Teoria e pratica del Copyleft*, cit., p. 41, where the author affirms that *copyleft* license «[. . .] sono state concepite in origine come "autorizzazioni" più che come "accordi," nonostante per la nostra cultura giuridica siano tecnicamente individuabili come contratti d'uso di opera dell'ingegno» (*author's note*, "were originally conceived as *authorisations* rather than "agreements," despite the fact that they are technically identifiable in our legal culture as contracts for the use of intellectual works"). *See*, for further details, *supra* § 1.

171 *See supra* § 4.

172 *See supra* note 54.

Exemplary, in this sense, is the reference that the codified definition of the right of ownership operates in favour of the power of enjoyment and disposition.

It is easy to understand, in fact, properties, on the one hand, lacking certain forms of enjoyment, or, on the other, lacking a certain power of disposition, without these characteristics being able to undermine their traditional consideration as undoubtedly proprietary schemes.[173]

Disposition and enjoyment, therefore, although interpreted as ordinary features of the proprietary scheme, may present themselves as features that are certainly not essential and typical of the right of ownership.[174]

That of enjoyment and that of availability are presented, in short, as concepts that are not unilateral and univocal, but changeable and different in the content that they can assume *de facto*, expressing, in this way, all their fungible nature, with the inevitable amplifications that derive from the digital world and its multifaceted diversity, especially if one were to necessarily link them to the trait of exclusivity that is commonly used to describe property and its link with the *res*.

Thus, the need emerges to envisage corrective measures to the transactional approach to the concept of property, both dominical and intellectual, which take their cue from digital circulation in the broad sense, understood not as a mere mode of distribution of intellectual works but as a mechanism that affects property, contract, technology, and enterprise, bending to concepts that have evolved and established themselves over time and bringing with them delicate aspects inherent to the protection of subjective situations.

Digital circulation, in fact, cannot be reduced to a simple matter of copyright, or contract, or the liability of the service provider, or the failure to protect the consumer.

It is no coincidence, then, that one encounters legal instruments, such as, among other possible hypotheses,[175] the non-copyleft, which can favour the emergence of proprietary schemes that are extraneous and autonomous with respect to the original one and from which they derive, and which, superimposed on it and living a life of their own, determine the formation of a series of subjective proprietary situations perhaps only divided *ab initio* by the owner of the original scheme.

Typical, in this sense, is, as we have already seen, free or open source software with a non-copyleft effect, which, born substantially as F/OSS, may, following subsequent modifications made to it by other users, turn into proprietary software, with all the consequent limitations in terms of use and distribution that follow.

And it is precisely in this multiplication of licences, which is relevant not only from a numerical point of view, but also from a substantial one, in that one cannot exclude, by the very nature of the model employed, the intervention of radical changes in the legal regime applicable to the specific open content and non-copyleft software, that all the revolutionary character that the non-copyleft is capable of imprinting on the proprietary model itself, as classically understood, is reflected, thanks to the facilitations coming from a changing informatics-digital reality.

173 P. Perlingieri, *Introduzione alla problematica della «proprietà»*, cit., p. 165 ff.

174 P. Perlingieri, *Introduzione alla problematica della «proprietà»*, cit., p. 165 ff.

175 Consider, just to give some examples, of the so-called public domain or participatory housing.

It is no longer possible, in fact, to identify and qualify a single subject, the original author/programmer, as the owner of the software he has created and which, by his own will, he can authorize others to use, but, in a framework made *ab initio* much more articulated in its free articulation, an indefinable series of subjects are grasped from the position of mere users of the software can, by their own decision, become its owners and place themselves in the condition of benefiting from all those prerogatives connected to their new position.

It could be argued, then, that the concept of ownership that we have tried to describe in the preceding pages, finding its own framing in the various passages analysed and finding an exemplary outlet in the non-copyleft, highlights how the digital world and the new technologies have favoured an acceleration and a strengthening of the process of innovation concerning the concept of ownership.[176]

This, in fact, in an evolutionary path that has started since the 19th century, has reflected the change that has marked the various epochs up to the contemporary age and will probably find ever new vigour in the future with the growth of technological potential,[177]

176 P. Grossi, *Il dominio e le cose*, cit., p. 246 ff., whose words, referring to the gradual affirmation of the domain of utility at the expense of the rigid Romanist construction of proprietary law, seem here to be echoed when the author, at p. 248, states «[A]lla costruzione tecnica del sistema si sostituisce ora la discussione delle sue strutture e delle sue categorie fondanti, l'erosione dei suoi materiali più sicuri alla luce della nuove acquisizioni culturali e dei nuovi fatti politici ed economici» (*author's note*, "the technical construction of the system is now replaced by the discussion of its founding structures and categories, the erosion of its most secure materials in the light of new cultural acquisitions and new political and economic facts").

177 J. Hamari, L. Keronen, *Why Do People Buy Virtual Goods: A Meta-Analysis*, cit, 59 ff., where the authors observe how in the last decade, virtual goods have become an important target of consumption online (especially in games, virtual worlds and social networking services) amongst physical and digital goods. They investigate the question of why do people purchase virtual goods by conducting a meta-analysis (random effects model) of the existing quantitative body of literature on the topic. The meta-analysis revealed an important aspect of value of virtual goods, because contrary to traditional goods, the reasons why people purchase virtual goods are tightly connected to the platform they are sold in. These findings underline the significance of service design and its relationship to the formation of value of virtual goods: the value of virtual goods is context-bound, and therefore, bound to the environment where they are usable in. Most factors that were found to be significant predictors of purchase behaviour (such as network effects, self-presentation, enjoyment, ease of use, flow and use of the platform) are directly related to the aspects and design of the platform beyond the general attitudes towards virtual goods themselves. Moreover, the authors found that enjoyment and prolonged use of the platform were more important predictors for purchases in virtual worlds than in games; A. Ronchi, *Rethinking the Role of ICTs-Digital Transformation and Culture Enjoyment Continuity*, in *Culture and Technology-Innovative Technologies in the Museum*, St. Petersburg, 2021, p. 1 ff., where the author, at p. 1, affirms that « Cyber technology is pervasive, and its key role is growing up every day, citizens consider cyber technology as a commodity. Mobile position aware devices represent the most recent revolution in both technology and society, they are perceived as something different from computers even if they play, among others, the same role and immediately became part of our daily life, a wearable accessory as our wallet or wristwatch. Extremely user-friendly devices are nowadays used with relevant satisfaction by formerly digital divided citizens [Ronchi A., 2020]. Accordingly with some technology forecast by the year 2030, half of the world population will adopt merely online and Internet-based materials, this is part of the so-called digital transformation even termed DT or DX. This is not the "full" scene, in 2020 an additional event took the stage: the pandemic. This unexpected event found major part of the countries unprepared even at public health level to do not mention all the other sectors. Extended lockdowns, a variety of national and even local policies, many times changed

since the proprietary logic represents nothing more than the "projection into the new world of a reassuring past."[178]

It is no coincidence, then, that the digital era seems to invert the transactional relationship established between property and goods,[179] according to which it was the former that affected the latter, since, as is well exemplified by the non-copyleft applied to software, digitality with its own particular space-time traits seems to operate in such a way that it is the very characteristics of digital goods that condition the new attitude of the proprietary model, without this leading, however, to the construction of a new category of *res*.

very quickly led to the paralysis of major parts of the activities including the traditional ones in the field of culture: concerts, operas, museums, exhibits, travels, etc. Citizens were forced to reinvent their "life"». Then, at p. 3, the author observes that «Digital transformation impacts the whole society. It's a cultural change that requires organizations and even citizens to continually challenge the status quo, experiment, and get comfortable with failure. Furthermore, on the citizens' side, even and more significantly, it is required the willingness to "go digital" even if sometimes this choice become a "must" to do not be "cut off." It is evident that digital transformation it is not a process "one size fits all," each specific sector and even activity requires a particular approach and custom solution; this starting from the three main branches: citizens, companies, public administrations. Because digital transformation will look different for every subject/service, it can be hard to pinpoint a definition that applies to all. Sometimes this means walking away from long-standing business processes that companies were built upon in favour of relatively new practices that are still being defined. In such a situation the "trial and error" finding by continues improvements the optimal solution is the practical approach».

178 S. Rodotà, *Il terribile diritto*, cit., p. 459.

179 R.P. Merges, *A Transactional View of Property Rights*, in *Berkeley Technol. Law J.*, 20, 2005, p. 1477 ff.; R.P. Malloy, *Applied Property Research: A Transactional Approach*, in *Researching Property Law*, edited by S. Blandy and S. Bright, London and New York, NY, 2015, p. 123 ff.

Index

For Product Safety Concerns and Information please contact our EU representative GPSR@taylorandfrancis.com
Taylor & Francis Verlag GmbH, Kaufingerstraße 24, 80331 München, Germany

www.ingramcontent.com/pod-product-compliance
Ingram Content Group UK Ltd.
Pitfield, Milton Keynes, MK11 3LW, UK
UKHW020007200926
475702UK00015B/2516
9781032543451